FOR FRANCES

Faithfully yours
Clark Gable

CINEMA

THE FIRST HUNDRED YEARS

—

DAVID SHIPMAN

Foreword by Barry Norman

PHOENIX ILLUSTRATED

FOREWORD

It's always gratifying to come across a man who has managed to turn a misspent youth to good effect. David Shipman, for example, appears to have idled away his formative years in the warm, dark womb of the cinema, there to be enchanted by the likes of Snow White and to thrill at the adventures of Robin Hood.

And yet, as this book provides ample evidence, he has skilfully turned that impromptu apprenticeship to the most satisfying advantage. Mind you, it is I suppose a sign of David Shipman's age (and mine) to call such a youth misspent; it would have been regarded so in the 1940s when the cinema was for grown-ups and children were allowed to go only to Saturday matinees or, as a special treat, to see the latest Disney.

But those were the days when, certainly in Britain, film was still not recognized for what it is – the art form of the twentieth century. Then, and for some time afterwards, our best actors, writers and directors looked upon the theatre as the place for serious work; the cinema was for light entertainment, for trivia and for picking up easy money between plays.

The world, however, has changed since then. Today, to be sure, people go to the movies far less often than they used to but now it's the young, not their parents, who make up the bulk of the cinema audiences. In fact the present generation, from quite small children to the thirtysomethings, is certainly more movie-literate than any that has gone before and general interest in films has had a quite remarkable resurgence, one that would have been unthinkable back in the 1950s when you could only see movies in the cinema and television was ruthlessly robbing that of its audience. One significant reflection of this renewed interest is the recent proliferation of TV programmes about the movies; people do not simply want to watch films, they are eager for knowledge about them.

And in this book David Shipman provides it. His theme is the development of film internationally, both as art form and escapist entertainment, and he sets the progress of the worldwide industry against the background of social and political changes. It's a timely work because it could be argued that the upstart television has already had its heyday and that movies are again, as they were for three decades from the introduction of sound, the world's most popular form of entertainment.

Cinema: The First Hundred Years will be invaluable not only to serious students of the cinema but also to those who merely want the facts to settle some heated argument about who made what and when. Of course, you will not agree with all of Shipman's opinions. I, for instance, am amazed at the small regard in which he holds Martin Scorsese's **Raging Bull** and the faint praise he accords to **The Godfather** and the genius of Woody Allen. Never mind. Disagreeing with the author's views is part of the fun of reading a book like this and is anyway no reflection on the accuracy of the information it contains.

I've been familiar with, and have held great respect for, David Shipman's work as a movie historian for many years and I have little doubt that here is yet another Shipman book of reference which I and others engaged in writing about the cinema will frequently consult and from which, if I'm to be really honest, we will on occasion cheerfully steal.   Barry Norman, June 1993

INTRODUCTION

I was first aware of movies on a summer outing to Great Yarmouth in 1938. A couple of weeks earlier I had been given a jigsaw puzzle featuring seven dwarfs. I had never liked a jigsaw so much, but I cannot recall whether I knew the dwarfs had an existence outside it. Yet I do remember that there were three others in the same series, under the title **Snow White and the Seven Dwarfs**, and I was saving my pocket-money to buy them. And there, on a cinema on Yarmouth front, were my seven dwarfs and the lady called Snow White. I bawled because I wanted to see them immediately and was told I would have to wait till the film came to Norwich.

I suspect that this was not the first film I saw, but it was the first I desperately wanted to see. I don't recall when I became hooked: perhaps seeing Deanna Durbin in **First Love** in 1940, after we moved to London, or when my cousin John told me about **The Adventures of Robin Hood** which, wonder of wonders, was in colour like **Snow White**. I longed to see it, all through evacuation, and in 1944 was at last able to, when a cinema full of like-minded children sat waiting for its first showing.

It was virtually impossible to see revivals (like **Robin Hood**) in those days. I remember the excitement of the whole family going to see **Rebecca** in 1946: in a suburb far away, in a cinema not much above those known as flea-pits. (Later it became a member of the Classic circuit and later still a tyre-store.) My parents succumbed to television around that time; I was allowed to go to the pictures only once a week. In the late 1940s television occasionally put on an old film, and to me both **Battleship Potemkin** and **The Blue Angel** were intolerably antique. But then the BBC telecast **Les Enfants du Paradis**, and I surrendered. Shortly afterwards I saw **Orphée** and then **Bicycle Thieves**. Virtually the first thing I did on returning from national service in Singapore in 1953 was to join the National Film Theatre, which had opened in 1952. It has been my spiritual home ever since, the place where I have discovered the masterpieces of the cinema's past – or have been equally excited by some more mundane piece, because I am seeing people caught on celluloid long before I was born.

Watching the century's films gives a fascinating insight into social changes. The screen can demonstrate and reflect our attitudes towards sex, religion, politics, racism and crime, as well as shifting tastes in fashion, architecture, interior design, travel and language.

From the outset the cinema was interested in current affairs, though it moved swiftly to fantasy as the pioneers sought ways of using the new medium – as opposed to what then was its closest relative, the theatre. Realism in cinema was never entirely swamped, and it was used for propaganda purposes in both world wars, not to mention many others. Horribly, the most recent ones have been projected into our living rooms. The cinema has been the tool of political parties of all creeds. It was influential in both the rise of Communism and its destruction, and the end of the Cold War.

In this book I have attempted to examine the way in which films, setting out primarily to entertain, have reflected the real world. I have regarded the century chronologically, looking particularly at social changes – most notably the more relaxed sexual attitudes of the 1920s, World War II and especially in the cinema, of the late 1960s. By its very nature sex plays a dominant role in the cinema's history: movies make voyeurs of us all, which is why films with a strong sexual content have usually proved very profitable. I wish it were possible to cover only the good movies, but the bad can be equally memorable. The reader will notice my reluctance to mention Hollywood's Academy Awards, partly because they are seldom a guide to excellence (and have been too much written about, in any case). Success at the box-office is important, but that was not my criterion. A hundred years is a long time, so I have varied my approach – usually by theme but from most of the 1930s to the 1950s with a monthly chronology (for Hollywood only) and for the 1980s by the measure of success.

I have dated films from the time they were first deemed ready to be seen by people not involved in their manufacture, whether journalists, others working in the industry or audiences for whom they were previewed. Titles of films can also vary, especially when crossing frontiers. I have given alternative titles when appropriate, but have usually used the name by which the film is best known. In the case of foreign language films, the Index lists both the original title and that (or those) given by British or American distributors.

Writing in 1942 the British critic C.A. Lejeune dated the birth of the cinema from 1896, when going to the movies became a habit. Others consider it began in 1895, when the Lumières first projected their films. My starting point is 1893 when Edison constructed the first 'studio'.

I have a number of people to thank for what has been a pleasurable experience: Frances Kelly, Coralie Hepburn, Lesley Baxter, Steve Pickles, Richard Chatten, Tom Vallance, Peter Downes, Tony Sloman and Felix Brenner.

David Shipman, Overton, Hampshire, May 1993

1893

Scientists and photographers the world over were trying to invent the movies, and it was only a matter of time before they succeeded. Leading the field was Thomas Alva Edison from his home in West Orange, New Jersey, where he completed the first film studio on 1 February at a cost of $637. Called the Black Maria, it was built on a pivot so that the set could be turned to follow the sun. Edison had already patented the Kinetoscope, a cabinet with a peephole through which one could view successive images by turning a handle. It was clear that these images would have greater appeal if projected, as in the popular device of the time, the magic lantern. Then, later in the year, one of Edison's assistants, Fred Ott, sneezed in front of a camera – and **Fred Ott's Sneeze** was the first film, copyrighted as 'Record of a Sneeze, 7 January 1894'.

Right: The scientific developments of the late nineteenth century, notably in electricity and photography, led inevitably to movies. Foremost among pioneers was Thomas Alva Edison, who had invented the phonograph in 1877. Below: Edison was also first to purpose-build a movie studio, in the garden of his New Jersey home. Opposite: He became determined to reproduce images as he had recorded sound, appointing his English-born laboratory head, W. K. L. Dickson, to research to that end. At one point, Dickson's assistant, Fred Ott, sneezed while the camera was pointed at him, and that became the first film to be copyrighted.

T he first Kinetoscope Parlor was opened in New York, and before the end of the year there were others in San Francisco, Chicago, Washington, Baltimore and Atlantic City. Among the images patrons may have viewed was a harmless little vaudeville, **Fun in a Chinese Laundry**, and the prize-fighters James J. Corbett and Peter Courtenay sparring,

1894

which had been filmed in the West Orange studio. Alexander Black began to use the magic lantern to project successive slides, at four a minute, with simple picture sequences accompanied by his own narration from the stage. The first of Black's picture plays was the 14,000-word **Miss Jerry**, which followed the adventures of a reporter – played by a well-known model, Blanche Bayliss – with William Courtenay as the leading man.

Above: Edison's renown brought to his studio such celebrities as Buffalo Bill Cody and Annie Oakley, to be filmed for a minute or so. Their actions could be glimpsed through the peephole of Edison's patented kinetoscope, synchronized to the music of his phonograph, which he considered by far the more important of his two developments. Right: The prizefighters Corbett and Courtenay re-enacted a moment of their famous fight.

10

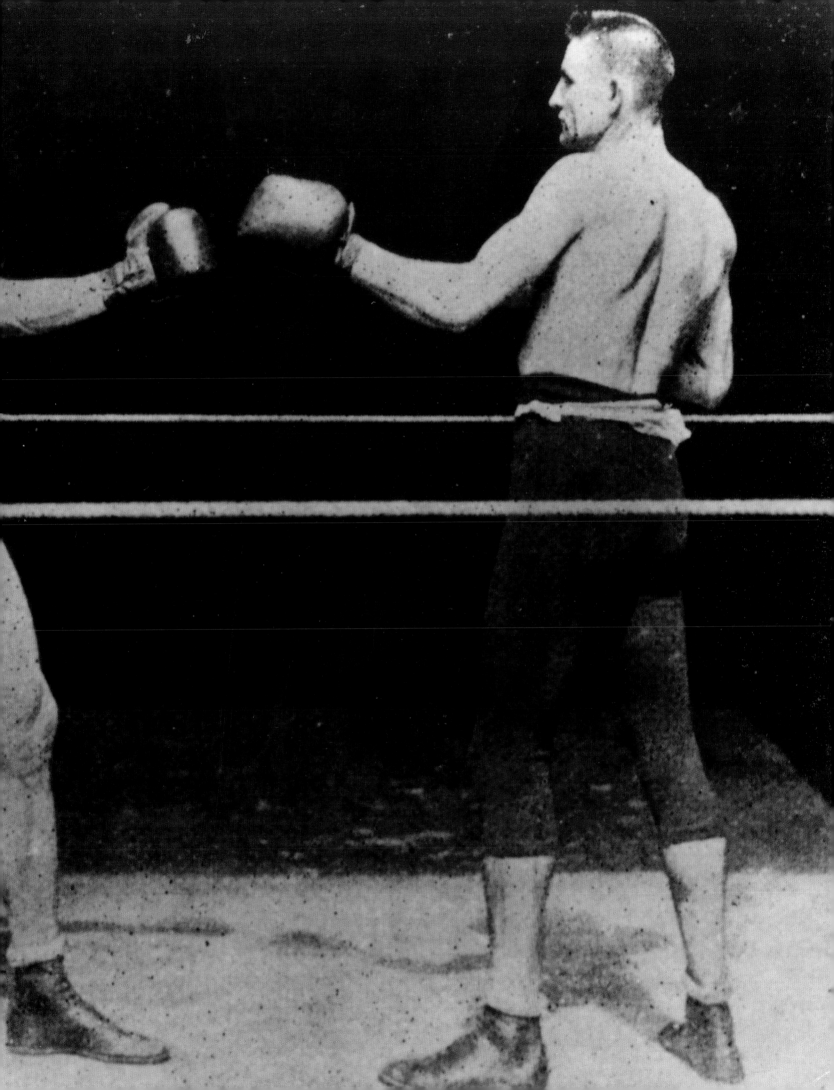

I n France, Auguste and Louis Lumière, working at their father's photographic factory in Lyons, filmed the workers leaving: **La Sortie des Ouvriers de l'Usine Lumière**. In February they patented a projector to show the images and did so on 22 March at 44 rue de Rennes, in the hope of interesting vaudeville or carnival showmen. Their efforts were in vain. Eventually,

1895

they turned entrepreneurs and hired the basement, the 'Salon Indien', of the Grand Café, 14 boulevard des Capucines. Posters outside advertised the event to take place on 28 December, entrance fee one franc, but of the hundred seats, only thirty-three were taken. Of the scores of Paris reporters invited, only two turned up. What they saw was **La Sortie des Ouvriers** followed by a number of other items. The brothers had stumbled on the newsreel, filming delegates arriving at the congress of the Société Française de la Photographie, which had taken place in July. But the most appreciated 'shot' was a joke, **L'Arroseur Arrosée** or, as it became known in English, **The Sprinkler Sprinkled**.

Above and opposite: Moving pictures were first projected to the public on 28 December 1895. Among the ten short items on the programme were some men playing cards, the arrival of a train in the station of La Ciotat on the Riviera (spectators fled from their seats as the train approached them) and a baby being fed. Below: The event was advertised thus, with the screen showing **L'Arroseur Arrosée** or **The Sprinkler Sprinkled**.

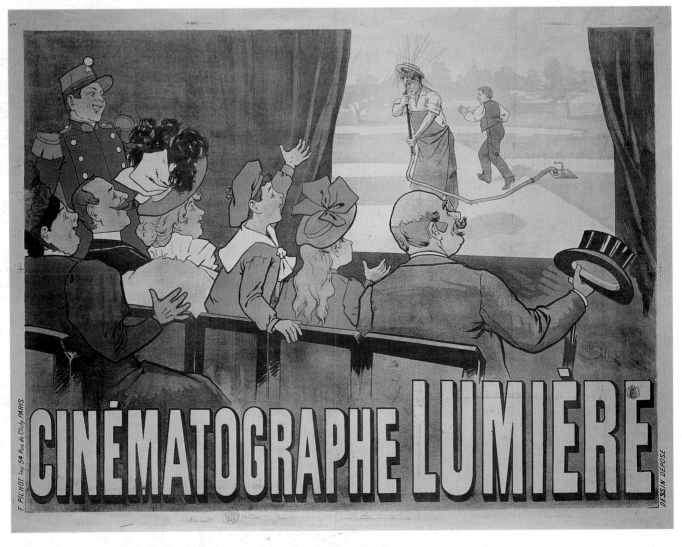

1896

By the middle of January the Paris public was flocking to the Salon to see these 'animated photographs'. Quinton Hogg of the Regent Street Polytechnic in London arranged a showing there on 25 February, and the Empire Music Hall immediately borrowed them, quickly moving them to the top of the bill. They were first seen in New York at Keith's Vaudeville Theater on 29 June – but with a little of the novelty lost, since Edison had shown his films at Koster and Bial's Music Hall on 23 April, using the Vitascope, a projector borrowed from its inventor, Thomas Armat, who doesn't seem to have minded that Edison passed it off as his own.

Feeling differently was W. K. L. Dickson, who had developed the movies, such as they were, for which Edison was now taking credit. Admittedly he had done so while on Edison's payroll, but he resigned and joined the company responsible for the Mutoscope, the Kinetoscope's chief rival. The outfit renamed itself the American Mutoscope and Biograph Company, projecting its first pictures in Pittsburgh in September.

In Paris, the life of one man had been irrevocably changed by a visit to the Salon Indien – Georges Méliès, magician, actor and designer at the Théâtre Robert-Houdin. When the Lumière brothers refused his overtures he went to London to buy the necessary equipment. He may have seen Edison's **The Execution of Mary, Queen of Scots** in which the camera was stopped twice, for a dummy to be substituted for the queen and then for her head to be raised aloft. Méliès himself claimed that he discovered the magical possibilities of the camera when it jammed, and a carriage turned into a horse. Later in the year, he built Europe's first studio, at Montreuil-sous-Bois.

Above: Movies quickly assumed their voyeuristic role – respectably so in the case of May Irwin and John C. Rice re-enacting their kiss from the stage success, **The Widow Jones**. Right: Georges Méliès, as a magician, appeared in most of his early films, including **L'Escamotage d'une Dame** – a lady who disappears and appears at the stroke of his wand.

1897

Most music hall owners thought that their customers would tire of moving pictures when the novelty wore off, but they simply began to demand more. Edison went for variety by offering **Fatima**, in a belly dance many considered obscene, and **The Corbett-Fitzsimmons Fight at Carson City**, which was actually filmed there. Since he could not meet the demand, he had no objection to the output of Biograph, as his only rival was now known.

Edison also sold a Kinetoscope to J. Stuart Blackton after putting together a film based on his drawings, **Blackton, the Evening World Cartoonist** (1896). Blackton was joined by a friend, Albert E. Smith, and in 1897 they formed the Vitagraph Company with another partner, William T. Rock, expressly to manufacture films to be projected. The first still exists: **The Burglar on the Roof**, but it consists only of a chase over their open-air studio on the Morse Building at 140 Nassau Street, New York. Sigmund Lubin in Philadelphia made his first film, **Horse Eating Hay**.

Méliès made **L'Auberge Ensorcelée**, in which a man – himself – in a hotel room finds his clothes disappear, his boots walking without him, a candle exploding, his bed and chair collapsing. Like everything put on film till this time, it lasts about two minutes.

Above: Edison invited the dancer Annabelle (Moore) to his studio to film some of the numbers for which she was famous. At least two survive, the 'Butterfly' and the 'Serpentine' (illustrated). Below: He also put on celluloid a more dubious personality, the dancer Fatima. Opposite: On 17 March 1897 Edison filmed 'Gentleman Jim' Corbett at Carson City – where he was defeated by the British boxer, James L. Fitzimmons.

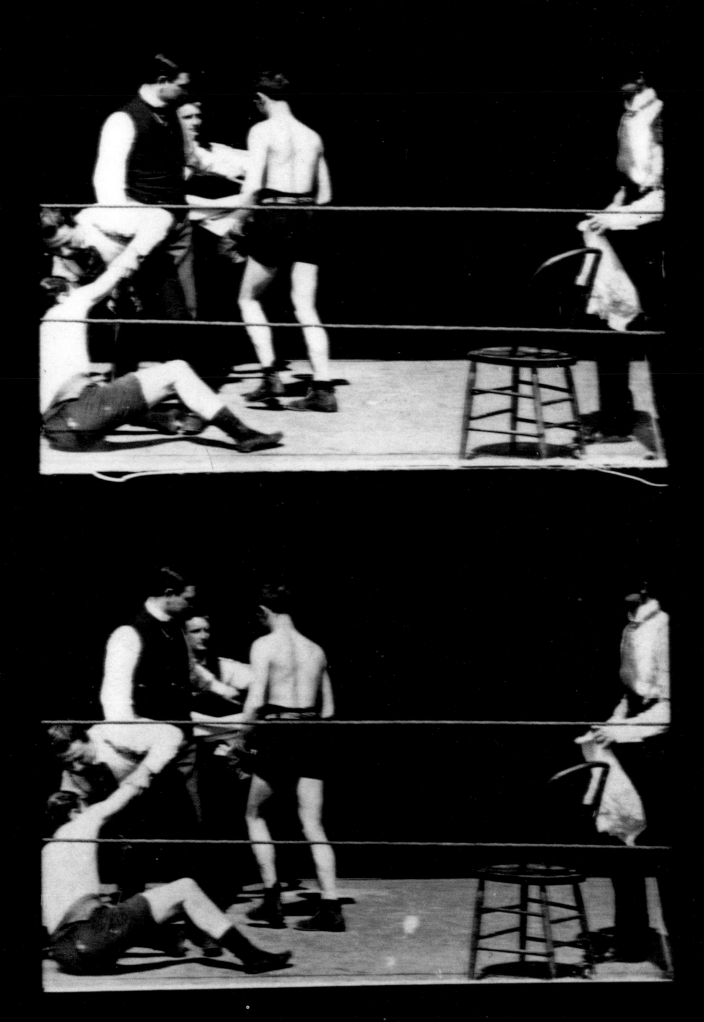

I f we discount Méliès's use of trick photography, the movies' first innovation occurred in Britain in August, when Robert Paul issued **Come Along, Do!** This consists of two scenes, of a couple eating in an art gallery, and gazing at a statue. Paul was immediately encouraged to make another, also a comedy, but with four scenes: in **Our New General Servant** a wife

1898

hires and fires a maid after seeing her husband flirting with, and kissing, the girl. G. A. Smith followed with **Santa Claus**, with five incidents and a 'trick' image of Santa as two little girls lie sleeping.

Vitagraph's second film, **Tearing Down the Spanish Flag**, expressed patriotic sentiment during the brief Spanish–American War and can be deemed the first propaganda film. The War began when the battleship *Maine* was blown up in Havana harbour, an event re-created to a degree by Méliès in **Visite Sous-marin du Maine**, as divers help a sailor out of a hole in the sunken ship. The vessel is obviously painted, but the fishes swimming between it and the camera show Méliès creating magic like never before.

Above: Films were getting longer. Robert Paul's **Come Along, Do!** was issued in two scenes in August, but the following month one of the many other pioneers, G. A. Smith, produced **Santa Claus** (illustrated), which had no fewer than five scenes. Right: Méliès presented **La Damnation du Docteur Faust** in just two scenes. He returned to the subject in 1903 and again in 1904, when it ran to an amazing forty.

1899

In the USA new companies were springing up without producing anything either innovative or original. In France people talked about little but the Dreyfus Affair, which concluded with Dreyfus's conviction on 9 September. Méliès rushed out **L'Affaire Dreyfus**, in no fewer than nine scenes, the last of which showed Dreyfus leaving for prison. The Lumières were still shooting life, whereas Méliès was using the camera to show reconstructions of life.

The great age of plagiarism was beginning. In Britain, G. A. Smith issued **The Kiss in the Tunnel**, in which the kiss concerned is framed with shots of a moving train. Riley Brothers-Bamford immediately followed with a less sophisticated version, with the same title. Both, of course, were titillating.

The great age of trick photography was also beginning. Robert Paul made **Upside-Down; or the Human Flies**, in which two couples are having such a wonderful time that they start to dance on the ceiling – with charming effect when the men take off their jackets, which float (down) to the floor, presumably drawn (up) by wires. Méliès was only one of many who subsequently copied this idea, but he did so with great ingenuity.

Above: Robert Paul's **Upside-Down; or the Human Flies**. Right: Méliès made his **L'Affaire Dreyfus** in nine scenes, of which this is the first, with Dreyfus on Devil's Island being informed that he is to return to France for a re-trial.

T he advance of movies was not in evidence as the pioneers struggled to copy each other. Among the most popular subjects were: a man kissing a pretty girl, only waking up to find himself in bed with his wife; children doctoring sick kittens; tea parties; courtships; children, usually seen large through magnifying glasses, or grown-ups watched in miniature by people of normal size; and peeps through bedroom door keyholes. While movies did little to acknowledge that the world was in a new century, they made much of automobiles, the telephone and the cinematograph, usually as new-fangled inventions with which the unworldly couldn't cope.

1900

Chiefly because of the innovations of Méliès, the French film industry was regarded as the most lively source of movies, but the Lumières still carried more prestige, and it was they who were invited to show their pictures at the Paris Exposition. Exhibition at the Exposition made many people realize that movies might be more than a nine days' wonder.

In the US a strike of vaudeville performers should have forced theatres to close, but their proprietors kept them open by mounting programmes consisting solely of movies. When audiences still turned up, the cinema habit was born.

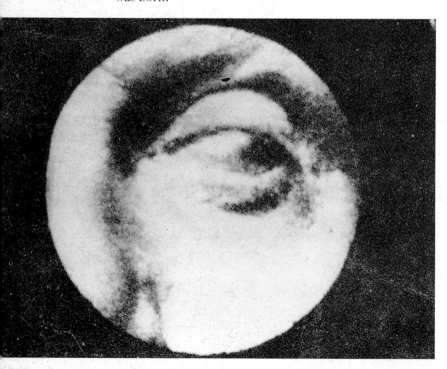

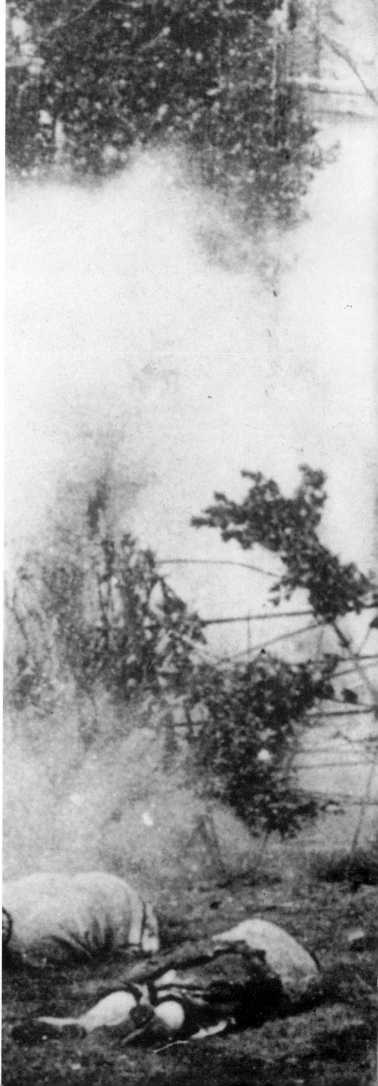

Above: In September G. A. Smith issued **Grandma's Reading Glass** (illustrated) and **As Seen Through a Telescope**. These were novel for their close-ups, not yet considered technically viable. Audiences still expected to see people whole. Right: James Williamson's **Attack on a Chinese Mission – Blue Jackets to the Rescue** was the longest British film yet, with four sequences, each lasting about a minute.

1901

It was the British, again, who moved the cinema forward. The previous year one James Williamson had issued **Attack on a Chinese Mission – Blue Jackets to the Rescue**, which was something more than the usual series of animated tableaux, if somewhat dowdy today. Now he came up with two little action films, **Stop Thief!** and **Fire!**, both of which have the tension and happy endings associated with the *Chinese Mission*. Will the thief be stopped? Will the fire brigade arrive on time? Yes, and far more urgently than anything attempted in the earlier film.

Queen Victoria died, and although the movies couldn't handle that, they would re-enact the coronation of her successor, Edward VII, none too convincingly in any version. The assassination of President McKinley also found its way onto film, again in a reconstruction of the event itself. Méliès was the foremost exponent of these movies. He was also making advertising films.

Robert Paul seized his chance: if Méliès could devote a whole reel – about ten minutes – to Dreyfus, one of the great unloved in French history, he could do the same with someone equally excoriated. **Scrooge; or Marley's Ghost** takes thirteen scenes to tell as much of Charles Dickens's perennially popular *A Christmas Carol* as was then possible. It's musty today, with Marley tripling up as the three Christmas spirits, but by no means the worst of the many film versions of this tale.

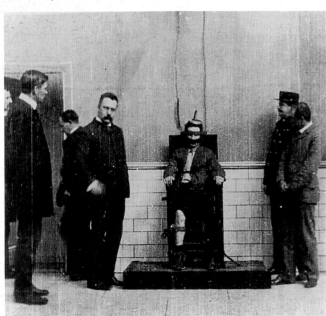

Above: The assassination of President McKinley and the death of his killer, the anarchist Leon Czolgosz, was one of several real-life events re-enacted in the studios. Right: **Are You There?** was a little joke film made by James Williamson. In a moment the girl's father will be seen listening to her, and a second later he will reappear at the right of the frame to beat the young man.

1902

The American film industry continued to grow without turning out anything of merit, but the first purpose-built cinema, the Electric, opened in Los Angeles on 16 April. The British stagnated, but in France things were humming. Since 1896, the Pathé Frères had been selling movie equipment, Edison phonographs and movies in the Lumière manner. In 1901 they had taken on board Ferdinand Zecca, an actor who, as producer-director, challenged Méliès at every turn. Charles Pathé then broke away from his brothers, and in 1902 built a studio in Vincennes. Pathé, confident of Zecca's skills, gave him his head, and what did it matter if Zecca was merely imitating Méliès? The two of them turned to history (Joan of Arc, Ann Boleyn), the Bible (Samson and Delilah), fairytales (*Cinderella*, *Puss in Boots*), the stage (*The Barber of Seville*, *Coppelia*) to feed audiences hungry for pictures. Zecca was the second person to put Christ on the screen, in **La Vie et La Passion de Jesus Christ**, after Alice Guy-Blaché had made a film of a similar title for Lumière.

Zecca had flair; Méliès had vision. In 1901 the latter had adapted Jules Verne's **Vingt Milles Lieues sous La Mer**, and with Verne in mind he wrote and directed **Le Voyage dans La Lune**, which comprised thirty tableaux. The itinerant showmen, who were his chief clients, refused to take it because it was too long and too expensive. He allowed it to be shown for nothing at a fair in Paris in August. The public hesitated at first, because no one had ever been to the moon, but the picture's easy humour and undeniable fantasy – not to mention the girls from the Folies-Bergères waving goodbye to the savants and welcoming them back – soon found favour. The film brought Méliès international fame, and he opened an exchange in the US (as did Pathé); but more than anything else it established the cinema's function, which was narrative. Trick films, reconstructions of actual events and animated views were soon yesterday's cold potatoes. The public wanted stories.

Below: While Britain and the US were wondering whether it was blasphemous to portray Christ on the screen, the French went ahead, with Ferdinand Zecca and Lucien Nonguet co-directing **La Vie et La Passion de Jesus Christ** for Pathé, in no less than eighteen parts. Right: France was the leader of the world's fledgeling movie industries – in part due to the productivity, energy and enthusiasm of Georges Méliès. This is a scene from **Le Voyage dans La Lune** or **A Trip to the Moon**.

1903

The second narrative film was made in Britain. **A Daring Daylight Robbery**, issued by the Sheffield Photo Company in April, comprised nine scenes featuring the local fire brigade as cops chasing robbers, with the final apprehension on a railway platform. It was seen by Edwin S. Porter, who was not only Edison's chief film-maker but who also inspected the films which Edison imported to distribute.

Porter remade Williamson's **Fire!** as **The Life of an American Fireman**, released in February with augmented fictional scenes – and in splicing them together he hit upon the technique of film editing. **A Daring Daylight Robbery** excited him because it was clear that the movies, unlike the stage, were perfect for showing chases. First, Edison wanted an **Uncle Tom's Cabin**, 'the longest and most expensive picture yet made in America'. Porter set the camera down as if in front of a stage, and it photographed vignettes from Harriet Beecher Stowe's novel and the stage adaptations of it. It was respectfully received, but he also attracted attention with **The Ex-convict**, a sympathetic study of one, and **The Gay Shoe Clerk**, in which a shop assistant begins to flirt with a pretty customer while her chaperone isn't looking. A close-up of the lady's ankle was considered very daring.

When Porter came to his own 'chase' picture, **The Great Train Robbery**, released in December, he vastly improved on Sheffield's effort. Although shot in New Jersey, he put the robbers into cowboy duds, to appeal to the audiences which flocked to the Wild West shows. He made the train an intrinsic part of the action, cutting from it to a dance hall and the telegraph office, where the operator lies bound and gagged; and he finished with a close-up of a man firing at the audience. He did not think of cutting from pursuer to pursued, but the effect was nevertheless sensational. It made moviegoers of those sceptical of this new entertainment, and it was the opening attraction of the renovated shops which were springing up all over the country. It very much over-shadowed **Rip Van Winkle**, in which Joseph Jefferson repeated, in abbreviated form, his stage success – the first noted actor to appear in a movie.

Below: It was common for the various film industries to copy each other, and Edison's **The Life of an American Fireman** was an extended variation on the British **Fire!**. Edwin S. Porter directed. Opposite: Porter was so excited by **A Daring Daylight Robbery** (above), the most elaborate of the several British cops and robbers chase movies that he put it into a Western setting as **The Great Train Robbery** (below).

1904

So bemused was he by the fantastic success of **The Great Train Robbery**, Porter did not attempt to follow it up. Instead, he made a two-reel **Parsifal**, based on Wagner's opera, though it did not occur to anyone to show both parts together – those who had liked the first were required to return the following week. The other American companies devised their own 'chase' movies and turned their attention to narratives – of widows wooed, husbands' deceptions and lovers' misunderstandings.

It was the British who benefited from Porter's advances, making a number of crime melodramas much more elaborate than the simple crook pieces of the past. A typical example is **Raid on a Coiner's Den**, directed by Alf Collins for the French company Gaumont, which had set up shop in Britain. Collins' film shows the activities of the coiners in detail, what they do to the copper who has hunted them down and how they are discovered in the bushes by police dogs.

Above: James Williamson's **An Interesting Story** was a punning title, for a man is so engrossed in his book that he pours tea into his hat. Later he is run over by a steam-roller, but thanks to trick photography he is put together again. Right: **Voyage à Travers l'Impossible** was Méliès's most ambitious and most expensive work to date; it cost the equivalent of $7,500. Otherwise it was strictly a repeat of what he had already done.

The only advances made were in Britain, where the formula of **The Great Train Robbery** – a crook, a train, the police – was applied to the famous Victorian criminal, Charles Peace, who could also be seen in the Chamber of Horrors at Madame Tussaud's. Sheffield's **Life of Charles Peace** was so popular that two other companies rushed out imitations.

1905

Crime was also a feature of the most successful British film yet made, Cecil Hepworth's **Rescued By Rover**, in itself inspired by Biograph's **The Lost Child**. Both were about kidnapped babies, but in Hepworth's version, Rover the dog rescues the baby from the gypsies. What made the film so sensational was Hepworth's cutting from the baby's fate back to the worried parents.

Above: R. W. Paul's **The Lover and the Madman**. Paul was drawn to films by virtue of his trade as a maker of scientific instruments. Below: Méliès's **Dêtresse et Charité** was typical of the little morality tales being manufactured by every film industry. Opposite: Cecil Hepworth's **Rescued by Rover** was the most successful British film yet made. Like many films of the time, it concerned a kidnapped baby.

1906

Cutting was the *raison d'être* of Porter's **The Kleptomaniac**. Following **The Ex-convict**, he decided to try another study of social injustice, contrasting the fate of a wealthy woman who shoplifts with that of a poor woman who steals on impulse. It was the only film of any consequence from any of the world's fledgeling film industries in 1906, apart from **La Vie du Christ**, directed in France by Victorin Jasset for Gaumont.

However, the American film-makers were now becoming much more adventurous: both Edison and Biograph employed for their one-reel crime adventures, **The White Caps** and **The Tunnel Workers** respectively, about twenty players each and over a dozen locations – in the case of the second, the Pennsylvania Tunnel, then under construction.

The new industry was burgeoning and the first 'Nickelodeon' was opened in Pittsburgh. Cinemas were opening in every advanced country, but the word 'Nickelodeon' was the generic name in the States for a movie-house.

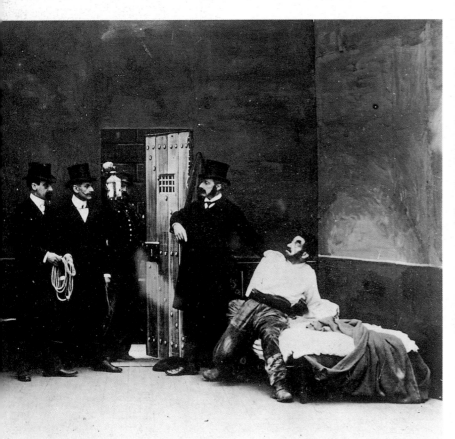

As the world's leading film-maker, Méliès found the demands being made on him were such that he was beginning to repeat himself. He burnt himself out and left the industry, bankrupt, in 1913. In 1906, he was churning out movies at the rate of more than one a month, most of them lasting about fifteen minutes. **L'Histoire d'un Crime** (above), in thirty scenes, was the sort of cops and robbers movie anyone could make, but **Jack le Ramoneur** (right) was uniquely his: the dream of a chimney sweep.

1907

France could now boast the world's leading film industry, in output, quality, variety, ingenuity and, not least, in its wonderful use of locations, both in Paris and the country. And, doubtless influenced by Méliès, the films are humorous and even satirical, a quality lacking elsewhere. However, the French were obsessively fond of chase movies, and the number of articles that could be knocked down by runaway people, children, horses, carriages and dogs was limited. There were variations, though, such as **Les Debuts d'un Aéronaute**, in which havoc is created by the dangling anchor of a balloon.

The lead in this Pathé film is the neat, moustachioed figure of Max Linder, uncredited as yet but destined to become the movies' first great clown. It was Pathé who recognized the drawing power of a resident clown, and they hired a music hall performer, André Deed, who launched a series of films about the accident-prone Boireau, or Foolshead. When he later went to Italy to become Cretinetti, Gaumont stepped in with Ernest Bourbon, known as Onésime, or Simple Simon.

Also coming into prominence in the US was another major figure, G. M. Anderson, who had acted for Edison and directed for Vitagraph. In 1907 he founded the Essanay Film Company with George K. Spoor, and they presented **The Bandit Makes Good**, featuring Anderson.

Another new company was Kalem, who in December issued **Ben Hur**, 'positively the most superb moving picture spectacle ever made in America in sixteen magnificent scenes with illustrated titles'. Kalem, alas, had not bothered to purchase the movie rights and were sued by the copyright owner, who settled for $25,000.

Below: The theme of small children being captured and restored to their parents remained popular – if carried somewhat far by Porter in his **Rescued From an Eagle's Nest**. Opposite: Bronco Billy – later Broncho Billy – was the screen's first cowboy. In 1907 he was one of the co-founders of Essanay and the following year he would be the first producer to move West. He was the first star known to audiences.

1908

If Boireau could attract audiences, then so might the American detective Nick Carter, or thus reasoned Victorin Jasset. The Nick Carter pulp novels were enjoying a vogue in France, and Jasset simply transferred their spirited tales of derring-do to Paris. Thus was born the serial, though for a while each episode was complete in itself.

France also led the way in regularly putting distinguished stage artists into movies. The first of these was a pompous, stagey reconstruction of an historical event, **La Mort du Duc de Guise**, with players from the Comédie Française. The admiration it aroused – incomprehensible today – persuaded Sarah Bernhardt to return to the movie studio (she had appeared briefly in **Le Duel d'Hamlet** in 1900) to play **La Tosca**, one of her famous stage roles.

The acclaim for the Duc de Guise's death was equally great in New York, where it arrived the following year and far exceeded that for Vitagraph's filmed Shakespeare: **Antony and Cleopatra**, **Richard III**, **The Merchant of Venice**, **Julius Caesar** and **Romeo and Juliet**. But taking into account such other Vitagraph historicals as **Francesca da Rimini** (1907) – while overlooking the over-age couple in Verona and disregarding some ham acting – these are conscientiously adapted, meticulously set and splendidly costumed.

In fact, faced with increased competition, Vitagraph had become the leader of the industry, turning out pictures of all sorts with skill and vigour. The company's chief asset was a pretty girl called Florence Lawrence, as Biograph recognized when they filched her by offering to

raise her salary by $10 to $25 per week – and by publicizing her as 'The Biograph Girl'. Biograph's own product began to improve when they took on an actor from Edison, D. W. Griffith, to direct half their output. He started with **The Adventures of Dollie**, which was issued in July. Its subtitle, 'Her Marvellous Experience at the Hands of the Gypsies', was something of a misnomer, since they kidnap her in revenge after one of them has been horse-whipped for stealing a purse and hide her in a barrel. There had been so many similar films that Biograph only made it at the insistence of Griffith, who played Dollie's dad – and who wanted to become a director, promising to return to acting only if it was unsuccessful. However, reaction to the film was such that he made at least two pictures a week, always on location – and would continue to do so for the next five years.

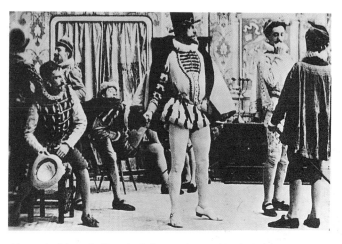

Above: **La Mort du Duc de Guise**, co-directed by André Calmettes and Charles La Bargy, was planned as the first 'art' movie. Below: **Le Bon Ecraseur** was a trick film, in which a car collides with a man and he loses his legs. It was just another variation on **How It Feels to be Run Over**, made in Britain as long ago as 1900. Many people in France felt that such films were holding back the cinema.

1909

The American film industry continued to burgeon. Among the new companies were Rex, Yankee, Powers Picture Plays and Imp, the last formed by Carl Laemmle. Bison, formed expressly to make Westerns, shot the first one in New Jersey, but soon moved to the West itself.

Only Edison, Vitagraph and Biograph had legal entitlement to manufacture motion pictures, and in an attempt to suppress any further competition they had formed the Patents Company, having invited Selig, Essanay, Kalem and Lubin to join, along with Méliès and Pathé. Legally, no company outside the trust could buy film stock. 10,000 exhibitors signed an agreement to show only those films made by the trust, which meant that the business was now, in effect, riddled with lawbreakers.

Above: **Gertie the Dinosaur** is the first animated film of any consequence. In France, Méliès and Emile Cohl had realized that films could be constructed from drawings, frame by frame. Gertie was commissioned from Windsor McKay, a newspaper cartoonist. Opposite: **The Lonely Villa.** Marion Leonard is the lady telephoning for help; Mary Pickford is the protective young lady, and one of the girls is Adele de Garde.

Of the members of the trust, only Vitagraph and Biograph were forces to be reckoned with, not just because they issued a picture every two or three days, but because the public liked the personalities in them. Both realized that it was only a matter of time before these players were named.

Vitagraph countered the loss of Florence Lawrence by signing Florence Turner and calling her 'The Vitagraph Girl'. Maurice Costello, a quondam matinée idol who had been acting for Edison, had joined the company in 1908 and was now advertised as 'The Dimpled Darling', which did not do justice to his considerable screen presence. Biograph retaliated by signing another well-known stage actor, James Kirkwood, but among the many new faces, one in particular found favour: Mary Pickford, who was soon known as 'The Girl with the Curls'. Her first picture, **The Violin Maker of Cremona**, was issued on 7 June, with **The Lonely Villa** following three days later.

Both were directed by D. W. Griffith, and they exemplify his work . . . but what's a fellow to do, turning out pictures at this rate? The first is an historical romance of horrible sentimentality, the second a 'will-they-get-there-in-time?' thriller. Cinemagoers had long shown a taste for both forms, the second of which had been refined in a French film of 1908, **Le Medecin au Chateau**. Cutting between the beleaguered or the threatened and the potential rescuer(s) was a device Griffith used – and would continue to use – much too often.

In France itself the only significant event was the continued rise of Max Linder, but one other country was now reaching out to the world's screens with its films – Italy, with **L'Inferno**, based on Dante, and **Giulio Cesare**.

Griffith's **The Drive for a Life** tells of rejected mistress who sends some poisoned candy to the fiancée of her erstwhile lover with a note forged in his handwriting. He gets to learn about it – but will he arrive in time?

Carl Laemmle quite consciously instituted the star system when he lured 'The Biograph Girl' to Imp for $1,000 a week and planted a story in a St Louis paper to the effect that she had been killed by a streetcar. He then announced in the trade press that not only was she alive but an Imp star, and when she appeared in St Louis to prove this, the crowd at the station was far greater than that for President Taft the previous week.

The resulting furore did not put Imp up there with Biograph and Vitagraph, but then there was competition from a slew of new companies – Majestic, Reliance, Thanhouser, Champion, American, Eclair and Nestor – not to mention Pathé, which opened an American studio.

Italy exported some relatively lavish productions,

Sarah Bernhardt conferred huge prestige on movies at a time when the legitimate theatre despised them. The world's most famous actress re-enacted her acclaimed role in **La Dame aux Camelias** before the camera.

including **La Caduta di Troia** in two reels, which had become quite common everywhere for the more ambitious films. Russia entered the world scene with **The Queen of Spades**, based on Pushkin's story. But it was Denmark which made audiences abroad think twice. Denmark offered sex. Other movie industries, desperate for respectability, had been ambiguous on the subject. Their sensibilities were in Victorian melodrama, in which rape and romance held sway, and never did the twain meet. They handled the subject gingerly, as in Vitagraph's **The Mill Girl** (1907), in which the vile, moustachioed mill boss is so overcome by lust that he doesn't notice that the place is on fire.

The Danes changed all that. They exposed **The White Slave Trade**. Everyone knew what the white slave

1910

trade was — virgins and other innocent damsels being shanghaied and forced to ply for trade in filthy foreign brothels. The bordello in this particular film is decorous by any standard – a cigarette is smoked, a piano is played, two ladies dance in their petticoats and (of course) the heroine is rescued by her sweetheart in the nick of time. The lesson conveyed was strong, but the American film industry gasped as the film was passed by even the puritan states, which had set up their own censorship committees.

The Danes made countless imitations, but in the meantime came up with an alternative: the Fallen Woman. She had been around for a long time, but not in movies, until Urban Gad was looking for a vehicle to showcase his wife, Asta Nielsen, whom he thought had been neglected by theatre producers. He directed her in **Afgrunden**, or **The Abyss**, which charts her downward spiral after she has 'given' herself to a passing circus performer — whom she stabs in the last reel after her former fiancé tries to redeem her from a life of sin.

Since she is last seen in the hands of the police, it is a highly moral film. It was a worldwide success, notably in Germany, where Gad and the great Nielsen went to work. She and Max Linder were the first internationally recognized movie stars; but more than that: at three reels, **Afgrunden** may be regarded as the first feature film.

This was an idea whose time had come, though it was not welcomed by the American film industry. Vitagraph had been issuing **A Life of Moses** in five reels over a fourteen-month period. In April one cinema in New Orleans showed all five reels together, and did sensational business. The lesson was not lost on the industry, but Vitagraph's rather pokey, three-reel **Uncle Tom's Cabin** was still intended to be shown over three successive weeks.

Below: Asta Nielsen succumbing to impulse and an itinerant circus performer. This was the start of her descent to **The Abyss** – or **Afgrunden**, to give it its Danish title. She wasn't seen to enjoy her sinning – though audiences were vicariously thrilled. Opposite: Puritan America left such subjects to Europe, hoping to make the movie houses – now springing up all over the country – respectable with such subjects as **Uncle Tom's Cabin**, based on the novel by Harriet Beecher Stowe.

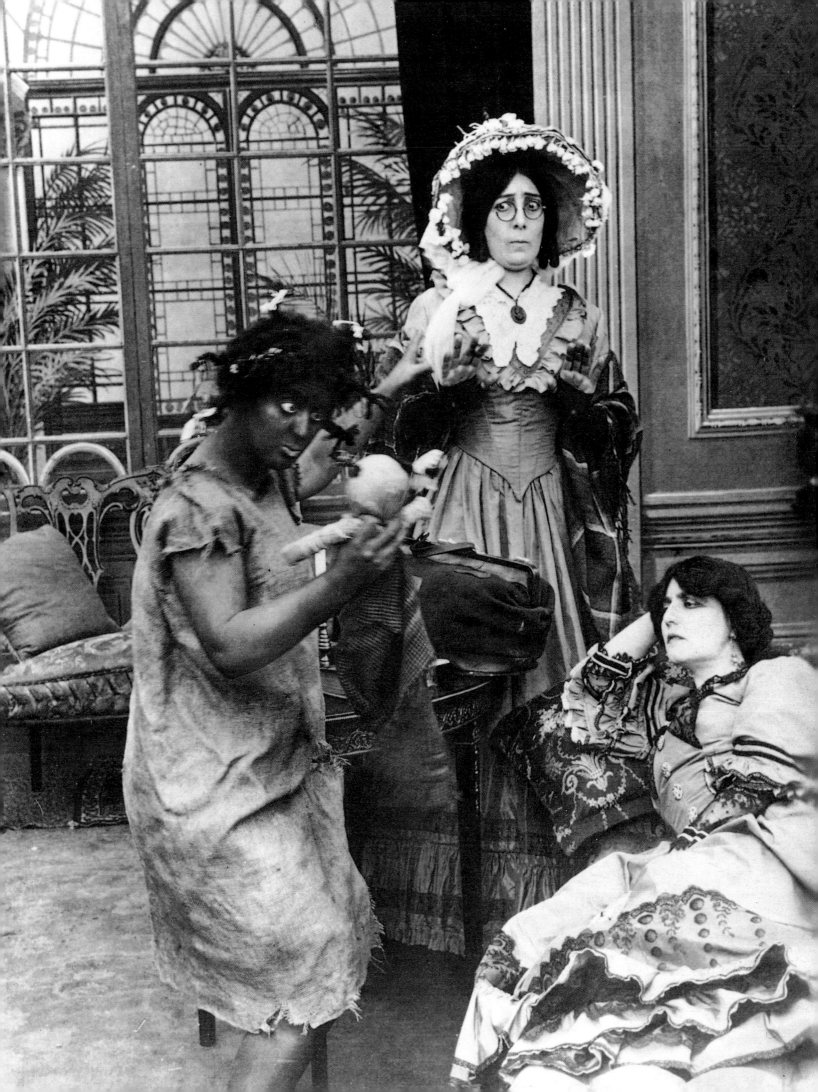

Vitagraph took note of the reception of **Uncle Tom's Cabin** and issued a three-reel **A Tale of Two Cities** (with Maurice Costello as Sidney Carton), to be shown at one sitting but with two breaks – partly because most cinemas still had only one projector, and partly because no one yet thought audiences could sit through a long story without a break.

1911

There was not much from anywhere else, though Denmark again advanced the cause of sex on the screen, with August Blom's taking little piece, **The Shop Girl**, about a young woman seduced by the boss's son, whose parents then refuse to let him marry her. The boot is on the other foot in **The Four Devils**, for the heroine makes it only too clear that she is willing to follow her lover into the bedroom. This is the first known reference to sexual intercourse in movies, apart from rape, and presumably the reason why the film enjoyed even greater success than the 'White slave trade' films.

France found an interesting new director in Albert Capellani, even if his **Notre Dame de Paris**, based on Hugo, is rather stodgy; but another old barnstormer, **Le Courrier de Lyon**, does create excitement while the audience waits to see whether an innocent man will go to the guillotine.

Above: **The Battle Hymn of the Republic** shows how Mrs Julia Ward Howe conceived the song of that title after visiting Lincoln at the White House. After a montage of battle scenes, it ends with a pageant of historic notables, including Napoleon and Jesus. Opposite: At three reels, **A Tale of Two Cities** was one of the longer films coming into fashion – but at that length it could accommodate only the rudiments of the plot.

The *Titanic* went to the bottom of the Atlantic, shocking the world not only because the ship was deemed unsinkable, but also because there were over 1,500 casualties. Denmark's **Drama at Sea** reflected the disaster, and although the drama is caused by a fire instead of an iceberg, the scenes of panic are filmed with virtuosity.

1912

The film event of the year, however, was rooted firmly in history. Sarah Bernhardt was persuaded to star in the first four-reel movie, **Les Amours de La Reine Elizabeth**, an inaccurate account of the Queen's relationship with the Earl of Essex (Lou Tellegen). During filming (in London) the company making it was forced into liquidation by Pathé. An American showman, Adolph Zukor, supplied the money to complete it, reasoning that the combination of star and subject would help his fight against the Patents trust. He retitled it **Queen Elizabeth** and opened it in July in New York to unprecedented acclaim. That enabled him to set up a new company, 'Famous Players', to bring the best of Broadway to the nickelodeons. Few of the results have survived, and in view of their renowned staginess that is neither regrettable nor surprising.

Above: D. W. Griffith's **The Musketeers of Pig Alley**, with Lillian Gish (left) as a poor girl who gets caught up with crooks when they steal her fiancé's money. The Americans still felt safe with the one-reeler. Right: Audiences, however, were ready for pictures of feature-length. Italy was at the forefront of those making longer and more expensive productions, such as the eight-reel **Quo Vadis?**.

1913

The only American feature film of consequence to survive is **Traffic in Souls** which slavishly copies the Danish 'White slave trade' movies, with a footnote or two on American hypocrisy (the mover behind the kidnapping of innocent virgins is an upright member of the community). Credibility, respectability and topicality were loaned to it when a decade-long investigation into prostitution culminated in the publication of a report on the subject in June. The film was instigated and directed for Laemmle's new Universal company by George Loane Tucker. The money it created put Universal on the map.

Britain's enthusiasm for longer movies of the classics resulted in a sluggish **Ivanhoe** and an even more torpid **David Copperfield**. Italy weighed in with **Gli Ultimi Giorni de Pompei**, which was livelier, as it couldn't fail to be. But Italy was poised to make a substantial contribution with the *divismo* movie, so called because the heroines were usually divas or actresses. Inspired by the success of Asta Nielsen and, above all, providing vehicles for the producers' paramours, they were a far cry from the dirndl charms of ringletted Mary Pickford, but the American film industry was preparing to cope with both images for the first time.

The cinema was twenty years old and growing up. Four countries each brought forth a masterpiece. From Russia came **Twilight of a Woman's Soul**, directed by Evgeni Bauer. An aristocratic woman turns to philanthropy and after too much wine at lunch lets the pauper she is visiting make love to her. She marries, and when she eventually confesses is disgusted by her husband's disgust, and has no forgiveness when he finds her after a two-year search.

In France **L'Enfant de Paris** was directed by Léonce Perret. A father returns to his 'orphaned' child to find her being shunted between a drunken shoemaker and his weak apprentice.

In Sweden Victor Sjöström directed **Ingeborg Holm**. The widow of a young tradesman is forced into bankruptcy by the actions of his assistant; she allows her children to go to foster parents, but despite their kindness becomes distraught to the point of insanity.

Germany issued **Der Student von Prag**, directed by Stellen Rye. An impoverished student is smitten by a countess, and is able to aspire to her hand after a stranger has offered him a fortune for his mirror reflection. In the end, however, he can no longer call his soul his own.

All four stories are bunkum, but they are told with a psychological insight, with superb locations, naturalistic acting and honesty.

Below: Paul Wegener in the title role of **Der Student von Prag**, a story he had concocted from several literary sources for a sinister tale of a student who trades his soul to the devil. Opposite above: In the nick of time! – a device used in just about every movie ever made. It had more than usual relevance, however, in **Traffic in Souls** because the heroine was in the clutches of White slave traders, but had managed to retain her virginity when the police arrived in the last reel. Opposite below: Hilda Borgstrom in Victor Sjöström's **Ingeborg Holm**, a strong social drama which follows the misfortunes of a young widow after her husband dies.

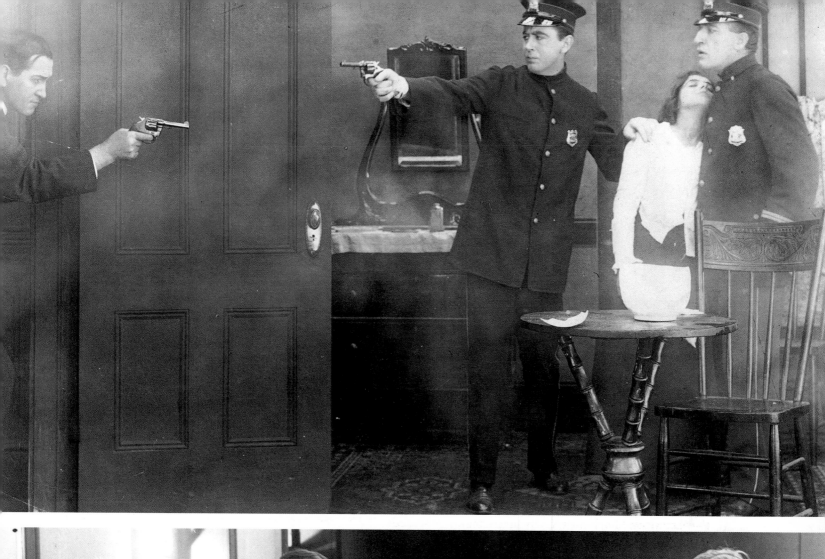
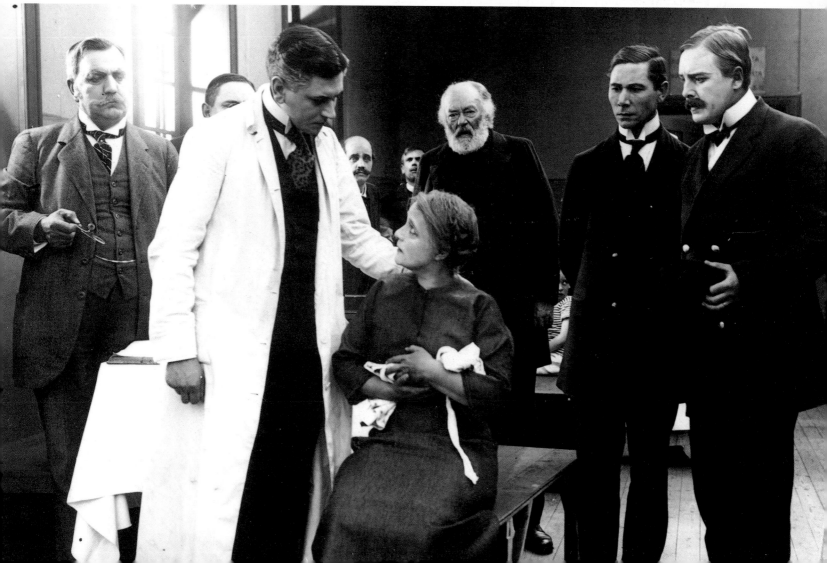

1914

Hollywood was born. Many companies were already shooting in California, which offered a) sunshine b) a variety of scenery, and c) an escape route to the Mexican border if the Patents Company should send out the lawmen. Jesse Lasky, emulating Zukor (they would later amalgamate to become Paramount), decided that he would film plays and sent Cecil B. DeMille and Dustin Farnum (who had starred in the original production) to Flagstaff, Wyoming, for **Squaw Man**. But it didn't look like the West, so they moved on to Los Angeles and rented a barn, preserved today as Hollywood's first studio.

The story, of a disgraced Englishman and the Indian girl who gives birth to his baby, holds no interest today, unlike **The Typhoon**, about a Japanese diplomat (Sessue Hayakawa) in Paris. This really does let us view a vanished world, as directed by Thomas H. Ince for Zukor. DeMille and Ince joined Griffith as America's three leading directors, the last of whom made **The Avenging Conscience**, one of the four films he directed for Reliance Majestic before opting for independence. It is a neatly made tale of murder and blackmail, but horribly melodramatic when compared with Reliance's two-reel **Detec-**

Above: Max Linder's popularity was at its peak when he was mobilized. Gassed at the front, he returned briefly to French films before accepting a Hollywood offer. Right: Winifred Kingston, Art Acord, Monroe Salisbury, Billy Elmer and Dustin Farnum in **Squaw Man**, the first picture to be made in what was to become Hollywood. DeMille brought a new vigour to movie-making, joining Griffith and Thomas H. Ince.

tive **Burton's Triumph**, which looks at the work of the police with a naturalism that would be rare in Hollywood for the next fifty years.

The year's most popular feature was a Keystone comedy directed by Mack Sennett, **Tillie's Punctured Romance**, in which Marie Dressler is a clumsy spinster pursued by a city slicker, Charlie Chaplin. Even the great Dressler cannot make this crude slapstick amusing today and its success then may have been due to Chaplin, who had arrived in movies earlier in the year and was making one-reelers for Keystone at the rate of almost one a week.

A well-known New York actor, Sidney Drew, arrived at Vitagraph, where he would make a series of fairly sophisticated two-reel comedies with the wife he met there. In the meantime he directed an extraordinary feature, **A Florida Enchantment**, in which the heroine, after taking some magic pills, starts dressing as a man and making love to her girlfriend. Her fiancé, scorned, also takes the pills and begins to wear dresses.

Among the foreign films were **Cabiria** from Italy, a spectacular set in Roman times which, at ten reels, was the longest film yet made, and **The Mysterious X** from Denmark, a convoluted thriller directed with skill by Benjamin Christensen. Denmark also produced a pacifist tract, **Down With Weapons!**, which was to have been premièred at the Vienna Peace Conference in September. The outbreak of the War in August put paid to that, and it was seen instead in the US, where it confirmed the view of many that the country should hold to neutrality.

The War was soon to have a serious effect on movie production in Britain, France and Germany, but before it did so a marvellous film was made in France, **Quatre-vingt-treize**, directed by Albert Capellani with the assistance of André Antoine. Capellani plays a landowner who becomes a revolutionary under the influence of a local priest and the canvas broadens, bringing in Danton and co., to finish with the guillotine.

Production was not affected in Russia, where Evgeni Bauer continued to make his amazing films. **Child of the Big City** tells of a wealthy playboy who, tired of his own set, takes up with a seamstress – who has only contempt for him after he has made her independently wealthy. The **Silent Witnesses** are the servants of a block of flats, whose wealthy inhabitants treat them cynically and cruelly. Bauer is easily the best director of this period: his films are psychologically complex, and he attempts zoom close-ups and panning shots.

Griffith's **The Avenging Conscience**, tells of the hellfire and redemption suffered by Henry Walthall (right) after murdering his uncle because he has forbidden him to see his sweetheart. It all turns out to be a dream.

The cinematic event of the year, alas, was **The Birth of a Nation**, which D. W. Griffith directed from a novel by the Revd Thomas Dixon, *The Clansman*. It opened on the West Coast under the latter title, and it was Dixon himself who chose the new one, which is both grandiloquent and dishonest. The Civil War was still fresh to many people and had been featured in countless one- and two-reelers. This film, lasting almost three hours, contains all the clichés of the genre – divided friends and families – as well as those of its maker, including the cutting between a mulatto governor trying to rape Lillian Gish and the Ku Klux Klan riding to the rescue. Its portrait of uppity blacks was considered offensive, even then, but the battle scenes are truly spectacular. It was road shown and extraordinarily popular, making converts of many who had previously despised movies.

The whole of it is not worth any one of the six reels of **The Italian**, co-directed by Reginald Barker and George Beban, who also plays the title role, an immigrant who because of poverty helps 'The Boss of the Underworld' to rig votes and become a 'Wealthy Politician'.

Also of the 'How the Other Half Lives' school is **Kindling**, with the star of the original Broadway play, Charlotte Walker, as a pregnant woman whose husband (Thomas Meighan) gets drawn into crime (again) because he doesn't want the baby born in the 'rat-hole' in which they live. This situation was repeated in **The Golden Chance**, the only difference being that the wife has previously succumbed to the advances of a millionaire (Wallace Reid). Both movies were directed, imaginatively and smoothly, by Cecil B. DeMille. Of the twelve features he made during 1915 the most sensational was **The Cheat**, about a silly society woman (Fannie Ward) who is branded, literally, by a Burmese playboy (Sessue Hayakawa) who has lent her money to replace the club funds she has embezzled.

1915

This film almost certainly came into being because of the sensation caused earlier in the year of a rather more hokey society tale, **A Fool There Was**, in which lust causes a decent man to abandon wife – and child – for a vamp who mocks her in the street. She has only to say 'Kiss me, my fool' to reduce him first to jelly, then to a falling-down drunk and, at the end, a corpse. All this owes

DeMille's **The Cheat**, in which Fannie Ward lets a Burmese playboy, Sessue Hayakawa, 'have his way with her' after he has helped her avoid a scandal. She's immediately sorry, of course.

as much to the *divismo* films as they owed to **Afgrunden**, even if Theda Bara as the vamp (the film coined this word) is a somewhat declassée version of the Italian actresses. William Fox, the showman who produced the film, did a mighty publicity job on Miss Bara, which was rather at odds with the mystery which was supposed to surround her. The film's success caused him to start the Fox Film Corporation, and the conjunction of the film and the new company enabled him to break the hold of the Patents Company, of which he, as exhibitor, had been its most powerful opponent.

Fox later issued **Regeneration**, directed by a former actor, Raoul Walsh, who described it as 'the first feature-length gangster film'. This may be true, but the crooks in it are closer to the counterfeiters of the first fiction films than the gangsters holding sway in the early Talkie era.

Lubin's **The Great Divide** must be mentioned, if only because the original play was being performed somewhere or other from 1906, when it first appeared on Broadway, till 1931, when the fourth and the last screen version was made. Ethel Clayton plays an Eastern girl who rejects the jolly young doctor who has followed her to Arizona. Saved from rape by a 'derelict', House Peters, she falls in love and marries him: but she cannot tell him so till the very end, long after *he* has raped her after a drink too many in a saloon with a Theda Bara lookalike.

The situation of effete Easterners in the Wild West was a popular one, exploited again in **The Lamb**, based on

a play which Douglas Fairbanks had done. He repeated it here, in his first film, and it was the year's most auspicious début.

In Italy, the *divismo* film went downmarket, but with a superb film, **Assunta Spina**, set among the launderers of Naples. Playing the wronged heroine is Francesca Bertini, the most accomplished of these actresses.

With the War worsening, nothing else of consequence was produced in Europe, though all governments realized the value of film as a panacea. In Russia, however, Evgeni Bauer made some more astonishing films, though their overall gloom may reflect the national mood at this perilous time. **Daydreams** examines the situation of a man who attempts to mould another woman in the image of his dead wife; **Children of the Age** finds a woman drawn by lust to a wealthy, ugly lecher instead of the handsome but impoverished husband whom she truly loves; **After Death** concerns a man attempting to find satisfaction with a strange woman after his mother has died, instead of the friend whom he really covets; and **The Happiness of Eternal Night** tells of a wealthy woman who rejects the doctor who has cured her blindness in favour of his worthless younger brother.

Below: Italy's *divismo* films found their finest interpreter in Francesca Bertini, here in the title-role of Gustavo Serena's **Assunta Spina**, the story of a Neapolitan laundress whose lover is sent to jail for wounding her. Opposite: William Fox's **A Fool There Was**, starring Theda Bara, was the first American version of these films. 'See what you have made me, and still you prosper, you hellcat,' says a bum as she departs for Europe.

1916

D. W. Griffith answered his critics with **Intolerance**, which was even more grandiose than **The Birth of a Nation**. Three hours long, it was divided into four parts, which ran concurrently: the fall of Babylon; the events leading to the Crucifixion; the massacre of the Huguenots in 1572; and a modern story on the bigotry of the self-righteous. An epilogue indicates that intolerance was responsible for the war in Europe. The film was a failure, as Thomas H. Ince was very pleased to find. He was Griffith's only rival as the artistic leader of the industry, making his own movie on the cataclysm in Europe. It went by the name of **Civilization**, ironically of course, since the monarch who forces his people into war is anything but civilized. As Europe collapsed, none other than Christ appeared to show him otherwise. The public turned up in droves.

Ince was everywhere, mainly in a supervisory role. **The Deserter**, directed by Scott Whitney and with the standard ingredients of the bar-room brawl, the covered wagons, the regimental dance and funeral, was one of the best of the Charles Ray Westerns he produced. Ince's encouragement also brought out the best in the gaunt-faced William S. Hart, whose position as the screen's most popular cowboy was confirmed with **Hell's Hinges**, directed by Reginald Barker. To the forsaken Western

Below: William S. Hart succeeded Broncho Billy as the screen's leading cowboy. He arrives bad, repents and reforms. This is **The Return of Draw Egan**, with Louise Glaum and Robert McKim. Opposite: Thomas H. Ince's **Civilization** was a riposte to Griffith, being not about the birth of a nation, but the end of one. It was also a response to several anti-isolationist movies, with no less than Christ (George Fisher) helping out.

town of the title comes the new parson and his sister; heading the lawless element are the saloon-keeper and Hart, but after one look at sister, Hart begins to convert. This became the Hart formula, and why not, since the film was extraordinarily popular?

Chaplin left Essanay for Mutual with his talent coming into flower: the tramp was sheer cheek, without the bombast and pathos with which Chaplin would later invest him.

In Germany, Asta Nielsen was clowning delightfully in drag in **Das Liebes ABC**. She decides that the fiancé chosen for her is too effeminate so she disguises herself as a man for a night on the town to show him how to be one. In Sweden, the homosexual director Mauritz Stiller adapted Herman Bang's novel *Mikael* (which would later attract Dreyer) as **The Wings**, in this version the story of two artists living together in harmony till the (much) younger one is smitten by a countess. Georg af Klercker made his best film, **Love's Victory**. An un-

happily married woman goes to Stockholm to become a star, but gives up the stage to live with the man she loves; she adopts her own child and her husband (the brute) turns up to blackmail her. In Denmark, Benjamin Christensen made **The Night of the Revenge**, casting himself as a convict with a seared soul, unable to go straight because his son has been adopted; and from August Blom came **The End of the World**, ostensibly about two planets colliding but in fact an allegory on the War, in which Denmark was neutral.

In Italy, the great actress Eleanora Duse made her only movie appearance, in **Cenere**, as a mother who abandons her son as a child. As an adult, he decides that they must make up for the years of separation by living together, but she commits suicide when his fiancée refuses to agree. Duse was then fifty-eight and is superb, virtually the only stage performer of this period to understand the demands of cinema.

In Russia, Yakov Protazanov directed **The Queen of Spades**, with Ivan Mosjukine as gambling Herman (a comparison with the 1910 version shows how far the cinema had developed in six years). Evgeni Bauer's **A Life for a Life** was intended to rival this, being an expensive and elaborate tale of adultery among the smart set. The scene in which the heroine waits in her negligée for her lover, her sister's husband, is quite remarkable for the time. The film has in common with Bauer's **Yuri Nagorni** the fact that both male protagonists are drunks, lechers and bounders. In the latter, a married woman sets out to seduce him in order to punish him. After they have made love she takes a lighted candle out of its holder and does nothing when, later, she sees the house burning.

Left: Douglas Fairbanks had been a Broadway favourite before moving into films in 1915. They were definitely more suitable for boundless energy. His co-star in his fifth film, **The Good Bad Man**, was Bessie Love. Above: Eleanora Duse in **Cenere** or **Ashes**, co-directed by Arturo Ambrosio and Febo Mari, seen on the right in the role of her son. Ambrosio and Mari wrote the screenplay together.

Three names dominate the industry in three very different types of film. Chaplin made his two-reel comedies, two of the best of which appeared in 1917: **Easy Street**, in which he joins the police force, and **The Immigrant**, which is self-explanatory. In both he finally gets the better of the gruesome bully Eric Campbell. Douglas Fairbanks was also appearing in a dozen pictures a year, five-reel efforts with interchangeable chin-up stories in most of which he was a ne'er-do-well who reforms at the end. Paramount restricted Mary Pickford's fans to about five films annually, running sometimes to six reels. These included, in 1917: **The Poor Little Rich Girl**, neglected by her parents until she nearly dies; and **Rebecca of Sunny-brook Farm**, ill-treated by two spinster aunts who don't want her. In both she played children, but the second of these started the habit of growing to adulthood for romance in the last reel. The public preferred her as a child, posterity as an adult, as in **A Romance of the Redwoods**, in which she keeps house for her uncle, a bandit, to discover at the end – after they have fallen in love – that he's neither. Cecil B. DeMille directed, as he did two elaborate vehicles for Geraldine Farrar, the opera star: **The Woman God Forgot**, the story of an Aztec maiden loved by a conquistador; and **Joan the Woman** – of Arc, that is – to remind audiences of the fighting in Europe. Indeed, an epilogue took place in the present day, making the film all the more topical in April when the US declared war on Germany after the sinking of the *Lusitania*.

Three other star vehicles: Helen Chadwick in **The Angel Factory**, escaping from brutal parents and given a home in a haven run by a wealthy philan-thropist (Antonio Moreno), who doesn't realize that he loves her until he's accused of murder several reels later; Pauline Starke in Frank Borzage's **Until They Get Me**, in a quandary because the Mountie she loves has to bring in someone she pities; and Molly King in **The On-the-square Girl**, a mannequin who discovers that one of her suitors is the man who deserted her mother years before. This is one of the growing number of films to suggest that an innocent glass of wine will lead to seduction or rape.

In Sweden, Sjöström made **The Girl from Stormy-croft**, concerning the tribulations of an unwed mother. For the period, this is a mature picture, but in turning to the epic he made two of his greatest films, both with

1917

As Charlie Chaplin's popularity continued to soar, Mutual (whom he had joined in 1916) allowed him longer to prepare his films. In one of the best of them, **Easy Street**, he swopped his bowler for a policeman's helmet.

himself in the leading role: **Terje Vigen**, about a sailor who breaches the British blockade, during the war with Napoleon, so that the family won't starve; and **The Outlaw and his Wife**, whose happy marriage deteriorates into hatred and ends in tragedy, because they are living in sin. God can't have that. Set in Iceland, in the distant past, it was influenced by the Norse sagas.

In Russia, Bauer was killed in an accident while making **The King of Paris**, the tale of a man who agonized throughout his marriage because he once allowed a homosexual to take him home. Bauer's other last films are equally extraordinary: **The Dying Swan** concerns a mute dancer whose artist discoverer becomes obsessed by the idea of painting her dying; **To Happiness** is about a widow who insists on making the sacrifice of giving her lover to her daughter because she, too, is in love with him and hasn't long to live; and **The Revolutionary**, whose adventures are followed from 1905 to exile in Siberia in 1917, when he discusses whether the country should stay in the War or sue for peace. The film, which was released in April, could only have been made because the Czar had conceded some power to the liberals, but nothing in it anticipates the convulsive events of October.

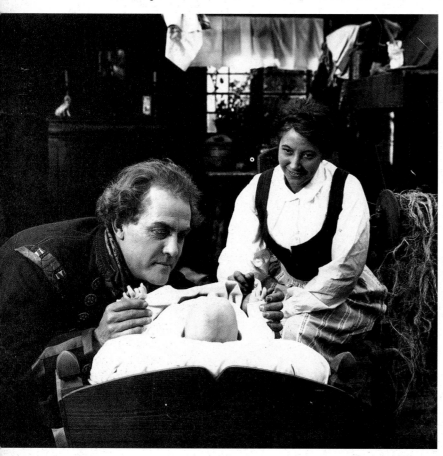

Above: Sweden was untouched by the War, but its grim, dour and heroic films suited the European mood. The best of them were made by Victor Sjöström, who usually played the lead. Here he is, a happy young husband, his troubles yet to come, in **Terje Vigen**, based on Ibsen's epic poem. Right: Mary Pickford out West in **A Romance of the Redwoods**, an unashamed star vehicle for 'America's Sweetheart'.

1918

The Armistice was signed on 11 November and the War in Europe finished. The world laughed when Chaplin was in the trenches in **Shoulder Arms**, his most successful film yet, justifying his decision to move to three-reelers and reduce his output. D. W. Griffith had also slowed down. **Hearts of the World**, started before the US entered the conflict, was the first major American film on the War, acknowledging that it brought heartbreak, shell-shock, the wounded and separation, as suffered by a French couple (Lillian Gish, Robert Harron), who spend their wedding night on the battlefield. Otherwise, however, it was the same old Griffith film as ever was, with audiences wondering which of the many dirty Huns would actually get to rape Lillian in the last reel.

The War was on DeMille's mind when he made **The Whispering Chorus**, since its subject was the responsibility for individual evil. It examines the fate of a couple whose troubles begin when the husband delves into embezzlement to buy his wife a new dress. In looking at the intricacies of marriage – thrown into relief by wartime separations – DeMille came up with the idea that till then had been ignored by American movies, that they (marriages) were not always harmonious. It was not a subject new to the theatre, where the concept had been propounded by Somerset Maugham, Schnitzler and Bernard Shaw. Where they were cynical, however, Mr DeMille was not. He called his next film **Old Wives for New**, an idea eventually declined by his protagonist.

The **Lady of the Dugout** is an astonishing film written and directed by W. S. Van Dyke, starring Al Jennings, who also produced. One of the country's most famous bandits has reformed, but he tells of the old days, of the lady of the title, turned out by her family because of her choice of husband, who subsequently becomes a surly drunk. Al and brother Frank heroically help her, but the film makes no bones about the fact that they had also once robbed banks.

Germany's Ernst Lubitsch made his international reputation with **Carmen**, starring Pola Negri, but the only foreign films of consequence were three made in Russia by Yakov Protazanov. **Jenny the Maid** is a rich girl who, impoverished on the death of her father, becomes a domestic; the young master, invalided home from the front, falls in love with her – and is surprised to find that she can play the piano and read English. A happy ending. **Little Ellie** has been murdered in a provincial town. The mayor (Ivan Mosjukine) later marries her mother, with whom he has been infatuated, but he behaves oddly and finally admits that the girl died while he was pursuing her because she looked like her mother. And Mosjukine was Tolstoy's **Father Sergius**, a courtier who enters a monastery when his future bride tells him she is the mistress of the man who ordered him to marry. She comes to his cell to seduce him and he cuts off a finger to prevent concupiscence.

Below: Ivan Mosjukine (right) in Protazanov's powerful **Father Sergius**. Opposite above: Dorothy Gish in **Hearts of the World**, filmed in Britain and France at the invitation of the British Government in order to sway American opinion. It was begun in the spring of 1917, but the US was in the War by the time it was finished. Opposite below: Raymond Hatton and Kathlyn Williams in DeMille's **The Whispering Chorus**.

1919

The world loves a love story: Mary Pickford married Douglas Fairbanks. They, with Griffith and Chaplin, formed United Artists, which wasn't actually their idea, but when suggested to them they jumped at the chance of enjoying the profits from their own films. Fairbanks's optimism was even more welcome as America recovered from the trauma of sending its young men an ocean away to kill and be killed. He upheld American democratic values as he inherited a European crown in **His Majesty, the American**: he wrote it himself, not with any great originality (since it had the same plot as **Hawthorne of the USA**, in which he had appeared on stage in 1912, and which Paramount now filmed, with Wallace Reid). The title of his other 1919 movie, **When the Clouds Roll By**, reflects the national mood: it is the same old Fairbanks vehicle, with as villain a sinister psychiatrist who thinks Doug's high spirits suspicious.

Griffith's first film for the new company was the successful **Broken Blossoms**, with Richard Barthelmess as the Chinaman who cares for Lillian Gish after she has fled her cruel stepfather, Donald Crisp. The stylized studio sets evoked much admiration, and when other studios learnt that they had cost so little they curtailed location shooting. The great age of production design had begun, but the loss is all the more evident in looking at Griffith's films on either side of it, **True Heart Susie** and **The Greatest Question**, when his cameraman, Billy Bitzer, makes such beautiful use of the rural settings. The first of these may well be Griffith's best film, a charming fable with Lillian Gish in the title role, paying to have Robert Harron educated, only to have him fall for Clarine Seymour, a hussy from Chicago.

DeMille's **Don't Change Your Husband** found Gloria Swanson discovering that the philandering of her new husband was no more satisfying than the dull life she had led with the old one. This director went on to Barrie's *The Admirable Crichton*, retitled **Male and Female**. Paramount reasoned that audiences would think it was about an admiral, whereas the material had been so adapted to be much like DeMille's other sex comedies. Swanson was Lady Betty, adoring butler Thomas Meighan when he lords it over the family after they've been shipwrecked. Paramount had offered DeMille Conrad's

Below: Paramount made **Victory**, the first of its three versions of Conrad's book. Seena Owen was the heroine, being menaced here by Lon Chaney. Opposite: Screen villainy was to find a virtuoso new interpreter in Erich Von Stroheim. His formula, however, was simple: there were many **Blind Husbands** and all he needed to do was exploit the situation. The lady being swayed by his sweet-talk is Franciella Beddington.

Victory, but he wasn't interested; Maurice Tourneur made a thrilling film of it, with Seena Owen as the girl who prefers nice Jack Holt to creepy Wallace Beery.

Another outstanding film was one more that questioned the sanctity of marriage, but on this occasion decadent old Europe could be blamed rather than confident young America. **Blind Husbands** was written and directed by Erich Von Stroheim, who had been playing nasty Huns in war movies. He loved donning uniform and did so again here, as a lecherous lieutenant at an Alpine resort taking advantage of the fact that an American husband neglects his wife.

From Germany, Ernst Lubitsch's **Madame Du Barry**, retitled **Passion** to disguise its origins, was successful enough to challenge Hollywood's pre-eminent position, but, beyond noting that Pola Negri had the title role and Emil Jannings was Louis XV, it is difficult now to see why. Lubitsch, a former comic actor, was happier with comedy and two vehicles for Ossi Oswalda remain charming and funny. Both **The Oyster Princess** and **The Doll** concern her wanting a husband: in the first she decides to marry a prince and gets an especially impoverished one through a marriage bureau, and in the second she pretends to be one of her father's life-size dolls in order to appeal to the man she has chosen. Richard Oswald followed his other films about sex with **Anders Als Die Andern**, in which concert violinist Conrad Veidt is blackmailed and driven to suicide after caressing the cheek of a male student.

Above: Victor Sjöström in his magnificent two-part **The Ingmarssons**, from Selma Lagerlof's series of novels, in this case about a troubled marriage with both parties haunted by grief. The film offers a fine portrait of life in rural nineteenth-century Sweden. Right: Paramount had no challengers as manufacturers of the most mature, sophisticated movies – notably exemplified by the marital comedies of Cecil B. DeMille: **Don't Change Your Husband** with Gloria Swanson and Lew Cody.

1920

A dismal year. It is hard to feel any enthusiasm for the products from the new United Artists, which included two sentimental pictures with Mary Pickford, **Pollyanna** and **Suds**, and Fairbanks's first eager, muddled foray into the swashbuckler, **The Mark of Zorro**. Of the major figures, only William S. Hart came through, with two major Westerns, **The Toll Gate** and **The Testing Block**, with direction by Lambert Hillyer and stories so similar that it's hard to tell them apart. After five years in movies, the director William DeMille, Cecil's brother, first showed his mettle with **Conrad in Search of His Youth**, in which Thomas Meighan is disillusioned when visiting his old flames.

Buster Keaton left behind a promising career as Fatty Arbuckle's sidekick to star in his own two-reelers, starting with **One Week**, released in August. He followed with **Convict 13**, **The Scarecrow** and **Neighbors**, to prove that we're not talking about sidekicks or Silent clowns but a comic genius.

In Sweden, Victor Sjöström confirmed his mastery with **Masterman**, a powerful and many-faceted study of a solitary, aged bachelor in a small seaport whose life is transformed when he becomes involved with a young couple in marital difficulties. The film dwarfs everything else made at this time, except **Karin Ingmarsdotter**, Sjöström's sequel to **The Ingmarssons**, which also beautifully celebrates the quiet rural life of the nineteenth century. The world's film industries, mesmerized by the cheap melodramatics of D. W. Griffith, didn't want to know, with the exception of France where Marcel L'Herbier directed **L'Homme du Large**, inspired by Sjöström's **Terje Vigen**. Roger Karl, even looking like Sjöström in that film, plays a dedicated fisherman grieving because his son prefers the pleasures of the town.

This was hardly seen abroad, while one German film takes its spurious place in film history by being discussed more perhaps than any film yet made. This is **Das Cabinet Des Dr Caligari**, directed by Robert Wiene with highly stylized sets – chiefly because they had no money for anything more solid. The story, in the German fantastic tradition, is satisfying in its Chinese box way. A showman (Werner Krauss) exhibits a somnambulist (Conrad Veidt), predicts a murder and is later found to be the director of a lunatic asylum. These fine players overact absurdly – just two of its many excesses. It was written by Carl Mayer (with Hans Janowitz) and produced by Erich Pommer, major talents who would go on to make some outstanding films. They knew better than to try to repeat this one, and the many imitations all failed miserably. But **Caligari** itself is an imitation, of George Kaiser's play **Von Morgens bis Mitternacht**, filmed earlier with direction by Karl-Heinz Martin. Both stage and film productions used stylized sets: they also play on the horror tradition and concern a man in a dark world which is getting the better of him.

Below: Thomas Meighan as **Conrad in Search of his Youth**. Opposite: German cinema benefited from attracting Berlin's intellectuals and major theatre talents. Its first great international flowering was the film now known just as **Caligari**. If still fascinating, it hardly justifies the acclaim it received, but there were powerful appearances by Conrad Veidt (in the foreground) and Werner Krauss (in the straightjacket).

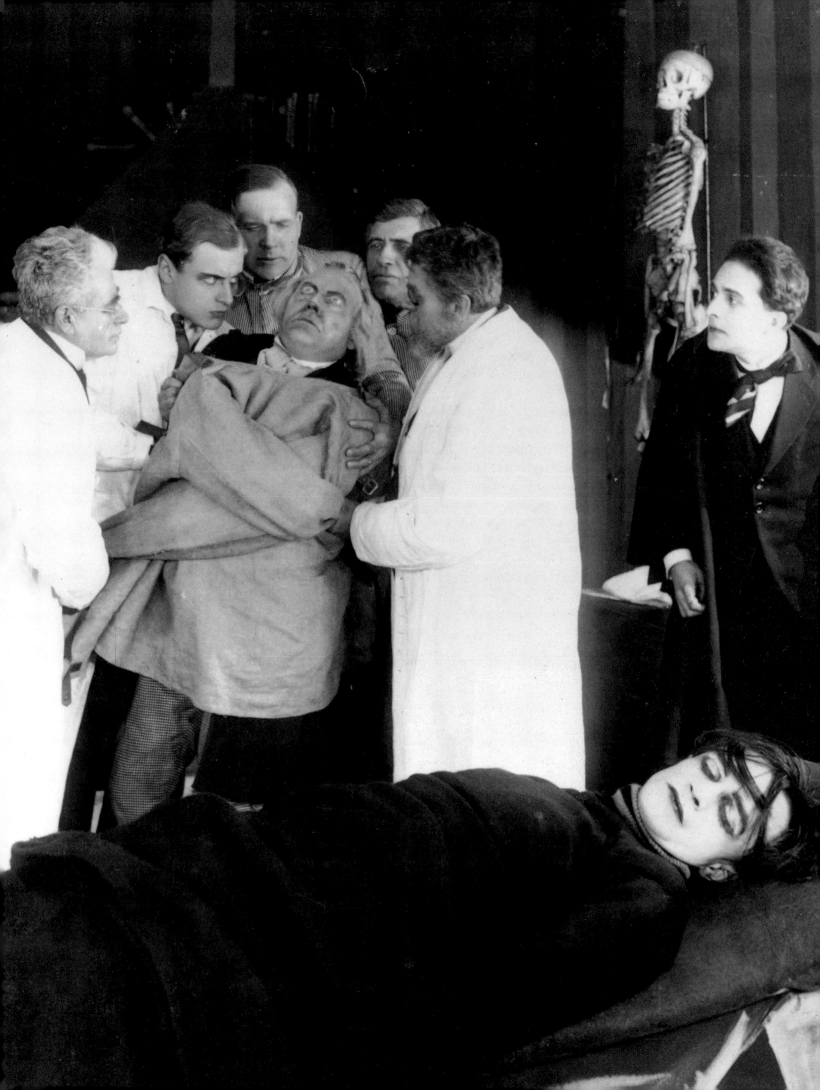

Audiences laughed and wept at Chaplin's **The Kid**, his first feature, in which he adopts and brings up a lovable waif, played by Jackie Coogan, who became a star in his own right. Technically it is little more than a series of music hall sketches and seldom as funny as **The Idle Class**, a return to two-reelers, in which he played both the tramp and a

1921

rich man. He was seldom as agile as when, having forgotten to put on his pants, he tries to cross a hotel lobby without anyone noticing.

Douglas Fairbanks forgot his pants in **The Nut** and exchanged them permanently for doublet and hose – during the Silent period, at least – in **The Three Musketeers**, a considerable improvement on his last swashbuckler. Mary Pickford played mother and son in **Little Lord Fauntleroy**.

Buster Keaton made his feature début in **The Saphead**, not a Keaton vehicle but a straightforward remake of Fairbanks's **The Lamb**. His wonderful shorts included **The Goat**, **The Playhouse**, **The Boat** and **The Paleface**. Harold Lloyd was edging towards features with **Now or Never**, **Never Weaken** and **A Sailor-Made Man**. Arriving in the US, Max Linder went straight into features with **Seven Years Bad Luck** and **Be My Wife**.

The title of the first of these must have brought an ironic smile to the lips of Fatty Arbuckle, whose career was ruined after being accused of statutory rape in a San Francisco hotel. Although clearly innocent and indeed acquitted, he was dropped by Paramount.

D. W. Griffith had two big, long ones with **Way Down East** and a story of the French Revolution, **Orphans of the Storm**. Both were based on antique stage melodramas. That audiences didn't laugh may have been due to the performances of Lillian Gish, though the climax of the first remains exciting, as Richard Barthelmess rescues her from the ice flow. Barthelmess himself was in the year's best movie, Henry King's beautiful **Tol'able David**, in the title role, the country boy who takes on the fearsome Ernest Torrence.

There was a polarization growing among American film-makers. Audiences were certainly happy with the galloping melodramas they were offered. King looked for more realistic subjects, as did Maurice Tourneur, co-directing **Foolish Matrons** with a newcomer, Clarence Brown. A foreword tells us that some women marry for love, some for ambition and some simply to have a

Below: Richard Barthelmess succeeded Robert Harron as Griffith's leading man. **Tol'able David** found him confronted by Ernest Torrence, perhaps the best of the many terrifying heavies of the Silent screen. Opposite: Rudolf Valentino, a former gigolo, café dancer and extra, achieved solid stardom in his second film of the year, **The Four Horsemen of the Apocalypse**. Alice Terry watches him teach one lucky lady to tango.

husband, and the film goes on to tell three separate stories.

The DeMilles came up with contrasting examples of the two forms in December, both of them special. William's **Miss Lulu Bett** concerns a slavey (Lois Wilson) in the kitchen, wondering whether to escape from it by marriage to the schoolteacher or her playful brother-in-law. Cecil's **Fool's Paradise** cannot be described as succinctly, moving as it does from a boom town near the Mexican border to a Siamese palace with an alligator pit, but suffice to say that the girl (Dorothy Dalton) from the cantina impersonates a famous French actress in order to marry the man (Conrad Nagel) she adores.

A month earlier, the same studio (Paramount) had come up with something even more exotic, **The Sheik**, with its new acquisition in the title role, Rudolf Valentino. He abducted an English milady, Agnes Ayres, who soon went native – as most of his female fans would gladly have done for him.

By this time **The Four Horsemen of the Apocalypse** should have gone, since it premièred in February; but it stayed for months in many cities, and not only because the new star, Valentino, plays an Argentine gigolo who becomes a war hero in the trenches of France. Rex Ingram directed from a novel by Vicente Blasco-Ibañez for the small Metro company, which spared no expense in re-creating the battlefields. At a time when war memorials were being erected on four continents, here was a romantic view of war – which clearly was what the public wanted, for with one exception, **The Singing Fool** in 1928, it was the biggest box-office success between **The Birth of a Nation** and **Gone With the Wind**.

The great Victor Sjöström continued to have no luck with foreign distributors, who imported **The Phantom Carriage** for quite the wrong reason, because it is a tract on the evils of drink. It was welcomed and much praised, but it confirmed the Swedes as gloomy film-makers; and it is far from being his best picture. He may, again, have been the inspiration of a French movie, **La Terre**, but the director, André Antoine, had once appeared in a dramatized version of Zola's novel.

The German industry again won foreign plaudits with its penchant for the mystical: F. W. Murnau's **Nosferatu**, based on Bram Stoker's *Dracula*, and Fritz Lang's **Der Müde Tod** which, in three separate tales, attempts to prove that 'love is stronger than death'. **Ich Möchte Kein Mann Sein** was a vehicle for Ossi Oswalda, who spends most of her time dressed as a man, with Consequences. It was a backward step for Lubitsch, but it had actually been made two years earlier.

German director Ernest Lubitsch came into his own with **Die Bergkatze**, a satire on military life with several moments of knockabout. Here, some officers cavort with Pola Negri, in the title role.

75

U niversal was publicizing **Foolish Wives** as its most expensive film to date and the most eagerly anticipated one yet made – a view with which its writer-director, Erich Von Stroheim, wholeheartedly concurred. Behind the scenes they were quarrelling about length. The studio eventually got it down to a manageable size and then it was mutilated by censors in virtually every country in which it was shown. For, like most show-off films, it was really a showcase for the director's fantasies. It is only too easy to be horribly fascinated by Von Stroheim's portrait of a cavalry officer, fetishistically uniformed, as he embarks on his schemes to seduce or rape most of the fairer sex living in or around Monte Carlo. In Von Stroheim's defence, a subtext suggests that the world is a very cruel place, which few American movies were prepared to admit.

The critics burbled over it in superlatives, which

1922

Above: Leatrice Joy in DeMille's **Manslaughter**: her proudest boast is that speed never stopped her. A traffic cop does, and she leaves him with a dropped diamond bracelet which she swears isn't hers. Right: The acclaim for Von Stroheim's first two films went to Universal's head, and he was allowed to duplicate half Monte Carlo on the back lot for **Foolish Wives**. He was also permitted to make a film of inordinate length (either thirty-four reels as he claimed, or twenty-one, as records suggest).

they trotted out again for what many think of as the screen's first feature-length documentary, **Nanook of the North**, a 'study' of life among the Eskimoes. For its maker, Robert Flaherty, it began what would become the most inflated reputation in cinema history after Chaplin – for one thing, all the scenes were staged, although the later ones do have a raw power.

Far preferable are Buster Keaton's **The Frozen North**, or any of his half-dozen two-reelers, two of which – **Cops** and **Daydreams** – are as bleak and funny as anything ever put on celluloid. The two opposing qualities are not unique to him, but no one else combined them with sheer genius.

The flapper appeared on the screen for the first time in **Manslaughter** in the comely person of Leatrice Joy, and just to make sure that she suffers for her sins, she goes to jail. Cecil B. DeMille directed, with little of his former verve and much of his later moralizing. Paramount further offered audiences vicarious thrills with **Blood and Sand**, when wealthy Nita Naldi plays around with matador Rudolf Valentino.

Love went no more smoothly in **The Toll of the Sea**, with a story as close to *Madame Butterfly* as made no difference; Anna May Wong was the wronged Lotus Blossom. This was the first feature in Technicolor, after a short – **The Gulf Between** – four years earlier, when the projectionist was required to have the knowledge of a scientist and the skill of an acrobat. The Technicolor Corporation had continued to experiment, and while this one was easier to show, it proved that the full palette was still lacking.

The **Cops** are out parading, and among them you may recognize a forlorn Buster Keaton. The two other great Silent clowns, Chaplin and Lloyd, were often society's rejects, but they were less original.

For many years Lon Chaney had been an admired villain, partly because of his extraordinary ability to change his appearance and partly because of his piercing eyes. Universal, which had been using him more than most companies (at one time he had been under contract to them), decided to star him in an expensive version – the sets were some of the biggest yet constructed – of **The Hunchback of Notre Dame**, based on Victor Hugo's novel. As the pitiable, deformed Quasimodo, Chaney confirmed his star status, and the film was one of the year's most popular; but Universal promptly blundered and did not sign him to a contract. The studio's brilliant young executive, Irving Thalberg, would take Chaney to MGM the following year.

Confident of its supremacy in the industry, Paramount poured a mint into one of its biggest productions: James Cruze's account of pioneer days, **The Covered Wagon**. It was regarded as a yardstick in the years to come.

Also among the year's biggest films were two from Paramount. Westerns had retained their popularity regardless of familiarity, but **The Covered Wagon** was something else. It was about the opening out of the West, the landrush which began in what became Kansas City. Many of the older pioneers were still alive, while their children and grandchildren were pleased to see their courage exalted on the screen. **The Ten Commandments** could not have been more different: after a long prologue featuring the events related

1923

in Exodus, cinemagoers were treated to an urban morality tale, showing what happened when one brother broke the commandments and the other didn't.

The habit of showing similar events in different

periods was satirized by Buster Keaton in **Three Ages**, which looked at courtship in the Stone Age, in the Roman era and in the present day. It was the first feature over which he himself had control, and as he himself pointed out was really three shorts packaged together. It has neither the quality of his best shorts or of the later features, including **Our Hospitality**, in which he is caught between two feuding families in the old South. Also in November Harold Lloyd was similarly involved, in **Why Worry?**, as an innocent very much abroad, caught up in a banana republic revolution. Splendid as both films are, Lloyd takes the year's comedy crown for his greatest stunt, climbing up a skyscraper in **Safety Last**.

There were echoes of the so-called Expressionist movement in both Robert Wiene's **Raskolnikov**, based on Dostoevsky, and Arthur Robinson's **Schatten**, known in English as **Warning Shadows**, but the strains of the movement are stronger and more haunting in Karl Grune's **Die Strasse**, in which a mild little man leaves home to spend the night learning about life in the company of a whore. The film's success will give rise to other dramas of prostitution and the underbelly of society. It was clearly far preferable for a defeated Germany, now facing inflation and mass unemployment, to exchange sour dreams for stark reality.

Below: Harold Lloyd climbs a Los Angeles skyscraper in **Safety Last**. It still works wonderfully well today. Audiences find it impossible to watch without feeling giddy with fear at one moment and hysterical with laughter the next. Opposite: Cecil B. DeMille's study of **The Ten Commandments** – how they got to be engraved on the tablets and how they might be interpreted in this modern but decadent age.

1924

American society was changing, but this was not reflected in the films of D. W. Griffith, whose decline continued with **America**, about the American Revolution, and **Isn't Life Wonderful?**, showing a Polish peasant family coping in a Germany in defeat after the First World War.

Lubitsch found his form in two marital comedies, **The Marriage Circle** and **Three Women**, the first set in bad, old Vienna and the second in good, new New York. He also made a delicious comedy about Catherine the Great, **Forbidden Paradise**. It was acknowledged, though, that Americans indulged in flirtations if not in actual adultery. The age of the flapper was just beginning and here they are, in **Wine of Youth**, drinking cocktails and going for midnight swims. The boys and girls sleep in separate tents, but there are misunderstandings about 'sinning' – as there would be in countless films over the next few years. The director in this case was King Vidor, who also offered the most exciting of the year's melodramas, **Wild Oranges**, in which an old man, his granddaughter and a stranger – the hero – are menaced by the brutal 'half-man half-boy' handyman.

Manhandled may have sounded much the same, but the title is a reference to the way Gloria Swanson feels as she travels to work in the subway. She had moved a long

Above: Life isn't easy for the great Buster, apprehensive in his love for Kathryn McGuire in **Sherlock Junior**. Opposite: Fox, challenged by the new rivalry between MGM and Paramount, threw down its own gauntlet in the shape of an expansive Western about the early days of the railroad. **The Iron Horse** was filmed almost entirely on location by John Ford, with George O'Brien and Madge Bellamy in the leading roles.

way down society since her previous film, which was Paramount's way of reflecting the changing times. DeMille did so for the same company with **Triumph**, in which the forewoman (Leatrice Joy) of a canning factory is wooed both by a manager (Victor Varconi), preaching socialism, and its playboy owner (Rod La Rocque).

Harold Lloyd was **Girl Shy** and in **Hot Water**, respectively hoping to publish a book on love (about which, predictably, he knows nothing) and trying to tame both a new car and his mother-in-law. But this year he takes second place, if not at the box-office, to the great Buster, at his most poetic as a dreaming cinema projectionist in **Sherlock Junior**, and at his most imaginative alone with his girl on a deserted liner in **The Navigator**. And Douglas Fairbanks flew over minarets on a magic carpet in **The Thief of Bagdad**.

There was magic of a similar sort in Paramount's much admired **Peter Pan**, directed by Herbert Brenon with Betty Bronson in the title role, but that was beaten for the year's weirdest film by Fox's **The Last Man on Earth**. The title says it all. It is set in a future, said to be 1940, which happily never came. Fox made amends with **The Iron Horse**, made precisely because of the success of **The Covered Wagon**. Again, the story is trite, but the background – the construction of the railroads over the Great Plains – is thrillingly depicted. John Ford directed, confirming his mastery of the epic style.

A new studio was born when the distributor Marcus Loew amalgamated three production companies he had bought because he needed product for the cinemas which

he also owned – Metro, Goldwyn and Mayer. With a former scrap-metal dealer, Louis B. Mayer, in command, and with Irving Thalberg from Universal in assistance, the company immediately went into overdrive. That said, it remains unclear which was its first production. Having taken on Goldwyn's roaring lion as its trademark, and its slogan, 'Ars Gratia Artis', the company released its new films under various forms of its name, Metro-Goldwyn-Mayer. The first may well be **He Who Gets Slapped**, an arcane circus melodrama featuring three people who would become glories for Metro (as we may sometimes call it): Lon Chaney, as the scientist who becomes a clown; Norma Shearer, as the bareback rider whom he adores; and John Gilbert, as Chaney's rival and her partner. The director was Victor Sjöström, whom MGM had anglicized as Seastrom. 'For dramatic value and a faultless adaptation of the play,' said the *New York Times*, 'this is the finest production we have yet seen.'

But the eulogies for this movie were as nothing for those for the Sjöström/Seastrom-influenced **Greed**, which MGM had most certainly inherited from the Goldwyn Company, none of whose executives were very enthusiastic about it. Its perpetrator was Erich Von Stroheim, who had seen in Frank Norris's novel *McTeague* a chance to make an epic in the manner of **The Ingmarssons**. The two have much in common: they are melodrama merging into tragedy as they examine a mismatched marriage; both are meticulous reconstructions of past times filmed almost wholly on location. **Greed** is set in San Francisco; the husband (Gibson

Left: The wedding night in **Greed**: Zasu Pitts was already thinking about accumulating money and Gibson Gowland had been imbibing too much to think about consummation. Von Stroheim directed. Above: King Vidor's masterly **Wild Oranges** took an equally sour look at a segment of American society, as half-witted handyman Charles A. Post tries to force his attentions on Virginia Valli. Opposite: The first real Metro-Goldwyn-Mayer (MGM) film was almost certainly **He Who Gets Slapped**. The director, Victor Seastrom (Sjöström in Sweden) is photographed here between the stars, Lon Chaney, Norma Shearer and John Gilbert.

Gowland) is a dentist; it is the obsession of the wife (Zasu Pitts) with money which spells their doom; and it is very long – but like most of Von Stroheim's other films, it was originally very much longer.

Speaking of epic, Fritz Lang went for broke in Germany with his version of the dark age sagas in his two-part **Die Nibelungen**. This country's varied output also included Arnold Fanck's **Der Berg des Schicksals**, which confirmed his – and his audiences' – fascination with the cleansing mountain spaces; Carl Dreyer's **Michael**, which daringly (for the time) examined the relationship of a painter (Benjamin Christensen) with his 'adopted son' (Walter Slezak); and F. W. Murnau's **Der Letzte Mann**, which brought international fame to both himself and Emil Jannings, playing a hotel doorman who cannot adjust, to put it mildly, to demotion to lavatory attendant. For reasons no longer apparent, this was for many years the most famous foreign film. Runner-up would be a Swedish film known under various titles, but which we shall call **Gösta Berlings Saga**. Mauritz Stiller

directed this enormously complicated and dusty story about an aristocratic family in the early nineteenth century. One reason for its fame was that it gave cinemagoers their first view of a girl who was to hold them in thrall for almost two decades, Greta Garbo.

Two important talents, both directors, made their film débuts in France: René Clair with a brief *jeu d'esprit*, **Paris Qui Dort**, and Jean Renoir with **La Fille de l'Eau**, a misguided attempt to make a star of his wife, Catherine Hessling: but at least its summery views reminded us that he was the son of the great painter. France's best film was Marcel L'Herbier's version of the Pirandello piece about a man who was thought dead till his past catches up with him, **Feu Mathias Pascal**, and its biggest film was Raymond Bernard's story of rivalry between the French and Burgundian courts, **Le Miracle des Loups**. At the other end of the scale is Léon Poirier's **La Brière**, which recommends itself to posterity for its portrait of life in the marshes of the Loire, where each village hates its neighbour and where life hasn't changed for centuries.

The new company, Metro-Goldwyn-Mayer, replaced Paramount as the leader of the industry with films such as **The Circle**, from Somerset Maugham's play about a wife tempted to run off with her lover. It starred Eleanor Boardman, as did **Proud Flesh**, directed by King Vidor, who was shortly to marry her. Perhaps that's why she's radiant here, as a Señorita

1925

staying with her down-to-earth San Francisco relatives, caught between her foppish Spanish suitor and a local plumber. But it took three films towards the end of the year to establish Metro's supremacy, two of them with John Gilbert. Despite the problems with **Greed**, there was never any doubt that Von Stroheim should direct **The Merry Widow** – as a vehicle for Mae Murray, she of the 'bee-stung' lips. Gilbert was cast as Danilo, the prince ordered to woo her because of the national debt, and Von Stroheim offers assorted lecheries and fetishisms before getting to the plot of Lehar's operetta. In King Vidor's **The Big Parade**, Gilbert is a playboy who joins the army and woos a French girl, Renée Adorée, before going into battle. The battle sequences were the best yet to depict the War and the film was a big success. **Ben Hur** was another property the new company inherited, undergoing many production changes and rising costs till it emerged, a colossus of the screen. Fred Niblo was the credited director and Ramon Novarro, who replaced the original lead, was confirmed as a star.

The only Paramount picture still quite as thrilling is a documentary, **Grass: A Nation's Battle for Life**, a record by Merian Cooper and Ernest B. Schoedsack of the Bakhtiari tribe's annual migration through dangerous territory. Adolphe Menjou was **The King on Main Street** for Monta Bell, and Paramount reprised the theme even more charmingly and amusingly in **A Woman of the World**, with Pola Negri set down in a small American town. The number of movies of the decade featuring royalty in the US had something to do with its fascination with the Prince of Wales and much with the republic's increasing interest in Europe since the War.

These movies also represent Hollywood's dilemma at this point: whether to make pictures about the rich and glamorous or about the people who actually went to see them. But because the film industry still yearned for respectability, there was a third option, and among the literary properties on display in 1925 were: **A Kiss for Cinderella**, from James Barrie's horribly fey play; **The Wizard of Oz**, directed by and starring Larry Semon as the Scarecrow, with Oliver Hardy as the Wood Tinman; and **The Lost World**, after Conan Doyle, with Wallace Beery as the professor who goes looking for dinosaurs – designed, by the way, by Willis O'Brien, who would do

Left: Harold Lloyd with Jobyna Ralston in **The Freshman**, pursuing a disastrous college career. Lloyd's *film* career was anything but: he was the most popular of the Silent clowns. Above and opposite: America's increasing interest in Europe since the War was reflected by Hollywood in two ways: in a series of gentle comic satires contrasting Continental sophistication with American down-to-earth common sense, and pictures about the conflict itself. King Vidor directed two of the best of both: **Proud Flesh**, with Eleanor Boardman and Harrison Ford, and **The Big Parade**, with John Gilbert and Renée Adorée.

much less primitive work on **King Kong** (1933).

Universal offered **Skinner's Dress Suit**, with Reginald Denny as a nice young husband who liked to charleston and couldn't get to work on time; but this studio's big picture was **The Phantom of the Opera**, with Lon Chaney in the title role. United Artists also thought big, and **Don Q, Son of Zorro** was Douglas Fairbanks's best film to date. William S. Hart retired after his first film for UA, **Tumbleweeds**, when it failed at the box office, perhaps because he departed from formula: instead of the Good Bad man he is good through and through, in the pioneer days.

Another good Western was Zane Grey's oft-filmed (the others: 1918, 1931 and 1941) **Riders of the Purple Sage**, with Tom Mix as the man bent on avenging the death of his brother-in-law and finding his kidnapped sister, only to find that the culprit has become a power in these parts. Mix went on to replace Hart as the movies' most popular cowboy. Fox also remade **East Lynne**, rather well, but including a scene of the wronged Lady Isobel (Alma Rubens) living in sin in Paris.

Opposite and above: The new Soviet government was entirely alive to the value of the cinema in establishing its legitimacy both at home and abroad – and it was fortunate to have a film-maker of genius to help them: Eisenstein. His propagandist tracts, such as **The Battleship Potemkin** and **Strike**, were usually seen abroad only at film societies, but they had a stunning effect on other movie-makers and those left-wingers who saw them. Right: 1925 was MGM's first full year in business, which it celebrated by having two of the biggest box-office films of the year – **The Big Parade** and **Ben Hur**.

Among the highlights of the French cinema were: René Clair's two fantasies, **Le Fantôme du Moulin Rouge** and **Le Voyage Imaginaire**; Jacques Feyder's **Visages d'Enfants** and **Gribiche**, with the talented boy actor, Jean Forest, in the first living in the Alps, where he finds that his new stepmother and stepsister both loathe him, and in the second living in Paris, where he is adopted by a wealthy American, Françoise Rosay; and a fine six and a half hour **Les Misérables**, directed by Henri Fescourt and originally released in four weekly parts.

In Germany the most valuable film was Gerhard Lamprecht's penetrating study of the underbelly of Berlin society as seen by an ex-con trying to get work, **Der Verrufenen**, but the one everybody went to see was E. A. Dupont's **Variété**, a triangle drama set in the world of trapeze artists. One of these was Emil Jannings, who played the title role in **Tartüff**, with Werner Krauss as Orgon and directed by Murnau, who made Molière's play a film within a film.

In the USSR, Sergei Eisenstein, in **Strike**, evoked the miseries of the Russians under the old regime, striving and failing to bring it down in 1907. He went on to show the injustices meted out to the crew of one particular ship, **The Battleship Potemkin**, originally meant to be part of a longer film, **1905**. These were his first two features and with them he re-invented cinema. Technically, they remain astonishing and are no less exhilarating as when they were first shown.

1926

The film event of the year took place at Warners' Theater in New York on 6 August, when Warner Bros introduced 'The Vitaphone'. 'The natural reproduction of voices, the tonal qualities of musical instruments and the timing of the sound to the movements of the lips of singers and actions of musicians is uncanny,' said *The New York Times*, which was impressed by the fact that lush orchestral sounds were produced with no musician present. The evening began with Will H. Hays on film congratulating the Warner Bros, the Western Electric Company, the Bell Telephone laboratories and Walter J. Rich for bringing Sound to the Cinema, and it was followed by shorts featuring such artists as the violinists Mischa Elman and Efrem Zimbalist and the tenor Giovanni Martinelli singing, 'Vesta la giubba'. The feature, **Don Juan**, starred John Barrymore, at the height of his screen popularity, as the Don. If the other studios had accepted Warners' lead, musicians in cinema pits would soon have been a thing of the past. But it has to be said that the only non-musical sounds emanating from the screen – bells and the clash of swords – were muffled.

The other significant event was the introduction of

Above: It wasn't till 1926, when the Civil War was sufficiently far in the past, that Hollywood thought that audiences were ready to laugh at it. Two very funny films set during that time were released this year. One was the **The General**, with Buster Keaton. The title referred to a railway engine. Right: Goldwyn had loaned Ronald Colman (left) to Paramount for **Beau Geste**, one of the actor's most popular films.

Greta Garbo to American audiences. This twenty-year-old Swedish girl had a run-of-the-mill role in **Ibañez' Torrent**, as a Spanish peasant who becomes a world-famous diva. Her welcome from the press was immediate and MGM rushed her into the second film under her contract, **The Temptress**, also based on a novel by Ibañez. Already typecast, she played a *femme fatale* who seduces a man (Antonio Moreno) in a Paris garden, only to meet him again when she and her husband arrive in the Argentine, where he is supervising the construction of a dam.

If stars shine, they also fade; and on 23 August Rudolf Valentino died of complications following an operation for peritonitis. He lay in state in a New York funeral parlour as thousands of bereft women filed past. United Artists, sorry to lose him, feverishly rushed his last film, **Son of the Sheik**, into cinemas only days later.

Two of the cornerstones of that company released two of their best pictures: the one with Mary Pickford was **Sparrows**, in which she cares for ten small mites on a farm in the middle of an alligator-infested swamp, and that of Douglas Fairbanks was **The Black Pirate**, whose title is self-explanatory. Trying as usual to give his fans better value for money, he filmed it in Technicolor, disguising its limitations as best he could, but the process remained unsatisfactory.

Ronald Colman, on loan to Paramount, played the title role in **Beau Geste**, an exciting version of P. C. Wren's novel about the Foreign Legion. Back with Goldwyn, he starred in **The Winning of Barbara Worth**, which marked the screen début of Gary Cooper. What

interested audiences most, however, was that the film, a Western, reunited Colman with Vilma Banky.

There was a novel screen teaming when MGM co-starred Lillian Gish and John Gilbert in **La Bohème**, based on Puccini's opera and directed by King Vidor; while later in the year Gish appeared in a beautiful version of Nathaniel Hawthorne's study of adultery, **The Scarlet Letter**, directed by Victor Sjöström.

All these pictures were great successes, but far and away the most popular movie of the year was **What Price Glory?**, based on the play by Laurence Stallings and Maxwell Anderson which had moved theatregoers two years earlier. There was too little irony and too much knockabout as filmed by Fox, but audiences enjoyed the comic rivalry of Captain Flagg (Victor McLaglen) and Sergeant Quirt (Edmund Lowe) so much that these two actors were to do variations on it for years to come. Dolores Del Rio played the heroine, Charmaine, and Fox distributed a copy of a song of that name to be played as an accompaniment to the film. Added to the track for those cinemas equipped for Sound, it grinded away monotonously.

The Bat, an old dark house thriller based on a Broadway play, was influential and a great crowd-pleaser,

Left: **Hands Up!** starred Raymond Griffith, seen here with Marion Nixon and Virginia Lee Corbin. Above: Rudolf Valentino and Vilma Banky in **Son of the Sheik**, which was no less hokey than its predecessor, but even more of a box-office bonanza, since Valentino died just before its release: women were anxious for a last look at their idol. Opposite: Miss Banky usually teamed with Ronald Colman and the movies of this much-loved romantic couple were among the most eagerly awaited of those produced by the Goldwyn company. **The Winning of Barbara Worth** was a modern Western – and the first film of Gary Cooper (right).

but seen today it is even sillier than most of its kind. Not dissimilar is **You'd Be Surprised**, a murder mystery set on a yacht, with Raymond Griffith as the detective in charge. The film is so stilted that it led to a temporary hiatus in his career, which is a pity, as earlier in the year **Hands Up!** had been one of his funniest films. And if Buster Keaton was fine in **Battling Butler**, as an effete young man who yearns to be a prizefighter, he was on sublime form in **The General**, as the engine driver who ignores the battle lines of the Civil War. Beatrice Lillie, after delighting Broadway, made her screen début to similar effect in **Exit Smiling**, a comedy about a third-rate touring company, but for some reason she made no other Silents – or, indeed, many films at all. Clara Bow had arrived at Paramount to achieve stardom in **Mantrap** – a title that referred to a town, though it certainly applied to the role she was playing. Female cinemagoers were

cutting off their long hair in emulation of Clara's curls, and those who weren't were copying Colleen Moore's bob, seen to good effect in **Irene**, based on the stage musical; in **Ella Cinders**, a tale of Hollywood; and in **Twinkletoes**, another show business tale, though in this one she wore a long blonde wing.

In Britain, Alfred Hitchcock attracted attention with his Germanic **The Lodger**, but spoiled good source material – Mrs Belloc-Lowndes' novel about Jack the Ripper – by making the lodger not a murderer after all. Foreign films of note included, from France, Jacques Feyder's **Carmen**; from Germany, Murnau's **Faust**, Pabst's **Secrets of a Soul** and two eloquent studies of Berlin low-life directed by Gerhard Lamprecht, **Menschen Untereinander** and **Die Unehelichen**; and from Russia, Pudovkin's **Mother** and Lev Kuleshov's **By the Law**.

1927

Warner Bros, having failed to interest anybody very much in synchronized Sound, had noticed much keenness for their Vitaphone shorts in the few theatres which were equipped to show them. Having added vaudeville stars to their classy assembly of concert artists, they decided to make a feature-length musical, **The Jazz Singer**. The leading role, that of a cantor's son who rejects his family's profession to go into vaudeville, had been played in the original stage version by George Jessel, but he turned down the musical when Warner Bros wouldn't meet his asking price. They subsequently agreed to pay more to Al Jolson, who thus was the first man to speak on the screen (that is, in a feature). He was not, however, the first to sing – that distinction fell to Bobbie Gordon, who plays Jolson as a child. No one believed that the Silent Picture would ever die and the entire industry was sceptical of this new gimmick, which was seen as an attempt by the pushy brothers Warner to elevate their company from its lowly position. But as the crowds flocked to **The Jazz Singer** it was clearly time to think again.

Elsewhere, the same stars dominated, with one newcomer being a vital exception. Flame-haired Clara Bow was the flapper personified – in the parlance of the day, the bee's knees – and clearly more to the public's

Above: Al Jolson blacked-up and sang in **The Jazz Singer**, the first feature-length Talkie. Except for Warner Bros, who produced, the industry thought Talkies were a flash in the pan. Right: Douglas Fairbanks and Lupe Velez in **The Gaucho**, perhaps the best of all Fairbanks's pictures. Miss Velez was a sweet silent heroine, but her career in Talkies is best described by the B-series she made as 'The Mexican Spitfire'.

sexual taste than the imperious Pola Negri. Paramount commissioned the romantic novelist Elinor Glyn to write a story for Clara, entitled **It**. Whether it was Mrs Glyn or a Paramount publicist who thought up 'it', Mrs Glyn obligingly defined it.

It was a good year for Paramount. **Wings** was voted the first Oscar (though it wasn't yet called that) by the new Academy of Motion Picture Arts and Sciences, an industry organization of artists and directors dreamed up (chiefly) by Louis B. Mayer, partly in an attempt to curb the growing power of the unions. This drama about the pilots of the Great War was directed by William A. Wellman, who had served with the Lafayette Escadrille. Interest in aviation had soared in May when Captain Lindbergh had made the first nonstop transatlantic crossing, and the film benefited as a result. It co-starred Miss Bow with two of the studio's reliable young leading men, Richard Arlen and Charles 'Buddy' Rogers, but it was Gary Cooper, in a cameo role, about whom most people were talking.

Miss Negri, however, did make two last excellent movies for the studio, also set during the Great War: **Hotel Imperial**, a cunning espionage drama directed by Mauritz Stiller, and **Barbed Wire**, a pacifist drama set among POWs, directed by Rowland V. Lee. And **Underworld** confirmed the stellar positions of Evelyn Brent, George Bancroft and Clive Brook. The two men played bums who become involved with a gangster's moll, Brent. Gangsters play only a small part in the film, but in writing

this first work for the screen, Ben Hecht drew upon his experiences as a reporter in Chicago.

Paramount also released the year's wonder-film, **Chang**, requesting reviewers not to reveal what the title meant. This semi-documentary about marauding elephants (yes, 'Chang' means elephant) in the Thai jungle is a beguiling entertainment with a thrilling climax and Merian C. Cooper and Ernest B. Schoedsack, producer and director, deserved all the plaudits they received. It was shown in some cinemas in Magnavision, a primitive version of wide screen.

Paramount and MGM were still battling for the supremacy of the industry. Metro discovered that it had a powerhouse combination in Garbo and (John) Gilbert when it released **Flesh and the Devil** in January. As adapted from the 1893 story by Hermann Sudermann, Garbo is (again) the enigmatic woman who comes between boyhood buddies John Gilbert and Lars Hanson, while all the while married to a.n. other. **Love** found her and Gilbert as modern reincarnations of Tolstoy's adulterous Anna Karenina and Count Vronsky.

Another Sudermann story provided the basis of Fox's memorable **Sunrise**, which transferred the action to

Left: Buster Keaton in **College**. He has a new suit for graduation, but it shrinks in the rain. Playing his mother is Florence Turner, whom audiences may have remembered from 1909, when she was known as 'The Vitagraph Girl'. Above: Garbo loves Gilbert in **Flesh and the Devil**. Their intensity was equalled by the public's interest in their own real-life affair. Opposite: Fritz Lang's vision of the future: **Metropolis** – life in the underground city, and a little light relief for the automatons.

the US but was otherwise Germanic. The images are always striking and sometimes dwarf the story, the tale of a country boy (George O'Brien) who plans to murder his wife after falling for a hussy on a trip to the city. Janet Gaynor played the wife, and won a Best Actress Oscar for it, for **Seventh Heaven** and 1928's **Street Angel**. Frank Borzage won the Best Director award for **Seventh Heaven** and became one of the handful of directors known to the public partly because this film was so popular. Fox sent **Seventh Heaven** out with a synchronized score and a tune, 'Diane', which became as ubiquitous as 'Charmaine' from **What Price Glory?** The extreme sentiment of both the Gaynor films tells us much about audience tastes. Set in a stylized Paris, **Seventh Heaven** tells how 'sewer rat' Charles Farrell saves waif Gaynor from a life of sin, and how they re-declare their love when he returns from the Great War, blinded.

In Britain, Michael Balcon's Gainsborough Pictures made an attempt at quality by filming two of Noël Coward's rather scandalous plays, **Easy Virtue** and **The Vortex**, but the results were tedious and, ironically, rather suburban. Alfred Hitchcock directed the first of these, and he was also responsible for the curious Ivor Novello vehicle, **Downhill**, based on a play which Novello had written for himself (with Constance Collier). Novello – rather too old to be a convincing schoolboy – is expelled after a girl accuses him, out of spite, of being the father of her child. He descends the primrose path till he becomes a gigolo in Paris. Hitchcock's borrowings from German cinema are more obvious than ever, but he was one of the few local directors with a flair for narrative, as he proved again in **The Ring**, his first film for B.I.P., which borrows from Dupont's **Variété** inasmuch as two men are in love with the same woman. The milieu is boxing instead of the circus, and instead of a *crime passionnel* there is a reunion: a very British solution.

Among the notable foreign films were, from Germany, Pabst's **Der Liebe Der Jeanne Ney** and Hans Behrendt's **Die Hose**, based on Carl Sternheim's 1911 small-town satire, with a lovely comic performance by Werner Krauss. The year also brought Fritz Lang's **Metropolis** which, though risible in many ways, still has power. From the Soviet Union there were two prime comedies, **Bed and Sofa** and **The Girl with the Hatbox**, as well as Pudovkin's **The End of St Petersburg** and Yakov Protazanov's drama set in the Turkestan desert, **The Forty-First**. France offered René Clair's sprightly bourgeois farce, **The Italian Straw Hat**, and two lumbering, grandiose historical spectacles, **Napoléon** and **Casanova**. At least the second of these serves its purpose, as a vehicle for the Russian *émigré* star, Ivan Mosjoukine, who is ardent, histrionically bold and somewhat cute.

1928

The year began with the year's most overrated film, Charlie Chaplin's **The Circus**, and it finished with **The River**, which conversely went completely overlooked, despite being directed by Frank Borzage. In April, Borzage had had another popular success with **Street Angel**, but then audiences couldn't get enough of the team of Janet Gaynor and Charles Farrell. The Naples of this movie was as stylized as the Paris of **Seventh Heaven**, and the story was similar; but the milieu of **The River** was starkly realistic and its story more adult, as an inexperienced boy (Farrell) becomes sexually obsessed with a bold, flirtatious woman-of-the-world (Mary Duncan).

One factor which marked this year was the number of superior films about fairly ordinary urban dwellers, including King Vidor's **The Crowd** at MGM and Paul Fejos's **Lonesome** at Universal. Victor Sjöström's **The Wind** is different inasmuch as it is set in the bleak West –

and it is certainly much more powerful, as a seemingly mismatched couple (Lillian Gish, Lars Hanson) gradually learn to love each other under harsh circumstances. **Our Dancing Daughters** represented the other America, the world of wild parties, with Joan Crawford continuing her advance to stardom as a misunderstood flapper (she was to remain misunderstood through most of her screen career).

Von Stroheim himself wrote, directed and starred in **The Wedding March**, set in Vienna, an anecdote about a dissolute prince who for money marries a lame rich girl (Zasu Pitts) instead of the waitress (Fay Wray) whom he loves: but this being Von Stroheim the film was very long, (two and a half hours), and the cut reels were released only in Europe, under the title **The Honeymoon**.

At MGM **The Viking** did not advance the cause of Technicolor, but that studio produced a ravishing rom-

Below: Lillian Gish and Lars Hanson in **The Wind**. It remains glowingly alive today. Opposite: Among the loose ladies of the period there was none more notorious than **Sadie Thompson**, a hooker who is reformed by a reverend but reverts to type when lust turns him into the same raging beast as ever she had in her room. The censor insisted that he became a religious fanatic. Gloria Swanson and Raoul Walsh, who also directed.

ance. Directed by W. S. Van Dyke and set in Polynesia, **White Shadows in the South Seas** was one of the rare starless films of the period – though neither Dolores Del Rio or Harry Carey in **The Trail of '98** were among Hollywood's biggest names. The spectacle was the thing, and this epic of the Yukon gold rush of 1898 remains breathtaking as directed by Clarence Brown.

Buster Keaton arrived at MGM after achieving one of his most brilliant stunts in **Steamboat Bill Jr**, and **The Cameraman** continued his high standard in getting laughs; but **Speedy** was below Harold Lloyd's usual standard. Keaton apart, the best laughs were to be had in some shorts: **The Best Man** with Billy Bevan, **Limousine Love** with Charley Chase, and **You're Darn Tootin'** with Laurel and Hardy.

All these films, including the short comic cut-ups, show the Silent screen language at its most eloquent, so that we must be sad that it was about to die. Or to be killed off. After the success of **The Jazz Singer**, it is not surprising that one of the assassins was Al Jolson. Warner Bros hesitated a surprisingly long while – eleven months – before assaulting an unsuspecting world with another maudlin Jolson vehicle, **The Singing Fool**. The world loved it. Jolson's song, 'Sonny Boy', had been written tongue-in-cheek by the team of Brown, de Sylva and

Below and opposite: The Soviets made two more propaganda films which coast the years with ease. Pudovkin's **Storm Over Asia** tells of a Mongol fur-trader who becomes a puppet king – against a background of the Civil War of 1918 and the dishonesty of Western and Imperial merchants. Eisenstein's **October** is a seemingly straightforward documentary account of the Revolution, **'Ten Days that Shook the World'** as its subtitle has it.

Henderson, but it was to become Jolson's biggest ever hit – and as the film went on to take in a record $5 million over the next eighteen months, all the studios geared themselves up to go over exclusively to Sound. The days of the Part-Talkie were over, and exhibitors would no longer have the luxury of choosing a Silent or Sound version of the same story.

Quickest off the mark was Walt Disney, the cartoonist, who had been having a mild success since 1924 with his 'Alice' comedies, combining animation and live action. In 1927 he dropped Alice for 'Oswald the Lucky Rabbit', but Oswald was replaced during 1928 by a mouse, Mickey. Disney cancelled the release of the first two cartoons featuring Mickey Mouse, and hurriedly added Sound to the third, **Steamboat Willie**. From the moment Mickey made his bow before the audience at the Colony Theater, New York, on 18 November, he was a world sensation. As much as Jolson he hammered a nail into the coffin of the Silent movie.

In Britain, there was E. A. Dupont, whose **Moulin Rouge** was yet another variation on **Variété**, and Geza von Bolvary, with **The Wrecker**, a thriller about trains which at least insulted its audience at speed.

In France, Luis Buñuel made his first film, the surreal short **Un Chien Andalou**, in collaboration with Salvador Dali. In the Soviet Union, Eisenstein's **October** and Pudovkin's **Storm Over Asia** overshadowed all else. And **Crossways**, Teinosuke Kinugasa's drama of a sister's sacrifice, became the only Japanese film seen widely in the West till **Rashomon** in 1950.

The most significant event of the year and, indeed, of the decade was the Wall Street crash in October, which would send the US and much of the rest of the civilized world into the Depression. Movies would be profoundly affected, but for the moment the talk of the industry was entirely about Talkies. There were Talkies Talkies everywhere.

1929

In January Fox released a Western, **In Old Arizona**, and cinema audiences heard for the first time the sound of bacon and eggs sizzling in a pan. MGM released **A Woman of Affairs**, and the only sound heard was music. As all the other studios turned their production entirely over to Sound, MGM produced three more Silents – **Wild Orchids**, **The Single Standard** and **The Kiss** which, like **A Woman of Affairs**, starred Greta Garbo. Picturegoers were excited by the prospect of hearing their favourites speak for the first time, but too many stars from Europe proved incomprehensible. A silent Garbo remained an asset, but for how much longer?

The company which had pioneered the change to Sound had become wealthy enough to buy up First National, just when the latter were shooting **The Divine Lady**, Frank Lloyd's eloquent re-telling of the romance between Nelson and Lady Hamilton. However, this suffered less from lack of Sound than Warners' decision to do little to promote it. Paramount had qualms about **The Four Feathers**, which had been long in production and would be too expensive to re-shoot with Sound. But with the promise of action so richly fulfilled, the studio had worried in vain. It came out in June, and a month later **Queen Kelly** became the most notable casualty of the rush to Sound. Gloria Swanson had halted production

because her director, Erich Von Stroheim, was unable to curb his extravagance; and his script became gamier – the scenes he had just been shooting were set not in an African hotel (as in the script) but a brothel – so that the Hays Office was likely to condemn the film outright. Shorn of these sequences and with a new ending, Swanson tried out the film in Europe, where its reception indicated that it would be wise not to release it in the US.

By April it was reckoned that 89 per cent of all pictures on release contained dialogue, but even more impressively, Silents amounted to only 4 per cent of those actually playing in theatres. A month earlier, Warners released the biggest spectacle yet in its history, **Noah's Ark**, which in the tradition of the time interwove a modern story with a biblical tale. The first thirty-five minutes were Silent, but the final sixty All-Talkie, including the sound of ancient and modern flooding.

Douglas Fairbanks did as well as he could by adding three speeches – at the beginning, in the middle, and at the end – to his rousing version of Dumas' **The Iron Mask**. At the same time Mary Pickford remained grown-up, playing a flapper, no less, in **Coquette**. This was an All-Talkie, and now that the screen's reigning sovereigns had shown themselves equipped for what Hollywood called 'King Mike', they dared to attempt Shakespeare, then considered too highbrow for movies. It was a typically bold gesture, even if almost the only play

Left: Garbo remained mute – in no less than four movies. They all had the same characters: a beautiful woman, compromised by the man who pays the bills, and an ardent young man who recognizes her True Worth. In one of them, however, she decides on **The Single Standard** (with Nils Asther) for men and women. Above: Gloria Swanson, prince's plaything in **Queen Kelly**. She was a Catholic schoolgirl and he, Walter Byron, the depraved fiancé of a dissolute monarch. Opposite: Anny Ondra in **Blackmail**. An artist had asked her to his studio at night and then to remove a few garments, so of course she had to defend herself.

suitable for them both could be much cut. In the event, **The Taming of the Shrew** was a travesty which was laughed off the screen. However, in the rush to Talkies it was the sort of mistake which could be forgiven.

Harold Lloyd, who had told the columnist Louella Parsons in July 1928 that sound was doomed, had second thoughts. **Welcome Danger** previewed successfully, but he decided to re-shoot most of it and dub the rest. Although he himself considered the result a success, and the public turned up in droves to find out what his voice sounded like, it's a dog's dinner of a movie. Laurel and Hardy, however, had perhaps their best year as they accustomed themselves to dialogue, with at least four masterly comedies: **Liberty**, **Big Business**, **Double Whoopee** and **The Hoose-Gow**. Mirth in the movies was given another lift by Walt Disney's 'Silly Symphonies', which began with **The Skeleton Dance**.

Following **The Singing Fool** and 'Sonny Boy' Hollywood was up to its ears in song. In February MGM released **The Broadway Melody**, which for many people the world over was the first Talkie they saw. The title song and 'You Were Meant for Me' became big hits, and later in the year another original, **Sunnyside Up**, offered 'If I Had a Talking Picture of You', 'I'm a Dreamer' and again the title song. Universal brought **Broadway** from Broadway and **Showboat**, throwing overboard most of its songs as being over-familiar, and then adding some of them to the prologue after converting the film to a Talkie. By keeping those of **Rio Rita**, RKO, then in its first year, had a success to rank with **The Broadway Melody**.

Among other popular Broadway shows filmed was **The Desert Song**, but more than Broadway, Hollywood loved its performers and those from vaudeville. Making their feature movie débuts were Gertrude Lawrence in **The Battle of Paris**, Helen Morgan in **Applause**, Ted Lewis in **Is Everybody Happy?**, Rudy Vallee in **The Vagabond Lover** and Marilyn Miller in **Sunny**. (For the record, Fanny Brice had appeared in a Part-Talkie at the tail end of 1928, **My Man**.) Few of these became successful movie players; the most impressive début in this field was Ethel Waters in **On With the Show**. Paramount had a major acquisition in Maurice Chevalier, initially in the indifferent **Innocents of Paris** and then in Lubitsch's risqué Ruritanian frolic, **The Love Parade**, his first teaming with Jeanette MacDonald.

It could be argued that music overwhelmed Hollywood in 1929, for it was not till the following year that it began to look at other stage stars; in the meantime many of its own stars were required to sing, including Marion Davies, Ramon Novarro, Nancy Carroll, Carmel Myers, Colleen Moore and Richard Barthelmess. In **The Holly-wood Revue of 1929** almost the entire star rosta of MGM

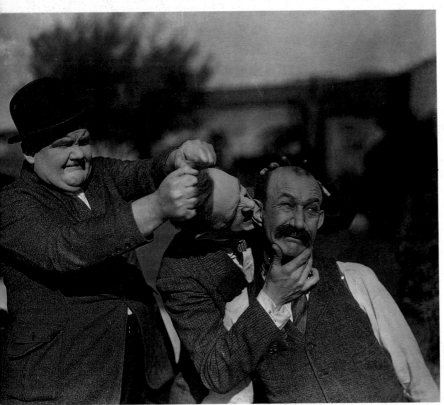

Left: Laurel and Hardy made the transition to sound with ease, and made one of their funniest two-reelers with **Big Business**. Above: Louise Brooks in **Diary of a Lost Girl**, the second of the two films she made for Pabst in 1929. In both, she embarked on odysseys of sexual delight. Opposite: Garbo again. In this picture, she starts a series of romances (including one with Johnny Mack Brown) after her husband commits suicide on their wedding night. Based on Michael Arlen's notorious novel *The Green Hat* the film version became **A Woman of Affairs**.

talent sang, danced or did sketches, which inspired Warner Bros to get their lot to do something similar in **The Show of Shows**. Like many of the year's musicals, these had sequences in Technicolor; and because MGM had let Norma Shearer and John Gilbert do the balcony scene from *Romeo and Juliet* (as well as spoofing it), Warners immortalized a few moments of John Barrymore's *Richard III*.

Although Gilbert had spoken at least adequately in that sequence, audiences laughed at his voice when Metro released **His Glorious Night**. He thus became the most famous victim of the Talkies, though most of his later ones reveals his voice as normally pitched and admirable, so the swift decline in his career may be mainly due to his quarrels with MGM executives, notably Louis B. Mayer.

In Britain, sound equipment was so primitive that for the first six months producers were restricted to making shorts to accompany American Talkies in those cinemas equipped to play them. When **The Broadway Melody** broke all records at MGM's flagship theatre in Leicester Square, playing to over half a million people in nine weeks, the message was clear. In March B.I.P. sent casts and crews of three Silent movies to the US so that dialogue sequences could be added. Even more enterprisingly, Herbert Wilcox filmed **Black Waters** entirely across the Atlantic, but since it had American money and American leads (Mary Brian, James Kirkwood), the first British picture was B.I.P.'s **Blackmail**, which had its dialogue sequences re-shot after the studio was wired for Sound. The imaginative use of Sound furthered the reputation of its director, Alfred Hitchcock.

German directors in their own country ushered out the Silent era in a blaze of glory with Joe May's **Asphalt**, Hannes Schwarz's **The Wonderful Lie of Nina Petrowna**, Leo Mittler's **Jenseits Der Strasse**, Phil Jutzi's **Mutter Krausens Fahrt in Glück** and **The White Hell of Pitz Palü**, directed by Arnold Fanck and G. W. Pabst. All of these except the last have a high sexual content, and Pabst made up for that in his two masterpieces, **Pandora's Box** and **Diary of a Lost Girl**, both with the luminous Louise Brooks. In Sweden Alf Sjöberg and Axel Lindholm collaborated on a powerful sea drama, **The Strongest**.

Two of the best French pictures were lost as the public clamoured for Sound: **Dans la Nuit**, a thriller directed by Charles Vanel, who also starred, and Jean Grémillon's **Gardiens de Phare**. Marco de Gastyne's **La Vie Merveilleuse de Jeanne d'Arc**, however, had a tremendous commercial career after its première at the Opéra. Abroad, few saw it, because distributors were looking the other way after the failure in 1928 of Carl Dreyer's **The Passion of Joan of Arc**.

1930

The first Talkies, however primitive, engendered an excitement, but many of those released in 1930 are static and stagey. One notable exception is **All Quiet on the Western Front**, directed by Lewis Milestone from the novel by Erich Maria Remarque. It holds its years with ease, partly because of its bitter anti-war sentiment. This is also a quality marking **Journey's End**, a British film but made in the US, and **The Dawn Patrol**, but both look musty today.

Beyond **All Quiet ...** the 1930 movie now best remembered is **Anna Christie**, because of its ad-slogan, 'Garbo Talks!' The suspense was over and her screen future assured, but it is a rather turgid piece, enlivened by the presence of the ageing vaudevillian, Marie Dressler, who again became a star in her own right, especially in the year's best rough-and-tumble comedy, **Min and Bill**, which teamed her for the first time with Wallace Beery.

The year's most sophisticated comedy was **Laughter**, directed by Harry D'Abbadie D'Arrast from a bittersweet screenplay by Donald Ogden Stewart. As acted by Nancy Carroll, Fredric March and others, it's revealing about the people of that time, at least in that area where the bourgeoisie meets Bohemia. Set in similar milieux were Columbia's **Ladies of Leisure**, directed by Frank Capra, with Barbara Stanwyck, and MGM's **The Divorcée**, directed by Rober Z. Leonard, with Norma

Above: Lew Ayres (left) in the moving final sequence of **All Quiet on the Western Front**. The dying French soldier who shares the bomb crater with him was played by the great comic Raymond Griffith in his last acting role; his voice was simply too light for the microphone. Opposite: Another of the year's acclaimed war films was **The Dawn Patrol**, starring Richard Barthelmess (centre) and Douglas Fairbanks Jr (left).

Shearer. Both reflected woman's growing awareness of her sexuality – a situation rendered in more exotic manner in Josef Von Sternberg's **Morocco**, inasmuch as a cabaret singer (Marlene Dietrich) prefers true love with a legionnaire (Gary Cooper) to baubles from her elderly 'admirer' (Adolphe Menjou). To an extent all these films were triangle dramas, as was the year's most underrated piece, **Passion Flower**, directed by William DeMille. If Kay Francis was the usual silly vamp, Charles Bickford was good as the bewildered husband and Kay Johnson something better than that as the wife who couldn't stop loving him despite his infidelity.

Equally valuable as a study of sexual mores is F. W. Murnau's drama of the Great Plains, **City Girl**, but Fox had delayed this Part-Talkie for much too long and it received few bookings. Its star, Charles Farrell, did much better with **Liliom**, reverently directed by Frank Borzage from Molnar's play. Fox also presented **The Big Trail**, a terminally dull Western which failed to make a star out of a young, callow John Wayne. Raoul Walsh directed. The novelty was that it could be seen in 70mm, in those cinemas which cared to install 'Fox Grandeur'. Few did, and the same fate awaited MGM's 'Realife', also applied to a Western, **Billy the Kid**. The Wide Screen would have to

wait more than twenty years for its renaissance.

Wallace Beery inherited the role meant for Lon Chaney in **The Big House**, when Chaney died after completing an indifferent remake of **The Unholy Three**. The big house was prison, and this was a rare Metro 'tough guy' drama. The genre fell decisively to Warner Bros, who began magnificently with Mervyn LeRoy's **Little Caesar**, which made a star out of Edward G. Robinson, in a role modelled on mobster Al Capone.

These pictures, 'torn from today's headlines' as Warners proclaimed, were just what Depression audiences wanted – something immediate and real. They didn't care, if indeed they noticed, that their favourites from the Silent era had almost all departed, associated as they were with the frivolities of a time that now seemed so long ago. All the same, Hollywood knew that escapism was an essential part of its output, and a panacea was needed more than ever, in the form of musicals. **Paramount on Parade** and Fox's **Happy Days** were as tedious as the earlier all-star movies – and the wide screen did less for the latter than the two Westerns of later in the year. Universal, having few stars, used the formula for roping in orchestra leader Paul Whiteman, the recognized **King of Jazz**. Bing Crosby made his feature début as one

of Whiteman's Rhythm Boys, while **Mammy** and **Big Boy** proved that Al Jolson was past his sell-by date.

The most bizarre musical was Fox's **Just Imagine** set far in the future, but it was closely rivalled by Cecil B. DeMille's **Madam Satan**, which begins as a sex comedy and adds songs and dances during a party held on an airship, till it is struck by lightning. 'Gay Party in Peril When Zep Hit: All Safe?' runs a headline, with horrible irony, for while the film was in release the British airship *R101* went up in flames at Beauvais, killing all aboard. It was one of the most sensational events ever caught by newsreel cameras.

With the divine exception of two songs by Lily Morris, **Elstree Calling** proved that Britain could produce all-star movies even more tedious than those from Hollywood. However, it was beaten as the year's worst British movie by **Knowing Men**, co-written and directed by Elinor Glyn. *The New York Times* considered that American audiences might like it because it showed the British aristocracy in its true light, but they didn't get the chance after the British had laughed it off the screen.

Opposite: Marlene Dietrich made **The Blue Angel** with Emil Jannings in her native Germany. It was later shown in the US, where audiences who had seen her in **Morocco** were able to judge how completely she had responded to Hollywood's glamour treatment. Above: Hollywood never permitted a female star to get out of bed with a hair out of place, but France preferred its women to be more realistic. This is Pola Illery in René Clair's **Sous les Toits de Paris**. Right: **The Divorcée** was about sexual emancipation: when Chester Morris proposes a 'free' marriage to Norma Shearer, he is horrified to find that she has followed him into infidelity.

The semiprofessional **People on Sunday** was precisely about that, Berliners on their day off. The directors were Edgar G. Ulmer and Robert Siodmak; the latter went on to make a touching portrait of boarding-house life, **Abschied**. Robert Wiene moved further up the social scale with **Der Andere**, in which the State Prosecutor (Fritz Kortner) goes hunting low life. That was also the theme of **The Blue Angel**, in which Professor Emil Jannings falls in love with Marlene Dietrich after hearing her sing the unforgettable 'Falling in Love Again'. Jannings remained in Germany, his heavy accent having ended his career in America. The director, Von Sternberg, returned, taking Dietrich with him -- and Americans found her somewhat more svelte and much less bawdy in **Morocco**, which they saw first. The Germans had such a success with **Drei Von Der Tankstelle** that it was imitated countless times, often with the star of this occasion — the coy, British-born Lilian Harvey — inevitably being pursued by two or more ordinary working guys.

This, in turn, had been inspired by René Clair's **Sous les Toits de Paris**, with its irresistible theme tune and its enchanting study of life in one *quartier*. After Luis Buñuel's brave, surreal **L'Age d'Or** only one other French feature is worth noting – **Prix de Beauté** – and that is because of the presence of Louise Brooks.

1931

It was the year of Clark Gable. In January, he was a rival of William Boyd in a Pathé Western, **The Painted Desert**. Signed by MGM, he was a laundry man in **The Easiest Way** and a bootlegger in a Joan Crawford vehicle, **Dance, Fools, Dance**. He was a reporter in **The Secret Six**, a gangster again in **The Finger Points** (at Warners) and a Salvation Army worker in **Laughing Sinners** – but although billed below Neil Hamilton, it was he who shared the fade-out with Crawford. He slapped Norma Shearer about in **A Free Soul** and she loved it. He returned to Warners and regressed with a smallish role, as a sinister chauffeur, in **Night Nurse**. But MGM finally realized what they had got and gave him top billing in a tale about race horses. He starred opposite Garbo and then Crawford in **Susan Lennox – Her Fall and Rise** and **The Possessed**, still effective melodramas, in both of which he becomes one of the powers about town. As John Gilbert and Ramon Novarro faded away, the studio had found the new male star it so badly needed. And he was a new breed of star.

Another such was discovered when Warner Bros promoted James Cagney to the lead in William A. Wellman's fine gangster drama, **The Public Enemy**, and

Above: Peter Lorre in his brilliant study of cowardly evil, a child murderer, in Fritz Lang's **M**. Right: The gangster films were 'torn from today's headlines', as the Warners claimed. Wellman directed one of the most celebrated, **The Public Enemy**, with Edward Woods (right) and James Cagney. A few days into shooting, Wellman made them change roles, and Cagney became a star overnight.

when he pushed a grapefruit into Mae Clarke's face, many women in the audience wished they had been in her shoes. Warners continued its racey melodramas with **Other Men's Women**, **Smart Money**, **Five Star Final**, **Blonde Crazy** and **Safe in Hell**. But its biggest achievement was William Dieterle's **The Last Flight**, an achievement to be overlooked for the next forty years, till it was rediscovered. This was Hemingway's Paris, with American expats drinking to forget the War, and the screenplay by John Monk Saunders is, because it is facetious and hence truer, better than *The Sun Also Rises*, which had used many of the same events. Helen Chandler's usual response to this unruly bunch is 'I'll take vanilla', the year's catchphrase. It is the year's best film.

At the time, however, the best was considered to be **City Lights**, and the 'genius' of Chaplin was much praised, in bucking the trend and staying Silent. It is true that no one wanted 'the little fellow', as Chaplin termed his screen character, to talk, but today the film is horribly sentimental and funny by turns. **Laughing Gravy** manages both qualities, but at the same time. At less than half the running time, Laurel and Hardy – in their masterpiece – manage to generate more laughter and more feeling than in the whole of Chaplin's film.

Funnier than either **Laughing Gravy** or **Monkey Business** – the Marx Brothers' contribution to the year's gaiety – was **The Struggle**, a tract on the evils of drink that would have seemed oldfashioned when D. W. Griffith began directing. He had put his own money into this and when it became a box-office fiasco overnight his career was finished.

A play successfully filmed was **The Front Page**, while **Platinum Blonde** also took a look at the press, as reporter Robert Williams (who died shortly afterwards) marries débutante Jean Harlow. It was one of the three Frank Capra pictures that year. The others were an action adventure, **Dirigible**, and an examination of the Aimée Semple McPherson type of evangelism, **The Miracle Woman**, with Barbara Stanwyck excellent in the title role. Capra's success was in attracting other major talents to Columbia so that it was no longer considered a Poverty Row studio.

Two expensive ventures paid off handsomely for other studios: **Trader Horn**, MGM's African adventure with Harry Carey in the title role, and **Cimarron**, the RKO epic which starts with the Oklahoma land rush of 1889 and follows Irene Dunne and Richard Dix as they age. And Universal had two immense successes with two horror pictures. Tod Browning returned to direct Bela Lugosi as a human vampire, Count **Dracula**, and as the grosses mounted, the studio set James Whale to direct Colin Clive to play Professor **Frankenstein**, who manufactures a monster, Boris Karloff.

Left: Warner Bros responded to the Depression with a series of gritty melodramas, like William A. Wellman's **Night Nurse** with Ben Lyon, Joan Blondell (centre) and Barbara Stanwyck. Above: Clara Bow, voted America's most popular star in 1929, made two pictures this year, **No Limit** and **Kick In**. However, a year later she was forced out of films following a series of sex scandals. Opposite: The new studio RKO had a gigantic success with **Cimarron**, based on Edna Ferber's novel of pioneer days and directed by Wesley Ruggles. Playing the central couple are a star on the way up, Irene Dunne, and one on the way down, Richard Dix.

But the year's best movie about 'jus' plain folks' was **Bad Girl**, a title at odds with its subject, which is the courtship and marriage of a shop clerk (James Dunn) and his girl (Sally Eilers). Frank Borzage directed sensitively, for Fox, which also offered one of the best additions to the gangster cycle, **Quick Millions**, in which Spencer Tracy swaggered and bootlegged it as king of the underworld. With Rouben Mamoulian directing, Paramount searched the same murky waters in **City Streets**, as Gary Cooper was persuaded to enter the rackets because his true love, Sylvia Sidney, is the daughter of someone much involved in them.

In Britain, Alfred Hitchcock returned to form with **Rich and Strange** – not a thriller, but a gently amusing study of a dreary suburban couple who learn about the great world out there – and themselves – when they take an ocean voyage to the Far East.

The only notable foreign-language films came from Germany and France. Germany contributed Pabst's **The Threepenny Opera** and **Kameradschaft**; Fritz Lang's chilling **M**, with Peter Lorre as a child murderer; Paul Czinner's romantic comedy, **Ariane**; Lamprecht's **Emil and the Detectives**; Fedor Ozep's surprisingly scintillating version of Dostoevsky, **Der Mörder Dimitri Karamasoff**, with Fritz Kortner and Anna Sten; and Phil Jutzi's **Berlin-Alexanderplatz**, based on Alfred Doblin's novel – and yet another astonishing record of the underbelly of Berlin at this time. Two German films had wide exposure abroad: Erik Charrell's **Congress Dances**, a musical set during the 1815 Congress of Nations in Vienna, and Leontine Sagan's **Mädchen in Uniform**, which dealt with lesbian passions in a girls' school.

France offered four singular triumphs, beginning with René Clair's **Le Million**, about a search for a missing lottery ticket. **Marius**, directed by the Hungarian Alexander Korda, was the first of what became playwright Marcel Pagnol's trilogy about the Marseilles waterfront, with the magnificent Raimu as a choleric bar owner. Jean Renoir, after several promising features, found his stride with **La Chienne**, in which the unhappily married Michel Simon surrenders everything for love of a *putain*. And Clair finished the year with **A Nous la Liberté**, a bubbling satire on capitalism, factory workers and the human condition.

N o studio tackled the Depression as well as Warner Bros, who did so head on in **I Am a Fugitive From a Chain Gang**. Strictly speaking, the hero (Paul Muni, magnificent at this point in his career) starts to bum around when laid off in 1925, but this is still the definitive portrait of the doughboys who came back from the War to find promises

1932

unkept. The year's best picture, **One-Way Passage** is the antithesis, the impossible shipboard romance between a dying woman and a man being returned to the US to fry in the Chair. Directed by Tay Garnett, the teaming of fragile, glamorous Kay Francis and suave, confident William Powell was magical. But the film triumphed because the kitsch was counterpointed by the crooks and conmen who surround the couple.

It is this demonic humour which makes the Warner films so cherishable today, and it would be unfair to move on without mentioning first, **Union Depot**, whose users included a hooker or so, a gigolo and a particularly unsavoury sex maniac; and second, **Three on a Match**, with Bette Davis, Joan Blondell and Ann Dvorak living on the edge of the underworld. A kidnapping in the plot is a reference to the year's most shocking event, the disappearance of the Lindbergh baby. Warners were inclined to throw in anything topical – and that could be a helluva lot for films sometimes lasting only an hour.

No one could remember a film so excitedly anticipated as **Grand Hotel**, because at a time when it was just becoming common to put two stars in a film, MGM offered no fewer than *five*. These were Garbo, Wallace Beery, Joan Crawford and John and Lionel Barrymore. Each played someone who was in some way a loser (if in the glamorous

circumstances of a luxurious Berlin hostelry) so it spoke directly to audiences; but they looked the other way when Paramount put a fistful of its stars into **If I Had a Million**. Its episodic structure was blamed, but most of the stories depended on the Depression for their effectiveness.

This studio reteamed Chevalier and MacDonald for two risqué comedies with music, **One Hour With You**, directed by Lubitsch, and **Love Me Tonight**, directed by Mamoulian. Lubitsch pulled off another corker with **Trouble in Paradise**, staring Kay Francis and Herbert Marshall as doublecrossing jewel thieves. Paramount also made **A Farewell to Arms**, based on Hemingway's love story set in the War in Italy. As directed by Frank Borzage it belongs to no recognizable world yet, as acted by Gary Cooper and Helen Hayes, it's a beautiful thing.

Back Street, directed by John M. Stahl, belongs right up there with it and **One-Way Passage**. The lovers, unable to live together because he is married, are Irene Dunne and John Boles. Garbo managed an erotic charge in her scenes with Melvyn Douglas in **As You Desire Me**, directed by George Fitzmaurice, reputedly from a play by Pirandello. Something similar happened when Clark Gable teased Jean Harlow in John Ford's **Red Dust**, in the tropics. Harlow was sensationally, unashamedly carnal in **Red-Headed Woman**, but when Clara Bow did the same in **Call Her Savage** she suffered almost every degradation available to ladies who sin, which may be why this attempt at a comeback failed.

Left: Kay Francis and William Powell in Warners' **One-Way Passage**. Impossible love stories were ten-a-penny in movies, but 1932 saw a number of superior examples. Above: **Grand Hotel**. Vicki Baum's novel had been a bestseller, but after an indifferent dramatization it looked like intractable movie material. MGM partially solved this by packing it with five stars, including John Barrymore and Joan Crawford. Opposite: In 1957 the wide screen, colour and some expensive talents were put at the service of **A Farewell to Arms**, but it doesn't begin to compare with this version, Gary Cooper and Helen Hayes.

Frank Capra looked at the formula of **Back Street** (Fannie Hurst's original novel, anyway), and came up with **Forbidden**, which he later dismissed as 'soap opera'. So it is, but so intelligently directed, written (by Jo Swerling) and acted (by Barbara Stanwyck as the unmarried mother) that criticism is stifled, if not stilled. Swinging back to reality, he looked at the disastrous economic policies of the past few years in **American Madness**, with Walter Huston on formidable form as a bank manager who refuses to panic when funds fail.

At RKO Gregory La Cava directed **The Age of Consent**, as accurate a picture of campus life as was then possible, as the students debate the wisdom of going 'further' than mere necking. La Cava also made **Symphony of Six Million**, from a novel by Fannie Hurst, about a Jewish doctor (Ricardo Cortez) who loses his idealism. It had been a long time since movies had attempted to encapsulate the American experience for many immigrants. And perhaps because of events in Germany, where the Nazis were emerging as probably the next ruling party, it was to be the last American film for over thirty years to acknowledge the existence of anyone of the Jewish race or religion.

Completely *hors série* is **Tarzan the Ape Man**, made by MGM in the hope that it would repeat the success of **Trader Horn** – and to utilize the studio jungle prepared for it when some African footage proved unusable. Edgar Rice Burroughs's *Tarzan of the Apes* had first attracted Hollywood in 1918. Until now, however, the necessary ingredients had never come together so well: Johnny Weismuller was the most athletic chap to have taken on the role, and his scenes with Jane (Maureen O'Sullivan) have a charge because he seems to respond to her sexual needs.

Real life and more weighty matters were reflected in **The Phantom President**. Following two political Broadway musicals by the Gershwins, Paramount commissioned Rodgers and Hart to write some songs for this movie. Neither the score nor it were memorable, but with Hoover's presidency drawing to an end and Franklin D. Roosevelt almost certain to be elected leader by a towering majority, there was intense interest in the subject. George M. Cohan made one of his rare screen appearances in the film – in a dual role, as a dour candidate unlikely to win and his double, a hobo whose personality make him eminently electable.

This studio offered another topical note in **Million Dollar Legs**, since the title referred to the athletes competing in the Los Angeles Olympics. What else it is

about is anybody's guess, except that it concerns the intrigues of Klopstockian politics: but as thought up by Joseph L. Mankiewicz and directed by Edward Cline, it is imperishably funny.

The Hollywood studios, however, decided that audiences cared to be scared rather than amused and each came up with its own solution. Following the Universal lead in horror, United Artists released the most inept, **White Zombie**, and Paramount made the most overrated, **Dr Jekyll and Mr Hyde**. RKO's **The Most Dangerous Game** concerned a mad baron (Leslie Banks) who sends his hound after two humans fleeing the jungle. MGM went furthest out, with its study of circus **Freaks**, which was banned for many years in several countries. Metro also did a fine job with **The Mask of Fu Manchu**, with its hints of sadomasochism and dreaded miscegenation, while Universal came up with the formulaic **The Mummy** and added laughs to **The Old Dark House**. The last three films, incidentally, starred Boris Karloff.

The most significant technical development was that

the Technicolor company finally perfected its system. Walt Disney immediately switched his 'Silly Symphonies' to colour, with **Flowers and Trees** in May and as the series developed it encompassed all his cartoons without Mickey Mouse. For the moment, the Mouse was too popular to need colour, and that was the way Hollywood felt about its output as a whole.

In Britain, **Wedding Rehearsal** plumbed new levels of gaucheness and Hitchcock's **Number Seventeen** new levels of silliness. At least it moved swiftly as did, more appropriately, Walter Forde's thriller **Rome Express**, the first British film in years to match Hollywood's professional standards.

From France, the best films were: René Clair's **Quatorze Juillet**; Jean Renoir's **Boudu Sauvé des Eaux**; Marc Allégret's **Fanny**, the sequel to **Marius**; and Julien Duvivier's **Poil de Carotte**, with its beautiful performance by Harry Baur. Jean Cocteau made his movie début as a director with **Le Sang d'un Poète**.

In Germany, Werner Hochbaum directed his simple but dazzling study of lowlife on the Hamburg waterfront, **Razzia in St Pauli**. Its antithesis was **Kühle Wampe** which, co-written by Berthold Brecht and directed by Slatan Dudow, manages to be didactic about the poor. Then, after a run of fine movies, Pabst chose to remake the dotty **L'Atlantide**.

Opposite: Paul Muni was on impressive form in Howard Hawks's **Scarface**, playing a mobster easily identifiable as Al Capone. Capone's unorthodox private life was reflected by giving him an incestuous passion for his sister, Ann Dvorak, here about to be punished for taking a lover. Above: Irene Dunne and John Boles as the frustrated lovers in **Back Street**. Right: **Tarzan the Ape Man** has been remade several times, but the one directed by W. S. Van Dyke remains the definitive version. It has mystery, excitement and, in the scenes between Johnny Weissmuller (in the title role) and Maureen O'Sullivan, an erotic charge.

1933

As President Roosevelt entered the White House Americans were revelling in Noël Coward's affectionate if jingoistic account of British life from the turn of the century to the present, **Cavalcade**. This was a present from Fox, who countered it with a charming piece of Americana, **State Fair**, directed by Henry King and proving that, at fifty-four, Will Rogers was still a national treasure. Radio City Music Hall opened with Capra's **The Bitter Tea of General Yen**, in which a missionary (Barbara Stanwyck) falls in love with a Chinese warlord (Nils Asther). A month later the theatre housed a giant gorilla, **King Kong**, clutching a screaming Fay Wray in its hand, and it towered over all competition.

And Warners made three musicals. The public had decisively rejected the operettas and frivolous backstage musical comedies which had been churned out for so long. In deliberately returning to the form, the studio confined the action to the theatre and rehearsal rooms, because these were exciting places to be; but they were now inhabited by hard-driving directors and venal angels, who knew that any showgirl was available, especially if an offer came with a diamond bracelet attached. Indifferent to the carnality around them and common to all three films are a singing duo, Dick Powell and Ruby Keeler, but around them are some more dynamic players, including Cagney, Aline MacMahon, John Blondell, Ruth Donnelly, Guy

Kibbee, Frank McHugh and hatchet-faced Ned Sparks. The lavishness, the sometime salaciousness and the sheer imaginative vulgarity of the production numbers, devised by a team headed by Busby Berkeley, remain astounding – and all in all (in order of release) **42nd Street**, **Gold Diggers of 1933** and **Footlight Parade** will endure as long as anything on celluloid.

As far as the Depression is concerned, it was (finally) safe in other hands, most notably Frank Borzage's, whose **Man's Castle**, for Columbia, takes a deeply romantic view of life in a shanty town, with Spencer Tracy and Loretta Young. But the most significant statement on the subject wasn't concerned with it at all. A Disney 'Silly Symphony', **The Three Little Pigs**, enjoyed outstanding popularity, returning again and again to the same theatres. Its theme song, 'Who's Afraid of the Big Bad Wolf?' became the anthem of the Depression, with Disney reputedly viewing the cartoon countless times in an effort to discover why.

MGM offered an all-star **Dinner at Eight**, directed by George Cukor, in which John Barrymore and Marie Dressler are down on their luck; but this was a comedy, meant to allow audiences to forget their own troubles, with laughs going not only to Dressler but to Billie Burke and Jean Harlow. Also in the cast, being mean, was Wallace Beery, and for him a reunion with Dressler, **Tugboat Annie**, was a huge crowd-pleaser. John Gilbert made his last film for the company, **Queen Christina**, at the end of which Garbo abdicated and went into exile, standing at the prow of the ship in one of the most

Left: **Duck Soup**. Groucho thinks up a new insult to throw at Margaret Dumont, the ultimate fall-girl, who won't understand it. Zeppo prepares to record it for the Freedonian history books. Above: Homosexual actor Charles Laughton played one of the greatest heterosexuals of history in **The Private Life of Henry VIII**. The images of the two, Charles and Henry, became irrevocably interwoven – as far as movie buffs were concerned. Opposite: Having astonished the world with the all-star **Grand Hotel**, MGM put another clutch of them, including Jean Harlow and Wallace Beery, into **Dinner at Eight**.

haunting images in the entire history of the cinema.

Posterity would also remember 1933 as the year in which Fred Astaire first danced with Ginger Rogers, in **Flying Down to Rio**, even if they only had supporting roles. Also at RKO Katharine Hepburn was an aspiring actress who didn't want to be just another **Morning Glory**, as she put it. In 1933 Mae West made a fortune for Paramount with **She Done Him Wrong** and **I'm No Angel** – the title song of which she sang with feeling. The studio had a box-office failure with a movie many now reckon is worth its whole output – **Duck Soup** – if only because it gives Margaret Dumont her richest role. 'They're fighting for your honour, which is more than you ever did,' says Groucho of the battles going on about them. Leo McCarey directed, getting the best of the Marxes with everything he had learnt from his years with Hal Roach and Charley Chase.

Finally, though it also belongs to the early part of the year, **Gabriel Over the White House** was produced by Walter Wanger, directed by Gregory La Cava and released by MGM to the fury of Louis B. Mayer, who quite correctly saw it as an attack on the policies of Herbert Hoover and an endorsement of those of Roosevelt. It put its case in supernatural fashion, by having a dead, corrupt president replaced by a far-sighted idealist who is his double. Walter Huston played both roles.

Among the stage stars now working in the British studios were Jack Buchanan and Jessie Matthews, both of whom sang and danced, but not together (at least on screen). The only reason for remembering Buchanan's **That's a Good Girl** is a song, 'Fancy Our Meeting', but **The Good Companions**, directed by Victor Saville from the novel by J.B. Priestley, is fine entertainment. Matthews plays a member of a concert party, the Dinky-Doos, whose efforts are helped by three others from different walks of life: Edmund Gwenn, John Gielgud and

Mary Glynne. The industry as a whole received a fillip when a comedy, **The Private Life of Henry VIII**, achieved worldwide success. It was produced and directed by Alexander Korda, and Charles Laughton, returning from Hollywood, scored a singular success in the title role.

In Germany, Max Ophuls came into his own after a few false starts with **Liebelei**, in which a handsome dragoon officer seduces the daughter of a musician. While keeping the unhappy ending of Schnitzler's original play, it manages to be more romantic than cynical. It was released in February as Ophuls, who was Jewish, prepared to leave Germany – as did Fritz Lang, who was half-Jewish, but who disliked the policies of the new Chancellor, Adolf Hitler. They were to be followed by many other prominent members of the German film industry over the next few years. With **Schleppzug M17** Werner Hochbaum made a film to equal **Razzia in St Pauli**, but his work began to decline slightly with **Morgen Beginnt Das Leben** – and it would plummet once the Nazis took control of the industry. The industry attempted to ingratiate themselves with their new masters with **S.A. Mann Brand**, about the enmity between themselves and the Bolsheviks before Hitler came to power.

In Czechoslovakia Gustav Machaty made **Ecstasy**, a tale about an old man, his young bride and the handsome fellow who diverts her while she's swimming in the buff. Her run through the forest, though chiefly hidden by foliage, was to confer notoriety on this film. For many years it was the only foreign-language Talkie many had heard of, but because of censorship few had actually seen it. The bride was played by Hedy Kiesler, who went to Hollywood to become Hedy Lamarr.

Left: Hedy Keisler looks apprehensive – will her new lover, Aribert Mog, be as tired as the elderly husband she has just shed? Because Mog first saw her swimming nude, **Extase** or **Ecstasy** was banned in most countries, which increased both its own notoriety and the curiosity of those unable to see it. Above: Fay Wray screams . . . and screams . . . and screams again, after being kidnapped by **King Kong**. Haunting, enthralling and unique (but the 1976 remake is not to be despised). Opposite: Dick Powell, Bebe Daniels and Warren Baxter in **42nd Street**, one of the three backstage musicals with which Warner Bros revitalized the form in 1933.

The world took one film, above all others, to its heart: **It Happened One Night**, directed at Columbia by Frank Capra, with Claudette Colbert as a runaway heiress and Clark Gable as a reporter who follows her across country for the story. It was a comedy of manners set aboard a Greyhound bus, and not till **One Flew Over the Cuckoo's Nest** in 1975

1934

would one film take the four leading Oscars. (For the record, when Gable was seen in one scene without an undershirt, men stopped wearing them.)

The other hugely popular film was a comedy-thriller, **The Thin Man**, directed at MGM by W.S. Van Dyke from a novel by Dashiell Hammett. Miss Loy and William Powell played a married couple who drink a lot and josh each other while hunting a murderer. There were subsequently five sequels, of which the first two (1936, 1939) were good and the last (1947) very bad.

Three Metro films are guilty pleasures: Edmund Goulding's **Riptide**, in which Shearer marries a British milord, Herbert Marshall, but dangerously dallies with an old flame, Robert Montgomery; Clarence Brown's **Chained**, with Joan Crawford behaving similarly after one look at Gable – this is True Love but the trouble is, she's being 'kept' by Otto Kruger; and Brown's **Sadie McKee**, with Crawford as a hat shop clerk who, seduced and abandoned by Gene Raymond, ups and marries a stout millionaire, Edward Arnold. That's not the end, as Crawford ultimately gets wealthy scion Franchot Tone. It was an established fact during the Depression that every working girl deserved a *decent* millionaire. Jean Harlow, Conway's **The Girl From Missouri**, went to look for one in New York and sleeps with Lionel Barrymore before

settling for his son, Tone. In both films the heroines get drunk before succumbing to sin, so are we to suppose that MGM thought that lushes made better lays?

All this was to stop. In the summer, the Production Code was tightened and bedroom scenes were banned. Movies were much less fun, and so was Mae West, even if in September, as the **Belle of the Nineties**, she was still able to tell her admirers, 'Well, I have my moments – all of them weak ones.' This was from Paramount, which made a glorious contribution to laughter by releasing no fewer than five movies with W. C. Fields, the Great Man himself. At least two of them are immortal: **It's A Gift**, in which he suffers like Sisyphus at the whim of wife, children, neighbours and assorted strangers; and the misnamed **Six of a Kind**. He (Fields) and Alison Skipworth are conners; Gracie Allen, George Burns, Charlie Ruggles and Mary Boland are the conned. **Cleopatra** is not quite in the same league, though it has its moments, as when Cleopatra (Claudette Colbert) waves away a pile of goodies which would not have disgraced Fauchon: 'We're not dining here after all.' Henry Wilcoxon was Mark Antony and Cecil B. DeMille directed.

Victor Schertzinger's **One Night of Love** was perfect as a star vehicle, though it helped if you liked the star, the rather formidable diva Grace Moore, returning to the screen after two earlier failures. The film was extremely popular, paving the way for 'classical' music in

Left: Gracie Allen, W. C. Fields, Mary Boland and George Burns in **Six of a Kind**. They were all amusing – especially Gracie, oblivious to anything beyond her own scatty logic. Above: Every Joan Crawford movie seemed to have the same plot – a shopgirl being misunderstood till she suffers in luxury in the last reel. She gets there long before that in **Sadie McKee**, though not helped by Esther Ralston (left) who had pinched her boyfriend after their first night together – the sort of situation to disappear with the Production Code in 1934. Opposite: Jeanette MacDonald and Maurice Chevalier on glittering form in MGM's **The Merry Widow**.

movies. Fred Astaire was reunited with Ginger Rogers, much to his indignation (he thought her miscast as an English society beauty, and she was) in **The Gay Divorcée**, a frivolous musical which at least had the sense to keep one Cole Porter song, 'Night and Day', from the stage version.

For Universal, Claudette Colbert, her black maid Louise Beavers and Ned Sparks all became rich manufacturing pancakes. This was in **Imitation of Life**, which was well titled inasmuch as Fannie Hurst's novel had taken some real life situations and turned them into nonsense. But in John M. Stahl's handling it is often persuasive, and it does have something useful (by the standards of the time) to say about race relations.

One actress made a huge advance: Bette Davis in **Of Human Bondage**, directed by John Cromwell from Somerset Maugham's autobiographical novel. The London chophouses and teashops are authentic, and Leslie Howard is fine as the medical student obsessed with a sluttish waitress, except that he's too old. The only other fault is the very thing for which the film was most praised: Davis's cockney accent.

The year's most worrying event in movies, along with the tightening of the Code, was the advent of a child star, Shirley Temple. She advanced to stardom with depressing rapidity, even capturing a gangster in **Baby Takes a Bow** which, despite its title (taken from a song

she had sung in an earlier picture), is a crime movie, if not a very gripping one.

In Britain, Douglas Fairbanks made his last picture, **The Private Life of Don Juan**, which did not deliver the delights promised by its title, but another erotic from the past got her just deserts when Anna Neagle became **Nell Gwynn**. Sir Cedric Hardwicke played her lover, the 'Merry Monarch' Charles II, who would have been falling on the floor if he'd had the luck to see Anna dancing to Edward German's music. Jessie Mathews danced on the ceiling in **Evergreen**, the only one of her star vehicles worth a light today, and Gracie Fields had her best screen moment in **Sing As We Go**, racing around Blackpool fun fair with a screenplay by J. B. Priestley and a title song which became Britain's anthem for the Depression.

Because of the success of **The Private Life of Henry VIII**, the increasingly ambitious local industry welcomed other American talents, if not rewardingly as far as they were concerned. Like **Henry VIII**, **Evergreen** was shown at Radio City Music Hall, giving an enormous fillip to Michael Balcon's Gaumont-British.

Two exiles from the Nazis, Billy Wilder and Robert Siodmak made charming comedies in France, respectively **Mauvaise Graine** and **Le Crise est Finie**, both

Left and opposite: There had been few sleuthing couples before **The Thin Man**, but carefree reporters and daffy heiresses were common enough in movies before **It Happened One Night**. The success of both films caused a hundred imitations, many of them very good – partly because their stars were as skilled as William Powell and Myrna Loy and Clark Gable and Claudette Colbert. Above: The great age of French movies was beginning, and with it a longing for the exotic – for Africa and the Orient. **Le Grand Jeu**, with Françoise Rosay and Pierre-Richard Wilm, is one of the most romantic pictures about the Foreign Legion.

with themes linked to the Depression. Two others, producer Erich Pommer and director Fritz Lang, tackled **Liliom**, with Charles Boyer as the big-headed carnival barker who goes to the bad. Raymond Bernard's very long **Les Misérables** has Harry Baur as Valjean and Charles Vanel as Javert, eclipsing any other actors in these roles. Jacques Feyder came up with two beauties, **Le Grand Jeu** and **Pension Mimosas**, both featuring his wife, Françoise Rosay. The former is a tale of passion in the Foreign Legion, with Pierre-Richard Wilm besotted with a coquette, Marie Bell; the latter is a loose retelling of *Phèdre*, set in Menton. With these a great period of French film-making begins, but not to be overlooked is **L'Atalante**, the masterpiece of Jean Vigo, who died this year at the age of twenty-nine. With both realism and poetry, it tells of a journey from Le Havre to Paris of two newly weds (Jean Dasté, Dita Parlo), uncertain of each other, and their relationship with the crusty barge-hand (Michel Simon).

The same qualities are to be found in **Il Canale Degli Angeli**, in which an unhappily married Venetian woman is tempted to stray when she meets a young seaman. It is the only feature made by the critic Francesco Pasinetti.

With most of its leading film-makers gone, Germany produced only one outstanding film, **Der Verlorene Sohn**, directed by Luis Trenker, who also plays the title role, a German adrift in a New York winter. The Russians had a big art-house hit (abroad) with a study of a Red commander during the civil war which followed the Revolution, **Chapayev**, directed by Sergei and Georgy Vassiliev. It was to influence every Soviet movie made up to the war years. Not exported then, but charming to see now, are several Japanese films, of which two may be singled out (invidiously, since this was an industry turning out 400 films a year): **Our Neighbour Miss Yae**, a gentle comedy of life in the suburbs directed by Yasujiro Shimazu, and **Street Without End**, a Silent soap opera handled with much skill by Mikio Naruse.

1935

N o one can be certain when the Golden Years of Hollywood began, but 1935 is one of them, with all the major studios turning out movies which are unmatched today. To marvel, without ignoring some clinkers along the way, the year (and those that follow) will be looked at month by month.

January   There's a pippin to start with, **David Copperfield**, directed by George Cukor for MGM with a cast which would have made Dickens dance in his grave. W. C. Fields as Mr Micawber, Edna May Oliver as Betsey Trotwood, Basil Rathbone and Violet Kemble Cooper as the Murdstones, Jessie Ralph as Peggotty, Roland Young as Uriah Heep, Lennox Pawle as Mr Dick. All of them more than make up for the two anodyne Davids – Freddie Bartholomew (boy), Frank Lawton (man). **Lives of a Bengal Lancer** directed by Henry Hathaway for Paramount. Rousing adventures on the Northwest Frontier, with a moustachioed Gary Cooper.

February   **Naughty Marietta**, an operetta, teams Jeanette Macdonald and Nelson Eddy for the first time. 'Ah! Sweet Mystery of Life' he bawls and she trills. Better, **Roberta** has a Jerome Kern score, Irene Dunne as a Paris couturier and Astaire and Rogers stepping-it after singing 'I Won't Dance'. **Ruggles of Red Gap**, directed by Leo McCarey, sees Charles Laughton as a British butler in the Old West heading a divine cast: Mary Boland, Charlie Ruggles (no relation), Roland Young and Zasu Pitts.

March   The formula falters with **Gold Diggers of 1935**, but the elaborate finale, 'Lullaby of Broadway', is smashing.

April   **Oil For the Lamps of China** is simply one of the best films to detail a man's working life. The man's Pat O'Brien; Josephine Hutchinson is his wife, with direction by Mervyn Le Roy.

May   John Ford's **The Informer** is one of the oddities which litter cinema history. It's not a bad movie, this tale of the 'troubles' in Dublin, with Victor McLaglen in the title role; but it's so derivative of European movies that you want to heave a brick at the screen. And it is precisely because it is so European that it was greeted by an avalanche of praise. Till then, RKO had loathed it.

June   **Becky Sharp** was the first feature in 3-strip Technicolor, and very handsome it is under Rouben Mamoulian's direction, especially when the officers whirl out of a Brussels ballroom to meet Napoleon at Waterloo. Whether it was wise to choose Thackeray's novel for this cinematic occasion is doubtful; it was certainly foolish to think Miriam Hopkins could play his nineteenth-century gold-digger. However, Cedric Hardwicke is superb as the Marquis of Steyne. Pioneer, which was set up to promote Technicolor, produced for RKO, who were not very

Left: Alfred Hitchcock (to the right) directing Robert Donat (centre) and Madeleine Carroll in **The 39 Steps**. Above: W. C. Fields as Mr Micawber with Freddie Bartholomew as **David Copperfield** which, as screen versions of Dickens go, is only rivalled by David Lean's **Great Expectations** and **Oliver Twist** in the 1940s. Opposite: Elsa Lanchester as **The Bride of Frankenstein**, one of the few sequels as good as the original. Curiously, they are not much alike: both chilled the blood, but while the grimness of **Frankenstein** was balanced by compassion, that in the second was leavened by a ghoulish humour.

happy with the box-office results.

July   A good time was had by all on the **China Seas**, including Clark Gable, Harlow, Wallace Beery, Rosalind Russell, Robert Benchley and Hattie McDaniel. Directed by Tay Garnett, it was perhaps the year's most enjoyable movie. With **She**, producer Merian C. Cooper was looking for something to equal **King Kong**, but he moved the setting (of Rider Haggard's novel) from Africa to the Arctic. She, who must be obeyed, is played by Helen Gahagan and if the result is less spellbinding than **King Kong**, it could be because the dialogue is unspeakable. John Ford's folksy, enjoyable **Steamboat 'Round the Bend** was the public's last view of Will Rogers, who had been killed in an air crash earlier in the year. He was on top form as the boat's captain. The film may be said to mark the emergence of a new studio, 20th Century-Fox, since Zanuck had left UA to take over the ailing Fox studio.

August   The **Man on the Flying Trapeze** was W. C. Fields, and who could ask for anything more? **Top Hat**: Astaire and Rogers with Irving Berlin songs. Garbo was **Anna Karenina**, Tolstoy's adulterous heroine, for the second time, with Fredric March as her lover and Basil Rathbone as her husband, directed by Clarence Brown.

October   For the delectation of future generation, the Marx Brothers spent **A Night at the Opera**, having moved to MGM to do so. Warners cast Paul Muni as a French chemist in **The Story of Louis Pasteur**, which began the rage in Hollywood for biopics. These denoted a new seriousness, and certainly this is not to be sneered at, as directed by William Dieterle. It was a Warner bid for

prestige, though dwarfed in that respect by **A Midsummer Night's Dream**, co-directed by Dieterle and the famed German man-of-theatre, Max Reinhardt. Mendelssohn, oodles of fairies, and players who may be a good thing (James Cagney as Bottom, plus the other rustics) or may not (the rest of the cast).

November   MGM brought out its big guns: **Mutiny on the Bounty**, directed by Frank Lloyd, and **A Tale of Two Cities**, directed by Jack Conway. In the former, Fletcher Christian (Clark Gable) revolted against the mean Captain Bligh (Charles Laughton) on the high seas. In the latter, Sidney Carton (Ronald Colman) did a far, far better thing by going to the guillotine after helping French aristos escape the Revolution. Both casts were sprinkled with Limeys, since the first was based on an incident in the British Navy in 1789 and the second on a novel by Dickens. Both heroes went unmoustached, to the dismay of their female fans.

December   A new actor, Errol Flynn, was pirate **Captain Blood** under director Michael Curtiz, because a number of other actors had turned down the role.

While Hollywood made two fine adaptations of Dickens, Britain could only manage an indifferent one, **The Old Curiosity Shop**, but it has a magnificent Quilp in Hay Petrie. The Silver Jubilee of George v was celebrated by an all-star **Royal Cavalcade**, which relived some events of his reign in a non-riveting way. A great actor, Harry Baur, was in **Moscow Nights**, with a young man who would become one, Laurence Olivier. He was impressive enough as a dashing officer with gambling

Left: Franchot Tone (left) and Clark Gable in **Mutiny on the Bounty**. Above: Greta Garbo in the title role of **Anna Karenina**, with Fredric March, a somewhat eager and callow Count Vronsky. Opposite: As **Becky Sharp**, Miriam Hopkins was even more puppet-like than Thackeray intended, but as she danced around this movie version of his *Vanity Fair* she encountered strong support from Sir Cedric Hardwicke (left) as the Marquis of Steyne and Alan Mowbray as Rawdon Crawley. It had taken Hollywood three years to use the much improved Technicolor for a feature, and the box-office results confirmed its hesitation.

debts. Anthony Asquith directed and other talents involved were Russian, Hungarian and German – the sort of combination which usually results in rotten movies, but not in this case. The producer Max Schach then united with other expatriates on **Abdul the Damned**, directed by Karl Grune with Fritz Kortner in the title role. The Turkish dictator Abdul Hamid was, till Hitler turned up, the most evil figure of modern civilization. All analogies were intended.

And what Hitler intended was clear enough from **Triumph des Willens**; thousands of marching, siegheiling young morons in Leni Riefenstahl's repellent record of the 1934 Nazi rally at Nuremberg.

In France, Pierre Chenal had an excellent Raskolnikov, Pierre Blanchar, and a magnificent police inspector, Harry Baur, for **Crime et Châtiment**. On the same level is Henri Poupon in Marcel Pagnol's affectionate study of a lonely schoolteacher, **Merlusse**, while Pagnol's rural dramas were being imitated by Jean Renoir in **Toni**. But one French movie wowed 'em the world over: Jacques Feyder's **La Kermesse Héroïque**, set in Flanders at the time of the Spanish invasion. Its purpose was comedy, expertly served by Louis Jouvet as a wily priest and Françoise Rosay, no less crafty as the mayor's wife. It set new standards for historical reconstruction, and hasn't dated an iota.

January Harold Lloyd did a nice turn as a milkman-cum-prizefighter in **The Milky Way**, but the big news was the 'Indian Love Call', warbled by MacDonald and Eddy in **Rose Marie**, a tale of how the Mounties always get their man. Directed by W. S. Van Dyke, it's their best film, because it is genuinely lighthearted.

1936

February **Follow the Fleet** sees Astaire, Rogers and some more peachy Berlin tunes. **Klondike Annie** has Mae West up North. In **Modern Times** Chaplin borrows jokes and situations from **A Nous la Libérté**. **The Trail of the Lonesome Pine** is the second Technicolor feature, with Henry Fonda, Fred MacMurray and Sylvia Sidney in a tale of feuding hillbillies, which was already dated when filmed in 1916 and 1923. Paramount atoned with **Desire**, which probably has the best opening ever of any comedy, as Dietrich cons a Paris Jeweller out of a priceless geegaw, and then pops it into Gary Cooper's pocket to get it past customs. It can only go down from there, and does. Lubitsch produced, Borzage directed.

March With **Mr Deeds Goes to Town**, Frank Capra was put at the head of the list of most admired American directors. It's a bit conventional now, full of smiles and tears, but there are wonderful things in it, especially the performances of Gary Cooper as the hick who wants to give away his unexpected inheritance, and Jean Arthur as the hard-boiled reporter who finds herself falling in love with him. **The Plow that Broke the Plains** wasn't a film many cinemagoers knew about since few

cinemas wanted to show it. A thirty-minute documentary made by a critic, Pare Lorentz, it's nevertheless a valuable historical document, telling as it does of how America's vast grasslands were turned into tillable soil.

May MGM had a good month with two movies which could not have been less alike. **The Great Ziegfeld** was a lavish musical biopic, with William Powell as the famous Broadway impresario and Myrna Loy as his second wife Billie Burke (who was independently carving out a second career in movies as a supporting actress). One set, like a giant wedding cake with a spiral staircase to accommodate hundreds of dancers, is excessive, as is the accompanying soundtrack, which blends 'A Pretty Girl is Like a Melody' with another dozen composers, from Mozart to Gershwin by way of Puccini. **Fury** is Fritz Lang's first American film, produced by Joseph L. Mankiewicz, a former writer at Paramount, and it concerns an innocent man (Spencer Tracy) who almost becomes the victim of a lynching. Louis B. Mayer loathed it; Lang was sacked; and it would be another twenty years before any Metro film suggested that the US of A was anything but heaven on earth.

That there was heaven on earth was something Warners also attempted in **The Green Pastures**, which re-created much of the Old Testament in terms of 'darkie' culture. It is a genuine curio, patronizing now, a brave achievement then, with a fine performance by Rex Ingram as the 'Lawd', dressed as an old-time preacher man. It was directed by William Keighley with Marc Connelly, author

Left: Madeleine Carroll and Tyrone Power in **Lloyds of London**, one of Hollywood's extraordinary historical epics of the period. It is fustian, but contains an immense amount of factual information. Above: Jacques Brunius and Jane Marken in Renoir's **Un Partie de Campagne**. Left unfinished in 1936, two intertitles were added ten years later to explain the missing action: it was greeted as a masterpiece. Opposite: Gary Cooper and Jean Arthur in **Mr Deeds Goes to Town**. Its populist attitude belongs to the Depression years, but Capra's understanding of comedy remains sure: by turns cynical, sentimental, cruel and farcical.

of the original play – and in view of the success of that a limited risk for the studio. Far preferable is **Bullets or Ballots**, with Robinson, Bogart and Joan Blondell, or **Anthony Adverse**, an exhilarating gallop through Hervey Allen's bestselling historical novel, directed by Mervyn LeRoy with a cast including Fredric March, Olivia de Havilland, Claude Rains, Edmund Gwenn and Gale Sondergard, all on considerable form. It also features Steffi Duna, who had to have the bad luck of simultaneously being on display in **Dancing Pirate**: she cannot carry the film and nor could Charles Collins, in the title role, a Boston dancing-master shanghaied and then let loose in a Spanish-Californian town. He *can* dance, but the film has no entertainment value – and was a distinctly unwise choice for Pioneer's second use of Technicolor. There would not be a third.

June This was MGM's month, by virtue of re-creating so magnificently the great **San Francisco** earth-quake under the direction of W. S. Van Dyke. Who could ever forget saloon owner Clark Gable and priest Spencer Tracy striding though the debris looking for Jeanette MacDonald? Universal was having a bad time, being in receivership after a number of expensive flops. La Cava's **My Man Godfrey** was too late to save it, but it gave a lot of people a good time as scatty Carole Lombard acquired hobo William Powell and made him the family butler. He then has to cope with her batty mother, Alice Brady, while the master of the house, stoic Eugene Pallette, looks the other way.

July Competing for the prestige prize of the month were MGM's **Romeo and Juliet** and RKO's **Mary of Scotland**. Both had major directors, George Cukor and John Ford respectively; miscast stars, Leslie Howard, Norma Shearer and Katharine Hepburn, Fredric March. If the first is to be preferred, it is because it has better decor and is much less silly.

August RKO atoned with **Swing Time**: Astaire-Rogers with a less puerile plot than usual, a sublime Jerome Kern score, and, under the guidance of George Stevens, the only one of their films as stylish as Astaire himself. If we exclude **The Plainsman** (see November), **The Texas Rangers** is the only major Western between **Cimarron** and **Stagecoach**. The poverty-row studios were churning them out for Saturday matinees, but Hollywood otherwise looked askance at the genre. This is a good one, made by King Vidor for Paramount, with Fred MacMurray, Jean Parker and an exceptional villain in Lloyd Nolan.

September William Wyler directed **Dodsworth**, one of the best films of the decade. Taken from the novel by Sinclair Lewis, it was superbly acted by Walter Huston as the wealthy middle-aged manufacturer who loses his silly, snobbish wife, Ruth Chatterton, on a trip to Europe and takes up instead with Mary Astor.

November If **The Plainsman** isn't a Western, it's a pioneer drama, or vice versa. Gary Cooper was Wild Bill Hickock and Jean Arthur was Calamity Jane for DeMille. Hollywood looked eastwards again as Fox unfolded the saga of **Lloyds of London**: it didn't seem a second too long under Henry King's direction, while the romantic team of Tyrone Power and Madeleine Carroll shows stars at their starriest. Such were notably absent from **Winterset**, since it was about poverty, the deprived and those living on the fringes of crime. Maxwell Anderson's earnestly poetic play had been inspired by the Sacco and

Left: Walter Huston may have been the best actor of his era, and he may never have had better material than **Dodsworth**. He played a business-man from the Mid-West, who begins to realize that his wife, Ruth Chatterton, is more attracted to a series of European gigolos and philanderers. Above: **Rembrandt**, with Charles Laughton, was the last film Korda himself directed in the post-war period. Opposite: Ginger Rogers and Fred Astaire in **Swing Time**. At the end, in 'The Waltz in Swing Time', several of the film's tunes were reprised in one of the longest and most captivating of all their dances.

Vanzetti case; it hasn't made an interesting film, as directed by Alfred Santell, but it is one of the great links, since it borrows heavily from **The Informer** and would, in turn, influence Marcel Carné's output over the next few years.

December The **Black Legion** was the Ku Klux Klan, and it showed that Warners still had a social conscience when needed. As a bonus, it has Bogart and Ann Sheridan. 20th Century (hereafter, Fox) showed how it could crank up a star vehicle by putting Sonja Henie into **One in a Million**. Here was a lady who couldn't do anything well but skate: and yet it entertains.

The year in Britain began with the death of the old king and ended with the abdication of the new one, Edward VIII. The local interest in royalty manifested itself in Lady Jane Grey, the 'Nine Days Queen', **Tudor Rose**, directed by Robert Stevenson for Gainsborough. In the title role, Nova Pilbeam was outshone by Gwen Ffrangcon-Davis as Mary Tudor. Korda's output included the prestige picture **Things to Come**. Directed by William Cameron Menzies from a screenplay by H. G. Wells, it predicted a world war in 1940, before moving on to the millenium and the first rocket to the moon.

In Germany, Luis Trenker, a former admirer of Hitler, went subversive in making **Der Kaiser Von Kalifornien**, a film with parallels so obvious that it is a wonder it wasn't banned. It was also much better than Universal's March release on the same subject, **Sutter's Gold**. The Italian cinema was now into turning out pro-Fascist propaganda: Augusto Genina's **Lo Squadrone Bianco** was meant to justify Italian intervention in Africa, and Goffredo Alessandrini's **Cavalleria** extolled the virtues of all matters military.

In the Netherlands Max Ophuls directed a biting satire on capitalism, **Komedie om Geld**, and in France he made one of his poorest films, **La Tendre Ennemie**. Pagnol did no better with **César**, an inadequate sequel to **Marius** and **Fanny**. Duvivier had a good year: a remake, **Le Golem**, with Harry Baur, shot in Czechoslovakia; **La Belle Equipe**, a jaunty comedy-drama about five work-mates, including Jean Gabin, who open a riverside restaurant; and the deeply romantic **Pépé Le Moko**, with Gabin as a fugitive from justice hiding out in the casbah. These were the cream of the year, with one exception, and that was not shown publicly: **Un Partie de Campagne**. Renoir adapted from a story by de Maupassant, a Sunday idyll for two randy Parisians bent on seduction. It is his most lyrical film, left unfinished because he was contracted to make **Les Bas-Fonds**, and at thirty-seven minutes no one knew what to do with it.

January   The year started with **Camille**, directed by George Cukor, with Garbo at her most luminous as the consumptive heroine and Henry Daniell at his most disdainful as her protector. The new management at Universal found a new formula called Deanna Durbin, a delightful teenager who sang soprano, and it saw its fortunes restored as she and her sisters reunited divorcing parents in **Three Smart Girls**.

1937

February   Without Garbo, MGM's France might be just a few more movie sets, but MGM's China, against all the odds, is a triumph. It may have been filtered through the sensibilities of a bestseller (Pearl Buck's) but **The Good Earth** never puts a foot wrong as it follows a young couple (Paul Muni, Luise Rainer) from poverty to wealth, to famine, poverty again and much else, including a revolution and a plague of locusts. The direction is credited to Sidney Franklin, though many hands worked on it. It was the last film produced by Thalberg, who had died in 1936 and is dedicated to him – the only time his name appeared on the screen.

March   There was the happiest casting in Hollywood history when Ronald Colman played the British diplomat in **Lost Horizon**, skyjacked to become the potential ruler of Shangri-La, a mysterious mountain country where no one seemed to age. James Hilton's novel had been a bestseller because it contained hope and many other messages as Europe darkened, and Frank Capra filmed it with such love that it is hard to scoff at its naivety. A flawless cast also included Thomas Mitchell, Edward Everett Horton, H. B. Warner and Sam Jaffe.

© Disney

Above: As the Disneyfication of the world accelerates, it is odd to reflect that the name once meant movie magic: with the early Mickey Mouses, the 'Silly Symphonies' and the first handful of features which began with **Snow White and the Seven Dwarfs**. Right: Ronald Colman in the superb **Prisoner of Zenda**, called up to defend the Ruritanian throne against the pretender, Rupert of Hentzau.

134

April   Errol Flynn was in a middling version of Mark Twain's tale, **The Prince and the Pauper**, which capitalized on the forthcoming Coronation in London by including a Tudor version of same. MGM threw out a programmer, **A Family Affair**, with Mickey Rooney as Andy Hardy. This would lead in time to a series about Judge Hardy and his family, bringing huge popularity to Rooney; by presenting a totally false picture of American life, all apple-pie sweetness, it would please L. B. Mayer and be the movies' most popular series till 007.

May   **Make Way For Tomorrow** was a brave and touching film about two aged parents, Beulah Bondi and Victor Moore, separated because none of their children wants them. Paramount disliked the film so much that they sacked its director, Leo McCarey. They would be sorry (see October).

July   **The Life of Emile Zola** was misnamed, since it concentrated on the Dreyfus Affair, but it brought much prestige to Warners, to director Dieterle and Paul Muni, who played Zola; it can still impress.

September   This has some beauties, including one that will be around as long as there is anyone left to watch it: **The Prisoner of Zenda**, with Ronald Colman heading a perfect cast (including Madeleine Carroll, Mary Astor, Douglas Fairbanks Jr and Raymond Massey) as the Englishman persuaded to impersonate the dissolute king of Ruritania. It was the Abdication which persuaded Selznick that Anthony Hope's old novel was worth another whirl; he got several hands to direct, but the one credited is John Cromwell. Musicals had a good month, with the imaginative, open-air staging of *The Donkey Serenade* in **The Firefly** – some nonsense set during the Peninsula War with Jeanette Macdonald and Allen Jones – and the presence of Deanna Durbin in her second starring vehicle, **One Hundred Men and a Girl**. The

hundred men were out-of-work musicians and she persuades Stokowski (as himself) to conduct them after singing Mozart at him.

October   Leo McCarey moved to Columbia, where he remade an indifferent marital comedy of 1929, **The Awful Truth**, but this time it scintillated, due chiefly to the playing of Irene Dunne and Cary Grant, whom he had persuaded to improvise; Ralph Bellamy, as so often, was 'the other man'. Charles Boyer was Napoleon to Garbo's Marie Walewska in Clarence Brown's **Conquest**, one of the few times she had a leading man to her measure.

November   John Ford directed **The Hurricane** for Goldwyn, and nothing much happens till the hurricane blows in, beyond some indifferent acting by Dorothy Lamour and Jon Hall as Polynesians and some excellent playing by Mary Astor, Raymond Massey and C. Aubrey Smith. Some of them get blown away in what is still one of the most exciting spectacles ever filmed.

December   **Snow White and the Seven Dwarfs** opened at Radio City Music Hall for Christmas. Disney had begun work on what the trade referred to as his 'folly' in 1934, a year before he put Mickey Mouse into colour. Only a couple of other people in the whole world felt that audiences would want to see a feature-length animated film. With Europe darkening, many regarded the Queen/Witch as an allegory for the dictators, but the film certainly made a lot of people very happy, including the

Left: Mischa Auer with Deanna Durbin in **One Hundred Men and a Girl**. Most of her early films were directed by Henry Koster and all were produced by Joe Pasternak, both of whom knew how to showcase her radiant high spirits. Above: Greta Garbo and Robert Taylor in **Camille**. She has left him at the request of his father and returned to her wealthy protector. Meeting again, her love for him overwhelms her, but she remembers the promise she made to Duval père. Opposite: There is no more sublime sound in movie history than the laugh of Irene Dunne as she gets the better of Cary Grant in **The Awful Truth**.

critics and Disney's accountants. As the public flocked, the industry decided that Technicolor might, after all, be a box-office attraction.

Britain's first Technicolor feature was **Wings of the Morning**, which had views of London and Killarny (while John McCormick sang about it) plus Annabella and Henry Fonda. The title referred to a horse. Korda had some successes, including **Fire Over England**, with Flora Robson as Elizabeth I delivering her Tilbury speech and Laurence Olivier and Vivien Leigh as the young lovers; and from Jacques Feyder came **Knight Without Armour**, with Robert Donat as a secret service agent in Petrograd and Marlene Dietrich as a Russian countess finding a ballgown in a White Army outpost. Among other unlikely costumes was the Catherine the Great fur-trimmed outfit worn by Anna Neagle in **London Melody** to sing 'Just a Jingle in the Jungle'. From this Neagle went on to play a real queen, **Victoria the Great** which, surprisingly for a Herbert Wilcox film, is actually worthwhile, as it runs through some of the great events of the reign. Anton Walbrook is superb as the Prince Consort, but that wasn't what one wag had in mind when he observed that this was the first time he realized that Albert had married beneath him. The film was made because of the removal of the ban on representations of the Queen, and also because of the euphoria surrounding the Coronation. But if there's one British film from 1937 to be preserved it's **Oh Mr Porter!**, which Marcel Varnel directed for Gainsborough. Will Hay, the music hall comic, finally came to his own in movies as the station master of a deserted station in Northern Ireland, staffed by the decrepit Moore Marriott and the juvenile Graham Moffatt, both exploring new horizons of contempt and incompetence – the latter being a quality with which Hay himself was richly endowed.

From the Soviet Union, a film at last that wasn't about tractors or Lenin or both: Vladimir Legoshin's **Lone White Sail**. It is set at the time of the disturbances of 1905, but is simply a marvellous boys' adventure set in Odessa. In Germany, Luis Trenker made **Condottieri**, which, although set in medieval Italy, is a thinly veiled study of the evils of Nazism. From Japan came **Humanity and Paper Balloons**, one of the two surviving films of Sadeo Yamanaka, who died young. A masterpiece, it examines the morals and mores of rich and poor – mainly poor – in one district of eighteenth-century Edo.

In France Jean Renoir made **La Grande Illusion**, a plea for France and Germany not to go to war again, but by making one of the characters a rich Jew (Dalio) he ensured that the film would not be seen in Germany. It is about many other matters, including patriotism, class and compassion, wonderfully expressed by Jean Gabin and Pierre Fresnay as French prisoners of war and Erich Von Stroheim as the camp commandant. This was one of the four French films which broke Hollywood's stranglehold on world cinema after the coming of Talkies. Another was Duvivier's **Un Carnet de Bal**. This is one of the first portmanteau films, taking several episodes to reveal what Marie Bell learns as she seeks out her partners at a dance long ago, including Raimu and Jouvet.

February   In **A Slight Case of Murder**, bootlegger Edward G. Robinson's plan to go straight is spoiled by the discovery of four corpses in the cellar of his new mansion. The source is a play by Damon Runyon and Howard Lindsay; the inspired supporting cast includes Ruth Donnelly, as Robinson's wife, Ed Brophy and Allen Jenkins. There were two decent pieces of Americana, much needed as Europe drifted towards war: **The Adventures of Tom Sawyer**, Mark Twain's story from Selznick in Technicolor, with Tommy Kelly as Tom; and Clarence Brown's **Of Human Hearts**, a family saga set on the Ohio River before, during and after the Civil War, with Walter Huston, Beulah Bondi and James Stewart as the family, plus such other nice people as Guy Kibbee, Charles Coburn and Ann Rutherford, as well as John Carradine as Abe Lincoln.

1938

March   **Her Jungle Love** is Ray Milland, and she's Dorothy Lamour, now in Technicolor, in perhaps the silliest of her sarong pictures, but Paramount makes up for this with **Bluebeard's Eighth Wife**, with Gary Cooper as a much-married millionaire and Claudette Colbert as the daughter of an impoverished count, Edward Everett Horton. Directed by Lubitsch and written by Charles Brackett, this was perhaps the best of the many comedies of this era on the non-consummation of a marriage – a subject to which the cinemagoer, because of censorship, had to bring much imagination.

April   **The Adventures of Robin Hood** was co-directed by William Keighley and Michael Curtiz, who was brought in to give the action more pizzazz. One of the cinema's enduring pleasures, unsurpassed as a swash-buckler, with a cast so perfect that most of it must be noted: Errol Flynn (Robin), Olivia de Havilland (Maid Marian), Claude Rains (Prince John), Basil Rathbone (Sir Guy of Gisbourne), Alan Hale (Little John), Eugene Pallette (Friar Tuck), Patric Knowles (Will Scarlet), Ian Hunter (King Richard) and Melville Cooper (The Sheriff of Nottingham).

May   There was more splendid stuff and another big one for director Henry King and stars Faye, Power and Ameche with **Alexander's Ragtime Band**, an American **Cavalcade** built around a score of Irving Berlin songs; Ethel Merman joined in to sing them, and not one of them aged a jot over thirty years. The **Three Comrades** are Robert Taylor, Robert Young and Franchot Tone, all understandably in love with Margaret Sullavan. Set in postwar Germany, it was taken from the novel by Erich Maria Remarque and directed by Frank Borzage. The film is anti-Nazi, though the word 'Nazi' wasn't used, by order of the MGM front office.

July   **Marie Antoinette** went to the guillotine again, in the person of Norma Shearer. Lavish, under the direction of W.S. Van Dyke, and better on the affair of the Queen's necklace than the Revolution; with Robert

Left: James Cagney going to the electric chair, watched by Pat O'Brien, in **Angels with Dirty Faces**. Above: Jean Gabin in Marcel Carné's **Le Quai des Brumes**. Opposite: Spencer Tracy and Mickey Rooney in **Boys Town**, which sealed success for both of them. Tracy, who had been an also-ran star in his days at Fox, advanced at Metro to be the studio's leading actor and one of its most popular stars. Rooney, a tot-around-town in parts large and small, had been signed by Metro in 1935. **Boys Town** was one of the steps which led exhibitors to vote him the biggest box-office attraction of 1939.

Morley as the King and Tyrone Power as Count Fersen.

August   'Frank Capra directed **You Can't Take It With You**, with an engaging cast including James Stewart and Jean Arthur. The thesis of the play, by George S. Kaufman and Moss Hart, is clear from the title; by adding a greedy developer and some thoughts on capitalism Capra was thought to have improved on it. In fact, he did it a disservice.

September   MGM took a rare look at contemporary life in **Boys' Town**, or at least an admiring look at Father Flanagan, who ran a reform school with benevolence. In that role Spencer Tracy is as good as ever.

October   In a not dissimilar tale, James Cagney goes cringing to the Chair so that the Dead End kids, the **Angels With Dirty Faces**, shan't admire him. This is the one about boyhood pals who grow up and go their different ways – Cagney to crime and Pat O'Brien to a dog-collar. Smashingly done, with Bogart as a really nasty gangster, Ann Sheridan, and direction by Curtiz.

The Prime Minister, Neville Chamberlain, returned from Munich after a meeting with Adolf Hitler, assuring 'peace for our time'. This gave a certain topicality to **The Lady Vanishes**, an espionage thriller set aboard a transcontinental train in which the 'enemy' is clearly German. It was Hitchcock's best film so far, splendidly written by Launder and Gilliat and with a fine cast, including Naunton Wayne and Basil Radford as two Britishers more interested in cricket. In the leads, Margaret Lockwood and Michael Redgrave lacked the insouciant style of their Hollywood counterparts.

The comic George Formby had a good year with **I See Ice** and **It's in the Air**, in which he joined the RAF, but his rival at the box office, Gracie Fields, had a bad year. Fox had signed this national treasure for 'the highest

salary ever paid to a human being' and they sent over Victor McLaglen and Brian Donlevy to scrap over her in turn-of-the-century South Africa: but **We're Going to be Rich** wasn't a good film, and the three she subsequently made for the company in Britain were hardly better.

Vivien Leigh was a don's flirty wife in **A Yank at Oxford**, who was Robert Taylor, and much to-do was made over this ordinary film because it was the first made in Britain by MGM, which had constructed a vast new studio and filched Michael Balcon to head production. Much better was its second film, **The Citadel**, directed by King Vidor from A.J. Cronin's novel about a doctor who loses his ideals when he gets to Harley Street. Robert Donat played him, with Rosalind Russell as his wife. At least these pictures were welcomed worldwide, as was one wholly British one, **Pygmalion**, directed by Anthony Asquith and Leslie Howard. (Only Howard was credited.) He was the only conceivable Professor Higgins until someone else came along, and Wendy Hiller was excellent as the cockney flower girl whom he turns into a lady.

In France, riches, amongst which is Pagnol's imperishable story of life in a Provençal village, **La Femme du Boulanger**, with Raimu as the baker who goes on strike until his wife, Ginette Leclerc, returns from her lover.

Left: Catherine Lacey, Margaret Lockwood and Michael Redgrave in Hitchcock's satisfying **The Lady Vanishes**. Above: Errol Flynn in **The Adventures of Robin Hood**. Not the screen's first Robin or the last, but the most gallant, the most blithe and the most lithe (actually, he wasn't a good fencer, but they managed to disguise that). Opposite: Ruth Donnelly and Edward G. Robinson in the hilarious **A Slight Case of Murder**. The repeal of Prohibition has put him out of work, but he's made a pile to impress the neighbours – to which end he has 'hired' an orphan, Bobby Jordan, who turns out to be the least of his troubles.

Jean Renoir, elsewhere a notable optimist, looked at the underbelly of humanity in **La Bête Humaine**, Zola updated, but at any other time it would surely have been done in period. An older man (Fernand Ledoux) is married to a tramp, played by Simone Simon, who has an affair with an engine driver, Jean Gabin. And after the murder the train speeds on . . . This actor was at his most Gabinesque in Marcel Carné's **Le Quai des Brumes**, an outsider, a deserter from the army, dour at worst, impassive at best. In a dank bar in a *quartier* of Le Havre, he is drawn to a whore, Michèle Morgan, who, at seventeen, finds life not worth living. It is no surprise to find Annabella and Jean-Pierre Aumont checking in to Carné's **Hôtel du Nord** with a suicide pact, or to find that its other inhabitants include Louis Jouvet, a fugitive from justice, and Arletty, cheerful but quite aware of how low they have sunk.

It has never been clear how much Carné owed to his collaborators – Jacques Prévert, who wrote the screenplay for the first of these (and with whom he worked most often), and Henri Jeanson, who supplied the dialogue of the second, from an adaptation by Jean Aurenche and Pierre Bost of the original novel (by Eugene Dabit). These are great screenwriters, as was Charles Spaak, who also contributed to this group of movies; and these film-makers had at their service superb art directors in Alexandre Trauner, George Wakhevitch and Jean d'Eaubonne. It is not surprising that the refugee Germans found France far more congenial than Hollywood or Britain, despite the fact that the producers were probably the least trustworthy of any industry.

Pabst was also working in France, but on trumpery melodramas, such as **Le Drame de Shanghai**, but at least it has the presence of Jouvet, as does Chenal's hugely superior **La Maison du Maltais**. Both films reflect the obverse side of the coin of pessimism, an obsession with the romance provided by the Orient and Africa. And every one of them has actors who makes you leave the cinema wondering at their wit, variety, subtlety and intelligence.

Fifty years later, in 1989, it was acknowledged that Hollywood had had its *annus mirabilis* in 1939. It was true, though it wasn't clear why it took the US Postal Service fifty-one years to note that fact (with four specially-designed stamps celebrating **Gone With the Wind**, **Beau Geste**, **The Wizard of Oz** and **Stagecoach**).

1939

January Robert E. Sherwood's play **Idiot's Delight** has as its setting a hotel lounge in Europe to which come, among others, a pacifist and an armaments manufacturer. A second world war has broken out – that seemed a distant possibility in March 1936, when the play opened. The prospect in 1939 and events since have done nothing to destroy or improve the highminded-ness of the piece, as directed by Clarence Brown. Clark Gable plays a song-and-dance man and Norma Shearer a phoney countess. The best thing about the film, however, is a long prologue about their days in vaudeville together – and that wasn't in the play.

February John Ford's **Stagecoach** was Hollywood's real return to mainstream Westerns in an age: the characters (played by John Wayne, Claire Trevor, Thomas Mitchell, etc.) and situation were from de Maupassant's *Boule de Suif*, with pursuing Indians added.

March **The Hound of the Baskervilles** sees Basil Rathbone and Nigel Bruce begin their screen careers as Sherlock Holmes and Dr Watson at Fox (to continue in B movies from 1942 onwards at Universal). Fred Astaire and Ginger Rogers part in an untypical film, **The Story of**

Vernon and Irene Castle which, based on fact, ended unhappily and used the songs the Castles danced to. There were two marvellous films. **Midnight**, written by Brackett and Wilder, directed by Mitchell Leisen, had Claudette Colbert as a penniless chorus girl pretending to be married to John Barrymore in order to make his wife, Mary Astor, jealous; with Don Ameche. **Love Affair**, deliberately, isn't quite so funny, because Irene Dunne and Charles Boyer don't meet up, as arranged, after falling in love on a transatlantic voyage. But in all cinema history no director balanced laughter and sentiment as adroitly as Leo McCarey.

April Don Ameche invented the telephone in **The Story of Alexander Graham Bell**. It took him years to live down the joke, but this is one of the best of the many biopics, as directed by Irving Cummings. Lew Ayres starred in **Calling Doctor Kildare**, which started a popular series for MGM. Cecil B. DeMille had Barbara Stanwyck and Joel McCrea on the **Union Pacific**, a spectacular Western and the last good film he made. Laurence Olivier was a fiery, powerful Heathcliffe in **Wuthering Heights**, eclipsing Merle Oberon's pallid Cathy: only the first part of Emily Brontë's great romantic novel made it to the screen, as directed by William Wyler for Goldwyn, but

Left: Cary Grant, Victor McLaglen and Douglas Fairbanks Jr as battling sergeants in George Stevens's **Gunga Din**, the tone of which was set by a statue of Queen Victoria under the credits. Above: The outbreak of war in Europe presented a problem for MGM, for Garbo no longer had much of a box-office following in the US, and the profits from her films came chiefly from the Continent. The problem was solved by putting her in a comedy, and an excellent one – **Ninotchka** with Melvyn Douglas – and advertising it with the slogan 'Garbo Laughs!'. Opposite: James Stewart as a young senator in Frank Capra's **Mr Smith Goes to Washington**.

can anyone remember anything about the British versions of 1970 and 1992? **Confessions of a Nazi Spy**, based on a little-reported trial of Nazi infiltrators in the US, has a Jewish actor, Edward G. Robinson, in the role of the F.B.I. agent who brought them to book. It is virulent in its condemnation of Nazism, which may not have been so brave after the annexation of Austria and Czechoslovakia, but is also imaginative and far-reaching. Anatole Litvak directed, and while you may just forgive the New York critics for choosing **Wuthering Heights** as the best film of the year, you cannot forgive *The New York Times* for not including it in its Top Ten.

June   Henry Fonda was the **Young Mr Lincoln** for John Ford, one of the most thoughtful of his movies. And **The Sun Never Sets** on the British Empire, which has obvious German spies trying to break it up: a fair-to-good adventure, and one of the earliest messages of solidarity which Hollywood would be sending across the Atlantic for the next few years.

July   William A. Wellman's splendidly remade **Beau Geste**, with Gary Cooper, Robert Preston and Ray Milland as the British toffs who join the Foreign Legion, with Brian Donlevy as their sadistic commander.

August   Judy Garland sang 'Over the Rainbow' and trod the yellow brick road to meet **The Wizard of Oz**, accompanied by a scarecrow, a tin man and a cowardly lion. Also from MGM, **The Women**, directed by George Cukor from Clare Boothe Luce's play, with Norma

Above: Laurence Olivier and Merle Oberon in **Wuthering Heights**, which is still the definitive version. Right: John Wayne and Andy Devine on the **Stagecoach**, with George Bancroft and Chris-Pin Martin before the start of their arrow-dodging journey. Opposite: The American public had turned a cold shoulder to Marlene Dietrich, and Paramount had paid her not to make the last film due under contract. At a much reduced fee she went to Universal for a comedy Western, **Destry Rides Again**, which brought her new popularity. That is James Stewart pouring water on her head, and Una Merkel with whom she is brawling.

Shearer, Joan Crawford, Rosalind Russell, Mary Boland, Joan Fontaine and Paulette Goddard bitching each other as they wait for divorces in Nevada.

September   Judy Garland got to sing again, with Mickey Rooney, in **Babes in Arms** – but not the songs from the Rodgers and Hart stage show, since most of these were jettisoned. Myrna Loy moved over to Fox to play an adulterous British milady in **The Rains Came**, directed by Clarence Brown from Louis Bromfield's novel. What with Tyrone Power as an Indian princeling, the time passes well enough till the rains come, when audiences discover that the Special Effects department don't let them down.

October   The Marx Brothers were **At the Circus**, and the decline has gently begun; but Groucho sings 'Lydia the Tattooed Lady' and still has Margaret Dumont to insult. Paramount remade **The Cat and the Canary**, with Bob Hope coming into his own as one of a group of legatees gathered at an old dark house in the bayous for the reading of the will; with Paulette Goddard and several sliding panels as sinister as Gale Sondergaard as the housekeeper. **Mr Smith Goes to Washington** in the person of James Stewart. Washington itself was distinctly unimpressed with this portrait of its worthy denizens, as played by Claude Rains, Edward Arnold, Harry Carey, Guy Kibbee, William Demarest, and others. One of the finest casts ever assembled includes Beulah Bondi, Thomas Mitchell and, best of all, Jean Arthur as the hard-boiled reporter converted by Stewart's naive idealism. Sidney Buchman wrote it for Capra, and it's a supreme moment in cinema history. And Ingrid Bergman arrived in Hollywood to remake one of her Swedish films for

Selznick, now called **Intermezzo: A Love Story**. It kept its theme tune, the first time a piece for violin made the record charts, and it made her even more spring-like, more radiant, as the piano teacher who falls in love with the famous father of one of her pupils, Leslie Howard. All in just over an hour, the shortest running time of any major movie in the Sound era.

November Garbo laughed, to lighten a world which now sadly needed as much laughter as it could get. The occasion was **Ninotchka**, directed by Lubitsch from a screenplay by Wilder, Brackett and Walter Reisch, and she was a stern Russian commissar in Paris sent to bring back three recalcitrant colleagues. It is suave Melvyn Douglas who converts her to western ways, and among the film's many enchantments is Garbo's vulnerability as the little girl in the big city. Her erstwhile rival, Marlene Dietrich, was also making people laugh, as a saloon floozie in **Destry Rides Again**, which revitalized her career. That wasn't something James Stewart needed, but he was on tip-top form as the slow-to-draw new deputy sheriff determined to clean up the lawless town of Bottleneck. Also at Universal, Deanna Durbin received her first screen kiss in **First Love**, an event which generated an immodest amount of publicity around the world. The film is a delightful modernization of *Cinderella*. Raoul Walsh

directed **The Roaring Twenties**, which offered a feast of Cagney, Bogart and some super montages concerning bootlegging, not to mention one of the most memorable endings in movie history. 'He used to be a big shot,' explains Gladys George, cradling Cagney's corpse.

December Paramount released the second full-length animated cartoon, **Gulliver's Travels**, based on just the first part of Swift's novel. Since its subject was war, it was timely, but the Fleischer brothers – creators of Betty Boop and Popeye – were discouraged from continuing in this field after the failure of **Mr Bug Goes to Town** in 1941. Partly because of the acclaim for **Wuthering Heights**, Hollywood was embarking on its great age of literary adaptations. They liked them old: **The Hunchback of Notre Dame**, William Dieterle for RKO, with Charles Laughton, unrecognizable and pitiable in the title role. And new: **Of Mice and Men**, Lewis Milestone for Hal Roach, untypically abandoning slapstick. It was based on John Steinbeck's novella about migrant farm workers during the Depression, with emphasis on the friendship between George (Burgess Meredith) and the mentally retarded Lenny (Lon Chaney Jr).

And then there was Margaret Mitchell's **Gone With the Wind**, which had sold eight million copies since its publication in 1936. From the day it came out there was speculation as to who would play what and the excitement engendered by the casting and the filming remains unique in cinema history. Selznick produced, the film was planned minutely by the designer William Cameron Menzies and George Cukor, who was replaced by Victor Fleming shortly after shooting began. Clark Gable played Rhett Butler, Leslie Howard was Ashley Wilkes and Vivien Leigh was the last-minute choice to play Scarlett O'Hara. The Melanie, Olivia de Havilland, once remarked that at the time Hollywood believed that it would be the only film to achieve immortality. At 3 hours 42 minutes it was also the longest, but it was quite clear that the public wanted the whole book and nothing but. So the Civil War in and around Atlanta, Georgia, was re-lived in Technicolor by these characters and an unprecedented number of cinemagoers. Ditto the Oscar nominations – thirteen, with eight wins, plus a special award to Menzies. Hattie McDaniel, who played Mammy, was the first black to win one, and at the ceremony she hoped she was a credit to her 'race'. The subject had a special significance now that Europe was in its third month of war, and it would run in London till the war ended.

Hollywood's interest in filming in Britain would be severely curtailed till then, but it concluded in 1939 on a high note when Sam Wood directed **Goodbye, Mr Chips**, with Robert Donat as the schoolteacher and Greer Garson as his wife. It was also a topical one, as Mr Chips sees his pupils leave for two previous wars.

A Hollywood director and actor, Victor Schertzinger and Kenny Baker respectively, had British employers on a Technicolor version of Gilbert and Sullivan, **The Mikado**. One of its financiers was a flour miller, J. Arthur Rank, whose distributing company had also handled **Pygmalion**. Deeply religious and high-minded, he believed in films as a force for good. As the Americans moved out of the three branches of movie-making – production, distribution and exhibition – he increased his control over all three, so that by 1942 he was by far the dominant figure in Britain and would remain so, if with an admirable 'hands-off' policy, allowing others to make all artistic and financial decisions.

Also of significance was **Cheer, Boys, Cheer**, made by ATP, which would soon re-name itself Ealing Studios at the behest of its new boss, Michael Balcon who, discouraged, had left MGM. He decided that the company's films should reflect the British way of life, but over the next few years Ealing's films would be mainly abysmal, especially its contribution to the war effort. The studio would lose George Formby (to Columbia-British) and gain Will Hay; and it would not really find its way till it realized that the British way of life could best be reflected by comedy. This particular film was a happy

precursor of Ealing comedy, telling as it does of the rivalry between two breweries, one aggressive and mechanized, and the other personal and old-fashioned. The former was headed by mean Edmund Gwenn, at one point seen reading *Mein Kampf*.

In retrospect the best British film would seem to be **I Met a Murderer**, low-budgeted and filmed on location with James Mason, who later wed his co-star, Pamela Kellino, then married to its director, Roy Kellino. The piece has an energy and a confidence common to the great Hollywood films of 1939, though the splendour of some of them is better found in another of Korda's dazzling tributes to the concept of Empire, the remake (in Technicolor) of **The Four Feathers**. He also produced **The Lion has Wings**, with Richardson and Merle Oberon, a tribute to the RAF with three directors and no discernible relation to either art or entertainment. But it was premièred in November, only two months after Korda had conceived the idea on 2 September, the day the Germans invaded Poland. The following day the British declared war on Germany.

With Europe in its uncertain state, its movie industries hesitated. The Soviet Union sent out the second of Mark Donskio's Maxim Gorky trilogy, **My Apprenticeship**, which is even better than the first, and one of the few films to convey the vastness of Russia.

In France, pessimism persisted. In Albert Valentin's **L'Entraîneuse**, set in a holiday *pension*, a nice, bourgeois boy falls in love with a girl (Michèle Morgan) not knowing – as his father does – that she's a whore; in Duvivier's **La**

Opposite: Howard Hawks's **Only Angels Have Wings** is by far the best of the many movies about small airlines, adroitly mingling laughs, sentiment and thrills. Cary Grant is the man running it and Jean Arthur a stranded showgirl. Above: Clark Gable and Vivien Leigh in **Gone With the Wind**, still the most successful and popular film ever made. If 1939 seat prices were adjusted to those of the last few decades it would easily regain its position at the head of all box-office charts. Right: Judy Garland in **The Wizard of Oz**, accompanied by Bert Lahr as the cowardly lion, Jack Haley as the tin man and Ray Bolger as the scarecrow.

Fin du Jour, set in a crumbling retreat for aged actors, Jouvet is the grandiloquent new arrival who drives his mistress to suicide and Michel Simon is an inmate with a fondness for boys. Charles Spaak wrote both. Three first-rate thrillers were no more optimistic: Pierre Chenal's **Le Dernier Tournant**, based on James M. Cain's *The Postman Always Rings Twice*, has Corinne Luchaire and Fernand Gravey as the lovers and Michel Simon as the husband they conspire to murder; Kurt Bernhardt's **Carrefour** sees Charles Vanel as an industrialist, an amnesiac, being blackmailed by Jules Berry; and Siodmak's **Pièges** tells of a series of chorus girls lured to their death by contact ads. Maurice Chevalier plays a nightclub owner, Pierre Renoir is his partner and Erich Von Stroheim is a mad couturier. All three films would be remade successfully by Hollywood, as was the Carné-Prévert **Le Jour Se Lève**, although regarded as the quintessential French film of the period. That was because of its fatalism, which was why the Daladier government banned it (a copy was smuggled out via North Africa in 1943, so it was then seen abroad). Jean Gabin is the factory worker chain-smoking through the night while the police wait outside, reflecting on why he shot Jules Berry and on the involvement of both of them with sweet Jacqueline Laurent and the rather more 'experienced' Arletty.

Jean Renoir also brought forth a masterpiece, **La Règle de Jeu**, in which a house party of people, foolish and spoilt, squander away their last minutes before war comes – not that war is mentioned, but the film's anti-fascist tone becomes stronger as their actions increasingly interweave with those of the servants.

1940

January There were at least five films that haven't dated an iota, and one of them still attracts huge audiences. That is Disney's **Pinocchio**, from Carlo Collodi's novel, the adventures of a puppet, including his trip to Pleasure Island with the bad boys who are then turned into donkeys, which is one of the most frightening sequences ever put on film. Howard Hawks's **His Girl Friday** is a remake of **The Front Page**, with Rosalind Russell at her formidable best in Pat O'Brien's old role as the reporter. Cary Grant is on similar form as her conniving editor. More charming, gentler but hardly less amusing is Lubitsch's **The Shop Around the Corner**, with Margaret Sullavan and James Stewart as Budapest colleagues who, unknown to each other, is the other's pen pal. After that, some seriousness, as Shirley Temple goes in search of **The Blue Bird**, Fox's answer to **The Wizard of Oz**. Its failure signalled the end of her career at the studio. Fox, conversely, had one of his greatest prestige successes with **The Grapes of Wrath**, directed by John Ford from Nunnally Johnson's screenplay, based on the novel by John Steinbeck. Henry Fonda (son) and Jane Darwell (mother) are two members of the Joad family migrating from the Oklahoma dust bowl.

February Mae West met W. C. Fields in **My Little Chickadee**, an occasion which should have been funnier than it was; Bing Crosby, Bob Hope and Dorothy Lamour met up for the first time and took the **Road to Singapore**; and Fred Astaire danced with Eleanor Powell to Cole Porter songs in **Broadway Melody of 1940**. The biographical mania continued with **Young Tom Edison**, who was Mickey Rooney; Henry King's **Little Old New York**, with Alice Faye and Richard Greene, who played Robert Fulton, the inventor of the steamship; and **Dr Ehrlich's Magic Bullet**, with Edward G. Robinson. His magic bullet was a cure for syphilis, a word mentioned only once in the film, which made it somewhat mysterious; but it fingered him as a Jew, and ended with a tirade against the fascism to come.

March Selznick produced Daphne du Maurier's **Rebecca**, directed by Hitchcock with a perfect cast, including Joan Fontaine and Laurence Olivier.

May There were biographies, with Spencer Tracy as **Edison the Man** and Alice Faye as music-hall beauty **Lillian Russell**. Husband and wife John Hubbard and Carole Landis changed sex for Roach in **Turnabout**, based on Thorne Smith's novel – odd then and odd now.

July Preston Sturges persuaded Paramount to let him direct his own script, **The Great McGinty**, a thesis to the effect that all politicians are corrupt; Brian Donlevy and Akim Tamiroff helped him prove it. In complete

Below: Henry Fonda (right) as Tom Joad in **The Grapes of Wrath**, with John Carradine as Casey, the priest who has lost his calling and who accompanies the Joads on their trek to California. Opposite: Arriving at Manderley for the first time: Joan Fontaine in **Rebecca**, with Laurence Olivier as the wealthy Englishman who met and fell in love with her on the Côte d'Azur. She is not made to feel entirely welcome.

contrast, **Pride and Prejudice** shouldn't have worked but does, despite Greer Garson's sometimes coy Elizabeth Bennett. Among its wonders: Olivier as Darcy, proud, charmless and exactly right; Edmund Gwenn and Mary Boland as Mr and Mrs Bennett; Edna May Oliver as Lady Catherine de Burgh and Melville Cooper as Mr Collins.

August   Hitchcock directed **Foreign Correspondent** for Wanger, who originally envisaged it as a serious study of an American reporter looking at the European 'situation'. What it has become is one of Hitchcock's funniest and most ingenious films, with some unforgettable sequences: the assassination in the rain and the chase through the umbrellas; the Dutch windmill with its sails going against the wind; Joel McCrea escaping his would-be murderers along the hotel parapet clad in only robe, socks and garters, landing in Laraine Day's room; and professional assassin Edmund Gwenn preparing to throw him off the tower of Westminster Cathedral.

October   In a doubtful début Carmen Miranda went **Down Argentine Way**. Betty Grable replaced a pregnant Alice Faye in the lead and after ten years in movies began a swift ascent to the top, helped by legs rather than talent. The situation in Europe was examined in two solid thrillers, Mervyn LeRoy's **Escape**, from MGM, and Mitchell Leisen's **Arise My Love**, from Paramount. The latter starts jokingly in Spain with Claudette Colbert as a reporter and Ray Milland as a flyer, but has serious matters on its mind, such as a torpedo attack in the Atlantic. The former has Robert Taylor in Germany looking for his mother, who disappeared after the Nazis came to power; with Norma Shearer.

November   In another doubtful debut Abbott and Costello were funny men in **One Night in the Tropics**, and if you're wondering why a second-string cast (Allen Jones, Robert Cummings, etc.) has a Jerome Kern score, it was written years earlier for a film which never got made. Katharine Hepburn arrived at MGM to repeat her

stage role in **The Philadelphia Story**, that of the haughty Tracey Lord who is rudely tamed by ex-husband Cary Grant as she's about to marry again; with James Stewart and Ruth Hussey as reporters and direction by George Cukor. **Fantasia** dies the death. Disney's publicists had warned him that this collection of snippets from the classics would need careful handling, but that didn't help it; nor did the public listen to the critics, who thought this a brilliant departure for popular culture. Some of them, however, pointed out that some sections were really quite vulgar. Disney nurtured the film, booking it into art-houses for short runs during the next three decades, but it wasn't till the 1970s that it achieved great popularity.

Europe needed laughter. The Germans invaded Denmark, Norway, Belgium, the Netherlands and Luxembourg. The invasion of France was equally successful, effectively allowing them to occupy one half of the country, including Paris, while the other part was ruled by a puppet government favourable to the Nazis. Later in the year they invaded Rumania. Winston Churchill became Prime Minister in a Britain now only supported by its overseas territories. British forces were evacuated from Dunkirk in June and, from September, London was under constant bombardment from the air.

The British film industry, including its ever-present comics, was uncertain how to treat the War – whether to

Left: 'The Lubitsch Touch' meant sexual innuendo, done lightly and subtly, but after he left Paramount in 1938 Lubitsch eschewed it completely, though still making comedies, like the charming **The Shop Around the Corner**, with Margaret Sullavan, James Stewart and Frank Morgan. Above: Universal teamed Mae West and W. C. Fields in **My Little Chickadee**, a somewhat careless comedy set in the Old West. Opposite: The climax of **Foreign Correspondent**, which takes place on a transatlantic clipper, with Joel McCrea, George Sanders, Laraine Day and Herbert Marshall.

make escapist films in order to let audiences forget it, or propaganda to show that the country was winning. Since the latter was manifestly untrue, the dilemma was solved for them by the government, which ordered the production of information shorts and documentaries to support the feature films – when, that is, cinemas were open. Government involvement with movies went back to 1928 with the formation of the Empire Marketing Board. This was absorbed in 1933 by the GPO Film Unit, which came directly under the control of the Ministry of Information on the outbreak of War. In May 1940 it was renamed the Crown Film Unit.

There was just so much propaganda audiences could take and there were too many untalented people creating it. This included most of the members of the Crown Film Unit, but there was one shining exception, Humphrey Jennings. He had been making beautiful documentaries on the British way of life for years, without the *de haut en bas* attitude of his colleagues. With the War he came into his own, leaving an invaluable record of those years, starting with **The First Days**, a montage he had assembled in the Autumn of 1939. The second, **London Can Take It**, co-directed with Harry Watt, is introduced by the American journalist Quentin Reynolds. Despite its

portrait of Londoners carrying on during the Blitz, it is less about that than the celebration of a spirit, that of the British people at the time.

One feature of merit made by the industry was **Pastor Hall**, based on fact and directed by Roy Boulting with Wilfrid Lawson as a priest who is sent to a concentration camp for opposing the Nazis.

In Germany, Viet Harlan's **Jud Süss** reworked that story as anti-Semite propaganda, made all the more effective by Ferdinand Marion's superb performance in the title role. Luis Trenker made another of his historical anti-Fascist films, **Der Feuerteufel**, and was banned from working again.

And in France, Edmond T. Gréville's remarkable **Menaces** focuses on life in a small Paris hotel from September 1938 onwards; it is melodrama, but a truer reflection of this period than any other film made. A sad history of the Hapsburgs, **De Mayerling à Sarajevo**, certainly contained resonances for this time. **Sans Lendemain** does not, though this romantic story of a woman trying to live down her past continues the down-trend of French cinema. Both films starred Edwige Feuillère and were directed by Max Ophuls. Both were still showing in Paris when the Germans marched in in June.

Hollywood was a long way from the War in Europe, but it made an occasional contribution to the conflict, mainly in the form of recruiting posters and messages of solidarity with the beleaguered British.

January **So Ends Our Night**, directed by John Cromwell from a novel by Erich Maria Remarque, is

1941

about those made homeless by Hitler's policies (though he goes unnamed, because the USA was still officially at peace). Margaret Sullavan is a Jewish girl, Glenn Ford a half-Jewish student and Fredric March an opponent of the regime.

February Two looks at the American past: **The Strawberry Blonde**, with James Cagney as a dentist loving Rita Hayworth but marrying Olivia de Havilland (that's bad?); and **Back Street**, remade with Sullavan and Charles Boyer. These backward glances were to increase over the next few years, because life seemed cosier and more comfortable then. Preston Sturges came up with **The Lady Eve**, a comedy with three qualities to show up those which strain to manage one — satire, romance and slapstick — with Charles Coburn and daughter Barbara Stanwyck fleecing Henry Fonda at cards.

March Mitchell Leisen came up with **I Wanted Wings**, starring Ray Milland, William Holden and Veronica Lake, whose peek-a-boo coiffure was to be much copied till, with America at war, the style was banned after too many women had caught their hair in machines in munitions factories. This picture has war on its mind: it invites bright young men to join the Army Air Corps. They were more likely to be persuaded by **That Hamilton Woman**, Vivien Leigh, as she ensnares Laurence

Olivier while Britain faces Napoleon's might. Directed by Alexander Korda, it was Churchill's favourite picture and played in the Soviet Union throughout the War. Anchors were aweigh in **The Sea Wolf**, Michael Curtiz's version of Jack London's novel and the best of the many which have been done, chiefly due to Edward G. Robinson's performance as the grim, haunted captain .

April **Penny Serenade** was George Stevens' adroit mix of comedy and pathos as Irene Dunne and Cary Grant meet, marry and break up after the death of their adopted son. Hard to know why anyone should prefer **Citizen Kane**, a Gothic melodrama with pretensions to social significance and many borrowings from **The Power and the Glory**. A dazzling piece of jewellery, but if you examine it closely, it's all paste. It does have wonderful things in it, including the cod newsreel with which it opens, the acting of Agnes Moorehead, Joseph Cotten and others, and Gregg Toland's cinematography. The New York theatre's wonder boy, Orson Welles, made his movie début as actor, director and producer and shares the writing credit with the experienced Herman J. Mankiewicz, though Welles's associate, John Houseman, declared that *he* wrote it with Mankiewicz. Because the tycoon Welles played was thought to be based on William Randloph Hearst, the film was ignored or reviled in his newspapers. Elsewhere, critics raved, as they have gone on doing till this day. You wonder what else they've seen.

Left: Preston Sturges's **Sullivan's Travels**: Joel McCrea as the Hollywood director who dons a hobo's outfit to discover what the real world is like, and Veronica Lake as the starlet who accompanies him on part of his journey. Above: Despite the War, British stars Laurence Olivier and Vivien Leigh stayed on in Hollywood to make **That Hamilton Woman** or **Lady Hamilton**, which was certainly about Lord Nelson's love for her, but it was also about one small, brave country standing up to a ruler who had conquered all Europe. Opposite: Alice Faye and Betty Grable, Fox's two singing blondes, as a sister act in vaudeville in **Tin Pan Alley**.

On the matter of capitalism, Sam Wood's deliciously funny **The Devil and Miss Jones** examines it more pungently. Charles Coburn's tycoon has more depth than Kane, but then he is helped by Jean Arthur as the fiercest of strike-minded employees in his department store. As an antidote, **Road to Zanzibar**, has Hope, Lamour and Crosby finding their uniquely free-wheeling style in the second of their journeys to exotic places.

July   Sonja Henie skated as a Norwegian refugee in **Sun Valley Serenade** – and people were getting a bit tired of Sonja skating. But accompanying her were Glenn Miller and his Orchestra, making a sound which meant much to many over the next few years.

September   Tyrone Power became **A Yank in the RAF** with Betty Grable, an American showgirl working in England. Also from Fox came **Weekend in Havana**, a Carmen Miranda musical. The ebullient, fantastically accoutred Miranda was so limited as singer and dancer that she could only support Alice Faye; but people talked about her, comics imitated her, so it suited Fox to set its musicals South of the Border. It also suited the government's 'Good Neighbor' policy, requiring neutrality in Latin-America in the event of the US being drawn into the War.

Following the example of Preston Sturges, John Huston made the transition to director with **The Maltese Falcon**, his own adaptation of Dashiell Hammett's thriller, unsurpassed and unsurpassable, and only partly because of the cast: Bogart as private eye Sam Spade, Mary Astor as the mysterious woman in the case, Sidney Greenstreet as the deceptively jovial Gutman and Peter Lorre and Elisha Cook Jr as his dangerous underlings.

October   There are songs in Disney's **Dumbo**, the tale of a flying elephant which, at sixty-four minutes, was his shortest feature. Garbo danced the Chica-Choca in

Two-Faced Woman, impersonating her supposedly amorous, more glamorous twin sister in order to win back husband Melvyn Douglas. With most European markets closed to her, MGM tried to win back her American audiences with comedy and had done so with **Ninotchka**, but this diminished her and no one liked it, including Cukor, who directed. She decided to retire until the end of the War (and then did not have the courage to face the cameras again).

Life in Britain was being studied in the immensely popular **How Green Was My Valley**, for which Fox constructed a Welsh mining village on the back lot. John Ford directed from the best-selling novel by Richard Llewellyn; the 'I' of the novel was played by young Roddy McDowall. Among others attempting Welsh accents were Maureen O'Hara (sister) and Sara Allgood (mother), who were Irish, and the Scottish Donald Crisp (father).

November   Hollywood presented its first picture of London during the Blitz, **Confirm or Deny**, an accurate portrait with, at the centre, two American journalists, Don Ameche and Joan Bennett. Unlike this, **International Lady** is not a good movie, but it features the Blitz, plus a gang of Nazi spies. There are even Nazi spies in the US in **Dangerously They Live**.

December   A surprise, **Hellzapoppin**, based on a Broadway show in which anything might happen, including patrons undressing in the stalls. Universal retained Olsen and Johnson, revamped it, put H. C. Potter to direct, and came up with a picture as anarchic and funny as any ever made. Martha Raye and Mischa Auer help. The wit of **Sullivan's Travels** is the highly individual one of Preston Sturges, in one of the best of all his films. Joel

Left: **King's Row** was one of those small towns behind whose shutters lurk self-righteousness and strange passions. The director, Sam Wood, got superlative performances from most of his cast, including Ann Sheridan; he even got an acceptable one from Ronald Reagan, here discovering that his legs have been amputated. 'Where is the rest of me?' he asked. Above: **Remorques** was finally shown, having been abandoned when war broke out. Michèle Morgan is unhappily married, Gabin is happily married, but they are doomed to fall in love. Opposite: Bette Davis, with Teresa Wright, as a Southern gorgon in William Wyler's **The Little Foxes**.

McCrea plays an earnest Hollywood movie-maker who puts on old clothes and goes out to find the meaning of life. MGM also put a topical note into its Rooney-Garland **Babes on Broadway**, with Judy giving out with a tribute in song to the British tommy and evacuees talking to their parents in London.

In March the United States Congress passed the Lend-Lease Act and in May President Roosevelt announced that the country was in 'an unlimited state of national emergency'. At the same time, he had to maintain a public stance of neutrality, although the German-Italian invasions of Yugoslavia and Greece meant that many first- and second-generations of Americans now had relatives living under foreign occupation. In June, in defiance of their treaty, Germany invaded the Soviet Union.

On 7 December Japan attacked Hawaii, Hong Kong, the Philippines and the Malay States by air and sea. The following day the Unites States declared war on Japan and on 11 December Germany and Italy declared war on the US. The conflict had widened, and no one could see it ending for years. Britain had entered the war with Germany as ill-prepared as that country was rich in armaments. The same was true of the USA and Japan. Although the US was no longer predominantly isolationist, Congress had made it clear to Roosevelt that it would not vote money for arms. It now regretted this.

The priority of the British film industry was to make films which might sway American public opinion in favour of Britain. The first of these was easily the worst, **This England**, with Constance Cummings as an American reporter who re-lives threats to British freedom in the past. More subtle were two historicals: **The Prime Minister**, with John Gielgud as Disraeli, and **Penn of Pennsylvania**, with Clifford Evans in the title role. The cause was enormously advanced by Leslie Howard, who had lived in both Britain and Hollywood. Because of his

popularity in the States, the two films he made were destined for American audiences: **Pimpernel Smith**, which he directed himself and in which he played a dreamy professor in fact involved in smuggling refugees out of Germany; and **49th Parallel**, directed by Michael Powell, with Eric Portman as a German on the run in Canada. Apart from himself, the actors to whom he was spouting Nazi slogans were all well known in the States: Howard, Olivier, Anton Walbrook and Raymond Massey.

Walbrook was a Polish airman and Sally Gray an American reporter in **Dangerous Moonlight**, whose theme, the 'Warsaw Concerto', became enormously popular on both sides of the Atlantic. Ealing's ambitious **Ships With Wings** was strictly for local consumption, but it has a bombing of a dam with models so obvious that Noël Coward stated it had given him his first real laugh since the War started.

Two literary properties all stood fine chances of American distribution: Shaw's **Major Barbara**, credited to Gabriel Pascal but actually directed by Harold French and David Lean, with Wendy Hiller, Rex Harrison, Robert Morley and Sybil Thorndike; and H. G. Wells's **Kipps**, with Michael Redgrave in the title role, Diana Wynyard as the rich girl who dallies with him, and Phyllis Calvert as the tweenie he marries.

Humphrey Jennings produced **Heart of Battle**, a companion piece to **London Can Take It**, a group portrait of some Midland and Northern cities as they are being bombed; and the **Words for Battle** are spoken by Laurence Olivier, beginning with Milton and moving

Opposite: Sidney Greenstreet (seated), Peter Lorre and (right) Humphrey Bogart in **The Maltese Falcon**. The film propelled Bogart towards stardom. Above: Bing Crosby and Bob Hope in **Road to Zanzibar**, the sequel to **Road to Singapore** (1940). Right: **The Lady Eve**, or love in the Preston Sturges manner. For decades, many of the best romantic comedies followed the same reliable formula: the two top-billed stars, he and she, fought for eight reels and didn't end up in each others' arms till the last one. Sturges had some variations on this, since here are Henry Fonda and Barbara Stanwyck in reel five.

through Blake, Kipling and others to the Gettysburg address. Olivier becomes increasingly forceful, but the images remain calm. **Listen to Britain** reminds us that Jennings had once acted in *The Voice of Britain* for the BBC. You would not have to be chauvinistic for it to be the one film to take to a desert island.

The War had a liberating effect on the Italian film industry. Between the pro-Fascist movies – never as virulent as those made in Germany – the film-makers had been turning out pleasing minor comedies and realistic dramas, most of them set in the open air. But Mussolini gave the country not only its railways but a real film industry. He built a giant new studio, Cinecitta, and had ordered a school of film to be opened, which created a new generation of film-makers.

For his first film as director, former screenwriter Mario Soldati chose the nineteenth-century novel by Antonio Fogazzaro, **Piccolo Mondo Antico**. Far from being studio-bound, it was beautifully shot in and around Lake Garda. Alida Valli and Massimo Serato play a young couple separated by the demand for the *Risorgimento*; no better portrait of the Italian past had been done. Approaching it in that respect is **Addio Giovinezza!**, with two sweethearts in Torino who split up when he is taken up by an older woman, Clara Calamai. The director, Ferdinando Maria Poggioli, also came up with **Sissignora**, an ingratiating comedy in which a young, spoilt lothario dallies with his spinster aunts' maid. Also sweetly amusing is **Teresa Venerdi**, directed by Vittorio De Sica, who plays a penniless young doctor saddled with a cantankerous actress, Anna Magnani, as mistress. Its uncredited writer, Cesare Zavattini, was soon to become the single most influential force in Italian cinema.

157

1942

January Several films with war-related themes were issued, suggesting that Hollywood had decided to throw in its lot with the Allies even before Pearl Harbor. In **Captains of the Clouds**, James Cagney listens to Churchill's speech, 'We shall fight in the fields and streets . . .' and says, 'Now there's a guy who knows how to issue an invitation.' He joins the Royal Canadian Airforce and at one point sings along in a rousing chorus of 'There'll Always Be An England'. Curtiz directed this not very good war picture, the only one for a very long while in colour. Michèle Morgan was **Joan of Paris**, falling in love with Paul Henreid, a Free Frenchman serving with the RAF. Nazi spies were hunted in **All Through the Night** and were present, less rewardingly, in two MGM Bs, **Nazi Agent** and **Joe Smith, American**. Spencer Tracy and Katharine Hepburn had their first and memorable meeting in **Woman of the Year** as, respectively, sports columnist and political pundit. As in most of their films, she was a hoity-toity lady to be converted by his more down-to-earth style. The famous last scene, in which she tries to prove she can cook breakfast, was devised by the producer, Joseph L. Mankiewicz; the film was directed by George Stevens.

February There was laughter, and much more, in Lubitsch's **To Be or Not to Be**, with Jack Benny and Carole Lombard leading an acting group required to impersonate Gestapo officers. For all the jokes about actors and Nazis, the film was accused at the time of making light of Polish suffering.

March A version of Graham Greene from Paramount, **This Gun for Hire**, which transposes the action from a 1936 Midlands town to Los Angeles and makes the criminal mastermind not an armaments manufacturer but a Fifth Columnist. Never mind, it is recognizably Greeneland, with Alan Ladd as the man with the gun and Laird Cregar as the greedy go-between.

April There was Disney's fawn **Bambi**, from Felix Salten's novel. Generations since have cried when Bambi's mother is shot and they have seen many, many other Disney features, only one of which (see 1961) has anything like the magic — if you forgive the excesses of **Fantasia** — of the first five. Rita Hayworth puts her hair up in a period musical, **My Gal Sal**, and thousands of women copy her.

May Greer Garson teamed for the second time with Walter Pidgeon, as Mr and **Mrs Miniver**, after which she became a blazing star and won an Oscar. The film, however, is far more important for other reasons: it won many more Oscars, was hugely popular and for many was the quintessential war movie. In the House of Commons, Winston Churchill expressed the view that it had done

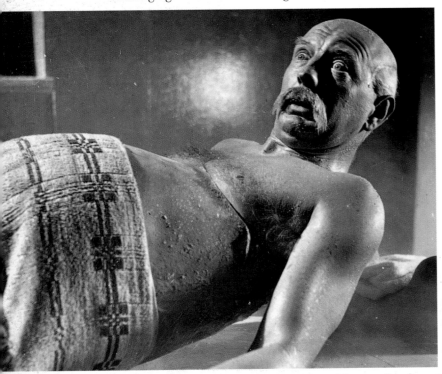

Above: Greer Garson (centre right) with supporting players in **Mrs Miniver**, in the dug-out. Right: Roger Livesey as Colonel Blimp, in Powell and Pressburger's film about a particular Englishman and a particular German — **The Life and Death of Colonel Blimp**. Opposite: **The Young Mr Pitt** was actually made by Gainsborough for 20th Century-Fox, who were glad to have it even if it was blatant propaganda. Firstly, it helped to fulfil their quota requirements in Britain, and secondly, it was one of the rare films of Donat, who was very popular in the US despite having made only one film in Hollywood almost ten years earlier.

20th CENTURY-FOX *Presents*

ROBERT Donat
IN

THE YOUNG Mr. PITT

WITH

ROBERT MORLEY
AND
PHYLLIS CALVERT & JOHN MILLS

DIRECTED BY
CAROL REED

PRODUCED BY
EDWARD BLACK

more for Britain than a flotilla of destroyers. It entirely betrayed Jan Struther's accounts of life in wartime Britain, and its distinguished director, William Wyler, admitted after arriving in Britain with the Army that he would have made it very differently had he seen Britain at war. It is a silly, phoney film, much less accurate than **Confirm or Deny**, which passed unnoticed; but it was the first film to feature people in air-raid shelters, i.e. in imminent fear of death, and to portray something which affected virtually every family in the US and Britain, the grief of separation. The portrait of wartime Britain in Fox's **This Above All**, directed by Anatole Litvak, is equally disastrous, and Joan Fontaine is not an actress who can get away with lines like, 'Look, they're bombing Dover – or is it Canterbury?' but it does have a slightly more genuine story, as she, an upper-class WAAF officer, falls in love with a working-class bloke, Tyrone Power, who deserted after Dunkirk.

June   A musical, **Yankee Doodle Dandy**, also benefited from the public mood, for as GIs prepared to ship out it celebrated the composer whose song had meant so much on the last occasion, 'Over There'. He was George M. Cohan, and he was played exuberantly by the great Cagney. Cohan had been a famous jingoist and the film, directed by Michael Curtiz, caught the imagination of the country in its flag-waving mood. There was nothing of the War in another musical, **Holiday Inn**, built around the romantic rivalry of Crosby and Astaire, each handling Irving Berlin tunes old and new. One of the new ones, 'White Christmas', would in any case have become the standard it is; but its lyric held a special meaning to those parted from their loved ones.

July   No war, either, in **The Magnificent Ambersons**. Based on a novel by Booth Tarkington, it was produced, written and directed by Orson Welles, and is as good a summation of the American past as exists. It centres on one particular wealthy family in the early years of the century, and it does so with intensity, compassion and imagination. RKO loathed it, and in Welles's absence cut fifty-three minutes, including a panoramic documentary which would have started the action in 1873. As it is, it is an extraordinary achievement, and one which cannot be left without a salute to Agnes Moorehead for her playing of Aunt Fanny.

August   Bette Davis changed from frumpish spinster to *soignée* woman of the world in **Now, Voyager**, asking Paul Henreid, 'Oh Jerry, why ask for the moon when we can have the stars?' – a reference to the fact that

he is married to a.n. other. With Claude Rains as Davis's psychiatrist and Gladys Cooper as her cruel mother, it is perhaps the most beloved sob-story of all. Audiences still applaud when daughter turns on mother. A popular success was **Orchestra Wives**, with Glenn Miller and songs like 'Serenade in Blue'. Clark Gable was making **Somewhere I'll Find You** when his wife, Carole Lombard, was killed in an air crash while selling war bonds; it was also his last film before joining the Army. Given the significance of that to audiences, it should have been better than it is. It starts well, with him as a journalist reporting from Europe and then tussling with Lana Turner; but when they both turn up in the Pacific war zone it becomes banal. **Wake Island**, the first film about US participation in the War, was put together so quickly that Robert Preston, Brian Donlevy, William Bendix and others could only re-enact the clichés of the war films of the 1920s.

October   Escapism with a moustached Tyrone Power swashing a buckle aboard **The Black Swan**. Directed by Henry King, from Sabatini, it was the first time since 1926 that audiences had seen skull and crossbones in colour. Crosby, Hope and Lamour were blithely on the **Road to Morocco**; Astaire and Hayworth danced to Jerome Kern's songs, including 'Dearly Beloved', in **You Were Never Lovelier**; and Claudette Colbert was undecided as to whether to leave husband Joel McCrea for millionaire Rudy Vallee in **The Palm Beach Story**. Mary Astor plays Vallee's sister and this comic masterpiece was written and directed by Preston Sturges.

Opposite above: As an actor, Orson Welles was magnificent on half-a-dozen occasions and unbelievably hammy on many others. He was equally variable as a director, but most regard **The Magnificent Ambersons** as a masterpiece. It is claimed that this was the first American film ever to show a ceiling – here is one, with Tim Hold under it and Dolores Costello watching him. Above: Bogart and Bergman in pre-war Paris, pre-**Casablanca**. Right: Carole Lombard, Jack Benny and Charles Halton in Lubitsch's **To Be or Not to Be**, exploring the premise that actors will always be actors – even when helping the Resistance in Warsaw.

November   A miracle: **Casablanca**. Sam plays 'As Time Goes By' as Ilsa walks into Rick's Café. They last met in prewar Paris. It had the perfect cast, including Claude Rains, Sidney Greenstreet, Conrad Veidt, Peter Lorre, Dooley Wilson as Sam and Paul Henreid as Ilsa's husband. Directed atmospherically by Curtiz and with more quotable lines than any other film, it is still moving, as when the 'Marseillaise' is sung as a gesture against the Germans. Perhaps because of the opposing qualities of Bogart and Bergman, disillusionment and devotion, it is also the most romantic movie ever made. It went on to win three of the most important Oscars (best picture, screenplay, direction) and then was completely forgotten for the next twenty years. Even at the time it was neither as popular nor as admired as **Random Harvest**, and that's not bad either, as shell-shocked Ronald Colman meets music-hall star Greer Garson on Armistice Day in 1918. Mervyn LeRoy directed, and its main trouble is the relentless MGM decor.

December   Paramount's **Star-Spangled Rhythm** was the first and least painful of the several movies showing the studios' stars entertaining servicemen. **Arabian Nights** was the first and least dreadful of Universal's Technicolor jungle epics, with Jon Hall and Maria Montez. The **Keeper of the Flame** was Katharine Hepburn, under Cukor's direction, and it was Spencer Tracy trying to expose her dead husband as a fascist. Thought important then, it seems now little better than **Reunion in France**, in which Joan Crawford is bored of the War in sixty different outfits until she sets eyes on a downed English flyer, John Wayne.

It is hard to tell who started the Resistance thrillers, each one worse than the last. The worst sort of all were those in which a dapper British cast went about trying to be French, as in **Tomorrow We Live**. At least in

Hollywood they had a lot of European ethnic types, even if they didn't cast them well.

As a variation on the theme, **Went the Day Well?** did very nicely, as a group of Germans speaking perfect English gather in a village to prepare the way for the invasion. Graham Greene had a hand in the story, Cavalcanti directed and its chief merit is in showing how badly some of the Britishers behave under stress. **Salute John Citizen** is not a good movie, but it was the first to show the War on the home front, with the black-out and air-raids.

The only three notable British contributions to the War effort starred four gentlemen well known in the US: Robert Donat was **The Young Mr Pitt**, facing up to the might of Napoleon (Herbert Lom) under Carol Reed's direction; Leslie Howard directed himself and played R. J. Mitchell, who invented the Spitfire, in **The First of the Few**, with David Niven; and Noël Coward was a captain in his tribute to the British Navy, **In Which We Serve**. He wrote and produced it, and co-directed with David Lean. It has some snobbery, much flag-waving, and

ratings, at least, loathed its portrait of life at sea. But where it matters, on the way the British behaved and felt from the summer of 1939 onwards, it is clear-headed. And there are some splendid performances, especially among the womenfolk – Celia Johnson, Kay Walsh, Kathleen Harrison and Joyce Carey. And a word for **The Great Mr Handel**, financed by Mr Rank, in Technicolor, with Wilfrid Lawson, because it was the first serious English-language film about a composer.

In France, two good thrillers: Clouzot's **L'Assassin Habité au 21**, about murder (or, rather, several) in a boarding house; and Henri Decoin's **Les Inconnus dans la Maison**, with Raimu as a drunken recluse trying to prove that his daughter was not responsible for the body in one of the upper rooms. And two full-blooded fantasies, which were much more subversive than the German authorities realized: Roland Tual's **Le Lit à Colonnes**, written by Charles Spaak, about a mean-spirited, adulterous prison governor (Fernand Ledoux), who passes off the musical compositions of one of the convicts as his own; and Jean Delannoy's **L'Eternel Retour**, Cocteau's updat-

ing of the story of Tristan and Isolde, with Jean Marais and Madeleine Sologne, which had a success abroad after the War out of all proportion to its merits. The same may be said of the other two films which made up the trio of allegories which the French themselves adored at this time: the Carné-Prévert **Les Visiteurs du Soir** and L'Herbier's **La Nuit Fantastique**.

In Italy, three splendid historicals: Renato Castellani's **Un Colpo di Pistola**, after Pushkin, about the tragedy which ensues after a girl flirts with a brother officer of her fiancé; Soldati's **Malombra**, from a novel by Fogazzaro, about the consequence arising when Isa Miranda decides that she is the reincarnation of someone who died in the chateau long ago and must therefore re-enact the tragedy; and, better still, Luigi Chiarini's **Via Delle Cinque Lune**, a vivid portrait of nineteenth-century Rome, about a pawnshop owner who loathes her daughter's beloved (Andrea Checchi) until he decides to seduce her – the sort of story unlikely to be sanctioned in either Britain or Hollywood.

Despite the decor, Chiarini was one of the leading believers of naturalism in films, or neorealism, as it came to be called. Zavattini was the leading exponent of this and

Opposite: The very first on-screen encounter of one of the screen's great teams: Spencer Tracy and Katharine Hepburn, watched by Reginald Owen, in **Woman of the Year**. Above: Judy Garland and Gene Kelly in **For Me and My Gal**, playing a vaudeville couple about to be caught up in World War I – common plot device at Fox, but MGM made it all seem fresh. Right: When the US entered the War, Americans felt closer to Britain, and in 1942 the New York critics voted a British film the best of the year for the first time (if we reckon that **The Citadel** was Hollywood-backed): Noël Coward's **In Which We Serve**, with Coward, at right.

had advocated a movie in which a camera simply followed an ordinary guy as he got up, breakfasted and went to work. He put these situations into a screenplay for Alessandro Blasetti to direct, **Quattro Passi fra la Nuvole**. They then added a trifling incident which will transform his life, temporarily, and after seeing a girl crying on a bus he finds himself going home with her, pretending to be her husband and the father of the baby she is carrying. Similarly, **Fari Nella Nebbia** is a simple story about a trucker and his wife who split up and become sexually involved with others. Giannia Franciolini directed, not well, but his portrait of life at this level had not been done so astutely for more than a decade. The aristocratic Luchino Visconti seized the ball and ran with it. His first film, **Ossessione**, is set in a drab little roadside café on the river Po, with a bored, tired wife (Clara Calamai) throwing herself at a vagrant (Massimo Girotti) after a mere glance has passed between them. The steamy scenes of passion were entirely new to movies, as was the suggestion that the man has a similar liaison with someone of his own sex during the time that he is apart from her. Since the film was based on *The Postman Always Rings Twice*, and MGM owned the rights when the War ended, it was not much seen abroad till the late 1950s. It was influential in Italy, as was the Blasetti–Zavattini film, **Quattro Passi fra la Nuvole** which, as **Four Steps in the Clouds**, enjoyed a great success in foreign art houses after the War. The two films had started a movement which would ineradicably change the face of world cinema.

1943

The year began with the Allied view that it could hardly be worse than 1942. Under their brilliant commander, Rommel, the Germans had recaptured Tobruk, and the British army was deadlocked with them in Egypt until the Battle of El Alamein, after which the Germans retreated. The U-boat presence in the Atlantic was so strong that supplies to Europe and, more importantly, to the Soviet Union were under constant threat. There was stalemate on the Russian front; after capturing several important cities the Germans were laying siege to Stalingrad. So, apart from El Alamein the only cheering news was that the American army was strong enough to invade Africa. The action moved to Morocco, Algeria and Libya, where the Allies were at last victorious. The Germans countered by violating their agreement with the Vichy government by marching into unoccupied France, and the French crews at Toulon scuttled the fleet, rather than have its ships fall into German hands. There had been a chilling moment back in July when the Germans had taken a reprisal for the assassination of Gauleiter Heydrich in Czechoslovakia by eliminating the village of Lidice.

1943 was only a month old when the German army surrendered at Stalingrad, and it was defeated in Africa in May, with prisoners estimated at over 50,000. Italy was invaded in July and Mussolini was forced into resignation, but when the new Italian government accepted the Allied terms of surrender, Hitler sent forces into Italy to seize every important city in the north of the country, including Rome. The Allies retaliated by making a second landing in Salerno, but although Naples was taken in October they had difficulty in moving further up the boot.

The year's movies:

January **They Got Me Covered** had Bob Hope and Dorothy Lamour involved with spies in Washington, most amusingly. Hitchcock had no truck with spies or anything else to do with the War in **Shadow of a Doubt**, which required Joseph Cotten to visit his sister's family in a small town in California. The title referred to the growing suspicion by his niece that he was a mass murderer, which spectators already knew, thus offering them (or not) 108 minutes of high suspense. By far the month's most popular film was an RKO B-movie, **Hitler's Children**, directed by Edward Dmytryk, about two Americans (Kent Smith, Bonita Granville) bewildered by the rise of the Nazi youth movement in pre-war Germany. Actually, it was no better than any other B-movie.

February At MGM Vincente Minnelli directed his first film, daringly choosing **Cabin in the Sky**, an all-black whimsy which had had a moderate success on Broadway. It had some great songs and some great performers: Ethel Waters, Eddie 'Rochester' Anderson as a couple whose marriage is threatened when vamp Lena Horne happens along, plus Louis Armstrong. Theatre managers in the South wouldn't book it. **The Outlaw** featured three legendary characters of the Old West, Billy the Kid (Jack Beutel), Pat Garrett (Thomas Mitchell) and Doc Holliday (Walter Huston), plus a new girl, Jane Russell, whom Howard Hughes (producing and directing) thought would become a legend in her own right. She posed on straw, sucking a stick of it as if enjoying fellatio,

Left: Eric Portman, Anne Crawford and Patricia Roc in **Millions Like Us**, Launder and Gilliat's enjoyable study of the women drafted into munitions factories. Above: Charles Laughton in Jean Renoir's Resistance drama, **This Land is Mine**, suddenly finding heroism by refusing the clemency of the Nazis and using the liberty of the court to denounce them. Opposite: **The Outlaw**, which made stars out of Jane Russell and Jack Beutel, was started in 1941. Howard Hughes took over from the original director, Howard Hawks, and tinkered with it for so long that it was not shown till 1943. It immediately ran into censorship difficulties.

and exposing the best of her body, which threatened to burst over the neckline of her tight dress. Hughes wanted to challenge censorship, in the belief that men on service installations would want to watch a sexually charged woman; he also wanted to make a fast buck. But he was no match for the censors, who began a battle which didn't finish till 1950, when the film was nationally released. It is not a good film, but the lady's two virtues are as persuasive as the censors feared and provided jokes for comedians for three generations – the film's most notable contribution to our culture.

March There were no fewer than four above-average films about Europe under German Occupation, as if Hollywood was ashamed, as it needed to be, about those it had already perpetrated. Fritz Lang's **Hangmen Also Die** is set in Prague after the death of Heydrich, and concerns the rounding-up of hostages and a quisling (Gene Lockhart) who has infiltrated a Resistance group. Renoir's **This Land Is Mine** is set in what is probably France, and shows the inhabitants of one town cooperating with the Germans or, in the case of one cowardly man, a teacher (Charles Laughton) finally speaking out against tyranny. Neither is as good as the other two, made by more journeymen directors. Both are set in Norway, Lewis Milestone's **Edge of Darkness** and Irving Pichel's **The Moon is Down**, from John Steinbeck's play. Both follow the theme of Renoir's film, the interplay of Germans, quislings and Resistance workers, the former with Errol Flynn, Ann Sheridan and Walter Huston, the latter with Cedric Hardwicke as a German commander hoping to win the respect of the locals. 'I guess you never really know your country till it's in trouble' might be a line from any of these films, but it is, in fact, from Clarence Brown's **The Human Comedy**, which looks at a small American town coping with wartime separations, news of death in battle, and so on. William Saroyan wrote the screenplay, which is maudlin and moving in turn.

April **Mission to Moscow** caused a stir, partly because Warners intended it should. Today it is dull and its distortions, including a kindly Stalin, even more glaring. Its source was the autobiographical book by Joseph E. Davies, American Ambassador to the Soviet Union from 1936 to the War, and he is played by Mr Huston. The rambling narrative covers a prescient Winston Churchill, played by Dudley Field Malone, and the Moscow Trials – a euphemism for what were already known as the Stalin purges. Two experts on these wrote to *The New York Times*, 'The film is, to resume, anti-British, anti-Congress, anti-democratic and anti-truth.' It was made at the behest of the War Office of Information, but the controversy it kicked up made Hollywood unwilling to cooperate on any further ventures.

May Fox released an all-black backstage musical, **Stormy Weather**, with Lena Horne and several speciality acts, including Fats Waller and the Nicholas Brothers, whose dance has audiences applauding fifty years on. There was also much applause in Borzage's **Stage Door Canteen**, as the stars (a mixed bag, for this was a UA film,

and most of them were freelance), playing themselves, entertained, danced with the boys or merely washed-up. Graciously. More tributes to the brave came in **Action in the North Atlantic**, with Humphrey Bogart and Raymond Massey in the Merchant Navy, and in **Bataan**, with Robert Taylor and others fighting against hopeless odds in the peninsula in the Philippines. Both films try to be responsible and serious, but you'd prefer Billy Wilder's remake of **Hotel Imperial**, which now has Rommel (Erich Von Stroheim) among its guests and has been retitled **Five Graves to Cairo** in deference to its new setting. Spies of varying nationalities, much suspense and as much fun.

July   Irving Berlin's **This is the Army** was originally a stage revue, but now becomes a film about soldiers putting on revues in both World Wars, with two future politicos, George Murphy and Ronald Reagan, playing father and son. Curtiz directed for Warners and Berlin wrote a new song, 'My British Buddy', and sang it in a postscript to the version shown in the UK. It had Technicolor and enormous popularity, qualities it shared with **For Whom the Bell Tolls**, directed by Sam Wood from the novel by Ernest Hemingway. This was expected to do for the Spanish Civil War what **Gone With the Wind** had done for the American, but it was flawed in many ways, not least by garish colour and some unlikely Spanish peasants, including Ingrid Bergman with a boy's bob which was much imitated. Gary Cooper is the American on the Loyalist side in love with her, and sometimes they get the earth moving.

August   There were some memorable moments: Claude Rains sawing away at the chandelier as **The Phantom of the Opera**, remade in Technicolor with Nelson Eddy and Susannah Foster; Bette Davis croaking her way through 'They're Either Too Young or Too Old' in Warners' all-star **Thank Your Lucky Stars**; and Roddy McDowall saying **Lassie Come Home** to a collie, said to be based on a book by Eric Knight but rather resembling a canine version of **The Perils of Pauline** (1912). Fred M. Wilcox directed for MGM, which had a huge hit on its hands, providing for several sequels.

September   Zoltan Korda's **Sahara** for Columbia had Humphrey Bogart and some other Yanks attached to the British Army. This was more responsible than most pictures about the current conflict, but unequivocally the best film made about the War during the War is **Corvette K 255**, which doesn't wave flags or indulge in heroics but

tells plainly of one voyage across the North Atlantic of a Canadian escort ship in convoy. Randolph Scott is the captain, Richard Rosson directed for Universal, and the producer was Howard Hawks, whose own **Air Force** had all the service stereotypes which this film sensibly eschews.

December   Deanna Durbin sang a Russian medley in the otherwise escapist **His Butler's Sister**, and MGM hymned the glories of life on the collective farm in **Song of Russia**, as seen by Robert Taylor, an American orchestra conductor visiting the country. This film would later be examined by the House of Un-American Activities, as would **Tender Comrade**, directed by Edward Dmytryk for RKO, for some alleged Communist remarks about the delights of a shared community, spoken as a group of women, including Ginger Rogers, decide to cope with life on the home front by living in the same house.

In Britain, George Formby was in the Home Guard in **Get Cracking**, his last acceptable film, and Will Hay was **My Learned Friend**, a barrister who is the sixth intended victim of a mad man, Mervyn Jones, whom he failed to defend successfully. A prime black comedy, it was Hay's last film – significantly, for the comics no longer dominated the British box-office lists. The change was wrought by one film, **The Man in Grey**, a Regency melodrama in which Phyllis Calvert and Stewart Granger are the victims. By being beastly, Margaret Lockwood and James Mason catapulted all four of them to immense popularity. The film has a certain panache, and it led to its producers at Gainsborough instituting many imitations. Those critics who despised it took some comfort from the fact that the same studio persuaded Launder and Gilliat to make **Millions Like Us**, producing and directing as well as writing the script, which chiefly concerns women working in a munitions factory. Anne Crawford and

Opposite: British documentary directors worked overtime during the War, with the Government commissioning propaganda items and the public anxious to know what was going on. These two strands were linked by a film-maker of genius, Humphrey Jennings. **Fires Were Started** was his only feature-length film. Above: Anne Baxter and Erich Von Stroheim in Billy Wilder's clever thriller, **Five Graves to Cairo**.

Patricia Roc play two of them; their men are, respectively, Eric Portman as the foreman and Gordon Jackson as one of Our Boys in Blue. The superb, long prologue, dealing with the British as they coped with rationing, air-raids, etc, was influenced by the work of Humphrey Jennings.

Jennings himself made his only feature, **Fires Were Started**, a salute to the auxiliary fire services which magnificently blended newsreel footage of dockland blazes with improvised (by amateurs) sequences of life in the fire station. About to be summoned, they sing 'Please Don't Talk About Me When I'm Gone', which by sheer understatement is one of the most moving scenes in cinema history. Jennings also re-created the tragedy of Lidice by setting it in Wales, **The Silent Village**. Hollywood had tried to come to terms with this, not only in **Hangmen Also Die** but also in **Hitler's Madman**, *nolo contendere*.

The other British war films were small beer compared to these, but they were honourable efforts. Leslie Howard was responsible for two tributes to women at war: **The Gentle Sex**, about the A.T.S. women recruits in the army, with Lili Palmer, Joan Greenwood and Rosamund John; and **The Lamp Still Burns**, with Miss John as the most dedicated of nurses. Howard directed the former and produced the latter, having in the meantime been killed when his plane out of Lisbon was shot down by German forces (he had been lecturing in neutral countries on behalf of the Allies).

Opposite: Jennifer Jones in **The Song of Bernadette**, directed by Henry King from Franz Werfel's bestselling novel. Above: Tim Holt (left, in uniform) and Bonita Granville in **Hitler's Children**, the first of several American films that tried to examine the roots of Nazism. It featured in the list of the year's most successful movies in the *Motion Picture Herald*. Right: Barry Fitzgerald, Thomas Gomez and Robert Mitchum in **Corvette K255**, a story of the Battle of the North Atlantic. Since the cast was supposed to be Canadian – and in line with wartime sentiment – it was retitled **The Nelson Touch** in the British Empire.

The German Occupation of France continued to influence the subject-matter of films produced, but did not diminish their quality: an acrid blend of humour, despair and mystery. Recognizing the exceptional talents of the French film industry, Goebbels had ordered a company to be started up, Continental. Some film-makers and actors preferred to retire when commanded to work for it; others decided to challenge it by making films with a subversive subtext. The most notable of these was **Le Corbeau**, written and directed by Henri-Georges Clouzot, in which a mild-mannered young doctor (Pierre Fresnay) receives some poison-pen letters, accusing him of being a lecher and an abortionist. The former he cannot deny, since he neglects the pure young thing who loves him and lusts after the cheap tramp (Viviane Romance) in the same boarding-house, who is also a cripple.

The Russians, for once, were glad to escape from grim reality. Their most talented film-makers were sent as far from the battlefields as possible, and in Tashkent Iakov Protazanov made his last film, an enchanting Arabian Nights-type adventure, **Nasreddin in Bukahra**. Lev Sverdlin plays, wonderfully, Nasreddin, a rogue who returns to his native city to outwit the evil Emir and rescue the girl the Emir has added to his harem. (Richard Williams' version of the same story, **The Thief and the Cobbler** was finally shown in 1993; he had been working on the project for twenty-five years.)

1944

The Allied advance up the boot of Italy was stopped by the strategic position of the Monastery of Monte Cassino, which the Germans held. It was eventually decided to bomb it, and rebuild. On 4 June Rome was liberated, and two days later Normandy was invaded by Allied forces. Two weeks after that Germany began to bombard Britain with pilotless planes, the V-1s. Intelligence knew that the Channel coast also was lined with launching-pads for rockets, the V-2s, so it became vital for the invading forces to reach them and put them out of action. On 20 July a group of German officers tried and failed to assassinate Hitler. On 15 August Allied forces landed on the Côte d'Azur; Paris was liberated on 25 August, a day after its citizens had rebelled against the German occupiers. Russian troops moved towards Berlin as, in the West, Patton's tanks moved into Germany. The V-2s began to fall in Britain on 28 December, but everyone knew it was the last Christmas of the War.

January **None Shall Escape** examined the career of one Nazi, Alexander Knox, from World War I till his trial *after* the present conflict; but it was worthy rather than convincing.

February Fox released two stories based on fact: **The Purple Heart**, directed by Lewis Milestone, about the trial in Tokyo of an American crew accused of strafing non-military targets; and **The Sullivans**, about five brothers who drowned when their boat was sunk at Guadalcanal. Both deal in clichés but the ending of the second is extraordinarily moving. From Fox, the defini-

tive **Jane Eyre**, if only for the early scenes with Jane (Peggy Ann Garner), Mr Brocklehurst (Henry Daniell) and Aunt Reed (Agnes Moorehead). Robert Stevenson directed, with Joan Fontaine as the adult Jane and Orson Welles as a Mr Rochester who glowers and frowns by turns. Paramount had two big ones: Leo McCarey's **Going My Way**, with Bing Crosby as a singing Catholic priest (among the songs he sang was 'Swinging on a Star'); and Mitchell Leisen's opulent Technicolored **Lady in the Dark**, with Ginger Rogers as a fashion editor with psychiatric problems. Neither stands up today, but the second, from the Moss Hart-Kurt Weill-Ira Gershwin stage musical, wasn't too hot back then.

March A peachy musical: **Cover Girl**, with Rita Hayworth heavenly in Technicolor, Gene Kelly and a Kern-Gershwin score which included 'Long Ago and Far Away', a song for lovers and families still separated by the War.

April Eddie Cantor, Joan Davis, George Murphy and Constance Moore experienced all the perils and joys of **Show Business**; and in **Two Girls and a Sailor**, a sister-act, June Allyson and Gloria de Haven, asked 'Doing anything tonight, soldier?', which has more serious implications in our less innocent age. Van Johnson plays the sailor of the title, the not-quite-so-shy sailor whom many a maid or man would have liked to take home to bed. Otherwise, the War: **Days of Glory**, with Gregory Peck (destined to be the big postwar glamour-pants; in his first film), as a Russian guerrilla; and **The Hitler Gang**, which follows Adolf's career from 1918 to the War with insufficient truth or ruthlessness. The same matters were

Left: Howard Hawks's **To Have and Have Not** was a **Casablanca** replay, in which a jaded Humphrey Bogart was again a neutral between the Free French and Vichy, in Martinique. He met his match in a sultry youngster, Lauren Bacall. With them is Walter Brennan. Above: Fred MacMurray and Barbara Stanwyck in **Double Indemnity**. Years later, Bette Davis commented that Stanwyck's ankle-bracelet was more erotic than all the naked couples of later films. Opposite: Laurence Olivier's **Henry v** paralleled current events in Europe and also proved that Shakespeare could be filmed triumphantly.

considered to an extent in **Address Unknown**, with Paul Lucas as a San Francisco art dealer who returns to his native Germany under Nazi rule.

May Esther Williams is the **Bathing Beauty**, swimming her way into the public's affection in glorious Technicolor, with Red Skelton plus Ethel Smith pounding out 'Tico Tico' on the electric organ.

June Preston Sturges produced two movies in one month, but that's because Paramount hated **The Great Moment** and cut and shelved it. Sturges upped and left. True, it is an odd mixture of slapstick and biography, with Joel McCrea and Betty Field acting out incidents in the life of W. T .G. Morton, the dentist who claimed to have discovered the anaesthetic powers of ether. But it also has the Sturges stock company, including Grady Sutton, Franklin Pangborn and William Demarest. The last had his biggest screen role in what may be Sturges's best film, **Hail the Conquering Hero**. He also had the key role, that of the sergeant who talks sad sap Eddie Bracken into pretending he is a much-decorated soldier when he returns home. The film is as cynical on military matters as it is on small town politics.

July More topical matters were covered in **Since You Went Away**, Selznick's first film since **Gone With the Wind**. He wrote it himself, but had the good sense to get John Cromwell to direct. For almost three hours Claudette Colbert and daughters Jennifer Jones and Shirley Temple showed how the women at home were coping; assisting them in a film remote from any real world were Joseph Cotten, Robert Walker and selfish (she doesn't care about the War) Agnes Moorehead. The

Seventh Cross, set in prewar Germany, has Spencer Tracy as an escapee from a concentration camp, seeking out friends who could help him flee the country. Fred Zinnemann, hitherto a minor director, signals that he has wisdom, compassion and is a master of his craft.

August Billy Wilder's third film as director is a classic, **Double Indemnity**. He wrote the screenplay with Raymond Chandler from a novel by James M. Cain, for a movie which defines the term 'film noir' for all those that followed. Rightly cheap are Fred MacMurray and Barbara Stanwyck, as the insurance agent who becomes her lover and conspires with her to murder her husband; Edward G. Robinson is MacMurray's boss, eventually realizing that the crime was committed under his nose. And there was **Wilson**, which Zanuck considered the most important movie in Fox's history, a study of the man who was president when the US entered World War I and who ended the country's isolationist policies in supporting the founding of the League of Nations. Technicolor, an above-average script, and direction by Henry King; but Alexander Knox as Wilson and the distinguished others are little more than waxworks.

September. Bob Hope was at Goldwyn for a hilarious spoof of swashbucklers, **The Princess and the Pirate**, in colour. And there were two thrillers directed by Fritz Lang: **The Woman in the Window**, with Edward G. Robinson as a mild-mannered professor becoming obsessed with Joan Bennett, who is double-crossing him with flashy blackmailer, Dan Duryea; and **The Ministry of Fear**, with Ray Milland always just a step away from the clutches of a Nazi spy ring. All the situations of Graham Greene's novel are intact, even if the portrait of London in the Blitz is slightly absurd. It was a good month for the genre: **Laura**, directed by Otto Preminger from Vera Caspary's novel, had a haunting theme tune, Gene Tierney as the girl who disappears, Dana Andrews and Vincent Price among the many obsessed with her, and Clifton Webb as an effeminate and acerbic critic, a character new to movies (at least in a leading role).

November MGM tremulously offered **Meet Me in St Louis**, not quite sure how audiences would like a turn of the century musical with much charm and virtually no plot. Will Judy Garland attract the boy next door, Tom Drake? And will the Smith family (Mary Astor, Leon Ames, Margaret O'Brien) have to move to New York? Vincente Minnelli understood this genre as no one before; Technicolor and the 'The Trolley Song' were plusses.

Above left: Judy Garland pining for the boy next door in **Meet Me in St Louis**, one of the most successful films in MGM's history. Opposite: In an era now long gone, Fox had filmed Noël Coward's **Cavalcade**, about life upstairs and downstairs in one English aristocratic household. In 1942, Coward returned to the theme, and David Lean directed the film version two years later: **This Happy Breed**, with Celia Johnson.

December Bette Davis may have been instrumental in setting up the **Hollywood Canteen**, but she didn't have to appear in this duff film about it, best remembered as the one in which a GI almost swoons because he's dancing with Joan Crawford. From Disney came **The Three Caballeros**, a hodge-podge of short cartoons, a mixture of animation and live action all designed to further America's 'good neighbor' policy.

In Britain, David Lean's second film was **This Happy Breed**, again based on Noël Coward material. A Technicolor chronicle of the life of one suburban London family during the 1920s and 1930s, it starred Celia Johnson and Robert Newton as the parents. Further study of the English way of life and why they were fighting was done well in Powell and Pressburger's **A Canterbury Tale**; but even better in **Tawny Pipit**, directed by Charles Saunders and Bernard Miles. In the second, Rosamund John and soldier Niall MacGinniss lead a campaign to prevent tanks disturbing a field in which nest some rare birds. In the first, there is an echo of Chaucer as a landgirl (Sheila Sim) and two soldiers, American (John Sweet) and British (Dennis Price), have each a reason to visit the cathedral city, but first, be warned, a magistrate (Eric Portman) creeps around in the blackout smearing girls' hair with glue. Carol Reed directed **The Way Ahead**, about some army recruits from induction to their first experience of battle, and the most honest portrait of service life till then – and for many years to come; with David Niven as their captain.

Britain's biggest propaganda effort saw Laurence Olivier producing, directing and starring in **Henry V**, based on Shakespeare's play about the English king who defeated the arrogant French at the Battle of Agincourt, here thrillingly re-created in Technicolor. With one bound it established Olivier as the country's foremost actor; it proved after many misses that Shakespeare was movie material; and, fondly nicknamed 'Hank Cinque', it was a big prestige hit the world over.

O n 12 January the Red Army took Warsaw and four days later it entered Germany. Allied forces crossed the Rhine on 7 March. By 11 April the United States Ninth Army reached the Elbe, where it greeted the Russians. German resistance in Italy collapsed on 28 April and partisans shot Mussolini as he tried to escape to Switzerland. With the Russians and Americans in Berlin, Hitler committed suicide and Germany surrendered unconditionally on 7 May. Roosevelt had died and had been succeeded as president by Harry S. Truman. In Britain, Churchill was replaced by Clement Attlee when the British voted Labour in with a landslide victory.

1945

The Japanese continued to fight on, and on 6 August the first atomic bomb was dropped on Hiroshima, destroying the entire city. But it was not until another was dropped on Nagasaki that Japan surrendered unconditionally, on 14 August.

For many, however, the most horrifying experience of the War came after the Fall of Berlin, when the newsreel pictures of the concentration camps were released.

It was another good year for movies. At least there would be no more Resistance dramas.

January **A Song to Remember**, from Columbia in colour, had Merle Oberon as George Sand and Cornel Wilde as Chopin. It was, quite rightly, much ridiculed, but it was a milestone in breaking down public resistance to classical music. Raoul Walsh's **Objective Burma** was execrated when it opened in Britain because, it was said, Errol Flynn liberated Burma without the help of the British. The film, however, made it clear that Flynn was leading one particular American patrol and it was, in fact, one of the better pictures about men in battle.

March From MGM came Minnelli's **The Clock**, in which a GI meets and marries a girl in New York while on a 24-hour furlough. He is Robert Walker; she is Judy Garland (who doesn't sing a note), and as this is the sweetest and most truthful of wartime romances, it hasn't dated a jot.

April One of the great exchanges of movie history. Esther Williams: 'I've enjoyed your singing.' Lauritz Melchior: 'I've enjoyed your swimming.' All this and Van Johnson too, in **Thrill of a Romance**. Van's a soldier, her marriage hasn't been consummated and Lauritz gives out with you-know-what from 'Pagliacci'. They're at a resort in the Sierra Nevada, and it's difficult to see why this Technicolor extravaganza was so popular.

May RKO did well with **The Brighton Strangler**, which has a convincing portrait of wartime London. The story is the old one about an actor who, playing a killer, finds a compulsion to do the same in real life. He's John Loder and June Duprez is the WAAF officer who is alone with him on a clock tower in the climax.

June With the war in Europe over there arrives the best film about it, William A. Wellman's **The Story of GI Joe**, based on the articles by war correspondent Ernie Pyle, who had not long been killed by a machine gun and who is played here by Burgess Meredith, following the campaign from North Africa into Italy. The film conveys the grind, the sheer tedium of war and helping verisimilitude is a cast little known except for Robert Mitchum as

Left: That the British could produce an outstanding film was proved by David Lean with **Brief Encounter**, starring Celia Johnson and Trevor Howard. Note her hat: a cap had been specially designed for Princess Elizabeth while serving with the ATS, and milliners all over Britain had copied it. Above: It wasn't till 1945 that anyone achieved a serious film study of the demon drink's consequences – Billy Wilder with **The Lost Weekend**, which starred Ray Milland and Jane Wyman. Opposite: Robert Walker and Judy Garland in **The Clock**, meeting and marrying because it's wartime, without really knowing each other.

the officer in charge. Also responsible, likeable and set in Italy is **A Bell for Adano**, directed by Henry King from John Hersey's novel about Americans trying to re-create democracy as they rehabilitate the country. A somewhat preachy tone is dimmed by beautiful performances by John Hodiak as the captain and William Bendix as his sergeant.

August   **The Lost Weekend** may be one of the best translations made from book to screen, even if the cause in Charles Jackson's novel is homosexuality rather than writer's block. In both cases the man is a dipsomaniac. Ray Milland plays him, with Jane Wyman as his fiancée and Howard da Silva, memorably, a barman. Directed by Billy Wilder, the movie stands above any other serious film of this period.

September   Fox exposed **The House on 92nd Street** in Washington, used by a German spy ring. The film claimed to be based on a true story, and had originated as a low-budget documentary for producer Louis de Rochement, one of the founders of the series *The March of Time*. The director Henry Hathaway liked the idea and decided to make the film on location when Zanuck refused to increase the budget; the final result was

given a commentary in the manner of *The March of Time* and was so much admired that Fox made several more in similar fashion.

October   **Mildred Pierce** was socially mobile, eventually running her own restaurant, but poor Joan Crawford has man trouble and a nasty daughter, Ann Blyth. 'Veta's convinced me that alligators have the right idea – they eat their young,' says Eve Arden. Michael Curtiz directed what is overall, compulsive stuff. And Ingrid Bergman was on the staff of a psychiatric home in **Spellbound**, with Gregory Peck as one of her patients. Hitchcock directed for Selznick, and nothing could keep the public away.

November   Ingrid Bergman again, as a nun for RKO in **The Bells of St Mary's**, a sequel to **Going My Way** and much to be preferred, if only because she's prettier than Barry Fitzgerald. And again, although **Saratoga Trunk** had been made two years earlier but, for reasons known only to Warners, shown only on service installations. Bergman was miscast as a mulatto vamp in nineteenth-century New Orleans; Gary Cooper follows her to Saratoga or vice-versa; Sam Wood directed. John Ford was on splendid form for MGM in **They Were**

Expendable, set in the Philippines just before the Japanese invaded in 1942. The mood is almost idyllic, and it somehow suits this tale of camaraderie among naval officers, who include John Wayne, and Robert Montgomery in a role based on the real officer who had pioneered the use of the PT boat in combat. Robert Barrat is 'The General' – clearly MacArthur.

December **A Walk in the Sun** is a fine, moving war movie directed by Louis Milestone, from Harry Brown's account of one week with his platoon in rural Italy. Dana Andrews does his best screen work as the sergeant, with Richard Conte and John Ireland among those under his command.

The British were taking longer to forget the War, but unlike the movies the Americans made, their fiction films were all set on their island. Launder and Gilliat's **Waterloo Road** had soldier John Mills going AWOL because a spiv, Stewart Granger, had been ogling his wife. From the same team, **The Rake's Progress** is only about the War inasmuch as it shows how it can make a hero out of a rotter, played by Rex Harrison. But it has some responsible themes, as when he marries a half-Jewish girl, Lili Palmer, so that she can avoid Nazi repression. **I Live in Grosvenor Square** was a plea by Herbert Wilcox for Anglo-American understanding, which is why stately Anna Neagle succumbs to the jitterbug. The plot has her trying to choose between British officer Rex Harrison and USAF sergeant Dean Jagger. **Great Day** is mild stuff, despite the presence of Flora Robson and Eric Portman, but it has a sweet idea: a village getting excited by a visit

Opposite: **The Seventh Veil**, with Ann Todd, made James Mason a name in the US. Above: Many reflected that too many of the films about the War had been at best superficial. William A. Wellman made amends for others with his moving **The Story of GI Joe**, with Robert Mitchum (left) and Burgess Meredith (centre). Right: Fox entrusted **A Tree Grows in Brooklyn** to a new director, Elia Kazan, who understood exactly the line between entertainment and an unpatronizing portrait of ordinary people; with excellent performances by Ted Donaldson, Dorothy McGuire and Peggy Ann Garner.

from Mrs Roosevelt. **The Way to the Stars**, directed by Anthony Asquith from a screenplay by Terence Rattigan, was the film the readers of the *Daily Mail* voted for when asked to name their favourite of the past few years: it looked back nostalgically to life on an RAF station (John Mills and Michael Redgrave were there), the pub they visited (Stanley Holloway, Rosamund John) and the Americans (Douglas Montgomery) who arrived to help them win the War. With the War over, Korda produced and directed (for MGM, a short-lived association) **Perfect Strangers**, which followed a fuddy-duddy couple (Robert Donat, Deborah Kerr) who joined up and, once returned from the War, transformed into rather glamorous people. The official British and American offices of information co-operated to make a valuable and moving contribution to the record of these times with **The True Glory**, an assembly of newsreel pictures by Carol Reed and Garson Kanin, taking the Allied forces from D-Day to VE-Day. A commentary, spoken by actors we recognize, by credited writers, comes across as having been collected from the people who were there.

It was James Mason's year. He drove his wife, Dulcie Gray to drink and suicide in **They Were Sisters**, while her siblings, Phyllis Calvert and Anne Crawford, had problems of their own. He was a highwayman in **The Wicked Lady**, and the lover of Margaret Lockwood. The film, however, belonged to the latter, who steals her best friend's fiancé and then gets so bored with him that she takes to the road. In **The Seventh Veil** Mason was Ann Todd's guardian, bringing his cane down on her hands while she is at the piano – but he got her at the fade-out.

These last two films were gigantic hits in Britain and the second, due to Mason, was a success in the States, thus causing Mr Rank to look in that direction. All but four of the films listed above were distributed by companies he owned (and he had a small financial interest in

Ealing). After **Henry V**, and with local audiences actually preferring British films to American for the first time, he decided to crack the American market. He had already invested in the most expensive picture yet made in Britain, **Caesar and Cleopatra**, directed by Gabriel Pascal, with Claude Rains and Vivien Leigh in the title roles. American critics liked it no more than their British counterparts, but it did what *Variety* would have called 'Okay-biz'. **Brief Encounter** was adapted by Noël Coward from one of his one-act plays. A happily married woman meets a doctor at a suburban railway station when

he takes a speck of coal dust out of her eye. Partly because of the superlative way the roles were played, by Celia Johnson and Trevor Howard, the critics raved – but the public was indifferent.

Germany saw the War out in an odd cinematic way with **Kolberg**, intended by Goebbels to be a Teutonic **Gone With the Wind** (a clandestine copy of which he had seen). The film had been initiated in 1941; filming had commenced in 1943, in Agfacolor, on a gigantic budget, with Veit Harlan directing and thousands of extras drawn from the Army. Kolberg was a small Prussian town which

had faced Napoleon's armies in 1807 before finally capitulating. As Germany crumbled, it was clear that the film's only possible ending could be that Kolberg's fate was that of the nation. It was premièred in 30 January, the anniversary of the Nazi rise to power, in La Rochelle, in a copy dropped by parachute. It opened in Berlin in March, in the only cinema to have escaped bombardment, but was immediately withdrawn because the last thing Berliners then wanted was the glorification of Prussian might. Another good reason might be that it is tedious in the extreme. At a private showing, Goebbels assured the audience that a similar film would be made about them a century hence.

France came up with a movie which would be coupled more appropriately with **Gone With the Wind**, because of its length and breadth, because it is also a deeply romantic portrait of a past age, and because the public immediately took it to its heart. There the resemblances end, for **Les Enfants du Paradis** is a work of art, and a very personal one as crafted by Carné and Prévert. Set in the world of Paris boulevard theatres of the 1820s it looks uncompromisingly at their people and at that point where they intertwine with those of the underworld and the aristocracy. If the mime actor, played by Jean-Louis Barrault, is an innocent, everyone else is almost wholly amoral, including the courtesan Garance, played unforgettably by Arletty. Their love for each other transcends her relationships with a count (Louis Salou), a pimp/thief (Marcel Herrand) and the actor Lemaître

(Pierre Brasseur).

Forty years later, French critics elected it the greatest French film ever made and although it is unique, it continues the tradition of sweetly sour movies. It was a mood not to change as the country continued to consider defeat and the extent to which many people had collaborated with the Germans.

Sweden came up with **Hets** (**Frenzy** in Britain, **Torment** in the US), the first dark melodrama exported since the heyday of Sjöström and Stiller. A schoolboy (Alf Kjellin) falls hopelessly in love with a slut (Mai Zetterling), who just happens to be the plaything of one of his teachers (Stig Jarrel), who is not known as 'Caligula' for nothing. Critics were carried away by its similarity to the German films of the 1920s, but it has bags of atmosphere which still impress today. Alf Sjöberg directed from a screenplay by Ingmar Bergman, a theatre man encouraged to continue in films as director as well as writer.

But as far as the 'cause' of world cinema was concerned, the overwhelming experience of 1945 was **Roma, Città Aperta/Open City** which, like **Les Enfants du Paradis**, had been begun under the Occupation. Its subject was a Rome in which the Germans bade farewell to their collaborators, including a party-girl and a lesbian, and fled. Filmed on location and partly improvised, it made *every* movie made until then seem old-fashioned and artificial, or so it seemed at the time. Critics in Italy were not amused, but its reputation began to swell when it was shown abroad. It made, and in spades, the reputation of its director, Roberto Rossellini, and its leading actress, Anna Magnani, who played a pregnant widow. She filled the screen without a vestige of youth or beauty – something, apparently, for which the critics had been longing for years. In the postwar climate, Magnani and Rossellini called the tune, allowing Hollywood to be attacked with a new virulence.

Opposite: James Mason with Margaret Lockwood as his female counterpart in **The Wicked Lady**. It was an absolute field day for her, stealing her best friend's fiancé, murdering a servant and robbing stage coaches in a mask on the King's highway. Above: Anna Magnani in **Open City**. Whether this is a better film than, say, **The Story of GI Joe**, is immaterial. It had an immediacy and impact which startled audiences then, and it can still do so today. Right: Joan Crawford, suffering in a chic mink outfit, as **Mildred Pierce**, with Moroni Olsen (left) and Bruce Bennett (hatless, to the right).

The Best Years of Our Lives caught the imagination of the public as no other contemporary drama since **Mrs Miniver**. They both had the same director, William Wyler, in this case working for Goldwyn, but this film is as honest as the other is not. Robert E. Sherwood, working from a story by MacKinlay Kantor, provided Wyler with a situation

1946

common to many families around the world: the returning soldier, and the moment Myrna Loy and Fredric March meet again struck a chord with all those couples who had been separated. The situation was repeated twice in this particular small town: by Dana Andrews, realizing that his hasty wartime marriage to trampy Virginia Mayo had been a mistake, and by Harold Russell (a veteran making his first film appearance), unwilling to commit himself to his fiancée because he has returned with hooks where his hands used to be. The various solutions are not without contrivances, but it remains clear why the film ran for months in cinemas when a two-week booking was considered a success. It actually opened in November. The year otherwise went like this:

March   MGM again fetched up its infinitely phoney Scotland for **The Green Years**, directed by Victor Saville from the bestselling novel by A. J. Cronin, with Dean Stockwell and Tom Drake as the orphan hero, boy and man respectively. The piece is now, quite rightly, forgotten, but its huge popularity at the time may have been due to the postwar feeling that even the humblest were entitled to the best education if they merited it. **Gilda**, Charles Vidor for Columbia, starred Rita Hayworth as the

wife of casino boss/killer George Macready, being unfaithful with his new aide, Glenn Ford. Not only did she know Ford Way Back When, but the dialogue suggests an equally intimate relationship between the two men – something no one commented upon in 1946.

June   Six months before **The Best Years of Our Lives**, **Till the End of Time** looks at the problems of the returning soldier: Bill Williams has artificial legs, Robert Mitchum has a silver plate in his head, and Dorothy McGuire hangs around bars because her husband isn't coming home. The trouble is that they're stuck in a glossy romantic drama, directed by Edward Dmytryk for RKO; but it does have a healthy comment on racism and occasional nuggets of truth, e.g. 'You didn't make yourself a soldier overnight. You cannot make yourself a civilian overnight.'

July   Cary Grant and Ingrid Bergman shared a record-breaking kiss in **Notorious**. They are both government agents working in Rio, and she marries Claude Rains in the hope of discovering whether he's a Nazi attempting a comeback. One of the classic Hitchcocks. Grant was simultaneously on view as Cole Porter in **Night and Day**, in which Monty Woolley plays himself – but as Porter's best friend, not as his lover. That wasn't the only liberty taken with the facts.

August   There was Raymond Chandler's **The Big Sleep**, but with Humphrey Bogart as Philip Marlowe and Lauren Bacall matching him, insolence against cynicism,

Left: A sticky moment in Hitchcock's **Notorious**, a film with many: Ingrid Bergman has married Claude Rains (right), whom she and Cary Grant think might become dangerous if he discovers the true reasons why. Selznick prepared the film, but at the last minute sold it to RKO for a cut of the profits. Above: Michael Hall (left), Myrna Loy (seated), Teresa Wright and Fredric March in **The Best Years of Our Lives**, a film with meaning for many families around the world. Opposite: Gloomy melodramas and thrillers that suited the post-war mood proliferated in 1946. One of the best was **The Killers**, with Burt Lancaster and Ava Gardner.

it doesn't matter if the plot isn't entirely clear. Howard Hawks directed, and the supporting cast plays the tacky Chandler-people to perfection. Ernest Hemingway's 'The Killers' is no more than a few pages long, but Universal's **The Killers**, directed by Robert Siodmak, examines at length in flashback why they had come to kill a broken-down prize-fighter (Burt Lancaster) in the first place. Thus we get to meet many devious characters, including Ava Gardner, Albert Dekker and Sam Levene.

September   The crowds roll up to experience **The Jolson Story**, in which Larry Parks mimed to the voice of you-know-who – who was launched on a new wave of popularity. It was no more accurate than **Night and Day**, and the songs weren't as good.

October   Walt Disney finds a solution to the undisputed fact that his full-length cartoons seldom show a profit. It is called **Song of the South**, a live-action picture of horrifying sentimentality with three animated sequences featuring Brer Rabbit and company. James Baskett is Uncle Remus and the very taking little boy to whom he tells his stories is Bobby Driscoll, who became the studio's first live star (and who later, as a young adult, would die forgotten and unrecognized, a drug addict). Fox did well because two old hands were at their best: John Ford with **My Darling Clementine**, which had Henry Fonda as Wyatt Earp, Victor Mature as Doc Holliday and Linda Darnell as a Mexican dancing girl; and Henry King with **Margie**, which had Jeanne Crain in the title role. Usually anodyne or sickly-sweet, this actress was winning as a high-school student in a small town in the 1920s.

December   **Duel in the Sun** has Jennifer Jones and Gregory Peck crawling over the rocks at the end, smeared in tomato ketchup. The film's nickname, 'Lust in the Dust', describes what these two miscast players get up to

in the old West, as produced by Selznick, whose passion for Miss Jones was now out of hand. This was his first and last attempt to compete with his own **Gone With the Wind**, but despite or because of a cast which included Joseph Cotten, Walter Huston, Lillian Gish and Herbert Marshall, the critics scoffed. The public, however, turned up in huge numbers. Neither cared much for Capra's first postwar movie, **It's a Wonderful Life**, in which a guardian angel appears to suicidal James Stewart to prove how different the town might have been but for his persistent do-gooding. Despite its warmth, the picture was simply too whimsical for the time, and admired far less than **13, Rue Madeleine**, the second of Henry Hathaway's documentary dramas for Fox. Despite the presence of James Cagney, as an instructor in espionage, it isn't even – with its hokey script – a half-decent movie. But with **Open City** opening around the world, this approach seemed to be the movies' way forward.

John Huston made **Let There be Light**, a documentary on the neuropsychiatric treatment of war casualties – that is, on the treatment of the shell-shocked in army hospitals. A foreword explains that nothing has been re-staged, but what was in the film was too much for the US War Department, who had commissioned it. They banned it, officially on the grounds that a public showing would constitute an invasion of privacy.

Left: Josette Day and Jean Marais in the title roles of Jean Cocteau's **La Belle et la Bête**. Above: Jennifer Jones as a half-breed girl and Gregory Peck as the lecherous Lewt in **Duel in the Sun**, directed by King Vidor. With the exceptions of **Gone With the Wind** and **The Best Years of Our Lives**, it took in more money than any other film yet made. Opposite: Judy Garland singing 'On the Atcheson, Topeka and the Santa Fe', lusciously staged in the best MGM manner, in **The Harvey Girls** – who were demure waitresses. George Sidney directed this underrated film.

The most remarkable film of the year was a documentary, Humphrey Jenning's **A Diary for Timothy**, a record of events great and small from Timothy's birth in September 1944 to the end of the War, some of which were re-staged and some of which were taken from newsreels. War-related themes appeared in a number of films, including Ealing's best serious film to date, **The Captive Heart**, which examined a group of POWs and their reaction to returning home. Basil Dearden directed a cast including Michael Redgrave, its weakest link as a Czech who assumes the identity of a British officer. This actor has a silly role in **The Years Between**, as a Member of Parliament who joins the Army. This is based on a play by Daphne du Maurier, and is no great shakes as directed by Compton Bennett; but it has a performance of such style and truth by Valerie Hobson, as the wife who takes Redgrave's place in the House, that single-handedly Hobson manages to indicate how the War changed women's conceptions of themselves. The reverse was done by Herbert Wilcox's **Piccadilly Incident**, in which a quick wartime wedding is followed by a long separation and the 'bride' returns after years on a desert island to find her husband has remarried. It gets loonier and loonier but the public adored it, pushing its stars, Anna Neagle and Michael Wilding, to the head of the box-office lists.

Rank made a more determined bid for the American market with a musical, **London Town**, with songs by the American team of Burke and Van Heusen, and direction by another American, Wesley Ruggles. The result finished his film career and set back those of its star, Sid Field, playing an ever-hopeful understudy, and Kay Kendall, his leading lady. Cut and retitled **My Heart Goes Crazy**, it played some US dates in 1953, after which it disappeared for thirty years. Rediscovered, it turned out to be even worse than its reputation allowed.

Stewart Granger had successes with two Gainsborough melodramas, **Caravan** – some nonsense set in Spain – and **The Magic Bow**, ditto about Paganini. Their sheer awfulness, however, is part of their charm. Among period dramas, **Great Expectations** established new standards or, at least, equalled those of the MGM **David Copperfield**. Deserting Coward for Dickens, David Lean (also one of the five credited screenwriters) did himself a favour in his casting: Anthony Wager and Jean Simmons as young Pip and Estella, John Mills and Valerie Hobson as them grown-up, Martita Hunt as the recluse Miss Havisham, Bernard Miles and Freda Jackson as the Joe Gargerys, Francis L. Sullivan as Jaggers and Alec Guinness (in his film début) as Herbert Pocket. The opening, when the convict Magwitch comes upon Pip in the graveyard, may be the most frightening ever filmed.

The French cinema refused to confront the real

consider astonishing in view of the location shots of a devastated Berlin. No mention of the Allied Occupiers, a heavy presence then in Berlin, suggests that Staudte thought that retribution was an entirely German matter. His message is framed inside a melodramatic story about a survivor (Hildegard Knef) of the camps who makes some strange discoveries because she has a letter to deliver.

Italy could match this, and did, with three films which emphasized the chaos which had overwhelmed the country. Aldo Vergano's **Il Sole Sorge Ancora** looks tellingly at a small provincial town between 1943 and '45, when its more volatile inhabitants were divided between collaborating with the German Occupiers and joining the partisans. The film is unjustly forgotten, perhaps because Vergano did little else of note (this should have been enough), and also because the two other great Italian films of 1946 were to confirm the reputation of their directors: Rossellini with **Païsa** and De Sica with **Sciuscià** or **Shoeshine**. De Sica, working from a screenplay by Zavattini, dealt with the aftermath of war and two urchins who scraped a living from selling black-market goods on the streets of Rome. Rossellini's film followed, in five episodes, the American army from the landings in Palermo to the retreat of the Germans from the Po Valley. But it is less concerned with these foreigners than the Italians' reaction to them, and the Italians include a sweet-faced Roman whore (Maria Michi) who isn't recognized by GI (Gar Moore) to whom she swore undying love before she took it up for a living. The movies, as ever, were growing up.

world, with one notable exception. Its film-makers had, indeed, started to turn out tributes to the Resistance, but these were too self-serving and silly to merit an export licence. René Clément's semi-documentary **La Bataille du Rail** was of another order. Not only was it immensely exciting, but it spoke with clarity and humour of the bravery of those who had attempted sabotage on the railways, of necessity the only connecting link between the France which was occupied by the Germans and that which, in theory, was not.

Clément also worked, uncredited, on the first of the two French masterpieces of movie fantasy. Both were also the work of Jean Cocteau, the dilettante writer who, with **La Belle et la Bête**, finally fulfilled Diaghilev's command to him to astonish. With imaginative camera-work and the romantic, surreal decor of Christian Bérard, he created the very world of fairy stories. Josette Day was Beauty, while Jean Marais doubled as her peasant admirer and the beast.

From a country now divided, East Germany sent out a powerful statement about war guilt, **Die Mörder Sind Unter Uns** or **The Murderers Are Among Us**, clearly considered by the writer-director Wolfgang Staudte to be more important than rehabilitation, which we might

Opposite: Rita Hayworth in **Gilda**, which wasn't very good, but it caught the public imagination. Above: He doesn't recognize her: whore (Maria Michi) and client (Gar Moore) in **Païsa/Paisan**. Opposite: Powell and Pressburger's **A Matter of Life and Death** has David Niven (centre foreground) being shot down in Technicolor and then listening in monochrome while a heavenly court argues the pros and cons for his recovery. Two Hollywood names, Kim Hunter (centre) and Raymond Massey (in 'Revolutionary' uniform), ensured the film's success in the US. To the left of Hunter, Marius Goring and Roger Livesey.

1947

Everything was quiet on the surface and the major studios were pouring out half-a-dozen films a month; but there was a subdued turmoil in the industry. In 1946 its turnover had been the highest yet, at $1,692 million, but it was an industry about to be divided, by government decree. For as long as anyone could remember, it lived by the rule of block-booking, by which theatres were forced to take a guaranteed number of films, sight unseen, regardless of merit. Since most of the production companies also controlled distribution and exhibition, this presented a problem only to Universal, Columbia and United Artists, none of which owned a circuit of its own. In 1938 the Department of Justice had started an investigation into industry practices, which had been postponed during the War. As the Department decided to break the monopolies, the industry issued writs to delay the inevitable (the last to capitulate was Loews Inc. which, in 1952, decided that its theatres were more profitable to its shareholders than MGM, and thus kept them and dropped the studio and its distribution company).

For the third year running, attendances were 90 million annually, though in Britain they had dropped from 30.5 million in 1945 to 28.1 million in 1947, perhaps because television was taken more seriously there. Only a few people in movies had regarded television as a threat since its inception in the 1930s. In both Britain and the US the service had been closed down during the War; it had been started up again with little interest, and in 1947 only 14,000 American homes possessed a set. The first television series were being created, but they were of amateurish quality.

What most concerned Hollywood was the move towards independence. Almost every film-maker who had served in the War had returned determined not to re-surrender to Cloud-Cuckooland which, in effect, meant making more serious films. Directors of the calibre of William Wyler, George Stevens and Capra were determined not to be subject to the whims of a handful of moguls, and at the same time a number of actors and writers were sufficiently powerful to start their own production companies. Among the distributors, RKO was the most welcoming. There were even new studios, such as Enterprise and Eagle-Lion, the latter set up by Mr Rank. Both of these were felled by box-office failures, but in the case of individual film-makers they were either plagued by bad luck or thwarted by the handful of moguls who controlled the industry. These admired talent, which was why so many of them made deals with the independents, but they were determined that it should not have its head.

Left: **Crossfire**, directed by Edward Dmytryk, was based on a novel about a GI who murders a man who made a pass at him. The Censor would not permit this; by making the victim Jewish the film is a valiant statement about anti-semitism. Robert Young (right) was the detective; Robert Ryan and Robert Mitchum (centre) were suspects. Above: Yves Montand and Nathalie Nattier as doomed lovers in **Les Portes de la Nuit**. Opposite above: Clark Gable and Deborah Kerr in **The Hucksters**, a satire on the world of advertising. Opposite below: James Mason and F. J. McCormick in Carol Reed's **Odd Man Out**, the year's most praised film.

186

January Elia Kazan consolidated his reputation with **Boomerang**, a thriller, filmed in Stamford, Connecticut, based on a true story much concerned with small-town corruption. Location filming had begun to herald the end of the great era of studio art direction, and certainly benefiting from it was **The Macomber Affair**, filmed in Kenya from the Hemingway story by director Zoltan Korda.

March **The Egg and I**, Betty Macdonald's bucolic comic novel about an urban couple starting a chicken farm, became one of Universal's biggest ever successes thanks, perhaps, to the stalwart efforts of Claudette Colbert and Fred MacMurray.

August **Life with Father** finally reached the screen after its record-breaking Broadway run, directed by Michael Curtiz at Warners in colour with William Powell as the irascible father and Irene Dunne the mother who is the true head of the household. It was also nostalgia time at Fox, with a vaudeville tale, **Mother Wore Tights**, starring Betty Grable and Dan Dailey, who would become a popular team for this studio.

October Henry James was filmed for the first time when *The Aspen Papers* became **The Lost Moment** for Universal, and that wasn't the only damage done to it. Why film James, when you can have Kathleen Winsor? Her **Forever Amber** had been more read and discussed than anything since **Gone With the Wind** and while no one thought it of the same quality, it raised temperatures and much else because Amber, to use a later phrase, slept around – around the court of Charles II, as it happened. The book was so notorious and its heroine such a hussy that it did nothing to change the image of women's sexuality that still lingered from the nineteenth century. The only question was, how many of Amber's lovers would the censor allow? Many people were curious, to the

gratification of Fox, which had spent a small fortune on the thing. What they saw was Linda Darnell being pert and pouting, with an occasional kiss proffered to the king (George Sanders) and her true love (Cornel Wilde).

November Elia Kazan directed **Gentleman's Agreement**, which he later dismissed as 'patronizing'. At the time, however, it brought prestige to him, to Fox, to Moss Hart (who wrote the screenplay from a bestselling novel) and Gregory Peck, playing a gentile journalist who poses as a Jew in order to learn about anti-Semitism – something he might have learnt from his best friend John Garfield, who is Jewish, as are several of the other characters. The piece does make some decent points among its many platitudes.

In Britain, Mr Rank's plans to assault the American market were in abeyance, partly because of the failure of **Caesar and Cleopatra**, and partly because he had started his own company. However, the film-makers within his empire were having a vintage year. Powell and Pressberger produced their most outrageous undertaking, **Black Narcissus**, a weird mélange of religious conviction and sexual frustration; and the Irish troubles were the focus of Carol Reed's **Odd Man Out**, with James Mason as a fugitive wounded after trying to rob a bank. Much too much 'Oirishness' all round, but it was the year's most praised film, almost certainly because it aped Carné's prewar movies.

The Boulting brothers looked responsible with **Fame is the Spur**, based on Howard Spring's novel, about a left-wing politician based on Ramsay MacDonald, played in the film – which upended Spring's whole point-

Left: **Dead Reckoning**, directed at Columbia by John Cromwell, with Humphrey Bogart up to his neck in mayhem while investigating the death of a buddy, and Lizabeth Scott, a nightclub chanteuse who might be as deadly as she looks. Above: John McCallum and Googie Withers in **It Always Rains on Sunday**, a vital look at life in the East End, centring on a bored wife sheltering an old boyfriend on the run. This is a flashback to a happier time. Opposite: David Farrar and Deborah Kerr in Powell and Pressburger's **Black Narcissus**, a tale of convent life in the Himalayas – which were superbly simulated in the studio by process work.

of-view – by Michael Redgrave. Also topical was Cavalcanti's **They Made Me a Fugitive**, with Trevor Howard as an ex-RAF man going to the bad and Griffith Jones as a major spiv, both of them mixed up in the postwar black market.

It was not a great year for Gainsborough, but the studio had a great success when Dennis Price played a character based on the ex-RAF sex murderer Neville Heath in **Holiday Camp**, a cross-section tale in the manner of **Grand Hotel**. The public's fondness for these establishments, and this film, may be because they reminded them of the regimentation and togetherness of the war years. The film also teamed Jack Warner and Kathleen Harrison as a cockney couple, Mr and Mrs Huggett, which led to three further films (all dire) and a radio series.

Ealing did well. **Frieda**, directed by Basil Dearden, sees David Farrar as a teacher who brings his bride to his home town, and she is German – hence the ad slogan, 'Would *you* take Frieda into your home?' The piece is somewhat loaded, as she helped him escape after his plane was shot down and is, in any case, played by a Swedish actress, Mai Zetterling. Ealing's best serious film to date, and the first honest movie look at the British working-class, which was **It Always Rains on Sunday**, which immediately established the reputation of its director, Robert Hamer. But Ealing's way forward was indicated by **Hue and Cry**, a boys' adventure in which a gang of them discover that some crooks are using an unworldly writer, Alistair Sim, to send code messages in their favourite comic. The film vividly records how blitzed London looked, as directed by Charles Crichton from a screenplay by T. E. B. Clarke, who would become the most influential force behind Ealing comedy.

Alexander Korda resurrected London Films with his Technicolored version of Oscar Wilde's **An Ideal Husband**, directed dully by himself, with Paulette Goddard as a vulgar Mrs Cheveley. The occasion was redeemed by Michael Wilding's debonair Lord Goring. This actor co-starred with Miss Neagle in 1947's top box-office film, **The Courtneys of Curzon Street**, a copy of **Cavalcade** so close that Coward could have sued producer-director Herbert Wilcox for plagiarism.

China's long-dormant film industry returned with two films about the country after upheaval, **The Spring River Flows East**, a melodrama about the fortunes (or lack of them) of a married couple from 1931 onwards, and the much less risable **8,000 Li of Cloud and Moon**, a brave autobiographical tale written and directed by Shi Dongshan, about another couple, actors and socialists, confronting corruption in postwar Shanghai.

In Italy, Giuseppe De Santis tackled the aftermath of war in **Caccia Tragica**, and Rossellini made his last considerable movie, on the same theme, **Germania, Anno Zero**, centring on one small boy and his family in the ruins of Berlin.

The French continued its pessimistic tales with Raymond Radiguet's autobiographical **Le Diable au Corps**, about a student and a married woman who embark on a passionate love affair while her husband is away at the Front (in the first World War). Mlle Presle and Gérard Philipe are memorable in the roles. Claude Autant-Lara directed. René Clair made his first French film for over fifteen years with the inventive and somewhat melancholy **Le Silence est d'Or**, starring Maurice Chevalier as a movie director at the time of Méliès.

René Clément's purpose in **Les Maudits** is allegorical, though it has a straightforward plot about some Nazis sailing to set up a new state in Latin America. One of them is a sadistic homosexual, or so we infer when he beats up the young friend whose eyes have strayed. Any form of sexual deviation in movies was so rare as to be remarkable, but there is a lesbian in Clouzot's enjoyable **Quai des Orfèvres**, and indeed much more than that, including a dirty old man played by Charles Dullin. However, the two chief roles go to Louis Jouvet and Suzy Delair, respectively a police detective and a music-hall star.

The outstanding French movie, now a valuable record of a past time, is **Farrebique, ou les Quatre Saisons**, which followed a peasant family for a year on their farm in a remote section of the Massif Central, enjoying pleasures and enduring hardships. It was made by Georges Rouquier, who in 1983 returned to the farm with a colour camera to show the changes. **Biquefarre** includes footage from the original film and shows the changes to be immense yet, curiously, it is excessively dull, demonstrating the advisability of Never Going Back.

Those professionally concerned with the cinema had recognized the paramount importance of the director since the days of Méliès, even if this was something that the studio moguls did not care to acknowledge. The studio system was still so strong, so intact, that directors did what they were told. But this was not always the case.

1948

January John Huston had been shooting **The Treasure of the Sierra Madre** on location in Mexico, a tale of down-and-outs hunting for buried bounty in bandit-infested country. The Warner Bros had not liked the enterprise in the first place and were appalled by the rushes but, encouraged by his star, Humphrey Bogart, and the critical response to the studio-free European directors, Huston continued to do things his way. The result was a resounding success for everyone concerned, especially the unshaven Bogart and Huston's father, Walter, as an ageing prospector. The extravagances and the acclaim for Von Stroheim had shaken the moguls; the acclaim and the popularity of Capra had cheered them. They were now having to consider the situation again.

Their difficulties were compounded by the fact that two dutiful studio directors turned out two movies in a way very much dictated by themselves: Henry Hathaway with **Call Northside 777** for Fox and Jules Dassin with **The Naked City** for Universal. Both were, or pretended to be, based on fact, which meant that they adopted a semi-documentary style. The first concerned a legal injustice, with journalist James Stewart campaigning for a wrong to be righted; the second follows a murder investigation in New York.

March MGM released one of the most unusual films in its history, **The Search**. Fred Zinnemann directed this location-filmed and moving drama about displaced persons in the wreck that was Europe, with beautiful performances by Montgomery Clift (in his début) as a GI, Aline MacMahon as an UNRAA official and Ivan Jandl as a Czech child.

April Billy Wilder's **The Emperor Waltz** was a lumbering, Lubitsch-like thing, with Bing Crosby as a salesman selling phonographs in the Tyrol and Joan Fontaine as a countess, whose dog is lusted after by his. This actress was luckier with Max Ophuls's **Letter From an Unknown Woman**, from Stefan Zweig's novel. No film-maker ever mined Old Vienna more hauntingly or got a more exquisite performance from Miss Fontaine, as a girl who loves, is seduced and left pregnant by a famous pianist, who doesn't recognize her when they meet years later.

May Winston Churchill, describing the division of the world as devised by the Soviet bloc, had spoken of **The Iron Curtain**, which gave Fox the title of an espionage thriller set in Canada, directed by William Wellman with Gene Tierney and Dana Andrews. (It also made, following Red Indians and Nazis, Commies official villains in Hollywood annals.)

June It was a bit late for an **Easter Parade**, but it was only an excuse for Judy Garland and Fred Astaire (coming out of retirement to replace an injured Gene Kelly) to run through a couple of dozen Berlin songs, including a divine comic number, 'A Couple of Swells'. Helping them were director Charles Walters and Ann

Left: Graham Greene, now being recognized as one of the century's leading writers, saw one of his short stories perfectly filmed, after Carol Reed had asked him to write the screenplay: **The Fallen Idol**. Ralph Richardson played the title role, the butler in a Belgrave Square embassy who causes the death of his wife while having an affair – both of which a lonely boy, Bobby Henrey, is party to. Above: Jane Wyman about to be raped by Horace McNally in **Johnny Belinda**. Curiously, given the taboos on sex, this still was used extensively in the advertising. Opposite: Laurence Olivier in his widely acclaimed **Hamlet**.

Miller, a B-movie actress who would be a tip-tappering asset to the MGM musical, here playing Fred's partner whom he replaces with Judy when she goes high hat. In Billy Wilder's **A Foreign Affair**, Congresswoman Jean Arthur goes to Berlin to discover that its American military officers are up to their ears in fraternization and the black market. One of them is John Lund; Marlene Dietrich is a nightclub singer; and this biting satire is, with **The Search**, the only American film of 1948 on an important contemporary subject.

August **Rope** had an interesting genesis when, in 1924, two young Chicago intellectuals, homosexual and Jewish, murdered a youngster picked at random to prove their Nietzschean superiority. The dramatist Patrick Hamilton re-imagined the situation, in which two students invite friends of the victim to their London flat to take tea on the trunk which contains the corpse. In filming it, Hitchcock transferred the action to New York, using Technicolor (it was the first-ever thriller in colour) and a much-publicized system of ten-minute takes borrowed from television, then always 'live', which was supposed to point the way forward for movies (but which he dropped as too constricting after his next movie). A generally dismal occasion was not improved by censorship (which was inevitable) and the miscasting (which was not) of

James Stewart as the professor who susses out the secret of the students, John Dall and Farley Granger.

September   Jane Wyman was violated in **Johnny Belinda**, but since she was a deaf-mute, she was unable to explain why she was pregnant. Lew Ayres played the doctor who is suspected of being responsible. The censor habitually allowed a couple of films annually (but no more) to deal with such serious matters, and director Jean Negulesco helped immeasurably by offering an affection-ate portrait of a poor Nova Scotia community and getting from Miss Wyman a performance of rare delicacy. Warners hated the film, but critical and public approval brought them a new star, Wyman, who had been standing in the wings for over a decade. Moreover, that approval, which had nothing to do with prurience for the film was both too warm and too harsh for that, caused many to think again about the way the subject of sex might be handled in movies.

October   Two old war-horses got a grim going over. Orson Welles's cut-price **Macbeth** for Republic offended eye and ear at every turn, as did Victor Fleming's glossy, expensive, garish **Joan of Arc**. It ended his career, sent its producer, Walter Wanger, into virtual bankruptcy, and didn't do much for Ingrid Bergman, either. 'They wouldn't even let me muss my hair,' she said later. Gene

Kelly went songless in **The Three Musketeers**, but he danced a lot, all in the cause of swashing a buckle as D'Artagnan. His muscular agility is one reason why this is the best of the several movie versions; another is that the sets are Technicolored versions of those in the Fairbanks version; yet another is the invigorating pace established by director George Sidney. On the debit side are the milque-toast milady of Lana Turner and the removal of the red robes of Richelieu (Vincent Price). The first of these matters is understandable, for MGM had had proof that the public liked Turner as a blonde schemer; the second is unfathomable, except to those – who would include the predominantly Jewish board of MGM – afraid of the pronouncements of the Legion of Decency. This was an organization of Catholic bishops set up in 1934 to combat immorality in movies. Ever since, it had been advising Catholics to avoid any which depicted it. Rather than have this film 'condemned' or considered 'morally objectionable' for showing the cardinal in a bad light, MGM simply unfrocked him.

November Columbia issued a B-movie, **Ladies of the Chorus**, starring a blonde who had been decorating the studio's films for years, Adele Jergens, and another whom it had just acquired, Marilyn Monroe. They played mother and daughter, with Monroe having two songs, one of which, 'Every Baby Needs a Dad-Dad-Daddy', is tailored to her unique gifts. Despite this and the fact that the *Motion Picture Herald* found her 'promising', Harry Cohn dropped her. He would regret this. **The Snake Pit**, directed by Anatole Litvak for Fox, saw Olivia de Havilland in a mental home – a bold film about a subject seldom tackled by an American movie, and one which remains strong.

December MGM released **Words and Music**, a biopic of Rodgers and Hart, with a dull Tom Drake and a libellous Mickey Rooney in their roles – the *only* thing Hart and Rooney had in common was diminutive stature. However, the musical numbers were often fine, and they included an interpretation of 'Slaughter on Tenth Avenue', danced by Gene Kelly and Vera-Ellen, that was the longest ballet so far in an American film.

The British had beaten them to it. Film-makers had long been fascinated by the relationship of Diaghilev and Nijinsky, always brought to the screen as a heterosexual couple. In Powell and Pressberger's **The Red Shoes** they were played by Anton Walbrook and Moira Shearer, in a story also resembling that one by Hans Andersen which

provided the basis for the climactic ballet. It is not an honourable movie, but it has the courage of its excesses, and when released in the US (just before **Words and Music**) became Rank's biggest success in that market.

David Lean and Laurence Olivier again triumphed on familiar territory, respectively Dickens and Shakespeare, **Oliver Twist** and **Hamlet**, again with magnificent art direction (Victorian London and a Danish castle at some vaguely defined time in the past) and casts to match: John Howard Davies (Oliver), Alec Guinness (Fagin), Robert Newton (Bill Sykes), Kay Walsh (Nancy), Francis L. Sullivan (Mr Bumble), Kathleen Harrison and Gibb McLaughlin (the Sowerbys); Olivier himself (the prince), Jean Simmons (Ophelia), Felix Aylmer (Polonius), Norman Wooland (Horatio), Eileen Herlie and Basil Sydney (the Claudiuses). It was particularly to Olivier's credit that the familiar story has an edge of danger, building to the final duel, one of the most exciting ever put on screen. No non-American film had before won an Oscar for Best Picture; Olivier also won an Oscar for his performance.

All these film-makers would leave Rank for Korda (Carol Reed had already gone). The reasons were simple: Korda's own charm and his greater love of the medium, which meant bigger budgets and a more personal choice of subject. Filippo Del Guidice, the Italian-born producer who had found the financing for most of these talents (that

Opposite: Robert Helpmann and Moira Shearer in **The Red Shoes**, the first major film about ballet in English. It made a movie name of ballerina Shearer. Right: Marlene Dietrich in Billy Wilder's **A Foreign Affair**. She played a dubious cabaret singer who has an American officer in her clutches – and both come under the scrutiny of a committee from Washington investigating the welfare of GIs in Berlin.

is, before Rank) and nurtured them (during their Rank days), retired. Rank's accountants were looking at budgets, and Gainsborough's executives had been replaced by Sydney Box, with instructions to turn out at least one medium-budget film a month. These were needed by Rank's cinemas because no new American films were coming in, the financially beleaguered Labour government having decreed that any profits made had to be kept and spent in Britain. Hollywood had responded by banning the export of its films to the UK.

The couple of dozen features released by Rank during 1948 are competent, but they included only three of passing interest. **Mr Perrin and Mr Traill**, adapted from Hugh Walpole's novel, is about the rivalry between two teachers – one stuffy and pompous (Marius Goring), and the other a carefree ex-rugger player (David Farrar) – in love with the school nurse (Greta Gynt). The novel was originally published in 1911 but, updated, has much to say about the pettiness and vindictiveness endemic in British society at this time. **Quartet** is the first really admired and successful omnibus film, consisting of four Somerset Maugham short stories, introduced by the Old Party himself, and **Good Time Girl** was Jean Kent as that postwar phenomenon, a contemporary Manon Lescaut,

moving from Soho clubs to reform school and back again, used by various bounders, including a GI deserter, Bonar Colleano, who involves her in murder (the film was inspired by a real-life case of 1944).

It is one of the anomalies of cinema history that you can learn more about Life As It Was from junky films than from Hollywood's smooth portraits of a nirvana-America. Two notorious (then) works show us how, and the negatives in the titles tell us as much as we need to know about expectations in austerity Britain. Neither, ostensibly, is set there and then. Both had been long-running plays: **No Orchids for Miss Blandish**, adapted from a pulp thriller by James Hadley Chase, is set in the world of New York gangsters, with Jack La Rue as a master kidnapper who is gratified to find that his victim, Linden Travers, is sexually insatiable; and **No Room at the Inn**, in which a petty officer (Niall McGinnis) is so entranced by the drinking skills and sexual advances of his daughter's foster mother (Freda Jackson) that he ignores the child's complaints and goes to bed with her. For this is a piece about evacuees and those people who took them in only for the money, a melodrama which is part Grand Guignol, part Dickensian, part 'Hansel and Gretel'.

The British looked much to the past in movies,

perhaps because they were in the process of divesting themselves of an Empire. Ealing made its first two Technicolor films: **Saraband for Dead Lovers**, which managed to be dull on the illicit affair between a Swedish mercenary (Stewart Granger) and Sophie Dorothea (Joan Greenwood), wife of the future George I of England; and **Scott of the Antarctic**, which perpetuated the lies told about that gentleman (John Mills). Basil Dearden directed the first and Charles Frend the second.

In France, Roger Leenhardt directed **Les Dernières Vacances**, a delicate study of the last summer of adolescence, and Christian Jaque did a terrific job on Stendhal's novel of political intrigue and ambition, **La Chartreuse de Parme**, with Gérard Philipe as Fabrice, Maria Casares and Louis Salou.

In Sweden, Ingmar Bergman directed the remarkably rich **Night is My Future**, about a pianist (Birger Malmsten) who simultaneously discovers that he is going blind, that he is not that good at his job and that he can't marry the girl he loves.

In Italy, Visconti returned to filming with **La Terra Trema**, a study of the lives of Sicilian fishermen exploited by the middlemen. He used the local dialect, which prevented the film from getting many bookings in Italy. Not seen abroad till much later, it was recognized as a masterpiece of realism, but not without some typically operatic flourishes. Four other films caused a great stir abroad. The Legion of Decency squawked about Rossellini's **Il Miracolo**, written by Fellini, with Anna Magnani as a peasant woman who takes a glass too many

with a man she thinks is St Joseph. (When her stomach starts to swell she believes she will be responsible for the Second Coming.) Elsewhere, at only thirty-eight minutes, it attracted little attention and was considered less about blasphemy than prejudice – that of the villagers who turn the woman out.

The Legion of Decency also banned **Riso Amaro** or **Bitter Rice**, with its promise of passion in the rice fields of the Po Valley, with buxom Silvana Mangano as a migrant worker oscillating between an honest police sergeant, Raf Vallone, and a petty thief, Vittorio Gassmann. Giuseppe De Santis, who directed, had been one of the leaders of the neorealist movement, which this film helped to destroy. He had injected melodrama to attract a wider audience, and when it attracted crowds all over the world, almost every Italian film-maker would try for the same success.

Two exceptions were De Sica and Renato Castellani. Castellani's aptly titled **E'Primavera**, fresh and full of vitality, finds a conscript pinching his best friend's girl in Catania and then, when he is posted to Milan, meets another whom he fancies as well. Among the three writers were the director and Zavattini, who alone wrote De Sica's masterpiece, **Ladri di Biciclette** (GB: **Bicycle Thieves**, US: **The Bicycle Thief**). The premise is simple: a man gets a job sticking up posters, but he cannot do it after his bicycle is stolen, so he sets off through the streets of Rome to search for it. Because he is accompanied by his small son and because of the ending, people wrongly remember this film as sentimental. It is, in fact, harsh to the point of cruelty, yet compassionate. The acclaim which greeted it outside Italy (where it was not liked) was tremendous, and it remains one of the greatest films ever made.

*Opposite: Howard Hawks put John Wayne and his ward Montgomery Clift on a cattle drive: and **Red River** has the distinction of being the only United Artists release to make a large profit during the post-War period. Above: **The Paleface**, with Bob Hope as a dentist trying to fleece a living out West, plus Jane Russell as Calamity Jane and a song that monopolized the air-waves, 'Buttons and Bows'. Right: Lamberto Maggiorani and Enzo Staiola in Vittorio De Sica's **Ladri di Biciclette**. Along with **Bitter Rice**, it was more popular abroad than any Italian film till that time; many regarded it as the greatest yet made.*

1949

August MGM struck lucky with Flaubert. For this studio and this time, **Madame Bovary** is exemplary, if filmed for the not-very-good reason that producer Pandro S. Berman thought he could get a risqué subject past the censor if taken from a classic novel. He put Minnelli in charge, cast Jennifer Jones and Van Heflin as the Bovarys, with Louis Jourdan as the squire and James Mason as Flaubert in the prologue. **Jolson Sings Again**, and again and again, as Larry Parks plays himself and Jolson in a film about the making of **The Jolson Story**. Weird. The month's high point – and indeed the year's high point – occurred when James Cagney yelled 'Top of the world, Ma!' from the top of a power plant at the end of **White Heat**. This actor, returning to Warner Bros and the gangster movie, was on terrific form as a psychopath whose gang is infiltrated by an undercover man, Edmond O'Brien. The crime business was much grimmer than before and might have pointed a way forward to the Bros,

Above: John Gregson, Morland Graham and Duncan Macrae in **Whisky Galore!**. Right: Orson Welles as black marketeer Harry Lime in Carol Reed's **The Third Man**. The film's four leads – Welles, Joseph Cotten, Alida Valli, Trevor Howard – were not box-office stars, and the Vienna of its setting was not the romantic one of 101 films about waltzes. The public, however, loved it, lured in by the Harry Lime theme, as played on a zither.

196

who were never afraid to repeat themselves; but in this case they made only one follow-up, perhaps because the acrid tone could not be copied. No one could be sure whether the director, Raoul Walsh, was responsible for this: he had made some striking entertainments in the past, but the handful of movies he subsequently handled were both clumsy and insipid.

October At last, an excellent movie on racial issues: **Intruder in the Dust**, directed at MGM by Clarence Brown from the novel by William Faulkner about a Southern town in lynching mood. Juano Hernandez, thought to be a killer, has only four whites on his side: the dead man's father, Porter Hall; old maid Elizabeth Patterson; lawyer David Brian and nephew Claude Jarman Jr.

November Married couple Tracy and Hepburn fight on opposite sides of the courtroom over would-be killer Judy Holliday in **Adam's Rib**, a delectable comedy written for this trio by married couple Garson Kanin and Ruth Gordon; with Tom Ewell as the unfaithful husband and Jean Hagen as his girl. Cukor directed.

December **Sands of Iwo Jima** is a really rotten movie, but it was by far Republic's biggest hit in its twenty-year history, thanks to the burgeoning popularity of John Wayne. Disney returns to what he once did superbly with **Cinderella**: saccharine songs, saccharine animation, but the returns encourage him to stay with full-length animation. And 1949 ends with its most enduring achievement, **On the Town**, with Gene Kelly, Frank Sinatra and Jules Munshin as three sailors with twenty-four hours to spend in New York, and Vera-Ellen, Betty Garrett and Ann Miller as the girls they meet. Kelly and Stanley Donen directed the Comden and Green script, from their Broadway show – some of whose songs get lost. Some location shooting, an air of fun and gaiety,

and the seeming spontaneity of the numbers make this the most innovative of all musicals.

The Hollywood presence in Britain is expressed in several films, but best in Vincent Sherman's **The Hasty Heart**, for Warners, based on a stage play set in a Burma Field Hospital, with Ronald Reagan and Patricia Neal as patient and nurse. Although she is as warm as ever, the film is memorable for Richard Todd as an antagonistic Scottish corporal who is fatally ill – something everyone but he knows.

Korda, after many expensive failures, had his fortunes restored by a zither playing 'The Harry Lime Theme' in **The Third Man**. Orson Welles was Lime, who has disappeared in Vienna, Joseph Cotten was the friend looking for him and Alida Valli the girl involved with both of them (and both of these were supplied by co-producer Selznick). Carol Reed directed from a screenplay by Graham Greene from a then-unpublished story; Trevor Howard was a British liaison officer in this city of shadows and mystery. Everyone involved was highly praised and the film was a big success worldwide.

This was something Rank still hoped for. And what could Americans want more than a film about **Christopher Columbus**? Rank insured his investment by bringing over Fredric March to play Columbus and his wife, Florence Eldridge, to play the Queen of Spain. It was generally agreed that until then the worst Rank film of the year had been **The Bad Lord Byron**, with Dennis Price in the title-role, but with British movies there always came along another to top it: **Diamond City** which, though set in South Africa, was so slavish of American Westerns that audiences could have chanted the dialogue along with the

Left: Ealing comedy arrived, gloriously, in three consecutive weeks, with **Passport to Pimlico**, **Whisky Galore!** and **Kind Hearts and Coronets** (illustrated). The last, with Dennis Price and Joan Greenwood, is inimitable. Above: Cecile Aubrey and Michel Auclair in Henri-Georges Clouzot's **Manon**, which caused temperatures to rise the world over. Opposite: DeMille's **Samson and Delilah**: a stuffed lion (not in this still) plus Victor Mature and Hedy Lamarr, neither of whom had drawn straws for years. Due to the subject matter – ? – this one mopped up, and despite notices as bad as those for **Duel in the Sun**, it did similar business.

characters. All three films were, as it happened, directed by David Macdonald.

At Ealing, Michael Balcon's team had been thinking hard about comedy and came up with a triple whammy, deliberately opening **Passport to Pimlico**, **Whisky Galore!** and **Kind Hearts and Coronets** in London in successive weeks. Later in the year came **A Run for your Money**, in which Alec Guinness was a timid gardening correspondent allotted the job of minding two Welsh miners in London for a rugger match which, of course, they don't see. Charles Frend directed. Alexander Mackendrick's **Whisky Galore!** was set in Scotland in 1943, when the inhabitants of a small island plot to get ashore a cargo of malt under the nose of the pompous British commander, Basil Radford. With the exception of Joan Greenwood, they are crafty and cunning, and the piece is chiefly recommended to those who think those qualities funny in themselves. T. E. B. Clarke wrote **Passport to Pimlico**, which supposes that some inhabitants of one London district can declare independence from Britain on discovering an ancient charter to prove that they may do so. The idea was taken from an old Gracie Fields film, **Look up and Laugh** (1935), but it had particular appeal in a country bound in red tape and still subjected to rationing. But Ealing's masterpiece is probably **Kind Hearts and Coronets**, a comedy of Victorian murders, stylishly directed by Robert Hamer from a screenplay by himself and John Dighton. Dennis Price is the impecunious heir who believes that eight Alec Guinnesses stand between him and the family fortune which is rightfully his, with Miss Greenwood and Valerie Hobson pretending that they can love him for himself alone. Ealing's contractual link allowed them the pick of Rank players, including those of the notorious Charm School, being groomed for stardom. Instead, they picked people whose fitness for the role was greater than their box-office standing.

China had more serious matters on its mind, as shown by Zheng Junli in **Crows and Sparrows**, a familiar tale of boarding-house life, but it is an authentic and powerful picture of life as the old régime crumbled.

In France, Jean-Pierre Melville made his first feature, **Le Silence de la Mer**, based on Vercors' clandestine bestseller of the Occupation years about a Francophile German officer billeted on a man and his niece, desperately demanding the friendship they refuse to return. The most discussed French film of the year was Clouzot's modernization of the Abbé Prévost, which starts with **Manon** (Cecile Aubrey) as a baby-doll collaborator. That fact and the scenes of the Paris black market upset the French; elsewhere, many were disturbed by the sado-masochistic implication of the sex scenes.

February Hollywood takes its first extended look at its rival, television, with good-humoured contempt, in **Champagne for Caesar**, with Ronald Colman as a know-all who wins so many game shows that a vamp, Celeste Holm, is hired to distract him.

1950

April Fox finally acknowledged that there was a real world out there, but **The Big Lift** is so terminally earnest about the Berlin airlift that it dwindles into an account of the duties of the Occupying Forces, who include Montgomery Clift and Paul Douglas. **Sunset Boulevard** was about a retired Silent star (Gloria Swanson) given, or so she thinks, the chance of a comeback by a failed screenwriter (William Holden) who has become a gigolo: 'If the lady's paying...?' says the menswear clerk – the sort of line not heard in an American movie since the pre-Code days. The man who put it there may have been the director, Billy Wilder, or one of his two co-writers. Between them, they came up with the definitive study of the has-beens, the never-wases and the failed of tinsel-town. At the time, critics admired the film, Hollywood loathed it and the public ignored it.

May Fred Zinnemann came up with a second consecutive film on contemporary problems. **The Men** may have its weaknesses, notably Teresa Wright's conventional gulp-in-the-throat performance, but it stated – boldly for the time – the dilemmas of those whose war wounds prevented them from functioning either physically or sexually. In his film début, Marlon Brando re-

invented screen acting by his refusal to invite pity for his literally intolerable condition.

June Bubonic plague was discovered in New Orleans in **Panic in the Streets**, shot excitingly in those self-same streets by director Elia Kazan. Two officials – Paul Douglas and Richard Widmark – search for a killer before he can pass it on. In an unnamed banana republic, an American surgeon (Cary Grant) is kidnapped to perform a life-saving operation on a dictator (José Ferrer) in **Crisis**, for MGM, with which Richard Brooks makes his début as a director.

July After aeons of neglect, Hollywood returns to science fiction – hereafter Scifi – as producer George Pal makes a gallant attempt to re-establish it. But the special effects of **Destination Moon** are derisory.

August Joseph L. Mankiewicz directs **No Way Out**, which checks out with **Intruder in the Dust** as the best movie yet on racial intolerance. It is also a thriller, and none the worse for that, as a nigger-hater (Richard Widmark) swears to kill the intern (Sidney Poitier) he thinks responsible for his brother's death.

September Writing his own script for the second time, Mankiewicz comes up with **All About Eve**, the best-ever film on theatre people, wise and so witty than some have memorized the dialogue. Bette Davis is on superb form as an ageing star actress, Anne Baxter is the protégée secretly scheming to take her place, Celeste Holm and Hugh Marlowe are friends, Gary Merrill and Thelma Ritter are Davis's lover and maid respectively.

November José Ferrer has a long nose in a cut-price version of **Cyrano de Bergerac** for Kramer-UA, and Judy Holliday becomes 'couth' (her word) in **Born**

Left: Jean Cocteau's **Orphée**, a dazzling fantasy which used some still potent tricks for Orpheus to enter Hades. Maria Casarès is the Princess, or Death, who takes him there. Above: Masayuki Mori (left) and Toshiro Mifune in **Rashomon**, the first Japanese film seen in the West for over twenty years. Opposite: Mala Powers and José Ferrer in **Cyrano de Bergerac**. Ferrer had played the role to great acclaim on stage, and he thought he should do so again on the screen. After all, if an Englishman, Olivier, could attract Americans to classic plays, why shouldn't he and Hollywood do the same? Except that it wasn't the same thing at all.

Yesterday. Both had done these on Broadway; both would win Oscars (she after considerable competition from Davis and Swanson). **Born Yesterday** is very funny and a considerable movie as directed by Cukor from Garson Kanin's Broadway play, and Holliday is incomparable as the dumb mistress of a scrap merchant (Broderick Crawford) who hires a teacher (William Holden) to wisen her up.

Korda produced the three most enduring British movies of the year, and **Seven Days to Noon** is far the best film with which the Boulting brothers were involved – a taut, well-written thriller about what happens when a scientist (Barry Jones) warns that he will plant a nuclear bomb in central London if the government doesn't stop their manufacture. Launder and Gilliat's **State Secret** took the premise of **Crisis** (see above), set it in an unnamed country (Italy doubled, but any connection to the Soviet bloc was not coincidental) and then gave chase in the manner of **Night Train to Munich** i.e., unless the hero can get out of hostile territory he is going to wind up

very dead. This team also filmed John Dighton's farce **The Happiest Days of Your Life** in which, by ministerial error, a girls' school is billeted on a boys' school. The situations are already funny and become hilarious because of the two prime comic talents of Alistair Sim and Margaret Rutherford as the head teachers, locked in loathing till it becomes necessary to cooperate to hide the blunder from visitors.

Ealing had a great success with a story about the police, **The Blue Lamp**, with Jack Warner as a bobby and Dirk Bogarde as a crook; and issued only one comedy, slight but pleasing, **The Magnet**. Written by T. E. B. Clarke, directed by Charles Frend and set on Merseyside, it examines the guilt of an eleven-year-old who tricks another boy out of his favourite toy.

The year's worst pictures were **The Dancing Years**, a schmalzy, garish Ivor Novello musical set in the Alps, and **The Astonished Heart**, based on a short play by Noël Coward, with Coward himself, Celia Johnson and Margaret Leighton.

In Italy, Ingrid Bergman gave birth to Rossellini's baby out of wedlock and by so doing shocked the world and rocked the film industry. **Stromboli**, the film she had gone to make, on her own initiative, was rushed into release by Howard Hughes, but an appraisal of its true merits was obscured. Seen after the dust had settled, it appears to have none in either the Italian or English versions. Bergman played a displaced person brought by her new husband to the volcanic island, where she dislikes everyone in sight except the lighthouse keeper and the priest, both of whom she would like to seduce.

The other Italian film most seen abroad was the antithesis, Luciano Emmer's sharply observed **Domenica D'Agosto** or **Sunday in August**, which looks at several different Romans enjoying a day by the sea; Zavattini was among the writers. Two films, not then exported, are excellent: **Luci del Varietà**, directed by Alberto Lattuada and Federico Fellini with a fondness for small-time vaudeville troupes and the even more run-down halls in which they appear; and Michelangelo Antonioni's amazing feature début, **Cronaca di un Amore**, in which a wealthy Milanese (Lucia Bose) persuades a past and present lover (Massimo Girotti) to murder her wealthy husband because she declines to give up her current standard of living.

In France, Cocteau wrote and directed his best film, a haunting and magical modernization of the myth of **Orphée** in the Underworld, with Jean Marais in the title role and Maria Casares as Death. Max Ophuls's return to France resulted in the equally masterly **La Ronde**, based on Schnitzler's play, in which each of the lovers is seen with a new one till we have come full circle. Signoret,

Philipe and Darrieux were among the stars, with Anton Walbrook as the master of ceremonies. In this respect – subjects with which the English-speaking cinema dare not attempt – is Jacqueline Audrey's **L'Ingénue Libertine**, a version of a Colette story about a young bride who cannot be aroused till two more experienced men have taught her. And France 1950 cannot be left without thought of **Paris 1900**, Nicole Védrès's entrancing collection of footage from the Belle Epoque, and Grémillon's amusing, brief study of the Academic painting of that era, **Les Charmes de l'Existence**.

There was sex, too, in Sweden when, one midsummer night, the young mistress of the house decides to surrender her virginity to the valet in Strindberg's **Miss Julie**, filmed by Alf Sjöberg with both erotic tension and mystery, with Anita Björk and Ulf Palme.

In Japan, Kurosawa made a film set in feudal times, **Rashomon**, when the almost ceaseless civil wars kept the country in chaos. In a forest, a bandit (Toshiro Mifune) rapes a woman (Machiko Kyo) while her husband looks on. Since he cannot be sure the extent to which the woman was pleased or shamed, the nature of truth is questioned, and the incident is told and retold from the point of view of all three participants – an idea whose time had come, since in 1950 Anthony Asquith's **The Woman in Question** also took a similar theme. But while that elicited only mild interest, Kurosawa's film created a furore when shown at the Venice Film Festival, going on to win the Grand Prix. The major reason was not the mysteries of the film itself, but the revelation of an Oriental movie culture of which the West knew nothing. The Japanese film industry had never expected foreigners to understand its films, but the floodgates had been opened, and by the end of the decade the best work of all movie-making nations would be international currency.

February   At MGM Fred Zinnemann directed **Teresa**, virtually the only film of the year with any pretension to topicality, looking as it does at the problems of a GI bride (Pier Angeli), adjusting to life in New York.

March   From Fox, the first of two superb films (see also November) directed by Henry Hathaway, both based

1951

on fact: **Fourteen Hours**, the story of a man on the ledge of a skyscraper, threatening suicide and bringing part of New York to a standstill.

April   MGM had a big hit with **The Great Caruso**, a cliché-ridden biography stuffed with opera pops, sung by Mario Lanza in the title role.

May   Kirk Douglas starred in **Ace in the Hole**, Billy Wilder's attack on journalistic ethics, which was so biting that this brilliant piece was poorly received by press and public.

June   MGM's remake of **Show Boat**, directed by George Sidney, confirmed the studio's supremacy in the field of musicals. At Warner Bros, Hitchcock found his old form with **Strangers on a Train**: one man (Robert Walker) proposing to another (Farley Granger) that they swop murders. Warners also brought **A Streetcar Named Desire** to the screen, and the Breen Office (formerly the Hays Office) had to give way on all but a few changes, since Tennessee Williams' play had been a sensation on Broadway. Rethinking his direction was Elia Kazan, with Marlon Brando, Kim Hunter and Karl Malden, all from Broadway, and Vivien Leigh, who had played the leading role in London – that of a nymphomaniac visiting her sister and brutish brother-in-law in New Orleans.

July   Like **Streetcar**, **A Place in the Sun** advanced the cause of sexual frankness in movies. This was a remake of von Sternberg's **An American Tragedy** and Paramount's most prestigious production of the year, directed by a newcomer to the studio, George Stevens, and starring Elizabeth Taylor as the rich girl and Montgomery Clift as the boy who murders his pregnant girlfriend, Shelley Winters, because she is an obstacle to their romance. The film would have been much less impressive if the first version had not been so long forgotten, since Stevens 'borrowed' so much from it. Disney tackled **Alice in Wonderland** and by sticking close to the plot and the Tenniel illustrations he brought it off acceptably; but it was one of his box-office failures.

August   Fox offered a Biblical, Henry King's ponderous **David and Bathsheba**, with Gregory Peck and Susan Hayward. MGM planned another such (see November), and hoped John Huston would direct. He had no intention of doing so, but strung them along in order to make **The Red Badge of Courage**, based on Stephen Crane's autobiographical novel, set amidst a battle of the Civil War: but the bigwigs, against the project from the start, ordered it to be cut to a mere sixty-nine minutes and sneaked it out without publicity. The studio was much

Left: When MGM issued **That's Entertainment** in 1974, celebrating the studio's musicals, it declared that its highspot was the ballet from **An American in Paris**, with Gene Kelly and Leslie Caron. Above: James Mason gave a very fine performance as Rommel in **The Desert Fox**, based on Desmond Young's bestseller. Opposite: Vivien Leigh and Marlon Brando in **A Streetcar Named Desire**. A husband (Brando) rapes his sister-in-law (Leigh) while his wife is in hospital having a baby. Because of this the censor insisted that the marriage is over, but because of the acclaim for Tennessee Williams' play most of it remained intact.

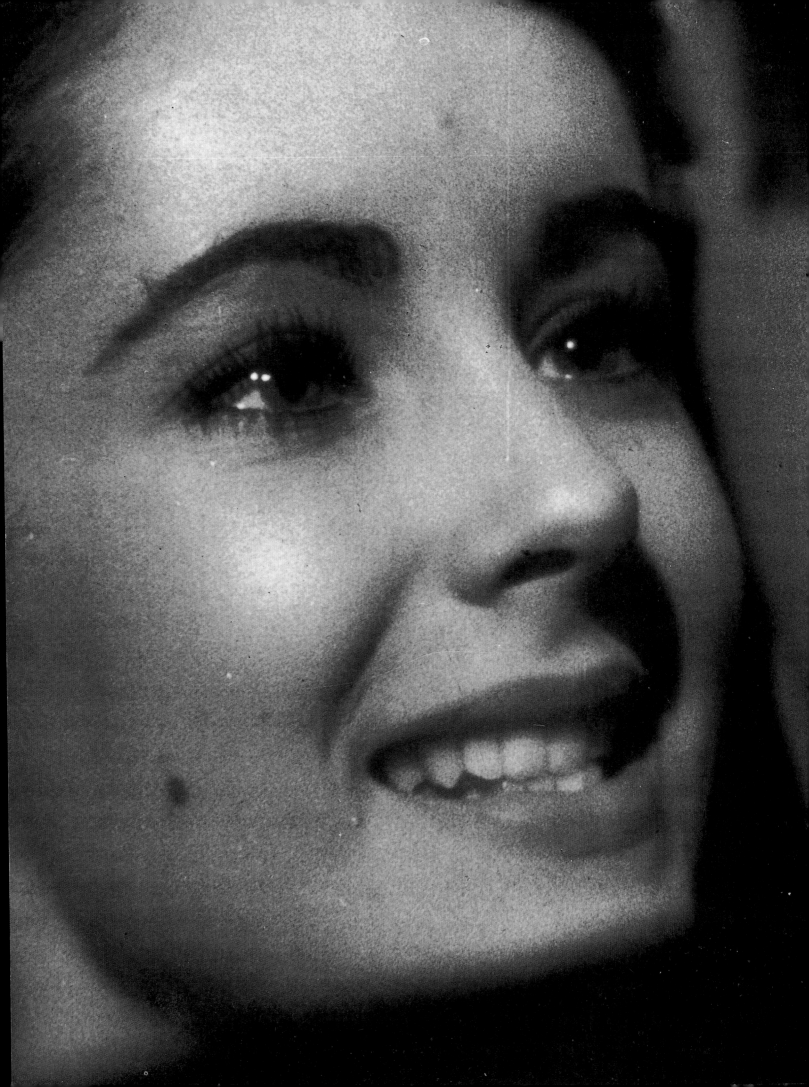

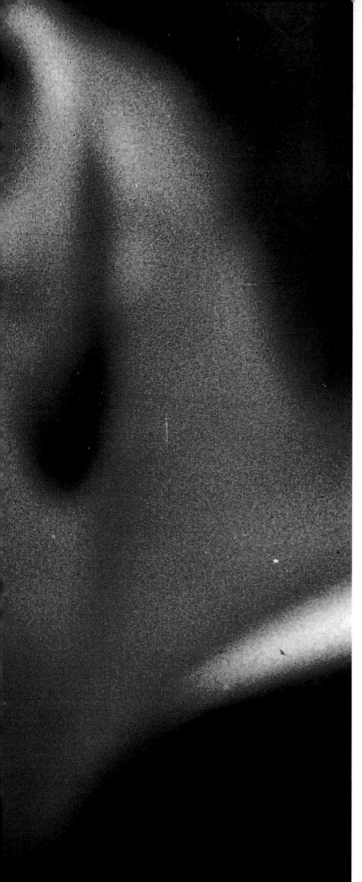

happier with **An American in Paris**, which became the first musical to win an Oscar for Best Musical since **Broadway Melody**. Although the director, Vincente Minnelli, packed some enjoyable ingredients into the film – the Gershwin songs, Gene Kelly's dancing and the charm of Leslie Caron – it was probably the climactic ballet which influenced the Academy voters, with its sets evoking the Impressionist painters and their successors. This was immediate, popular culture of the sort Hollywood understood, but not to be preferred to the less pretentious **Show Boat**.

September After Hitchcock, another old master wonderfully on form was Jean Renoir, with **The River**, made in India from the novel by Rumer Godden. It was an India seen by westerners, specifically a British family living on the banks of the Ganges.

October Hathaway's second outstanding picture was **The Desert Fox**, a portrait of the great German military tactician, Rommel, played by James Mason.

November MGM had another big one with a new version of the old story of Christians versus the lions, **Quo Vadis?**, directed by Mervyn Le Roy, but beyond Peter Ustinov's camp Nero there was little to enjoy.

Austerity in Britain seemed finally to be coming to an end as the country, or at least London, celebrated with the Festival of Britain. The film industry's contribution was **The Magic Box**, a tribute to William Friese-Greene, coyly described as 'one of the inventors of cinematography'. The year, however, belonged to Ealing. Two contrasting comedies, but both with Alec Guinness, consolidated its reputation in the field: **The Lavender Hill Mob** and **The Man in the White Suit**.

Among all the jungle movies ever made, pride of place would still go to **The African Queen**, in which a Canadian drunk and a prissy spinster travel up river to do their bit for the British in World War I. They were perfectly interpreted by Humphrey Bogart and Katharine Hepburn under John Huston's direction.

Among foreign-language films, the big news was the re-emergence of Luis Buñuel. **Los Olivados** was an acrid portrait of life among the down-and-outs of Mexico City. Trying something similar in Italy, Vittorio De Sica and his writer, Cesare Zavattini, came up with **Miracle in Milan**. In France, Robert Bresson made an austere and utterly compelling version of the novel by Georges Bernanos, **Diary of a Country Priest**. And, Fernandel and Françoise Rosay teamed well in Claude Autant-Lara's chilling comedy of murders, **L'Auberge Rouge**.

Left: Elizabeth Taylor and Montgomery Clift in George Stevens' **A Place in the Sun**, the second much-praised film in 1951 to deal honestly with sexual matters – and the censor allowed those, not only because of Stevens' reputation, but because it was based on Theodore Dreiser's classic novel, *An American Tragedy*.

1952

February Two major movies showed off the art of Fox's two best directors: Elia Kazan's multi-layered and vivid **Viva Zapata!**, with another astonishing performance by Marlon Brando as the Mexican Indian revolutionary who, briefly, became president of the country; and Mankiewicz's elegant, exciting spy thriller, **Five Fingers**, based on the incident during the Second World War when an Albanian-born valet in the British embassy in Ankara sold documents to the Germans, including the plans for the Normandy landings, which they chose to ignore. There are superb performances by James Mason as the valet and Danielle Darrieux as the impoverished Polish countess who sets the events in motion.

March A masterpiece: **Singin' in the Rain**, about Hollywood in the days when it was harried by the coming of Sound, with Gene Kelly as a star, Debbie Reynolds as the chorus girl he makes into a star and Donald O'Connor as his sidekick. Few musicals were more melodic and none was ever funnier, partly because of the performance of Jean Hagen as a dumb, vain star who isn't going to make it in Talkies – a character created by Comden and Green in homage to their old partner and chum, Judy Holliday, in her **Born Yesterday** role. At Paramount Robert Walker was **My Son John**, a Commie. Since 1947, the country had been wracked by the House of Un-American Activities Committee, investigating Red infiltration into American life. Hollywood's high-profile people were particularly vulnerable and the naming of names in 1950 – and the jailing of some of them, the 'Hollywood Ten'– had divided

the community. Since the furore had not died down, this inept film came at an unfortunate time. Its director and co-writer was the once-estimable Leo McCarey, whose thesis was that even the best American home could raise a Red, a veritable viper in the nest. Helen Hayes and Dean Jagger were the parents, and the occasion was worsened by the death during shooting by Walker, leaving a messy last reel with in-cuts from **Strangers on a Train**.

April A Western beauty, **High Noon**, with Gary Cooper as a sheriff waiting for three released prisoners who have sworn to kill him. As others look away as danger threatens, so this was an allegory on the Communist witch-hunt, written by Carl Foreman and directed by Fred Zinnemann. This may be the only Western liked by those who usually don't.

December For those who despaired of movies ever growing up came Fred Zinnemann's delicate version of Carson McCullers' play and novel, **The Member of the Wedding**, with the Broadway cast: Julie Harris as the tomboy longing to be the member of something – anything; Ethel Waters as her wise old Mammy; and Brandon de Wilde as the earnest little boy from next door. There was more superior Broadway with Shirley Booth as the slatternly, dreaming, middle-aged heroine of **Come Back, Little Sheba**, who once drove her husband to drink

Left: Gary Cooper in **High Noon**, which was admired and very popular. It was decidedly not hurt by the driving theme tune, sung intermittently by Tex Ritter throughout the film. Above: The century's greatest actor gives his best, most moving performance in old Chicago as a prosperous restaurateur who loses his wife, bread and everything, ending on skid row: all for love of **Carrie**. She is Jennifer Jones, he is Olivier, the source is a novel by Theodore Dreiser. The film, directed by William Wyler, was a box-office failure. Opposite: José Ferrer as Toulouse-Lautrec in John Huston's **Moulin Rouge**.

and may do so again. He is played, atrociously, by Burt Lancaster; but even the heartrending performance of Miss Booth can't persuade us that Daniel Mann's film or William Inge's original play are first rate.

Lancaster atoned with a British-based swashbuckler, **The Crimson Pirate**, directed by Robert Siodmak. Other Americans in Britain included John Huston, whose **Moulin Rouge** has a stunning re-creation of the Paris of Toulouse-Lautrec and a fair stab at what made the artist tick.

The critics liked David Lean's **The Sound Barrier**, his first film for Korda, written by Terence Rattigan and adequately described when you know that that Americans made 'Breaking' a prefix to the title; but this drama of test flights holds little interest today. Conversely, Zoltan Korda's **Cry, The Beloved Country**, adapted by Alan Paton from his novel, can still make people angry. Malan had been elected on the Apartheid ticket in 1948, and people were angry then; the mechanics of the plot – a black priest (Canada Lee) searching for his son, who has killed a white boy – work well around its portrait of injustice.

Among Rank's directors tackling literary sources was Anthony Asquith, with **The Importance of Being Earnest**, Oscar Wilde's comedy. As the two men, Michael Redgrave and Michael Denison struggle to find the right style, but the film preserves Margaret Rutherford's Miss Prism, Joan Greenwood's Gwendoline, Dorothy Tutin's

Cecily and especially Edith Evans's Lady Bracknell, all of which are definitive interpretations.

Spain sent out **Bienvenido Mr Marshall** or **Welcome Mr Marshall**, its first movie export for as long as anyone could remember. However, it wasn't until 1956 that it reached America, the country most likely to be amused, since the title referred to Marshall Aid, a Congressional Bill aimed at helping the European economy recover from the War. Luis G. Berlanga's gentle and occasionally biting satire found one rundown Castillian town turning itself into the haven of mantillas and castanets which its American visitors expected to see.

India's contribution to the international scene was its first colour film, **Aan**, but in all other respects this was just another of the hundreds of similar films its industry made, an extraordinary mélange of songs and dances, chases, duels, all slotted uneasily into an overlong tale of princely revenge. Its success in the West was due merely to its curiosity value.

In Japan, two directors forged their way towards greatness: Mizoguchi with **Life of Oharu** and Kurosawa with **Ikiru** or **Living**. No two films could be, superficially, less alike, for the first deals with a samurai's daughter (Kinuyo Tanaka) forced into prostitution, and the second with a minor civil servant (Takashi Shimura) dying of cancer. But both are questioning, in the most complex terms, the reasons for human existence.

Both films were not known by foreign audiences till

Left: Aldo Ray and Judy Holliday in **The Marrying Kind**, as an ordinary couple reflecting on the ups and downs of life together – and because of Miss Holliday the comic ups are very high indeed. George Cukor directed. Above: The French comic actor Fernandel became an international favourite in a French-Italian co-production, **The Little World of Don Camillo**, directed by Julien Duvivier. Fernandel was well cast as the cunning parish priest who wrangles with the Communist mayor of the village. Opposite: Simone Signoret (centre) in Jacques Becker's **Casque d'Or**, with Claude Dauphin (to her left) and Dominique Davray.

later, as is true of two of Buñuel's Mexican ventures, **El Bruto** and **El**, with two of his most tormented protagonists, respectively an abattoir worker (Pedro Armendariz) in thrall to lechery, and a wealthy man (Arturo de Cordova) so certain of his wife's infidelity that his jealousy ruins three lives. He is also a foot fetishist, but audiences did not have to share these obsessions. They had read about them in plays and novels; they did not find them in **The Crimson Pirate** or **My Son John**.

France continued to maintain its position as a purveyor of quality cinema. Many people regarded Jacques Becker's **Casque d'Or** as the best historical film since **La Kermesse Heroïque**. Certainly it contained a wonderful re-creation of the Paris of the Belle Epoque, with superb performances by Simone Signoret and Serge Reggiani, as a gangster's moll and the carpenter with whom she falls tragically in love. Max Ophuls' **Le Plaisir** was another stunning period piece, three stories by de Maupassant. The longest and most beguiling was 'La Maison Tellier', about the annual visit of the madame and her ladies to the country, with Danielle Darrieux and Jean Gabin. René Clément's **Les Jeux Interdits** was considered one of the greatest of films, as it tells of a little girl (Brigitte Fosey) just orphaned by the War and the country boy (Georges Poujoly) with whom she plays funeral games.

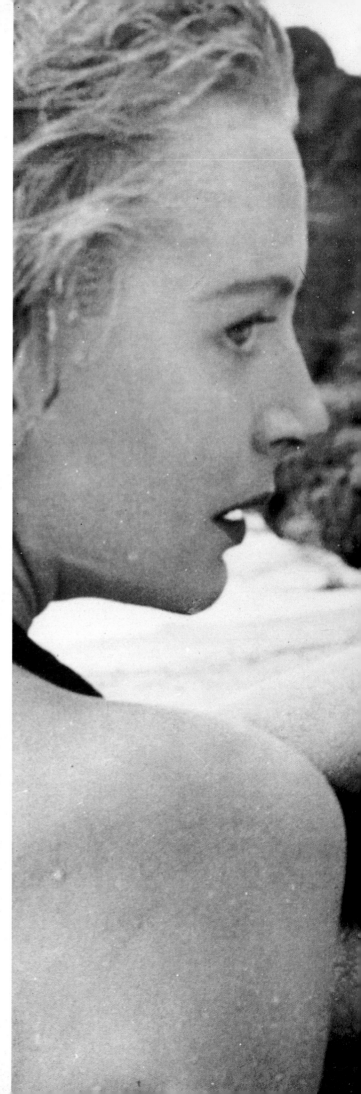

1953

Audiences were deserting cinemas for television and Hollywood, worried, tried some panaceas. One was Cinerama, which was shown on giant screens from three projectors. It produced two quivering lines between the images; it also meant conversion for theatres – limited to those cities with a large catchment area – and higher prices and seats only bookable in advance. A company had been formed to exploit the device, offering rollercoaster rides and such as the camera roamed the world's more striking scenery: and audiences endorsed **This is Cinerama**, which ran for years and had a handful of successors till it ran out of steam in the early 1960s. The industry also looked more closely at 3-D after audiences began pouring in to the critically despised **Bwana Devil**. But 3-D required the issue of special spectacles. Fox was convinced that the battle against television could be won by introducing a wider screen for its patented CinemaScope, but again this required costly conversion, especially as Fox refused to 'rent out' its patent unless it was shown with Stereophonic sound. The end of the dominance of Technicolor was in sight as the studios obtained their own colour systems. Cinecolor, without the true palette, had

Above: Alan Ladd and Brandon de Wilde in **Shane**, George Stevens' acclaimed Western. Right: Enlisted man, Burt Lancaster, with officer's wife, Deborah Kerr, on a deserted beach. Their roll in the foam was much enjoyed by cinemagoers. **From Here to Eternity**, based on James E. Jones' novel, and Norman Mailer's The Naked and the Dead – filmed less successfully in 1958 – extended what was sexually permitted in novels.

been a remote option in the 1940s, but Kodak had developed Eastmancolor, developed from the Agfacolor 'captured' by the Allies at the end of the War. In Europe this had become Sovcolor and Gevacolor, but in the US it was termed Metrocolor, Warnercolor, De Luxe (Fox).

January Marilyn draped all over **Niagara** – a wonderful conjunction of talents, for her mock-innocence was matched by Henry Hathaway's feeling for cod melodrama. She and Joseph Cotten are honeymooners – but not, she hopes, for long, since she is trying to persuade her new man to push him into the Falls.

April MGM anticipated the Coronation in Britain with **Young Bess**, the story of the early life of the first Elizabeth (Jean Simmons). Stewart Granger, Simmons' husband, played the Seymour suspected of being Bess's lover, and Charles Laughton got to re-play Henry VIII in Technicolor. Alan Ladd was **Shane**, the stranger who rides in from the faraway hills and tames a town; Jean Arthur (in her last film), Van Heflin and Brandon de Wilde comprised the family he stayed with, and George Stevens' Western, an instant classic, now seems a little too well-bred. Warners dusted off **The Mystery of the Wax Museum** and remade it as **House of Wax**, with Vincent Price as the genius who finds it easier to coat corpses with wax than to build models from scratch. Audiences screamed as objects were flung at their 3-D glasses.

June Marlon Brando emoted over the body of **Julius Caesar** (Louis Calhern), enhancing his reputation (unfairly – heard today, he slurs many more words than he should) and that of director Joe Mankiewicz, who proved

that Hollywood could film a Shakespeare play as it deserved, even if MGM's motive in backing it was to use the costumes left over from **Quo Vadis?** James Mason (Brutus) and John Gielgud (Cassius) helped immeasurably. **Gentlemen Prefer Blondes** – well they do when one of them is played by Marilyn Monroe, never more bewitching than when discovering that 'Diamonds Are a Girl's Best Friend'. She and Jane Russell, as her sidekick, keep vulgarity at bay – a considerable achievement in view of Howard Hawks's attempts to inject it at every turn into this frail little piece, originally devised by Anita Loos as a tribute to that quintessential figure of the 20s, the gold-digger. The robust Broadway show based upon it – songs by Jules Styne and Leo Robin – was recognizably set at that time, which the film is not. As sex symbols go, Maggie McNamara, an otherwise winsome chick, quickly went, but before she did so she created a storm by saying 'Would you try to seduce me?' William Holden and David Niven were the two men who wanted to, in **The Moon is Blue**, a Broadway comedy which producer-director Otto Preminger insisted on bringing to the screen intact. That meant McNamara banging on about being a 'virgin' and wanting to become a 'mistress' – words not heard in

Left: Yves Montand and Charles Vanel in **The Wages of Fear**, which had audiences sitting on the edge of their seats. Above: Audrey Hepburn on the Spanish Steps in **Roman Holiday**, taking a couple of days off from being a princess. Watching her is a journalist, Gregory Peck, who knows a scoop when he sees one. Opposite above: Jean Simmons, Ernest Thesiger and Richard Burton in **The Robe**, the first film in CinemaScope, a wide screen process meant to lure people from the small screens at home. It did – taking almost twice as much at the box-office as its nearest competitor, **From Here to Eternity**.

cinemas since the pre-Code days. And that meant that the Legion of Decency and the industry's own censorship board kicked up their skirts in horror, refusing their seals of approval, which in turn meant that no theatre could book it. But many did, fired by the furore, and this tedious, verbose enterprise became the first bastion in the fight against censorship.

July The battle, however, had not been truly joined, and the hooker of James E. Jones's novel, **From Here to Eternity**, had become the usual euphemism, a dance hostess (Donna Reed). The GI prepared to surrender his All for her is Montgomery Clift, a boxer who won't box till ordered to do so by sergeant Burt Lancaster. The sergeant is having an affair with an officer's wife, Deborah Kerr, and their tussle in the surf makes its mark in Hollywood history. It all takes place in Hawaii just before Pearl Harbor, and it was directed for Columbia by Fred Zinnemann. A new star enchanted: Audrey Hepburn as a princess who whisks herself off for an incognito **Roman Holiday**. She is recognized by American reporter Gregory Peck, who sees a story and didn't reckon with falling in love. The world fell in love with Miss Hepburn, even if Peck and William Wyler's direction aren't as sprightly as she is.

September Fox launched CinemaScope with **The Robe**. Biblical spectaculars seldom failed at the box office, and Lloyd C. Douglas's 'inspirational' novel, with Romans being converted to Christianity all over the place, was no exception. Among those playing them are Jean Simmons, Richard Burton, Victor Mature and, as St Peter, Michael Rennie. Henry Koster's direction and the wide screen reduced them to cardboard, as the critics pointed out, but the public turned up in large enough numbers for Fox to announce that all future productions would be in CinemaScope and colour.

October There were two bumper musicals: **Calamity Jane**, too much like **Annie Get Your Gun** (1950) for its own good, but with three assets – Doris Day, Howard Keel and a fine score; and Cole Porter's **Kiss Me Kate**, well done by MGM, with George Sidney at the helm, with Mr Keel and Kathryn Grayson as the shrew who needs taming, plus Keenan Wynn and Ann Miller, whose numbers are particularly invigorating. If today Miller seems to want to dance in your lap, it's because the film was originally shot and shown in 3-D. Disney offered his first full-length 'True-Life Adventure', **The Living Desert**. Since the series had started in 1948, four of them had carried off the Oscar for Two-reel Short Subjects. This would be Oscared, too, and the praise of the press brought out the queues at least for the first two or three features. Today, though, the relentless facetiousness of commentary and score make them hard to sit through.

November **How to Marry a Millionaire** was Fox's perennial about girls looking for rich husbands. They'd filmed it at least three times before, twice with music, but the idea this time seems to have been that a large cast could be strung out on the CinemaScope screen. The girls are Lauren Bacall, Betty Grable and Marilyn Monroe, who stole the film as a myopic blonde who refuses to wear glasses.

In Britain, two documentaries: **The Conquest of Everest** and **A Queen is Crowned**. Rank rushed the second into cinemas to compete with **Elizabeth is Queen**, shown on a rival circuit. Laurence Olivier had pre-recorded the commentary for Rank, but his own filmic contribution to Coronation year was coolly received by the press and shunned by the public, few of whom had heard of **The Beggar's Opera** in its previous existence. Peter Brook directed.

Ealing comedy wasn't what it once was but the studio had its greatest box-office success with **The Cruel Sea**, written by Eric Ambler from Nicholas Montserrat's bestselling novel and directed by Charles Frend. The book had sold more copies than any other in the history of British publishing, but its guts had been removed; and while Jack Hawkins was undeniably strong as the captain, the novelty of his authority wore off as he donned some sort of uniform for every other film of his career.

Ealing might have had another success had anyone there liked the script of **Genevieve**, by William Rose. Director Henry Cornelius took it to one of Rank's companies, but during filming (in Technicolor) no one involved held out much hope for it either. Its concern was the annual race of vintage cars to Brighton, and particularly those of two smart couples, married John Gregson and Dinah Sheridan, and Kenneth More and Kay Kendall, a bachelor and the model with whom he hopes to spend an amorous night. The slapstick of the piece would have been enough, but the bantering between the couples, sophisticated with sexual undertones, had long been considered the prerogative of American films (Rose was American). Critics and public were delighted, and Rank reissued the film almost annually over the next few years.

A popular film from Sweden was Arne Sucksdorff's **The Great Adventure**, in which two small boys adopt a pet otter, but like the Disney nature films it doesn't stand up now that television has shown us how such matters should be handled. One of Ingmar Bergman's films was finally seen abroad – **Sawdust and Tinsel/The Naked Night/Gycklarnas Afton**, a tale of adultery among

circus people, set in a small resort town. It wasn't much liked, but after the world discovered Bergman (see 1957), there was a warm welcome for **Summer with Monika**, equally misogynist but affecting, as a clerk (Lars Ekborg) lights out from his job to spend a woodland idyll with a slut (Harriet Andersson) who is clearly using him.

The reason he puts up with her behaviour is obviously sexual, and after several lifetimes in which Hollywood had reinforced the Victorian view that sex was only indulged in (but never enjoyed, except momentarily) by oddballs, deviants and hookers, the art-cinema was saying something different to its patrons. They could identify with Bergman's young couple as they couldn't – for all the sexual innuendo – with honeycombed Hollywood people like Cary Grant or Paulette Goddard.

Japan sent out two films which were much admired: Kinugasa's **Gate of Hell**, a tale of infidelity, murder and revenge among the samurai set, in exquisite Eastmancolor: and Kaneto Shindo's **Children of Hiroshima**, with some shattering documentary footage amidst its slight plot.

Clouzot provided France with one of its biggest successes with **Le Salaire de la Peur** or **The Wages of Fear**. It was acclaimed everywhere, this tension-packed tale of four unemployed men (including Yves Montand,

Opposite: Betty Grable, Rory Calhoun, Lauren Bacall, Cameron Mitchell and David Wayne in **How to Marry a Millionaire**, the second film in CinemaScope. Above: Ingmar Bergman was just becoming known outside Sweden, but **Summer with Monika/Monika**, with Harriet Andersson and Lars Ekborg, would not be seen abroad for a few years yet. It became one of Ekborg's most admired films. Right: Charles Boyer, Danielle Darrieux and Vittorio De Sica, husband, wife and lover respectively, in Max Ophuls' ironic study of romantic intrigue in the Belle Epoque, **Madame de ...**, known in the US as **The Earrings of Madame de ...**.

Charles Vanel) in Mexico who are hired by an American oil company to do a job for which they cannot get union labour – to drive two trucks containing nitroglycerine along rough jungle roads.

In Italy, De Sica directed the third and bleakest of his great films, **Umberto D**, the study of an old man so penniless, so despised (by his landlady), so friendless (except for the maid and his beloved pooch) that he decides that suicide is the only solution to his wretched existence. It was written by Zavattini, who was the guiding force behind **Amore in Città**, an omnibus picture intended to be the first of a series allowing directors to tackle short subjects of their own choosing. There were no follow-ups, which is a pity in view of the quality of Fellini's contribution. This director was also in splendid form with **I Vitelloni**, which followed the lackadaisical lives of some layabouts in a small seaside town out of season. Among the others contributing to **Amore in Città** was Antonioni, who was in variable form on his own episode film, **I Vinti**, which looked at delinquent youngsters in London, Paris and Rome, each filmed in their respective languages. But he did marvellously with **La Signoria Senza Camelie**, a story about a girl too intelligent to be a starlet but not sufficiently talented to become a star. Significantly, this was a movie about movie-making which demonstrated that, until now, its approach to storytelling had always been too literal. Except in thrillers, when they set out to scare audiences, film-makers set the scene as if for the stage. Antonioni never divulged everything immediately, but moved his camera only when he decided that it was time to change audience perception about his characters and their problems. Even more than **Cronaca di un Amore**, he showed how he would change the language of the cinema.

1954

The studio system was finally beginning to fall apart. For a while, some directors – Wilder, Wyler, Zinnemann, Mankiewicz, Stevens, Hitchcock, Cukor, Kazan, Huston – had chosen their own material but now, free of contracts, they also chose the studios at which they wished to work. And they were joined by actors like Burt Lancaster and Kirk Douglas, who refused to be tied down by long-term contracts and basically selected their own material.

January   At Columbia studios, for producer Stanley Kramer and director Laslo Benedek (who did little else of interest) Marlon Brando was **The Wild One**, a motor cyclist whose rivalry with Lee Marvin has both their gangs terrorizing a small town. Based on an actual incident, the film was banned outright in Britain in case its bikers decided to do likewise.

February   MGM peeked into the boardroom, the **Executive Suite**, with Robert Wise directing the corporate body, who included Barbara Stanwyck, William Holden, Fredric March, Paul Douglas and Walter Pidgeon, plus June Allyson and Shelley Winters.

March   MGM used CinemaScope for the first time for its remake of **Rose Marie**, with Ann Blyth and Fernando Lamas sharing the 'Indian Love Call'.

April   An indifferent show about putting on a show, **Lucky Me**, with Doris Day, was advertised by Warner Bros as 'The first CinemaScope musical', which they were able to do as MGM hadn't yet released **Rose Marie** and had understandable reservations about **Brigadoon**. In the latter two cases, too many studio pine-trees.

May   Negulesco's **Three Coins in the Fountain**, for Fox, is the story of three American girls (Jean Peters,

Dorothy McGuire, Maggie McNamara) living in Rome and their suitors (Rossano Brazzi, Clifton Webb, Louis Jourdan). Fair soap opera. And bad: the remake of **Magnificent Obsession**, which is glossy, vulgar, artificial and solemn, with Jane Wyman and Rock Hudson. Both films were extraordinarily popular, the second unfortunately so, for it persuaded its producer, Ross Hunter, to churn out many similar soaps, some of them again directed by German-born Douglas Sirk, who had already made some interesting films during his ten years in Hollywood. As he now began to make rubbish for Hunter and Universal, he found himself a cult figure. He could never understand why.

June   **Seven Brides for Seven Brothers**, with Howard Keel and Jane Powell, is a taking fable about six backwoods bachelors who emulate their eldest brother by taking their wives by force. Despite two singers in the leads, Stanley Donen's film is at its most exhilarating in the dances, notably the barndance wooing. It was much liked and no one could have foreseen that from this time on, the MGM musical would slowly die.

July   A major thriller: Hitchcock's **Rear Window**, with James Stewart as a photographer, Grace Kelly coming into bloom as his fiancée, Thelma Ritter as his nurse and Wendell Corey as a detective. Stewart is laid up with a broken leg and what he thinks he sees from his window is a murder. The exposition is clumsy, but the piece is genuinely macabre and amusing. What made it notable then was that what Stewart sees across the courtyard is his neighbours indulging in sex which,

Left: Judy Garland and James Mason in **A Star is Born**, which was even better than the 1937 original. Above: Grace Kelly and James Stewart in **Rear Window**, one of the two 1954 Hitchcock movies that made her a star. Opposite: Marlon Brando in **The Wild One**, which influenced men's fashions the world over. These had previously been impervious to Hollywood, but by the mid-Fifties Levis were being worn outside North America for the first time – and leather became the *sine qua non* of bikers and other butch guys.

though mostly implied, was rare in films at the time. Two explicit examples: the spinster who drinks to give herself courage to pick up a man and the honeymooners who only appear at their window between bouts.

And: a powerful, exciting thriller deliberately exposing corruption **On the Waterfront**, specifically the racketeers who had infiltrated the longshoremen's union. Kazan directed, from a screenplay by Budd Schulberg, with a heartrending performance by Brando as the inarticulate ex-prizefighter who, in a wintry Hoboken, reluctantly finds himself becoming the voice of conscience. The scene with his brother, Rod Steiger, in the cab has been much anthologised: 'I coulda been a contender'. Excellent performances, too, by Eva Marie Saint as Brando's girl and Karl Malden as a priest.

August   From Paramount came **White Christmas**, which introduced VistaVision, the company's answer to CinemaScope, a deeply-focused image which could be projected onto a screen of any size – but which wasn't around very long. Everything else is strictly recycled, including the plot.

September   Judy Garland returned to the screen in **A Star is Born**, remade by George Cukor with a screenplay by Moss Hart and songs by Harold Arlen and Ira Gershwin. They include 'The Man That Got Away' and a long melody-mélange by other hands, 'Born in a Trunk', in which her rendition of 'Swanee' demonstrates unparalleled star power. James Mason played the Hollywood star who discovers her, marries her and watches her rise to fame as his own recedes. As a satire on Hollywood this bites a bit more than even **Sunset Boulevard**, but the public was less impressed than the press. At three hours, this was the longest American film since **Gone with the Wind**; cut to two and a half it did no better, and when it went Oscarless, snubbed, in 1955, Warner Bros simply buried what they had expected to be the greatest success in their history. At that time it had just opened in Britain to fantastic notices for the two stars and business to match; but Warners had already announced that they did not intend to proceed with the other two contracted films with Miss Garland. Her private behaviour – drug addiction, lateness, non-appearance and temperament – had as much to do with this as the film's failure.

The very nature of stardom brought difficulties, which Mankiewicz examined in **The Barefoot Contessa**, which was expected to be as pungent on movie-making as **All About Eve** had been about 'theatre'. He starts well, with Humphrey Bogart as a disenchanted, ex-alcoholic director, Ava Gardner as the flamenco dancer he propels towards stardom, and Edmond O'Brien as a press agent. The Gardner character had been based on Rita Hayworth, who had married one of the major figures of the Moslem

world, Prince Aly Khan. She was also based on Garland, whom Mankiewicz had helped to discover and who later became his lover. Garland then married a homosexual, Minnelli, and to demonstrate the way movie stars mess-up their lives, Mankiewicz made the Khan character gay, which Khan definitely wasn't. James Mason had committed himself to the role, but changed his mind. Faced with non-talent as a replacement, Rossano Brazzi, and the fact that the Hollywood censorship board made him change the man from being homosexual to impotent, Mankiewicz simply let his subject matter get away from him.

December   The producer-director team of Seaton and Perlberg offered **The Bridges at Toko-Ri**, with Grace Kelly and William Holden, and in fact directed by Mark Robson. Based on the novel by James A. Michener, it was the first major movie about the Korean War (1950–53). Since Miss Kelly was getting prize projects on loan-out, she was irritated when MGM cast her in a simple jungle adventure, **Green Fire**. The dispute, though minor, was another fissure in the break-up of the star system. Meanwhile, since she was one of the half-dozen female stars with box-office clout, Metro promised to try harder. Spencer Tracy was about to leave MGM with whom he had been so long associated (Clark Gable had left earlier in the year) but he went out in glory, as a one-armed visitor, a man spending a **Bad Day at Black Rock**. The time is 1945 and the locals, like Robert Ryan, Ernest Borgnine, Lee Marvin, are either unhelpful or dangerous. John Sturges directed this classic of suspense.

Hollywood people were congregating in Europe, especially Britain. There were three reasons for this: lower production costs, and in Britain the added bonus of supporting players popular because of their exposure on American television (which was still denied major movies, except British ones); the increased preference for location-shooting over set-building; and, most importantly, the US Government had granted tax exemption on foreign earnings for anyone working out of the country for eighteen months or more. But this was not a mere question of self-interest or greed: the great age of air travel had just begun.

Stewart Granger returned to be a dreary **Beau Brummell** for MGM, which produced the first British film in CinemaScope, a pallid **Knights of the Round Table**, with Robert Taylor as Sir Lancelot, Ava Gardner as Guinevere and Mel Ferrer as Arthur. Paul Douglas arrived to play in one of Ealing's best comedies, **The 'Maggie'**, as an American travelling on a barge through Scotland with furniture for his new home. The film's real subject, though, as written by William Rose and directed by Alexander Mackendrick, is the triumph of local guile over American efficiency. This was the studio's only notable movie of the year.

The only movie of note from Korda's set-up was Launder and Gilliat's **The Belles of St Trinians**, which brought Ronald Searle's ghastly schoolgirls to the screen, with Joyce Grenfell and Alistair Sim in a dual role, as headmistress and her brother, a bookmaker. Despite their contributions, however, the humour was not subtle. Even more popular was **Doctor in the House**, with Dirk Bogarde, Kenneth More, Donald Sinden and Donald Huston as medical students in conventional bed-pan situations. Both films would have several sequels: it was a grim outlook for British comedy.

France's biggest international success was **Touchez Pas au Grisbi**, an underworld tale with Lino Ventura matching up to Jean Gabin, and Jeanne Moreau among the *gens du milieu*. The word *grisbi* (loot) passed briefly into the English language. Jacques Becker directed.

Outside Italy, Visconti's **Senso** was retitled **The Wanton Countess**, and as such received a few bookings. Later the world was to learn that the full-length Italian version was immeasurably better, a sensuous, beautiful movie about a tragic romance at the time of the Risorgimento, when a noblewoman, Alida Valli, betrays the cause and her husband for love of an Austrian officer, Farley Granger, who in turn betrays her.

In Mexico Buñuel got backing for a film in English with an American actor, Daniel O'Herlihy, and **The Adventures of Robinson Crusoe** was an impeccable version of Defoe's book, in colour. He also filmed another

great English novel, *Wuthering Heights*, which he had been hoping to do for years, but in this case the same backers forced compromises in the casting and insisted on the action being transferred to Mexico. The result, **Abismos de Pasión**, is fascinating. Everything that happens after Cathy's death is worthy of the original, though we may wonder how a protestant vicar's daughter might have reacted at seeing her tale transcribed to a subtropical climate, with crucifixes dominating every room in which the passions are played out.

Japan sent out a great movie, which for many years was also its most widely seen: **Seven Samurai**, Akira Kurosawa's spellbinding movie set in and around a small village, whose inhabitants hire a motley group of warriors to guard them against marauders. A very long film (3 hrs 10 mins), it seems to pass in seconds, and has the feel of the primitive epics. There are outstanding performances by Takashi Shimura as the leader and Toshiro Mifune as the braggadocio maverick. Japanese cinema was moving to its great flowering. Ichikawa's **The Heart**, based on the autobiographical novel by Soseki Matsume, is about a married professor realizing, in 1912, that his regard for one of his male students is more than that of teacher-and-pupil; and **An Inn at Osaka**, based on the novel by Takitaro Minakami, is Gosho's reflective study of the inhabitants of a hotel, most of whom are frustrated. Mizoguchi made three of his last films: **A Woman of Rumour**, about the madam of a geisha house whose much younger lover is drawn to her daughter; **Chikamatsu Monogatari**, about a couple who flee rather than have their adulterous love ended; and **Sansho the Bailiff**, which vies with **The Life of O'Haru** as the greatest Japanese historical film ever made – both explain the past while **Seven Samurai** exploits its legends.

February   A new era is born when, for $4,000, MGM buys a record which till then had passed unnoticed, and puts it with the title credits. That song was 'Rock Around the Clock', played and sung by Bill Haley and the Comets. The studio had never spent so little money for so large a return, for the mainly youthful spectators went back time and again. The film

1955

was **Blackboard Jungle**, written and directed by Richard Brooks from Evan Hunter's novel, with Glenn Ford as the new teacher facing up to the fact that every pupil in the school is delinquent. In many ways the film was more honest than most – another reason it endeared itself to its audience. Youth got a further insight into itself watching James Dean misbehaving in Elia Kazan's rather languid version of the first part of John Steinbeck's long novel, **East of Eden**: Cain and Abel relocated to a California valley.

March   **Run For Cover** had James Cagney getting besotted with John Derek. Nothing unnatural about this, because there was a lot of it about: teaming stars of the past with those of the present.

May   Monochrome films were a doomed species, but their cause was given a huge temporary fillip by **Marty**, put into production by Burt Lancaster's company as a prestige item and a hoped-for tax write-off. It had been a television play by Paddy Chayevsky, directed by

Above: Betsy Blair and Ernest Borgnine in **Marty**, the success of which was supposed to drive glamour and fantasy from the movies. It didn't happen. Right: James Dean, who died in an auto accident in September, was the **Rebel Without a Cause**, quarrelling with his parents and anyone else over the age of consent. Nicholas Ray directed this hyped-up, corny melodrama. It also made a star out of Natalie Wood.

Delbert Mann, who was invited to reprise for the film, which featured Ernest Borgnine as a pug-plain thirty-four-year-old butcher who decides to marry after meeting a passed-over spinster, Betsy Blair, at a hop in the Bronx. It won the Grand Prix at Cannes, was mightily Oscared and influential without being imitated. From **The Italian** to **Ladri di Biciclette** the best film-makers had opted for the 'real', and the second-best had sometimes copied them. What could not be copied was the authenticity of Chayevsky's dialogue: 'What 'ya doin' tonight, Marty?' 'I dunno, Ange, what' you feel like doin'?'

August   A masterpiece, and *sui generis*, unless you count its symbolic borrowings from Grimm, Disney and Dickens: **The Night of the Hunter**, the only film directed by Charles Laughton, written by James Agee from a novel by Davis Grubb. Robert Mitchum may play an itinerant preacher, but he's prepared to kill to get his hands on a small fortune. His victim is Shelley Winters, and since her kids have got what he wants, he pursues them through a dream-like West Virginia, becoming a nightmare as they shelter with a spunky old lady, Lillian Gish.

October   **Oklahoma!** finally lumbered onto the screen in Todd AO, another short-lived wide-screen system. Rodgers and Hammerstein, who were among its backers, had simply left it too long – there had been too many like it. Still, their score came up freshly, especially when sung by Gordon MacRae as the cowboy and Shirley Jones as his girl. Fred Zinnemann directed on Arizona! locations. Celeste Holm wants fiancé Frank Sinatra to name the day, but he wants to continue to play the field: **The Tender Trap**, directed by Charles Walters, isn't much funnier than **The Moon is Blue**, but together they ushered in a decade of semi-salacious comedies, almost all from Broadway, about the need of swinging bachelors to swing.

November   Joan Crawford is a **Queen Bee**, stinging everyone within reach, except an old lover: 'Any man's my man if I want it that way,' she boasts.

December   Two books provided the basis for Hollywood's new frankness: Lillian Roth's autobiography, **I'll Cry Tomorrow**, about her descent into dipsomania, and Nelson Algren's **The Man with the Golden Arm**, about a man living in a drug-induced hell. These were directed respectively by Daniel Mann for MGM, with Susan Hayward mistakenly doing her own singing, and by Otto Preminger for UA, with Frank Sinatra, who doesn't sing a note. There was a surprise with **Helen of Troy**. It had a weak Italian Helen and an even weaker French Paris, and a host of British stalwarts going about with names like Menelaus and Agamemnon, but it works, thanks to Robert Wise, designer Roger Furse

Above: **1984** was hastily filmed by Associated British after a BBC version of Orwell's book caused more comment than anything yet seen on television, including the Coronation. Edmond O'Brien was brought over for it. Opposite: **To Catch a Thief**: the best of the Hitchcocks with weak plots – but with Grace Kelly and Cary Grant looking gorgeous and views from the Haute Corniche, who cares about the plot?

and cinematographer Harry Stradling.

After almost a decade of lousy war movies the British (Associated British, in fact) produce one to stand honourably with the most honest and intense of the past: **The Dam Busters**, written by R. C. Sheriff (he of **Journey's End**) and starring Michael Redgrave and Richard Todd, respectively, as the man who invented a device to flood the dams of the Ruhr and Guy Gibson, who led the raid which dropped it.

There were some botched Anglo-American ventures – **The End of the Affair** and **I am a Camera**, but one transatlantic venture did work beautifully because of the conjunction of two wonders, a woman and a city: Katharine Hepburn as a spinster schoolteacher finding a late love affair while vacationing in Venice, with a married man (Rossano Brazzi) for whom she is just another passing fancy. The film was **Summer Madness** (US **Summertime**), based on a Broadway play by Arthur Laurents, directed by David Lean. Britain's other leading director, Carol Reed, made a miscalculation with his East End fable, **A Kid for Two Farthings** – but then, Powell and Pressburger filmed *Die Fledermaus* as **Oh Rosalinda**!!!, which had the distinction of opening at the same time as Herbert Wilcox's version of Ivor Novello's **King's Rhapsody**, with Anna Neagle and Errol Flynn. Thus

November was a black month for British musicals, a species most people avoided in the first place.

From Ealing came the glorious comedy **The Lady-killers**, directed by Alexander Mackendrick from a script by William Rose, about a gang of inept crooks planning a bullion robbery. Their plotting is done in the house of a dear old lady (Katie Johnson), who thinks they are playing chamber music. Alec Guinness plays their leader, with Cecil Parker and Peter Sellers among his followers. Laurence Olivier produced and directed the third of his Shakespeare films, **Richard III**, playing with wit and relish one of the Bard's most famous villains. There was also some equally clever playing among his distinguished cast: Ralph Richardson as Buckingham, John Gielgud as Clarence, Claire Bloom as the Lady Anne and Cedric Hardwicke as Edward IV. Both films marked the end of an era. **Richard III** was produced by Korda's London Films, an organization which folded on his death early in 1956: **The Ladykillers** was the last film under Ealing's contract with Rank, which would not renew unless given more control over content. Balcon indignantly took his unit to MGM, but the handful of films subsequently released by the company showed that the heart of Ealing had gone.

France had big international hits with two taut thrillers. Indeed, Clouzot's **Les Diaboliques** was much more than taut, being scary if not horrific, as a head teacher (Paul Meurisse) is gruesomely murdered by wife (Vera Clouzot) and mistress (Simone Signoret), both of whom are disconcerted to find that he might, after all, be alive. The detective is Charles Vanel. **Du Rififi chez les Hommes**, directed by Jules Dassin, who had settled in France, centred on a brilliant heist from a jeweller in the rue de la Paix.

In Italy, Antonioni returned with an adaptation of Pavese, **Le Amiche**, set among the smart set of Turin who have little to do but make love and trouble for each other.

In Mexico, Buñuel turned out his darkest, funniest and richest film yet, **Ensayo De Un Crimen** or **The Criminal Life of Archibaldo de La Cruze**. Archibaldo's life is a rake's progress and he has the wealth to indulge his fetishes, which include the purchase of a life-size doll after women prove unsatisfactory. He is, of course, a dead ringer for all that is evil in the bourgeoisie, as are the representatives of church, state and army, clearly about to orgasm as they discuss the rituals of ceremony.

In Sweden, Bergman was also preoccupied with the odd ways of humanity, and this too meant sex, which he regarded with the same combination of fascination and contempt as Buñuel. It is unlikely, though, that this latter sentiment is shared by his characters in **Smiles of a Summer Night**, who assemble at a house party at some time much earlier in this century and lightheartedly pursue it, sex that is, mostly with the wrong people.

In Japan, Mizoguchi made his first two films in colour, **Shin-Heike Monogatari** and **The Empress Yank Kwei-Fei**, both wondrous to look at, but without the weight of his other feudal tales. Kurosawa looked at what he called the problem of 'atomic extinction' in **I Live in Fear**, in which the family of an elderly foundry-owner, Mifune (with white hair), want him committed because he wants to emigrate to Brazil to escape death. It was not a success, because the Lear-like situation is examined technically but not emotionally. Gosho made the best Japanese film of the year, on **Marital Relations**, an ironic title since its subject is adultery and the relationship between siblings. No Western film had handled such matters with such perception.

Out of the East, however, another voice spoke, and it was an astonishing one. It belonged to Satyajit Ray, a Bengali blue-blood who had abandoned a career in advertising when, while posted to London, his lifelong interest in film had accelerated on seeing **Ladri di Biciclette**. That determined him to film a book he loved, **Pather Panchali**, the autobiography of Bibhuti Bhoshan Banerjee, a tale of a poverty-stricken childhood in a remote Indian village. A great humanist director had arrived and, as the young boy, Apu, looked at a train, wonder of wonders, across the fields, the cinema was changed irrevocably. A special prize at the Cannes Film Festival also helped.

February John Wayne was Genghis Khan in **The Conqueror**: see it and you still won't believe it. This was a favourite, expensive, project of Howard Hughes; it wasn't released till he had sold RKO, and its failure hastened the demise of the company.

1956

March Wayne again, going from his worst picture to his best: John Ford's **The Searchers**, a myth-like story of a cavalry officer on an odyssey to find the niece abducted by Indians years before; she's Natalie Wood and he's accompanied by her half-brother, Jeffrey Hunter.

June **The King and I** is **Anna and the King of Siam** (1946) remade, with the score Rodgers and Hammerstein provided for Broadway. As on that occasion, Yul Brynner is the king, irreplaceably (though few of his later performances would be half as good); Deborah Kerr is the governess. With **The Killing** Stanley Kubrick leapt to the forefront of contemporary directors; he also wrote the twisty screenplay, about the planning of a racetrack heist by some of the seediest characters ever to plan a racetrack heist: ex-con Sterling Hayden, ex-alcoholic Jay C. Flippen, bent cop Ted de Corsia and inside-men Joe Sawyer and Elisha Cook Jr.

Above: There were so many war movies in this period that you wondered whether the British weren't trying to make up for their loss of an empire by re-living their finest hour. **Reach For the Sky** was not the best of them, but Kenneth More was ideally cast as Douglas Bader. Right: **Baby Doll**, played by Carroll Baker, whose husband would respect her virginity, which would fall to another man.

August After many a plan, Tolstoy's **War and Peace** finally came to the screen, as an American-Italian co-production directed by King Vidor for Paramount. This particular novel, about the vicissitudes of a family and its friends during Bonaparte's invasion of Russia, could never be filmed except in reduced form, but as long as Audrey Hepburn is around, as Natasha, that doesn't matter. Henry Fonda, wrongly cast as Pierre, is still good value, but if others in the injudicious cast are better left unnamed, this is still entertaining, and a more than brave shot. Like Miss Hepburn, Miss Monroe could stun audiences into compliance, and not in this case, **Bus Stop**, by mere personality or looks. She acts touchingly, and as long as she's on screen this – William Inge's play, screenplayed by George Axelrod, directed by Joshua Logan – is first-rate stuff. She plays a third-rate (but could you ever forget her 'That Old Black Magic'?) chantoosie whom a simple-minded rodeo star (Don Murray) impulsively decides to marry. Which man wouldn't. No question mark.

September There were two from MGM, both directed by Minnelli, who was helping that studio to adulthood. **Tea and Sympathy**, from Robert Anderson's play about a student (John Kerr) confused about his masculinity because he has been cast as Lady Teazle in the school play, till his housemaster's wife (Deborah Kerr) shows him how to be a man – not that the piece was very frank about this. **Lust for Life**: Van Gogh in Arles and other places. Hollywood had tried and tried with the great European writers, musicians and artists, usually failing dismally. Kirk Douglas looked like the self-portraits, and for him and Minnelli this was clearly a labour of love, and not to be despised today. Anthony Quinn was Gauguin.

October The public flocked to producer Mike Todd's **Around the World in 80 Days**, directed by

Michael Anderson from Jules Verne's novel for UA, with David Niven as the intrepid traveller Phileas Fogg and the Mexican comic, Cantinflas, as his valet, plus a host of stars in cameo roles, including Noël Coward, Buster Keaton, Fernandel, Marlene Dietrich, Ronald Colman, Hermione Gingold, Beatrice Lillie, John Gielgud, Charles Boyer and Trevor Howard; and to DeMille's **The Ten Commandments**, which had another cluster of stars, notably Charlton Heston, who parted the Red Sea.

November A rock-and-roll singer, Elvis Presley, was singing up such a storm that Fox put him into a Western, **Love Me Tender**, supporting Richard Egan, whom Fox was publicizing as the new 'King of Hollywood', succeeding Clark Gable. No one believed the hype, least of all Fox. The film was made in monochrome. A month earlier, Fox had decided that **Teenage Rebel** (with Ginger Rogers as the rebel's mother) was too stark to command colour, but this one? With their claimant to king, and the man who would be king?

December Tennessee Williams drove like a rivet into the sex fantasies of this time – or, rather, Elia Kazan did, for he took two one-act plays by Williams and turned them into a movie with only minimal help from him. **Baby Doll** was condemned by the Legion of Decency, still unwilling to recognize that we are all sexual beings. The plot is basically one of revenge: Vacarro (Eli Wallach) wants to get even with Archie Lee (Karl Malden), so he decides to seduce the child-wife (Carroll Baker) whom Archie Lee has agreed not to 'touch' for a year. But Archie Lee is panting to, and Vacarro knows that his scheme will wound him more than anything. After he has executed his

Left: Deborah Kerr and Yul Brynner in **The King and I**, one of the prize Broadway properties filmed around this time – more successfully, many thought, with Walter Lang at the helm than those with more prestigious directors. Above: Jeremy Brett and Audrey Hepburn, Rostovs both in **War and Peace**. Every pitfall awaited this venture: a certifiably great book and an international cast, crew and creative team, but the producers Carlo Ponti and Dino De Laurentiis were rewarded with glowing notices and business to match. Opposite: Jeffrey Hunter, John Wayne and Ward Bond in **The Searchers**, directed by John Ford.

plan, it is clear that the guileless Baby Doll had never enjoyed anything as much in her life.

Britain's film industry was still fighting the War: the year's most popular film was **Reach for the Sky**, directed for Rank by Lewis Gilbert with a genuine feeling for banality, which is not to detract from Douglas Bader, the legless pilot who rejoined the RAF at the outset of war, or Kenneth More, who played him so cheerily.

Among the foreigners working in Britain were Ingrid Bergman (welcomed back to the fold) and Yul Brynner in **Anastasia**, directed by Anatole Litvak and based on a play about the claimant to the Russian Imperial throne. John Huston attempted the unfilmable, **Moby Dick**, with Gregory Peck as an inadequate Captain Ahab, but Oswald Morris's photography of seas and such memorably emulates old whaling prints.

In France, Robert Bresson returned to filming with **Un Condamné à Mort s'est Echappé**, based on André Devigny's reminiscences of his attempts to escape from a wartime jail. Also looking back – courageously, terrifyingly and harrowingly – was Alain Resnais's **Nuit et Brouillard**, which intercut colour footage of the German concentration camps as they are with newsreel footage of the period. This is an important document but, thankfully, a short. The most popular French film was **Et Dieu Créa la Femme...**, produced by Raoul J. Levy, who gave Roger Vadim his first chance to direct – a story they had written together as a vehicle for Vadim's wife, Brigitte Bardot. She is first glimpsed sunbathing naked, on her tummy, and as the camera surveys her, Vadim changed sex in the cinema for ever. It was so obviously an innocent shot, and she was such a child. She subsequently seduces almost every man in sight, including her brother-in-law on her wedding day. They called Bardot 'the sex kitten'. The Legion of Decency condemned her, and while those who went to **Baby Doll** disregarded its ban, even more so did the American art-house public, making this the most successful film yet to play at those theatres.

From Japan, Ichikawa's **The Burmese Harp** follows the fortunes of a POW who, making his way home in 1945, finds his life transformed after entering a Buddhist monastery. Few films have better expressed the futility of war. Another great film, from India, was **Aparajito** or **The Unvanquished**, from Satyajit Ray, which shows Apu coming to manhood in Benares and realizing that the only way to escape poverty is through education.

1957

I f there was any one year in which the American film industry changed, it was 1957. It forgot its simultaneous fear of and contempt for television, partly because it was selling its old films to the medium and partly because it knew that television's directors, writers and actors could inject new ideas into movies; they could also work more quickly and more cheaply than the old guard. Hollywood changed tack as traditional, expensive films went unheeded after being decried by the critics, who were increasingly relied upon to persuade the public to seek entertainment outside the living room. An exception was Elvis Presley. The critics didn't like him, nor the industry, but he saved MGM. His third film, **Jailhouse Rock**, was no better or worse than the first two, or those to come, all of which were low-budget efforts in keeping with Hollywood's view of him; but it wiped out the red ink in Metro's ledgers.

January **Edge of the City**, from television, edged the movies into its new era. MGM presented it, modestly rather than proudly, and Martin Ritt directed for the second time. Written by Robert Alan Aurthur and originally called *A Man is Ten Feet Tall*, it was a melodrama about corruption on the waterfront, as experienced by mixed-up John Cassavetes and black Sidney Poitier. While pernicious – if Cassavetes hadn't been a mental mess he would never have had a black for a pal – it was also wonderful, because of Sidney's sane, cheery disregard of that fact.

April There were three from television. John Frankenheimer arrives to direct **The Young Stranger**, Robert Dozier's drama that Frankenheimer had already prepared as a teleplay. James MacArthur has the title role,

a youngster whose relationship with his father spirals ever downwards after a minor fracas in a cinema. Everything that **Rebel Without a Cause** does badly, this does well. Another newcomer, Sidney Lumet, repeats **Twelve Angry Men**, Reginald Rose's television drama about a hung jury, chiefly notable for the acting. Henry Fonda is the man who starts the doubts growing, with E. G. Marshall, Jack Warden, Jack Klugman, Lee J. Cobb, Martin Balsam. And Delbert Mann directs Paddy Chayevsky's **The Bachelor Party**, with Don Murray as the man about to be married and Mr Marshall among the other four accountants enjoying a night on the town. Since it doesn't try as hard as **Marty**, it has dated less – indeed, not at all. Because it is also starless, low key and in monochrome, **The Strange One** might seem to be of this group, but in fact it comes from a stage adaptation of Calder Willingham's novel, *End as a Man*, about bullying in a military school. Again repeating are director Jack Garfein and actor Ben Gazzara, neither of whom fulfilled their promise on this occasion. Since the film has more than a hint of homosexuality, it's surprising to find Gazzara has a girl, Julie Wilson.

May It was a good month for Paramount: Burt Lancaster was Wyatt Earp and Kirk Douglas played Doc Holliday in John Sturges's superior Western, **Gunfight at the OK Corral**; and Audrey Hepburn was an ugly duckling Greenwich Village bookseller turned into a Paris model by photographer Fred Astaire – and you never saw a lovelier ugly duckling. Stanley Donen directed Leonard Gershe's book, to music by the Gershwins for an occasion as stylish as the stars, but perhaps a

Left: Bengt Ekerot and Max von Sydow in **The Seventh Seal**, with which Ingmar Bergman became the king of the world's art houses. Above: Alexei Batalov being carried by Vasily Merkurev in **The Cranes are Flying**. The US was still so scared of Communism that in their publicity Warners claimed that they were distributing it at the request of the State Department as part of a cultural exchange with the Soviet Union. They needn't have bothered: it was a good picture, liked by everybody, with no ideology. Opposite: Kirk Douglas, man of integrity in Kubrick's **Paths of Glory**.

little too chic: **Funny Face**. At Warners Andy Griffith was **A Face in the Crowd**, an itinerant singer who rises from local radio to national fame, but whose ambitions do not stop there. Kazan directs Budd Schulberg's satirical script, which is really about the misuse of power, and it hasn't dated a jot, with excellent performances by Patricia Neal as the reporter who discovers Griffith, Lee Remick as the drum majorette who throws herself at him and Walter Matthau as a cynical reporter.

June On the same theme was another hard-hitting, undated movie, **Sweet Smell of Success**, with Burt Lancaster as a Broadway columnist – a thinly-disguised Walter Winchell – and Tony Curtis as his boot-licking press agent. Screenplay was by Clifford Odets and Ernest Lehman, from the latter's story, and the film was directed by Alexander Mackendrick, who on this showing should have had a distinguished American career.

October Joanne Woodward was a surburban housewife for Fox in **No Down Payment**, an examination of four couples who lived in those lawn-infested places – which until now Hollywood had always presented as happy haunts for happy people. For the first time they were seen to have problems, financial and sexual, and the movie, directed by Martin Ritt, was a pungent one.

November MGM advised, with assistance from director Charles Walters: **Don't Go Near the Water**, and Glenn Ford agreed, as a sceptical young lieutenant. But he needn't have bothered, since the film was taken from him by Keenan Wynn, as a war correspondent glowing with his own self-importance, and bald-pated Fred Clark, a commanding officer who smiles but never exactly knows what he's doing. They're all, after a fashion, bringing democracy to a small Pacific island. In the Eisenhower era, when America was obsessed with reds under the beds and the possibility that the USSR might become the dominant partner in the Cold War, it was comforting to be reminded of the time when America was boss.

December Hollywood went serious – indeed, glum – on the related subject of the American Occupation of Japan, from James A. Michener's novel, **Sayonara**, the idea for which had been suggested to him by Joshua Logan, who lumberingly directs. A GI (Red Buttons) is given permission to marry a local girl (Myoshi Umeki), but she is not allowed to follow when he is repatriated so they enter into a suicide pact – which persuades the officer (Marlon Brando) who had been his best man to seek out the local girl with whom he has fallen in love. He had originally been a bigoted Southerner, indifferent to his American fiancée (Patricia Owns), who asks him whether

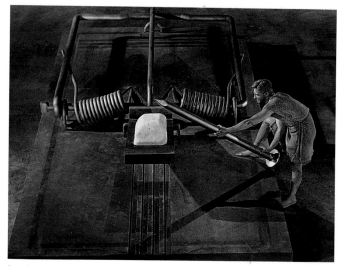

he has ever wanted to drag her back to some shack – dialogue which would have been unthinkable before **Baby Doll**. Such matters were the whole point of **Peyton Place**, which has a couple sending away for a manual in plain wrappers. 'Norman,' says the girl, 'it's time you knew girls want to do the same thing as boys.' It has a girl (Hope Lange) raped by her drunken stepfather (Arthur Kennedy), plus a frigid widow who was badly played by Lana Turner. The opportunist whole was brought to the screen by two respectable talents, producer Jerry Wald and director Mark Robson, and there was little the censor could do: Grace Metalious' autobiographical 'lifting the lid off' novel had been an enormous bestseller, and Peyton Place became a synonym for all small towns where passions heaved behind lace curtains.

World War I was the subject of **Paths of Glory**, in which a French unit mutinied rather than go over the top to face cannon and machine guns. Directed and written with passion by Stanley Kubrick from Humphrey Cobb's novel, the film's subject is primarily the blinkered mentality of the officer corps, chiefly represented by Adolphe Menjou and George Macready, who are unable to comprehend why colleague Kirk Douglas chooses to represent the defendants at the subsequent court martial. The film remains one of the finest achievements in Hollywood history.

At the time, it was completely overshadowed by an American film with British nationality, **The Bridge on the River Kwai**, directed by David Lean for Sam Spiegel and Columbia, with William Holden, Jack Hawkins, and Alec Guinness as a brave little officer who defies his

Opposite: The climax of **Gunfight at the OK Corral**, one of the two outstanding Westerns built around the relationship of Doc Holliday and Wyatt Earp. The other is John Ford's **My Darling Clementine** (1946). Above: Jack Arnold directed **The Incredible Shrinking Man** at Universal, from a story by Richard Matheson. Here's Grant Matthews doing battle with a spider. Right: Brigitte Bardot, known as the 'sex kitten', and a household name throughout the US after **And God Created Women** in 1957. Hollywood beckoned, but she resisted its blandishments. As she said, after she retired (in 1973), she simply did not enjoy stardom.

Japanese captors during the building of the Burmese railway. A spurious epic with all the old notions of the fighting spirit and the bravery of the British, it made a few genuflections towards War Being a Bad Thing. Much to-do was also raised by **Island in the Sun**, forerunner of **Peyton Place** for Fox, based on Alec Waugh's bestseller, written again for the screen by respected Alfred Hayes and directed by Robert Rossen. The issue of the novel was the manner of self-government on a Caribbean island after the British have withdrawn; what was foremost in the film was a landlord (James Mason) who takes to rape and murder, and two inter-racial romances. Since that between Dorothy Dandridge and John Justin was mainly talk, few eyebrows were raised; what caused the outcry was that Harry Belafonte (playing a political activist) actually had a clinch with Joan Fontaine.

The best British film of the year was **The Smallest Show on Earth**, an affectionate and funny comedy about a London fleapit movie-house, with Virginia McKenna and Bill Travers as its young owners, with Margaret Rutherford, Bernard Miles and Peter Sellers comprising its antique staff. Basil Dearden directed William Rose's script for producers Launder and Gilliat. The Boulting Brothers' **Lucky Jim** has Ian Carmichael in the title role, an accident-prone professor thumbing his nose at the conventions of university life. The pretensions, complacency and pomposity of Kingsley Amis's characters remain; but the Boultings chiefly offer tomfoolery for wit. It was not a great book, but it was one of the literary artefacts of this time that changed Britons' perceptions of themselves. There were too many people in the British industry, like the Boultings, determined that such revelations should not get into films.

France's biggest international success was Jules Dassin's **Celui Qui Doit Mourir**, based on Kazantzaki's novel, *Christ Recrucified*, set in Greece in 1921, when people fleeing Turkish domination are welcomed only by those rehearsing the annual Passion play. These include Pierre Vaneck as the shepherd playing Christ and Melina Mercouri as the Magdelene.

In Italy, Antonioni's harsh, bitter **Il Grido** was shot on location in the bleakest part of the Po delta. It is about a drifter, Steve Cochran, a refinery worker shocked into drifting when the woman (Alida Valli) with whom he lives tells him she plans to marry another man.

Japan sent out **Throne of Blood**, Kurosawa's visually and aurally stunning version of *Macbeth*, with Toshiro Mifune in that role. It increased the country's movie-making reputation even more than **Seven Samurai**. Masaki Kobayashi's aptly named **Black River** is a dark comedy about the inhabitants of a flophouse and their inter-relations with a gang boss (Tatsuya Nakadai); and Gosho's **Elegy of the North**, set among the bright young set of a coastal town in Hokkaido, which centres on one girl whose meddling proves fatal.

From Greece, Cacoyannis' best film, **A Matter of Dignity**, is an unblinking satire on an Athenian family hoping the daughter (Elli Lambetti) can latch onto the scion of a wealthy family before he learns how little money they really have. From the Soviet Union, and the first film for a long time from this country to be widely seen outside, was Mikhail Kalatozov's **The Cranes are Flying**, about the exploits of one girl (Tatiana Samoilova) during the War and just afterwards. From Argentina came the first of Leopoldo Torre-Nilsson's baroque movies to be known abroad: **La Casa del Angel**, the study of a lonely, dreamy senator's daughter (Elsa Daniel) in the 1920s, who has an affair with one of her father's colleagues.

From Sweden, Ingmar Bergman's **The Seventh Seal** recounted the adventures of a knight (Max von Sydow) returning from a crusade and playing chess with Death (Bengt Ekerot). It was heavily symbolic, with a theme with which we will grow familiar: a quest for the nature of God. The film makes Bergman's international reputation, but many people prefer the warmer and less schematic **Wild Strawberries**, in which an aged professor (Victor Sjöström) reflects on his life past and present – and on death – as he journeys across the country, visiting the family home *en route*. Ingrid Thulin is the daughter-in-law who accompanies him; Bibi Andersson has a dual role as a hitchhiker to whom he gives a lift and his first love; and von Sydow has a small role as a garage attendant.

(From left to right) E. G. Marshall, Henry Fonda, Lee J. Cobb, Edward Binns, Jack Klugnam (at the back), George Voskovec, Joseph Sweeney and (with his back to the camera) Martin Balsam in **Twelve Angry Men**.

1958

March Two musicals, a mountain and a mouse. **South Pacific**, from Rodgers and Hammerstein's show, had a wonderful score, a funny comment or so on the wartime Navy and some decent ones on race relations as a lieutenant (John Kerr) falls for a Polynesian maiden (France Nuyen). Both roles are inadequately cast, but not as much as the two leads, the nurse (Mitzi Gaynor) who falls for an ageing French plantation owner (Rossano Brazzi). Even more at sea is director Joshua Logan, whose idea it was to pop a colour filter into the camera every time anyone feels a song coming on. There were some real talents: Nat 'King' Cole, Eartha Kitt, Ella Fitzgerald, Mahalia Jackson, Pearl Bailey and Cab Calloway, in the story of W. C. Handy, who wrote the **St Louis Blues**, but the film had a B-budget. Fox should be ashamed of the first; Paramount of the second.

June You don't expect Hollywood to excel at **The Vikings**, but it's equally as good as that 1955 expedition to the Trojans, with the same feeling for primitive epic and, in this case, the sea. Richard Fleischer directed for Kirk Douglas, who plays the lead; Tony Curtis, Earnest Borgnine and Janet Leigh support.

Ingrid Bergman's restored popularity is confirmed in two British pictures: Donen's slight comedy, **Indiscreet**, in which she and Cary Grant spend several reels pretending they don't want to marry; and Mark Robson's **The Inn of the Sixth Happiness**, in which she plays

Gladys Aylward, missionary in China during its war-torn years (Robert Donat made his last screen appearance, as a kindly local despot). Other Americans around included John Ford directing **Gideon's Day**, a Scotland Yard tale with Jack Hawkins, which was unique inasmuch as Columbia released it in colour in Britain and black and white in the US; and William Holden in Carol Reed's flawed but fascinating movie **The Key**, which Trevor Howard hands to Holden, believing him to be the next of a long line of naval officers wanting to sleep with Sophia Loren. She wasn't too pleased about this, but the film did advance the cause of sex in the cinema, because it was the first to demonstrate that nice people could be promiscuous, too.

West Germany sent out two films just above its low average, but both of them are historically important. Rolf Thiele's **Das Mädchen Rosemarie** was based on the case of a Frankfurt callgirl who, when found murdered, was revealed to have been blackmailing her powerful clientele. Kurt Hoffman's **Wir Wunderkinder** is a cabaret-style history of the country from 1913 to the present, featuring an anti-Nazi wimp and a shady friend who prospers under the Nazis and even more during the economic miracle, Germany's recovery. This recovery is the true subject of the first film, for Rosemarie could not have flourished had there not been so much money about.

Left: Ernest Borgnine, Janet Leigh and Kirk Douglas in **The Vikings**, one of only two Hollywood pictures about The Dark Ages – since the coming of Talkies anyway. The other, **The War Lord** (1965), is also outstanding. Above: Hitchcock's **Vertigo** concerns an ex-cop, James Stewart, making-over brunette Kim Novak into the blonde Novak he had failed to prevent being killed. Opposite: **Cat on a Hot Tin Roof**, from Tennessee Williams' play, which is jointly about Big Daddy dying of cancer and the son who won't sleep with his wife. Paul Newman is fine as the son, Elizabeth Taylor is not, as his wife.

There were a fair number of masterpieces elsewhere. Japan had an incredible year with Kurosawa's **The Hidden Fortress**, an energetic adventure yarn with Toshiro Mifune escorting a princess and some treasure through hostile territory; Tadashi Imai's **Night Drum**, like **Rashomon**, an investigation into the nature of truth, with a court official (Rentaro Mikuni) unwilling to believe that his beloved wife has been unfaithful in his absence; Gosho's beautiful, complex **The Fireflies**, a study of the inhabitants of an inn as the country leaves its feudal period; and Ichikawa's **Conflagration**, based on a novel by Mishima in turn based on an actual incident when a student priest with an inferiority complex burned down

the Golden Pavilion temple in Kyoto to get even with the world. Most of these were in wide screen which, in the tradition of scrollpainting, the Japanese were using with a virtuosity unequalled elsewhere.

In Sweden, Bergman made his most Shakespearean film, **Ansiktet** (GB, **The Face**; US, **The Magician**), concerning the leader (Max von Sydow) of a troupe of strolling players trying to decide whether he is a charlatan, a seeker after the truth, or a monster. The film is quite terrifying, in a Grand Guignol manner.

In India, Ray completed the Apu trilogy with **The World of Apu**, which manages the considerable feat of being even better than its predecessors. After losing his

wife, Apu deserts his son to go on an expedition, which is to explore himself as much as the vast subcontinent. The adult Apu is played by Soumitra Chatterjee, who would become to Ray what von Sydow was to Bergman – his favourite interpreter and alter-ego.

In Poland, Wajda had found someone similar in Zbigniew Cybulski, which may be why **Ashes and Diamonds** is by far the most haunting and compelling of what became known as his 'war' trilogy. It takes place as the War ends, in Warsaw, with Cybulski as a Resistance worker not knowing where to turn for a new cause.

Italy did not produce anything of this quality, but two movies stand out: Mario Monicelli's delightful and

influential **I Soliti Ignoti** (GB, **Persons Unknown**; US, **Big Deal on Madonna Street**), a comedy about a gang of incompetent crooks planning a heist; and Francesco Rosi's debut feature, **Il Sfida**, a melodrama about corruption among the local wholesalers.

In France, Gerard Philipe was in Autant-Lara's **Le Joueur** with Françoise Rosay, adapted by Bost and Aurenche from Dostoevsky. Autant-Lara was not one of the directors liked by the vociferous critics of the magazine *Cahiers du Cinéma*, who would themselves soon enter movies in a challenging way and, with their first films would change cinema, though most of their subsequent movies would not stand up as well as the least of those of Autant-Lara. They would be called the *nouvelle vague* or 'new wave', and lumped among them was Louis Malle, who had been assistant to Jacques-Yves Cousteau, the underwater documentary director. Malle's own first feature is a true precursor of the movement. It stars Jeanne Moreau (Malle's mistress at the time), its favourite actress; and it features extensive Paris locations photographed by Henri Decae, its favoured cinematographer. **Ascenseur pour l'Echafaud** (GB, **Lift to the Scaffold**; US, **Frantic**) is a good film in its own right, a thriller about a killer (Maurice Ronet) trapped in a lift while about to retrieve some incriminating evidence. Moreau is both his victim's wife and his lover. She and Jean-Marc Bory were **Les Amants**. She was a bored wife and he a friend of friends staying the night. On a whim, perhaps, they couple, and continue to do so in the garden, in the bath, in his room. Malle's approach is erotic but also lyrical – one reason why the censorship boards of most countries passed it. They didn't realize that they had opened the flood gates.

Left: Three films established Satyajit Ray as one of the great humanist directors and they comprise what we usually call the Apu trilogy. The last of them, **The World of Apu** is, if anything, even richer and denser than the first two, and it was incomparably acted by Soumitra Chatterjee and Sharmilla Tagore. Above: Another trilogy, the 'war' trilogy, was completed in 1958. The first two films are uneven, but **Ashes and Diamonds** is unquestionably a masterpiece; and it made Zbigniew Cybulski an international name.

1959

March Billy Wilder's glorious **Some Like It Hot** was one of the funniest movies yet made. Jack Lemmon and Tony Curtis are two musicians who drag up and join an all-girls' band after witnessing the St Valentine's Day Massacre. They meet Marilyn Monroe, and Curtis can only woo her by putting on pants and pretending to be a millionaire. Joe E. Brown, who is wealthy, dances with Lemmon, and then the gangsters turn up ... Audrey Hepburn plays Rima the bird girl in **Green Mansions** with Tony Perkins (ridiculous as a treasure-seeker); directed by her husband, Mel Ferrer, it only proves that W. H. Hudson's novel is unfilmable. She turned down George Stevens' offer of **The Diary of Anne Frank** because of her own memories of living in the Netherlands during the Occupation, but without her – with Millie Perkins, a former model – it's not far from disaster, despite the appropriately sober approach.

April **It Happened to Jane** at Columbia has Doris Day as a lobster-farmer, Jack Lemmon as her lawyer boyfriend and the magnificent Ernie Kovacs as the railroad proprietor she sues because he closes down her branch line. Richard Quine directed on sunny Maine locations, and the whole is just dandy, like the best comedies of the 1930s – which was what producer Ross Hunter intended with **Pillow Talk**, a salacious comedy with Day and Rock Hudson, to come out in October. Ironically, Quine's film failed, while the Hunter film led to several others depressingly like it.

June Audrey Hepburn appears in a class movie,

Zinnemann's **The Nun's Story**, from Kathryn Hulme's autobiographical novel about a novice who, in the end, does not have sufficient faith. Zinnemann approaches his subject with respect but not piety, allowing us to make up our own minds about the philosophy of the convent system. Peggy Ashcroft and Edith Evans play mothers superior far more bigoted than they think; Peter Finch plays a doctor Hepburn meets in the Belgian Congo.

July In **Anatomy of a Murder** Preminger uses words not then used in movies, on the grounds that the novel – by a judge under a pseudonym – had been a bestseller. A lieutenant (Ben Gazzara) is on trial for shooting the man who raped his wife (Lee Remick).

September **That Kind of Woman** said a mouthful. 'I'm kept by a very rich man,' says Sophia Loren as she seduces GI Tab Hunter. Naturally he falls in love. The man is a Washington big shot, played by George Sanders in one of the first 'also starring' roles, listed under the title. Due to Loren and Sidney Lumet's handling, it seems better than it is. King Vidor's **Solomon and Sheba** was a more punchy Biblical than usual, but not when either monarch is on screen: Yul Brynner (who replaced Tyrone Power, who died during shooting) and Gina Lollobrigida. The film passed virtually unnoticed.

Left: Francois Trauffaut established himself as a major talent with his stunning feature debut, the autobiographical **Les Quatre Cents Coups**, with Jean-Pierre Léaud. Above: Laurence Harvey and Simone Signoret in **Room at the Top**, based on John Braine's mediocre novel. The film was much praised and was a big box-office hit. Opposite: 'Nobody's perfect' became the most famous last line in movie history. It's an ironic finish because **Some Like it Hot** is as close to perfection as any comedy ever made. The reasons, beyond the screenplay by Billy Wilder and I. A. L. Diamond: Marilyn Monroe, Jack Lemmon and Tony Curtis.

November **Ben Hur**, on the other hand, started runs of several months in several cities, while not being noticeably more lively – though the chariot race is as exciting as the one in the 1925 version. Nothing else is, but the results and the fistful of Oscars were handy to MGM which, in a parlous state, had thrown everything they'd got into this, including a handsome fee to William Wyler. Charlton Heston was Ben, Stephen Boyd his boyhood friend, now his foe, and Jack Hawkins a Roman officer.

British movies had been transformed by 'Free Cinema', a movement which amounted to less than a handful of films, all shorts and unseen outside London's National Film Theatre and a few independents foolish enough to book them. These were made by people scornful of the complacency of the British industry, aware of the documentary tradition, but knowing that the only figure of importance in it was Humphrey Jennings. Just as his films caught a particular time, so did these, perhaps the best of which was Karel Reisz's fifty-two-minute **We are the Lambeth Boys**, about a South London youth club.

Meanwhile, there was the untalented Laurence Harvey. His decade in movies, some of them in Hollywood, could not have happened if he had not a lover, James Woolf, who was also a film producer. Woolf brought John Braine's bestselling novel, **Room at the Top**, as a starring vehicle for Harvey, and assigned director Jack Clayton, whose credits as a producer (he had directed one short) showed no indication that he would change the British

film industry. Nor was Braine's bestselling book anything more than a sub-Orwell text about an ambitious climber who pushes his mistress aside in order to marry the boss's daughter. Seen today, it is loud, obvious, pushy, its only virtue being Simone Signoret as the mistress (English in the novel). She was much praised and became the first actress to win a Best Actress Oscar for a foreign film.

Meanwhile, there was John Osborne, a former actor whose play **Look Back in Anger** had transformed British theatre in 1956. It wasn't a good play – the plot derived from **A Streetcar Named Desire** – but it hated the Establishment, which was a Good Thing in 1956. Suddenly, the cobwebs were swept away, and whatever the nonsense talked about 'angry young men', the play's protagonist, Jimmy Porter, was their leader. Osborne decided that the film version should be directed, as on stage, by Tony Richardson. Associated British decided to give them a deal provided that Porter was played by Richard Burton, who had achieved little of consequence after a decade alternating between Hollywood and the Old Vic. Richardson, influenced by Free Cinema, filmed on location and with natural sound. Burton, faced with his first movie role of merit, attacks it like a lion, ably supported by Mary Ure as his abused wife and Claire Bloom as her best friend, who despises Jimmy but surrenders to him immediately Ure is out of the picture. With its gritty portrait of Britain in 1959, **Look Back in Anger** was everything that **Room at the Top** would like to have been.

In France the *nouvelle vague* had a false dawn – a draggy, bucolic drama, **Le Beau Serge**, with Jean-Claude Brialy as a student who, returning to his native village,

Left: There were two things the British cinema had never been very good at: sex and the working class. That was to change with **Look Back in Anger**, starring Mary Ure, Richard Burton and Claire Bloom. Above: Audrey Hepburn, believable and magical in **The Nun's Story**. Zinnemann directed. Opposite: Rouben Mamoulian had directed the Gershwins' tragic folk opera, **Porgy and Bess**, on stage in 1935, but Goldwyn fired him from the film after a few days shooting, replacing him with Otto Preminger – which was a mistake. The film tells of the crippled Porgy, played by Sidney Poitier, and Bess, Dorothy Dandridge.

finds that his old friend, Gerard Blain, is a consumptive and a drunk. There was no indication that critic Claude Chabrol had learnt much from a life of watching movies, nor when he directed a thriller, **A Double Tour**, later in the year. But in the meantime, he came up with **Les Cousins**, a totally amoral tale about a country mouse, Blain, who in Paris is spectacularly caught up in Brialy's world of parties, booze and sex. The Paris of movies had never been as decadent before, nor as lovingly photographed. The freshness of Chabrol's approach was surpassed by his *Cahiers* colleague, François Truffaut, in his first feature, **Les Quatre Cents Coups**, an autobiographical tale of an unwanted child (Jean-Paul Léaud) who turns to mild crime and ends up in a reform school. This was shown at the Cannes Film Festival, along with **Hiroshima, Mon Amour**, directed from a screenplay by Marguerite Duras by Alain Resnais, his first feature, and **Orfeu Negro**, directed by Marcel Camus, his second. The first concerns a romance between a French actress (Emmanuele Riva) with a local man (Eiji Okada) while in Japan, with flashbacks to her disgrace for having loved a German soldier; the second, in blazing colour with a score by Antonio Carlos Jobim and Luis Bonfa, is a retelling of the Orpheus story in Rio at carnival time. Resnais was to make many more remarkable films, but not Camus (though this one breasts the years splendidly). The two films have nothing in common beyond a sensuality new to the cinema – in say, the way the camera plays on the naked bodies in the opening scene of Resnais' films, and in the gyrating bodies of the carnival.

In Italy, after his unremarkable film about young married couples, **Giovani Mariti** (1958), Mauro Bolognini made **La Notte Brava**, written by Pier Paolo Pasolini. Its resemblence to **Les Cousins** is not incidental. Disillusioned, aimless youth is the subject common to both films, and quick, easy sex – which in this case includes Laurent Terzieff accepting money from a wealthy young homosexual who has invited him back to his home.

From Argentina came two films by Torre-Nilsson: **La Caida** and **Fin de Fiesta**, both about the pain and misery of entering the adult world. The first is set in a town, the second in the country, respectively about a girl lodging with some children disinclined to bury their mother and a boy realizing that his grandfather, a senator, is the centre of a web of corruption. In Mexico, Buñuel made his greatest film, **Nazarin**, a rich and complex narrative – from the nineteenth-century novel by Benito Pérez Galdós – of a priest (Francisco Rabal) whose humility is so complete that he is regarded with contempt both by the fat cats of the church and the poor whose lot he seeks to share.

Elsewhere, the war was being relived. In Poland,

Wajda directed **Lotna**, set in 1939 when a cavalry unit attacked German tanks. In West Germany, Bernard Wicki directed **Die Brücke**. Set in 1945, it was the story of young conscripts guarding a bridge, and one of the few German films to confront defeat. In the USSR, Grigori Chukhrai directed **Ballad of a Soldier**, the adventures of same as he travels to visit his mother.

In Japan, Ichikawa's **Kagi** or **The Key** is a black comedy about a young doctor (Tatsuya Nakadai) swept into circumstances he can't control when his prospective father-in-law suggests that he sleep with his wife. Ichikawa followed it with the extraordinary **Fires on the Plain**, the odyssey of one soldier in the Philippines, in defeat in 1945. This theme would be taken up by Masaki Kobayashi in Part III of **The Human Condition**, which we shall look at in 1961 when the trilogy is complete. But you may be only part-way through Part I (1959) when you're aware that you're watching the greatest film ever made.

The age of television had finally arrived. Cinemas began shutting. Production in Hollywood was decreasing rapidly, with the major studios offering an average of one movie a month, plus another half-dozen or so bought – mainly from Britain and Italy – to keep their distribution offices busy.

1960

John Sturges, who had made half a dozen good Westerns, now came out with an outstanding one, **The Magnificent Seven**, a reworking of **Seven Samurai** with Yul Brynner, Steve McQueen, James Coburn, Charles Bronson, *et al*, with Eli Wallach in fine form as the bandit leader. John Huston made his first Western and re-thought the genre, for not till **The Unforgiven** did any film show the vastness of the territories, the loneliness, the distances. The story, that of Indians trying to reclaim Audrey Hepburn, raised by Lillian Gish alongside Burt Lancaster and Audie Murphy, reverses that of **The Searchers**, which was also by Alan le May.

Another director on fine form was Billy Wilder with **The Apartment**, a prime comedy with a melancholy edge. Jack Lemmon plays a lowly office schmuck who lends his apartment to his superior for trysts, only to find that one of them, Fred MacMurray, is using it for the lift-girl he's getting a crush on, Shirley MacLaine. It was the year's best film. The public enjoyed it in large numbers, and similar crowds were terrified during Hitchcock's **Psycho**, when Janet Leigh is knifed in the shower of a run-down motel run by a twitchy Anthony Perkins. There's more to it than that, though.

Hollywood was changing and two films proved it: the first male nude (from behind – Anthony Perkins) in a college comedy with Jane Fonda (her first film), **Tall Story**, directed by Joshua Logan; and Hollywood's last quaint London in **Midnight Lace**, a thriller in which Doris Day is convinced that husband Rex Harrison is trying to murder her.

The most significant event in American cinema in 1960 happened in London's National Film Theatre, when it premiered **Shadows**. The actor John Cassavetes, tired of Hollywood banalities, had gathered money from friends to direct, on New York locations, a partly improvised movie about race relations. It's about three siblings: Hugh Hurd sings with a jazz band, Ben Carruthers hangs out with white buddies; and light-skinned Leila Goldoni loses her virginity to a man who doesn't know she's black, a daring scene for the time. The Academy, a London art cinema, welcomed the film, where it ran for months, as it did throughout Europe. New York gave it short shrift when it opened there in 1961, but the industry recognized a vital talent and flirted with Cassavetes as a director. He later worked independently, without achieving much success either artistically or commercially; but the young film-makers who saw **Shadows**, raw and jagged, knew that there was no going back. As with the *nouvelle vague*. The fact that they came at the same time was merely coincidental.

Britain was much entertained by the battle of the Oscars. Robert Morley had played Wilde in 1936, in a club theatre, and in the more relaxed climate – Wilde's homosexuality could now be acknowledged – had decided

Left: Jack Lemmon in **The Apartment**, the idea of which came to Billy Wilder when he considered the assignment in the borrowed flat in **Brief Encounter** and wondered about the man who owned it. Above: In Italy, Antonioni was changing the language of movies, but in a very different way from the young French directors: Monica Vitti and Gabriele Ferzetti in **L'Avventura**. Opposite: Anita Ekberg in Fellini's **La Dolce Vita**.

that there was a film in the playwright. It was to be backed by Warwick, a production company run by two Americans, Harry Saltzman and Albert 'Cubby' Broccoli, who specialized in making cruddy movies starring American names. A number of these had been directed by Ken Hughes, and suddenly it was all systems go, with Hughes making **The Trials of Oscar Wilde** for Warwick with Peter Finch and Fox agreeing to release **Oscar Wilde** with Morley, directed by Gregory Ratoff. The latter opened first, by five days, in Fox's London showcase; the best that Warwick could do, despite the advantage of both Technicolor and CinemaScope, was a West End arthouse. *Nolo contendere* as James Mason said (in fact, after reading critics wrongly claiming that Ralph Richardson's defence counsel was superior to his). **Trials** has it over no-trials, though both films work up a storm because of the sheer drama of the whole business.

Laurence Olivier played Archie Rice, **The Entertainer**, a seedy music hall comic, which had been one of his greatest triumphs on stage. John Osborne wrote it, and, as with **Look Back in Anger**, it was to re-unite producer Saltzman and director Tony Richardson for Woodfall. It was to première at Rank's flagship Odeon till someone told a high-up at Rank that it was an allegory of the decline of Britain; the première was cancelled and it

went out on the lesser of the two Rank circuits in summer. Playing Archie's children in the film were Joan Plowright (who became Lady Olivier), Alan Bates and, in a brief role, Albert Finney. Woodfall backed Karel Reisz when he wanted to make **Saturday Night and Sunday Morning**, written by Alan Sillitoe from his own novel. Finney starred as a Nottingham factory worker having an affair with a married woman (Rachel Roberts) when a nice girl (Shirley Ann Field) decides to marry him. It was by far the most authentic picture of British working-class life, and after the critics told the public so, it became a huge success. The British cinema would never be the same again.

French cinema had changed irrevocably; every movie buff everywhere was talking about the *nouvelle vague* and especially about Jean-Luc Godard, whose **A Bout de Souffle** (aka **Breathless**) was even more free-wheeling than what had gone before. Largely improvised on the streets of Paris, it had little more to offer than a relationship between an aimless, amoral young hood, Jean-Paul Belmondo, and an American girl, Jean Seberg, who hawked the *New York Herald Tribune* on the Champs-Elysées. It was enough, and still is: the years haven't dimmed its freshness. Time has been equally kind to Truffaut's second feature, **Tirez Sur le Pianiste**, based on an American pulp thriller, its action transposed to France, about mob betrayal and revenge, starring Charles Aznavour as the unsuspecting pianist of the title; to Chabrol's mordant black comedy, **Les Bonnes Femmes** – four assistants in a dry-goods store near the Place de la

Left: **Spartacus**, from Howard Fast's novel, was directed by Stanley Kubrick as a favour to Kirk Douglas, producer and star, for having helped him set up **Paths of Glory**. This epic of Rome's gladiator days snared a number of major talents, including Charles Laughton, Peter Ustinov and (illustrated) Laurence Olivier and Jean Simmons. Above: Jean-Paul Belmondo and Jean Seberg in Godard's **A Bout de Souffle**. Opposite: Anthony Perkins as the proprietor of the Bates Motel in **Psycho**. Hitchcock saw the film as a new departure – horror – never dreaming that many future movie-makers would institute a series of 'slasher' pictures.

Bastille; and to Louis Malle's jokey, irreverent **Zazie dans le Metro**, based on Raymond Queneau's comic novel about – if it's about anything at all – the relationship between a young hetero female impersonator (Philippe Noiret) and his precipitately mature niece.

Sweden had a big international success with **Mein Kampf**, a life of Hitler made up from newsreel footage by Erwin Leiser, a refugee from Germany. It is simple and it is overpowering: you may see this movie and still not understand that it could have happened.

The year's biggest international movie was from Greece, in English, **Never on Sunday**, directed by Jules Dassin with Melina Mercouri (whom he married). Sunny Athens and the score by Manos Hadjidakis unquestionably helped, but the public treasured the film because its hooker heroine wasn't remotely ashamed of what she did for a living – only she never did it on Sunday.

Sea and sex were also vital ingredients in a very different film. From the Soviet Union, **The Lady with the Little Dog** was directed by Josif Heifitz from a short story by Chekhov, and set in Yalta during the summer. A dog-owning lady (Iya Savvina) and a Moscow banker (Alexei Batalov) are married, but not to each other. They decide to go to bed together, and the scene in which they do so may be the most delicately handled seduction in all movie history.

The cinema of sensitivity was also wonderfully served by Satyajit Ray with **Devi** or **The Goddess**, a many-textured film about a young wife (Sharmila Tagore) who comes to believe that she is the reincarnation of the goddess Kali, to the consternation of her husband (Soumitra Chatterjee) who, till then, had believed that he was the master of all things rational.

In Japan, Naruse's **When a Woman Ascends the Stairs** is the study of a Ginza bar hostess; Shiro Toyoda's **Twilight Story** the study of a novelist examining the red light district. Tomu Uchida's striking **Killing in Yoshiwara** deals with similar matters, but back in feudal times and with a magnificent climactic duel; and Kurosawa's cool, cunning **The Bad Sleep Well** transposes the plot of *Hamlet* into the corrupt world of big business.

The whole world was being stunned by Fellini's statement about **La Dolce Vita** on the via Venato. It is trivial and exaggerated as it looks at some Roman whores and pleasure lovers through the eyes of a jaded journalist, Marcello Mastroianni. Despite its length (173 minutes) and air of self-importance, it was in fact only mildly received until the Americans went mad for it, presumably on the grounds that they, discovering tourism, now had it proved to them that old Europe was as decadent as they had always suspected.

Equally ambitious, Visconti's **Rocco e i Suoi Frat-**elli (**Rocco and his Brothers**) offered a similar view of Italian society – in this case a Southern family which had settled in Milan. This is melodrama masquerading as tragedy, unbelievably cast with Alain Delon as the noble Rocco: but it is his brother, Simone, played by Renato Salvatori, who gets most of Visconti's attention. He seduces Rocco's boss (Suzy Delair); rapes Rocco's girl (Annie Girardot), a prostitute, while friends hold Rocco down; murders her with a flick-knife; and accepts cash from a gay boxing impresario (Roger Hanin) who lusts after him.

The disenchantment of both films is superficial, but disenchantment is the key to understanding the protagonist of Antonioni's **L'Avventura**, as he, Gabriele Ferzetti, comes to realize in the final reel. The film begins as a mystery story: Ferzetti's girlfriend has disappeared on one of the Lipari islands. As he searches for her, he is drawn to her best friend, Monica Vitti, but they search ever inwards, into themselves, in images provided by the director, often without words. It is Antonioni's masterpiece and one of the milestones in cinema history.

Mike Todd had died in a plane crash in 1958. He had been one of the industry's new players – one of the few known to the public since Hollywood's heyday: he had made sure of that. Others to be reckoned with in that respect were DeMille, who died in 1959, and Hitchcock, who had achieved even greater fame since introducing his half-hour television series in

1961

1955. Samuel Bronston and Joseph E. Levine had now joined the line-up: whether they cared that the public knew who they were is immaterial. Both ensured that the public had heard of their films. In 1955 an American muscle man, Steve Reeves, went to Italy to star in what became known as the 'sand-and-sandle' movies. In 1960 Joseph E. Levine bought one of these cutprice epics, rechristened it **Hercules Unchained**, and spent a fortune promoting it. It paid off.

The industry was gripped by road show fever, partly because it had to get it right. To raise the prices and invite bookings for two shows a day could only be disastrous if the public didn't care and didn't come. But the notion paid off handsomely with **West Side Story**, officially directed by Jerome Robbins (as on Broadway, though he only shot the electrifying opening sequence; but he planned and rehearsed the musical numbers, written by Leonard Bernstein and Stephen Sondheim) and Robert Wise. Today this *Romeo and Juliet* of gang warfare is dangerously heavy, and those two roles are undercast with Natalie Wood and Richard Beymer.

Other examples of 1961 gigantesque include Stanley Kramer's **Judgment at Nuremberg**, overcast with Spencer Tracy, Burt Lancaster, Marlene Dietrich, Richard Widmark, Maximilan Schell and, in cameo roles as witnesses at the trials, Judy Garland and Montgomery Clift. Also expensive was **One-Eyed Jacks**, a wonderfully authentic-looking Western directed by Marlon Brando (who took over from Stanley Kubrick), with himself masochistically vowing to wreak vengeance on sheriff Karl Malden – who had deserted him once, when they were robbing a bank.

There were traditional pleasures with Disney's **One Hundred and One Dalmatians**, showing a decently designed London and countryside. It was his best animated movie since **Bambi**, and maybe his last really good one. Melvin Frank's **The Facts of Life** made gentle fun of two married people conspiring to commit adultery – an unusual situation for a movie comedy at this time, especially as they are Bob Hope and Lucille Ball, both now idols of the small screen. Blake Edwards' **Breakfast at Tiffany's**, written by George Axelrod from Truman Capote's novella, started Audrey Hepburn (at her most enchanting) as Holly Golightly, New York party girl who is practically anybody's, and George Peppard, who is definitely Patricia Neal's.

One, Two, Three, set in Berlin, concerns a Coca-Cola executive (James Cagney) who discovers that his boss's dizzy daughter (Pamela Tiffin) intends to marry a militant Communist (Horst Buchholz). Directed by Billy Wilder and written by him and I. A. L. Diamond, their fourth collaboration, it is even more brilliant than the

Left: There was much speculation about the teaming of two sex symbols from different eras, Clark Gable and Marilyn Monroe, in **The Misfits**. Its rather acrid tone was initially disconcerting, but under John Huston's direction it *was* the deeply romantic film anticipated, as a later generation realized. Above: Silvia Pinal and Fernando Rey in **Viridiana**, Luis Buñuel's full-frontal attack on the hypocrisies and naiveties attendant on religious faith, at least as practised in Catholic countries. Above: Charlton Heston and Sophia Loren in a long film about Spain's legendary medieval hero, **El Cid**. Anthony Mann directed, offering some haunting visual images.

others (**Love in the Afternoon**, **Some Like It Hot**, **The Apartment**) in terms of in-jokes and bull's-eye zingers. There would be more to come but nothing else like **The Misfits**, America's other most enduring film of 1961. Arthur Miller wrote it as a vehicle for his wife, Marilyn Monroe (though by this time the marriage was crumbling), who plays a sweet, lost lady, in Reno for a divorce. She meets another divorcée, Thelma Ritter; two cowboys, Clark Gable and Montgomery Clift; and a mechanic, Eli Wallach. They inter-react, and memorably, under John Huston's clinical direction.

Cagney retired after **One, Two, Three**; Gable died within a few days of completing **The Misfits**; Gary Cooper died before the release of **The Naked Edge**, a British film in which wife Deborah Kerr thought he was a wife-murderer . . . a likely story.

Lewis Gilbert directed a film of Rumer Godden's novel **The Greengage Summer**, about four English siblings having to stay in a French hotel when their mother is taken ill. Susannah York is the eldest of them, experiencing all that it means to grow up, including a 'period' (movies had never mentioned this before) and fending off a boy rapist. Kenneth More was a mystery man who befriends the family and Danielle Darrieux the manageress with a lesbian assistant. Well, after all, she was French.

Dirk Bogarde was unquestionably English when he told his wife in **Victim** that he loved a man. Director Basil Dearden and producer Michael Relph, the team responsible for **Sapphire** (1959) had turned from blacks to gays for an equally facile thriller, about a barrister whose rough-trade lover is being blackmailed. Homosexuality was about to come out of the closet. Some plays touching on the subject had been performed at club theatres in the 1950s; but one, Terence Rattigan's *Ross*, was seen in the commercial theatre with the consent of the Lord Chamberlain. Its subject was Lawrence of Arabia, once more – after many plans – to be biographed by the screen (indeed, *Ross* had originally been a screenplay). The two Oscar Wilde films had had no effect on public thinking, for he was too flamboyant, too clever. The parliamentary committee charged with examining the laws relating to consenting males over the age of twenty-one had produced the Wolfenden Report, which was favourable to them. But another play had also been instrumental in forming public opinion. **A Taste of Honey** was filmed by Woodfall, with Tony Richardson directing. Shelagh Delaney's original script had had little merit, but had been worked up for the theatre by Joan Littlewood, a radical and far-seeing director who had had many of her works from Stratford East transferred to the West End, including this one. The film was a touching one, about a

teenager (Rita Tushingham) whose flighty mother (Dora Bryan) and mother's fancy man (Robert Stephens) don't give a damn about her. When she is impregnated by a black sailor, she is cared for by a shop assistant (Murray Melvin), who is quite frank about being gay.

The French cinema in 1961 made four notable contributions to the more open acceptance of sexuality: Alexandre Astruc's **La Proie pour l'Ombre**, in which Annie Girardot consoles herself for her husband's neglect by taking a lover (Christian Marquand) and not feeling the least regret about it; Jean-Gabriel Albicocco's **La Fille aux Yeux d'Or**, in which colleagues (Paul Guers, Françoise Prevost) in a Paris fashion house are in love with the same girl (Marie Laforet) – an updating of Balzac which is much more explicit than the original; Jean-Luc Godard's otherwise irritating **Une Femme est une Femme**, in which *copains* Belmondo and Brialy share Anna Karina; and Jacques Demy's **Lola**, which centres on a happy hooker (Anouk Aimée) working in a Nantes bar. She is idealized by both Demy and her customers, and it should be emphasized that the film is less about sex than the hopes and dreams of all its leading characters – for that is what they have in common.

There were two outstanding shorts: **La Rivière du Hibou** or **Incident at Owl Creek**, written and directed by Robert Enrico from a story by Ambrose Bierce, about a man being hanged during the Civil War; and **Heureux Anniversaire**, written and directed by Pierre Etaix and Jean-Claude Carrière, with Etaix as a man delayed in the Paris traffic as he attempts to get to his wife for their anniversary.

In Italy, Sophia Loren made **La Ciociara**, produced

Left: In **Il Posto** Ermanno Olmi brought to the cinema many of the skills he had learnt in making documentaries – plus wit and compassion. A non-professional, Sandro Panzeri, was his young hero. Above: Pamela Tiffin, Horst Buchholz and James Cagney in **One, Two, Three**, Billy Wilder's satire on several matters, including a divided Berlin and Coca-Colonialism. Right: **A Taste of Honey**, which broke a number of movie taboos. For instance, Dora Bryan (left) played a woman who cared more for booze and men than her daughter, Rita Tushingham, who became pregnant without the benefit of a wedding ring. Audiences were cheered.

by Joseph E. Levine and Loren's husband, Carlo Ponti, very much aware that her international career had been spotty. She dubbed it into English as **Two Women** – for which she won a Best Actress Oscar. It was directed by De Sica, who had returned to acting after the critical and commercial failures of **L'Oro de Napoli** (1954) and **Il Tetto** (1956); he also wrote it with Zavattini, from the novel by Alberto Moravia, and while it is not on the level of their masterpieces, neither is it comparable to the abysmal films in their future. Its best feature is its portrait of a time out of joint, as the Germans leave and the Americans arrive; food is short and the villages are full of refugees. Loren is excellent, as is Belmondo as a pacifist; and the scene where Loren and her teenage daughter are gang-raped in a church by Moroccan soldiers is still shocking.

Marcello Mastroianni had a very good year, both in Antonioni's **La Notte** as a famous writer locked into a loveless marriage with Jeanne Moreau; and Pietro Germi's funny **Divorzio all' Italiana**, as a seedy Sicilian baron whose only hope of getting rid of his wife – so that he can marry his pretty young cousin – is to kill her when he finds her *in flagrante delicto*. But the film of the year was Ermanno Olmi's endearing **Il Posto**, the study of a young Milanese in his first job.

From Spain came the year's most talked-about foreign-language movie, Buñuel's **Viridiana**. He had returned to Spain to make it but knew that it would never be sanctioned by the Franco regime, so he smuggled it out to show at the Cannes Film Festival, where it re-established him as one of the world's leading film-makers. Viridiana (Silvia Pinal) is a novitiate who goes to live with her uncle (Fernando Rey), whose sexual fantasies she is supposed to fulfil. Her innocence and naivety destroy

him, and they look like destroying her when she is faced with his more pragmatic son, Francisco Rabal.

Poland was the more likely source for an anticlerical diatribe, and Jerzy Kawalerowicz provided one when, with **Mother Joan of the Angels**, he transferred the story of the witches of Loudon to that country. Andrzej Wajda was in Yugoslavia making an even more powerful film, **Siberian Lady Macbeth**, about the lady of the manor whose love with a stranger is discovered by her father-in-law. She becomes murderess as well as adulteress as she and her lover wait for her husband.

In India, a great film-maker made a virtually flawless film, **Three Daughters**, a triptych of stories by **Rabindranath Tagore**, about whom he – Satyajit Ray – also made a beautiful documentary. Each story settles on a relationship: between the new rural postmaster and his 11-year-old housekeeper; between a couple trapped in a loveless marriage; and between a westernized young man (Soumitra Chatterjee) courting the village tomboy (Aparna Das Gupta).

In Japan, Shohei Imamura made one of his most astonishing films, **Hogs and Warships**, a tale of petty crime in Yokosuka – and since the ships in the harbour are American, that's what's responsible for the wholesale corruption. The title of Kurosawa's **Yojimbo** means 'bodyguard', and at a time of strife, Mifune is a samurai prepared to sell himself to the highest bidder. Two merchants in this bleak, warring town both want him, but they're both dangerously mean. This is a film about greed on a massive scale, enormously exciting and perhaps the most satisfying that Kurosawa made.

Masaki Kobayashi completed **Ningen no Joken** or **The Human Condition** in three parts, each over three and a half hours long: **No Greater Love**, **Road to Eternity**, **A Soldier's Prayer**. They are taken from a six-volume epic novel by Jumpei Gomikawa and concern Kaji (here, Tatsuya Nakadai). In Part I, he is seconded to a steel factory in Manchuria under Japanese Occupation; in Part II, he is conscripted into an army where brutality is the rule; and in Part III, Japan has surrendered and he is trying to walk his way home. Kaji is a humanist and a pacifist in environments where these words are unknown; he is a survivor; but he is also somewhat arrogant, so he has to fight for our sympathy. It is also clear that this tense, dense polemic is tackling some immense subjects – imperialism, fascism, militarism, Japanese war guilt and, most importantly, man's inhumanity to man. In the cinema's first hundred years, **The Human Condition** is one of its most extraordinary achievements.

The Hustler was a movie about losers but it was boom time for others, including audiences, as Paul Newman schemed to take on a pool-table champ, Jackie Gleason. Directed and co-written by Robert Rossen.

MGM went into partnership with Cinerama to make fiction films – a logical conjunction since Cinerama's documentaries had lost their appeal, and MGM had always considered itself the biggest company. The titles of **How the West was Won**, a three–parter, and **The Wonderful World of the Brothers Grimm** are self-explanatory: the former, boasting a host of stars, was widely seen; the second, without that advantage, did poorly. MGM and Cinerama decided to bide their time; besides, Metro had too much money bound up in the remake of **Mutiny on the Bounty**. That was initiated in another of the studio's attempts to raid its profitable past, but Brando's antics during the shoot in Polynesia had sent costs soaring (this was not so much his fault; he had asked for the moon and got it, including the replacement of Carol Reed by Lewis Milestone, with whom he then didn't get on).

Fox, having its own troubles with star behaviour (see 1963), were banking everything on Zanuck, asked to return to run the studio, and on **The Longest Day**, his most promising venture after several years of failures. The film of Cornelius Ryan's account of the D-Day landings was stuffed with stars like plums in a pudding. The gamble paid off.

Warners filmed two of the great Broadway shows, **Gypsy** (music: Jules Styne, book: Arthur Laurents, words: Stephen Sondheim) and **The Music Man** (everything: Meredith Willson). The first was based on the autobiography of stripper Gypsy Rose Lee and her bossy mother, in which stage role Ethel Merman was incomparable. The second was a fable about a small Iowa town buying seventy-six trombones at the behest of a fast-talking travelling salesman (Robert Preston). Preston made it to the screen and The Merm didn't, though she was conceivably a bigger name in movies. Posterity is grateful, even if Warners' accountants weren't. Posterity is not grateful for Rosalind Russell, who played Mama Rose, or Natalie Wood, as Gypsy.

Among the plays filmed was Lillian Hellman's **The Children's Hour**, with its lesbian theme restored. Wyler again directed, but although Audrey Hepburn and Shirley MacLaine are better actresses than the two in **These Three**, the film is much less effective. Homosexuality was something else, as Sidney Lumet found in planning to film Arthur Miller's **A View From the Bridge** – to which it is only incidental, as longshoreman Eddie, in love with his wife's niece, kisses the cousin she loves to prove that he's gay. Hollywood thought that the damned kiss would get the film into trouble, so that it couldn't return its costs. It was therefore made with French money (**Vu du Pont**) in New York in English, with Raf Vallone, Maureen Stap-

Left: Peter O'Toole (centre) as **Lawrence of Arabia**, with Anthony Quinn. Robert Bolt's literate script did not shrink from examining dubious British interests in the Middle East or from showing Lawrence as a poseur. Above: Marlon Brando in **Mutiny on the Bounty**. Seen today, Brando's foppish, lisping Fletcher Christian soon becomes tiresome, so the film belongs to Trevor Howard's fierce Bligh. Opposite: Alan Bates and June Ritchie in **A Kind of Loving**. He plays a young northern draughtsman, not quite wanting to marry her after getting her in the family way.

leton, Carol Lawrence and Jean Sorel.

The first gay bar in movies was in **Advise and Consent**, since that was where one of the Washington high-ups had spent much time in the past. This was otherwise an absorbing drama about political ambitions, with a cast that included Henry Fonda, Charles Laughton, Lew Ayres and Walter Pidgeon, from the novel by Allen Drury. It's probably Preminger's best movie. A better director, George Cukor, found himself with a less distinguished bestseller, **The Chapman Report**. He thought it gave him a chance to satirize such reports; he also owed Fox a picture, but after trouble over the content, Zanuck took it to Warners and then the MPAA made cuts, which Cukor thought ruined it. There were still matters new to the American screen: a widow (Jane Fonda) consults a psychiatrist (top-billed Efrem Zimbalist Jr) about frigidity; a silly wife (Glynis Johns) picks up a beach boy who is almost certainly gay; and a nymphomaniac (Claire Bloom) puts the come-on once too often and is gang-raped by some jazz groupies. Few commented on the sexual content, possibly because it was recognized by now that Hollywood's ideas on sex were hopelessly out of date and this wasn't that much of a step forward.

The Manchurian Candidate, directed by John Frankenheimer from Richard Condon's novel, has Laurence Harvey returning brain-washed from a Korean prison. Worried are a buddy (Frank Sinatra), his Commie-bating stepfather (James Gregory) and his monster of a mother (Angela Lansbury). There were also thrills of an unusual sort in Robert Aldrich's **Whatever Happened to Baby Jane?**, as two grotesque sisters (Bette Davis, Joan Crawford) live out Grand Guignol lives in isolation and mutual hatred. Both, clearly, were subjects for **Freud**, John Huston's tribute to his researches into the psyche, here reduced to just two patients, Susannah York and David McCallum. Montgomery Clift played Freud. Burt Lancaster was the **Birdman of Alcatraz**, directed by Frankenheimer. It told the true story of Robert Stroud, a two-times murderer who spent a lifetime in jail, which he used to become a world authority on bird diseases.

A modern Western, **Lonely are the Brave**, had Kirk Douglas as a cowboy pursued across the mountain by a helicopter; Walter Matthau was the sheriff. And in **Ride the High Country** Joel McCrea and Randolph Scott are two old-timers transporting gold from the mines. We all know that one of them is going to depart with it, but which? A clever, if unremarkable, plot, but what marked the film was Sam Peckinpah's command of period detail. It was seminal, too: there's hardly been a Western since without cowboys in long johns and whores in their underwear.

In Britain, **Lawrence of Arabia** happened. So did **Lolita**. David Lean directed the first for Sam Spiegel and Columbia, with Peter O'Toole in the title role. It had startling desert locations, plus a large cast of names, including Claude Rains, Jack Hawkins, Anthony Quinn, Anthony Quayle and Omar Sharif, the only Egyptian actor to achieve world stardom. **Lolita** was directed by Stanley Kubrick from Nabokov's novel, with James Mason as the middle-aged man who marries Shelley Winters so that he can be around her nymphet of a daughter. Fearing wholesale censorship, MGM insisted on shooting in Britain, thus losing the tacky drive-ins of middle America which are such a feature of the book. Oh, and **Dr No** happened. Ian Fleming's thrillers about a snobbish and sex-mad secret service man, James Bond, had been around about a decade, not even selling well till comparatively recently. With fiendish masterminds and treacherous women, few thought they were movie material for the 1960s, including the considerable number of actors who turned down the chance to be the screen Bond. Producers Broccoli and Saltzman persisted and, *faute de mieux*, got Terence Young to direct and Sean Connery to play Bond. He could have been better. So could the film. So could the grosses. A reissue or ten would help that side of things.

A new director came along, from television. John Schlesinger, a former actor, looked at that grey area in which the working class aspire to suburbia. He did it with humour and insight, much helped by a screenplay by Willis Hall and Keith Waterhouse, based on a novel by Stan Barstow, **A Kind of Loving**. Alan Bates plays a young northern draughtsman, not quite wanting not to marry Ingrid (June Ritchie) after getting her in the family way one rare Sunday afternoon in the living room when the house is deserted – till confronted by her mother (Thora Hird), ablaze with affront that he doesn't share her enthusiasm for her high street purchases and TV quiz shows. Audiences loved it when, living with her after the wedding, he comes home drunk and vomits all over her favourite carpet.

In France, Chabrol made two haunting, elusive and unsuccessful films about young men determined to destroy because they are consumed by sexual fantasies: **L'Oeil du Malin**, in which Jacques Charrier visits a famous writer and, when his wife (Stéphane Audran) doesn't respond to him, imagines her in another man's bed; and **Ophélia**, in which André Jocelyn goes to see Olivier's **Hamlet** and wonders about the remarriage of his mother (Alida Valli) to his uncle. Much more popular was Truffaut's oddly admired **Jules et Jim**, with Jeanne Moreau as the apex of a ménage à trois.

In Italy, Bolognini filmed Pavese and Moravia, respectively **Senilità** and **Agostino**, wonderfully set in Trieste in the 1920s and present-day Venice. In the first, a man (Antony Franciosa) goes to pieces over a whore (Claudia Cardinale), and in the second a young wife (Ingrid Thulin) has an affair with a playboy (John Saxon). Her teenage son, meanwhile, gets a crush on a handsome fisherman, and *that* was something which turned up in three further movies: Damiano Damiani's **L'Isola di Arturo**, based on a novel by Elsa Morante (Signora Moravia), in which another teenager has to accustom himself to the fact that the young man his father brings home is more than just a friend; Giuseppe Patroni Griffi's **Il Mare**, a game for three (Umberto Orsini, Dino Mele, Françoise Prevost) in a wintry Capri, during which it's clear that the lady is *de trop*; and **L'Italiane et l'Amore**, an omnibus film organized by Zavattini with new talent, in which in one episode the young husband is seen holding hands with another. Dino Risi's **Il Sorpasso** is, after those, healthy, with a young law student (Trintignant) overwhelmed by a wealthy neighbour (Vittorio Gassmann) who takes him joyriding.

In Greece, Michael Cacoyannis makes **Electra** on location at Mycenae, with Irene Papas in the title role, the first Greek tragedy (it's the Euripedes version) to be filmed. In Sweden, Ingmar Bergman makes one of his bleakest but strongest films, **Winter Light**, in which a country pastor (Gunnar Björnstrand) doubts his faith and thus fails his mistress (Miss Thulin) and his friends (Max von Sydow, Gunnel Lindblom). In Mexico, Buñuel makes the extraordinary **El Angel Exterminadór**, about some party guests who fall into disarray and then degradation rather than leave.

In Japan, Kenji Misumi directed the first film about the blind masseur and swordsman, Zatoichi, which would have over thirty sequels. Tomu Uchida was halfway through his exciting five-part series on the seventeenth-century warrior, Musashi Miyamoto. Inagaki made **Chushingura** to celebrate Toho's (the largest Japanese company) anniversary, which isn't terribly good, despite the presence of Mifune; but this Kabuki story should be mentioned, for as *The Loyal 47 Ronin* it has been filmed so often, since the first version in 1913, that even *aficionados* have lost count. Set in the early eighteenth century it starts with a quarrel between two noblemen and follows the consequences to their followers when their overlord orders one of them to commit harakiri.

The huge success of **Yojimbo** called for a sequel, so Kurosawa made **Sanjuro**, but it is deliberately much lighter in tone, with Mifune allied to some inferior samurai before changing to the enemy – who are even worse. Naruse directed **Her Lonely Lane**, from a novel by Fumiko Hayashi, whose work had often attracted him, partly because of her pessimism. And Kobayashi made two films: a dark comedy, **The Inheritance**, about a dying man who, like Volpone, resolves to put his heirs to the test; and **Harakiri**, which may not be the greatest Japanese picture about feudal times, but it is the most complex, cruel and riveting.

Opposite above: There were strange thrills in Robert Aldrich's **Whatever Happened to Baby Jane?**, as two sisters – Bette Davis (illustrated), with Victor Buono, and Joan Crawford – co-exist in isolation and mutual hatred. Right: Gregory Peck as the perfectly liberal Southern lawyer in **To Kill a Mockingbird**, defending a black man on a charge of raping a 'poor white'. Robert Mulligan directed from Harper Lee's novel.

1963

On 22 November President John F. Kennedy was assassinated in Dallas, Texas.

It's A Mad, Mad, Mad, Mad World was the first film in single-lens Cinerama (there would be nine more before it was abandoned in 1969, as no longer having box-office appeal). This one, as the title implies, was a comedy, and over two dozen comedians supported Spencer Tracy, as a detective, in a tale about buried loot. It was written by William and Tania Rose, and produced and directed by Stanley Kramer; and had the singular virtue of not raising a titter during its three-hour-plus running time. It also gave the industry the notion that anything exploding, crashing or falling apart, be it boat, plane, building or, in most cases, automobiles, would automatically attract audiences. That was true only for a while, and when the public lost interest in comedies about destruction, it was given chase thrillers instead.

The industry's eyes were on **Cleopatra**, modestly budgeted till Elizabeth Taylor was cast. When her illness halted production in 1960 a new creative team was put in place, including Mankiewicz as writer-director, Richard Burton as Mark Antony and Rex Harrison as Caesar. Cleopatra fell in love with Antony in real life, too, and costs mounted; only a miracle could make it financially successful, and it didn't happen. Mankiewicz, Harrison

Above: Tom Courtenay as **Billy Liar!**, with Julie Christie, who was photographed as lovingly as Godard did with Karina, but the film otherwise owes nothing to anyone else. Right: Steve McQueen in John Sturges's exciting film about POWs, **The Great Escape**. There were several Britishers in the cast, to remind us how many British films there had been on this subject: this was worth all of them put together.

and some supporting players emerged with credit. Nobody else did.

Miss Garland was in Britain, making her last film: **I Could Go On Singing**, about an American star who, while appearing at the London Palladium, wants her son back. Dirk Bogarde was the father, and this was the only film she made to indicate what she was like as a stage performer; Ronald Neame directed. Bogarde had his finest screen hour as **The Servant**, as did director Joseph Losey and Harold Pinter, who adapted it from a novel by Robin Maugham. James Fox was the wealthy Chelsea boy whose life is taken over by the servant.

John Schlesinger's **Billy Liar!** rewardingly reunited him with Waterhouse and Hall (Hall had written the original novel). Billy (Tom Courtenay) works in a Yorkshire funeral parlour and dreams of escaping to London – dreams not encouraged by his fiancée, who hasn't a mind above her bottom drawer, but by a radiant stranger, Julie Christie. She is photographed as lovingly as Godard was doing with Karina, but the film owes nothing to anyone else.

Britain's other leading purveyor of 'ordinary' people moved upwards and backwards, to the eighteenth century. Tony Richardson directed **Tom Jones**, adapted from Henry Fielding's novel by John Osborne. Tom (Albert Finney) is a bastard son of the squire class, and the way he behaves he's likely to have plenty of his own. Among his conquests are Joan Greenwood, Diane Cilento and Joyce Redmond, whose lickin'-chicken scene with him was much appreciated by audiences – who turned up in record numbers the world over. Classy bawdiness had never been seen in movies before.

Also new to movies were masturbation and stand-up sex. It was Sweden which introduced them, the latter in Jörn Donner's study of a troubled marriage, **A Sunday in September**, with Harriet Andersson and Thommy Bergren. Of course the other film, **The Silence**, was about more than self-abuse (as it was then called), because it was directed by Ingmar Bergman – and because it was directed by him, no one complained. Ingrid Thulin was the lonely lady in her hotel room, while her sister, Gunnel Lindblom, finds similar satisfaction with a waiter, Birger Malmsten.

In India, Satyajit Ray's **Mahanagar** (or **The Big City**) is an eloquent study of a woman forced to find work because her husband cannot. It was the last thing she had expected to do; but she flowers because of it. The feminist movement didn't notice that one of its first major statements was made by a man.

From Japan, Imai's **Cruel Tales of the Bushido**, a pocket history of the rules governing the samurai class and its predisposition towards death. Kurosawa's **High and Low** was a thriller originating from Ed McBain, with Nakadai as a police chief and Mifune as a businessman with a dozen choices to make when the chauffeur's son is

Left: It was easy to see why Billy Wilder was attracted to **Irma la Douce**, a Paris *poule* who is visited by a cop she knows, only she doesn't recognize him because he's disguised. Shirley Maclaine (illustrated) and Jack Lemmon are fine, but it was a mistake to cut the songs. Above: Dirk Bogarde in **The Servant**, with Wendy Craig as his boss's fiancée, rightly suspecting that something strange was going on. Still, it ends with a strictly hetero-orgy, which was not in the original novel. Opposite: Claudia Cardinale dancing with Burt Lancaster in Visconti's **The Leopard**. This ballroom sequence takes up the last forty minutes of the movie.

kidnapped. Ichikawa alone made two masterpieces, as unlike each other as could be, beyond the fact that both are star vehicles and that their use of colour and wide screen surpassed anything that had gone before. **An Actor's Revenge** stars Kazuo Hasegawa (who had played the role in Kinugasa's 1936 version) in a dual role, as actor and a thief; and **Alone on the Pacific** stars Yujiro Ishihara (who also produced), as the young man who sailed to San Francisco in a small craft in 1962.

In France, two of the *nouvelle vague* directors came up with unforgettable and unsettling works: Alain Resnais with **Muriel, ou le Temps de Retour**, and Louis Malle, with **Le Feu Follet**. The former has Delphine Seyrig clutching at bits of her old life while waiting for her lover; the second has Maurice Ronet visiting old lovers while deciding whether to end his.

In Italy, Monicelli's **I Compagni** concerns itself with the formation of trade unions in Turin in the 1880s, with Mastroiannia as a professional agitator sent to aid the strikers; and Olmi's **I Fidanzati** is a gentle and loving look at an engaged couple separated when he is seconded to work in Sicily. Sicily is the setting of a movie quite without equal: Visconti's evocative, magisterial **Il Gattopardo** or **The Leopard**, based on Lampedusa's novel about one aristocratic family during the Risorgimento, with Burt Lancaster as the patriarch. Its costs were so great that Visconti had persuaded Fox to put money into it; but their dubbed, cut, reprocessed (in DeLuxe color) version was a travesty which quickly failed. Why do they do these things?

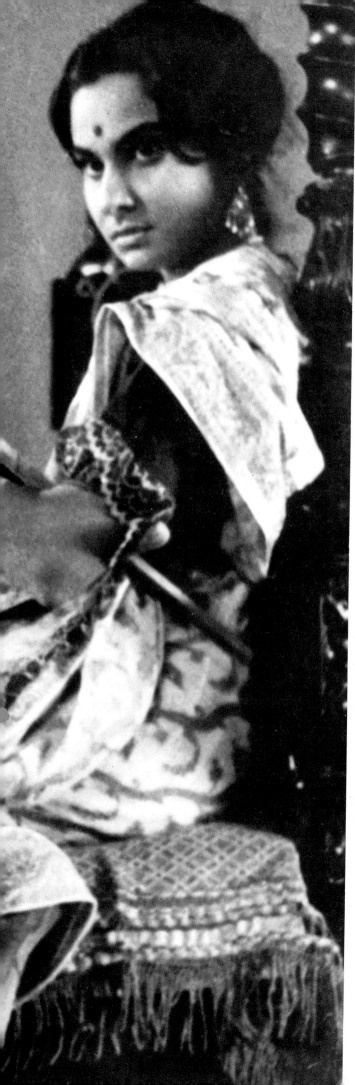

To get the worst over with: Peter Glenville's **Becket** has Richard Burton in that role and Peter O'Toole as Henry II; and Cacoyannis' **Zorba the Greek** has Anthony Quinn as that life force and Alan Bates as the man who, inheriting property in Crete, learns how to lose his English inhibitions. Both were Well Thought Of – and travesties of their source material, respectively Jean Anouilh's play, which was a comedy, making much fun of the differences between the English and the French, and

1964

the novel by Nikos Kazantzakis which, unlike the film, liked Crete.

Cary Grant was back, and co-starring with two younger actresses. In Ralph Nelson's **Father Goose** he plays a beach bum on a desert island disapproved of by French teacher Leslie Caron as the Japanese are invading all around them; and in Stanley Donen's **Charade**, he scares Audrey Hepburn in Paris (but not as much as James Coburn, George Kennedy or Ned Glass). The first was a comedy, the second a comedy-thriller.

He might have been in **My Fair Lady**, but he refused so that Rex Harrison could reprise his stage Higgins; Stanley Holloway was again Mr Doolittle. Warners had paid a record $5.5 million for the rights and needed a box-office name to ensure their investment, so Audrey

Left: Soumitra Chatterjee and Madhabi Mukherjee in Satyajit Ray's haunting, moving **Charulata**, perhaps his greatest film. Above: In the Soviet Union Grigori Kozintsev made **Hamlet** with Innokenti Smoktunovsky in the title role, borrowing much from Olivier, but emphasizing the ritual of a Renaissance court. With Smoktunovsky is Elza Radzin-Szolkonis, who played Gertrude.

Hepburn came in as Eliza, under the rather stately direction of George Cukor. The dropped Eliza, Julie Andrews, was compensated by Disney, who cast her as **Mary Poppins**, a very proper English nanny – and one who could fly, among other things. She was also romanced by cockney chimney sweep Dick Van Dyke, whose accent remains legendary. Andrews had not been at Disney long before word was out that she was a special screen presence.

In **The Best Man**, adapted by Gore Vidal from his own play, rival presidential candidates each have a host of guilty secrets. The intellectual Henry Fonda had once had a nervous breakdown and arrogant Cliff Robertson used to smile at young men – facts which the schemers around them won't hesitate to use. Franklin Schaffner directed, underlining Vidal's premise that politics was only for the crazy or the crooked. Doing the same were John Frankenheimer with **Seven Days in May** and Sidney Lumet with **Fail Safe**, both of which are set mainly inside the White House, whose Top Man is working away like Hercules to avoid a nuclear war. The respective Top Men are Fredric March and Henry Fonda, the all-time integrity actors, like no US presidents since. The first film, presaging Kissinger, has Walter Matthau as a German-Jewish professor who wants to get the Reds; the second has Burt Lancaster, Kirk Douglas, Ava Gardner and Edmond O'Brien, all of whose aims are by no means so clear. Beside them, Vidal's politicos are sheep.

In Britain, Kubrick's people are scary as they, too, contemplate a nuclear war. Most of them love the idea of it: the obtuse, batty military men (George C. Scott, Sterling Hayden, Keenan Wynn), a mad scientist, an RAF

liaison officer and the US president (all Peter Sellers). **Dr Strangelove, Or How I Learned to Stop Worrying and Love the Bomb** is a film of gleaming brilliance, a 'nightmare comedy' as Kubrick himself put it.

Sellers was the bumbling French detective, Inspector Clouseau, in Blake Edwards' **A Shot in the Dark**. It is a one-joke movie, but there were, surprisingly, a number of sequels. Sean Connery was James Bond, 007, for the third time in **Goldfinger**, and he's getting more adept. Because of the Bond movies, because of **Tom Jones**, most British movies were being backed by the Hollywood companies.

The most eagerly awaited cinematic event of 1964 was the début of the fab four, the Beatles, in **A Hard Day's Night**, playing themselves and singing their songs, in bits, all over London. Richard Lester directed, only too jokingly, and the anti-pseud script now seems somewhat tiresome.

Japan had some of its greatest successes outside Kurosawa with two curious, cruel films, both set in a remote limbo, both by directors whose other work was little exported. Kaneto Shindo's **Onibaba** is about two women grieving for a loved one and murdering passing samurai for their possessions; and Hiroshi Teshigahara's **Woman of the Dunes** makes a passing scientist (Eija Okada) prisoner, lover and slave in her underground home. Imamura's **Unholy Desire** studies the relationship between a rapist and his victim. Their mutual fascination has all the more piquancy because he is a nice man and her husband is a nasty piece of work. This was little seen outside Japan, unlike Kobayashi's **Kwaidan**, an exquisitely coloured, 'Scope collection of ghost stories,

Left: George C. Scott and Tracy Reed in **Dr Strangelove**, directed by Stanley Kubrick – who would end a remarkable run of masterworks with **2001** four years later. Sadly, the four since have all been duds. Above: Almost overnight, it sometimes seemed, a pop group had become four of the most famous men in the world: John Lennon, Ringo Starr, George Harrison and Paul McCartney in **A Hard Day's Night**. Opposite: It was a mere coincidence, but following the assassination of President Kennedy there were three excellent films about American politics. This is **The Best Man**, and it's Henry Fonda's face you can see on the posters.

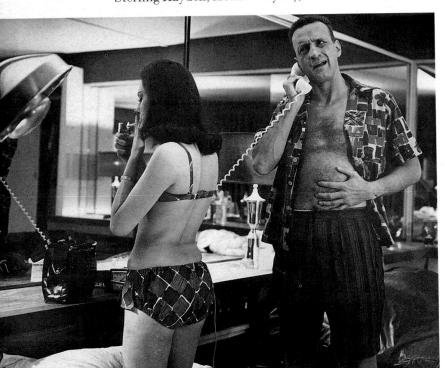

four of them, in fact, based on Lafcadio Hearn.

In India, Ray turned again to Tagore for what may be his masterpiece, **Charulata**, about a proudly westernized publisher, his young wife and the young cousin (Soumitra Chatterjee) he invites to live with him. Because he loves them both, he doesn't know how to react when he believes that they are falling in love.

In Czechoslovakia, Milos Forman made his feature début with **Peter and Pavla**, influenced by Olmi, about a boy's first job; and Jan Kadar and Elmar Klos jointly directed the moving **The Shop on the High Street**, which was owned, in 1942, by an elderly Jewish lady. The film concerns the relationship between her and her 'Aryan controller'.

In France, Buñuel made a great movie, **Le Journal d'une Femme de Chambre**, with Jeanne Moreau. It is harsher and grimmer than Renoir's version, and funny in a more acid way. Jacques Demy scored a triumph with his pretty, all-sung (to music by Michel Legrand) **Les Parapluies de Cherbourg**, with Catherine Deneuve as the girl who helps her mother in the shop, and the *garagiste* who leaves her pregnant when conscripted.

Antonioni made the best Italian picture of 1964, **Deserto Rosso** or **The Red Desert**, set in Ravenna, where a neglected wife (Monica Vitti) begins an affair with her husband's best friend (Richard Harris). It was not his most profound film, but because of its colours (it was his first in colour, and he had a street in Ravenna painted especially) and an Anglo-Saxon star name, it was the most widely seen abroad and therefore influential.

Another name in Italy was Clint Eastwood, best known as a television cowboy. He went downmarket, to be mean if still heroic as 'The Man With No Name' in Sergio Leone's **Per un Pugno di Dollari**. It was not the first spaghetti Western, a species which had already replaced the sword-and-sandal epics as the Italian film industry's chief exports. It was not even a very good one. Release was delayed because the plot plagiarized **Yojimbo**; but when it appeared as **A Fistful of Dollars** it made a mint. Hundreds of spaghetti Westerns followed, mainly shot in Spain, often with Anglicized names (here, John Wells is recognizably Gian Maria Volonté). There have even been books written about them. The world is certainly a strange place.

1965

The **Sound of Music** mowed down all competition to become the most successful film at the box office since **Gone With the Wind**. The Rodgers and Hammerstein musical had known some popularity on the boards, even if critics had unanimously deplored the combination of nuns, Nazis and kids. The prospect of having these in close-up on the wide screen was daunting, but we weren't reckoning with the location photography (in Salzburg and its environs), imaginative handling by Robert Wise and, above all, the sparkling personality and soaring voice of Julie Andrews in the leading role. Whatever humour was in her lines she jumped at, and the film confirmed her as a blazing new star. As money poured into the coffers, 20th Century-Fox could forget the débâcle of **The Greatest Story Ever Told**, with which director George Stevens told, yet again, the life of Christ. Sunday-school stuff, despite the great Swedish actor, Max von Sydow, as Jesus. It wasn't helped by an all-star cast, many of whom were miscast, especially John Wayne as a Roman soldier.

There might be divisions of opinions on the merits of Boris Pasternak's novel, **Doctor Zhivago**, but it was a bestseller and so was brought to the screen by heavyweight British director David Lean, working again from a screenplay by Robert Bolt. The result was enormously popular, despite a vacuous performance by Omar Sharif in the title role.

Lee Marvin gave a jolly account of himself in a fine comic Western, **Cat Ballou**, with Jane Fonda cleverly kidding herself in the title role. Rod Steiger played the title role in **The Pawnbroker**, contrasting his life in Spanish Harlem with memories of Auschwitz. Those around him include junkies and whores, one of whom exposes her breasts to him – the first time anything like that had been seen in a mainstream film since the ethnic movies of the late 1920s. Sidney Lumet directed.

Lumet was one of several American directors working profitably in Britain. **The Hill**, set in a British army

Below: Jane Fonda in the title role of **Cat Ballou**, directed by Eliot Silverstein. With her are Michael Callan and Dwayne Hickman. Opposite: You either loved **The Sound of Music** or loathed it. Those who loathed it were the very few who hadn't seen it. Those who loved it did so mainly because of the comic verve Julie Andrews, with the guitar, brought to her role. Oh yes, and there was the scenery.

prison in North Africa in 1942, was more accurate on the military mentality than anything seen before and also proved that Sean Connery was wasted as James Bond (whose outing this year was **Thunderball**). Another foreigner working locally was Roman Polanski, whose **Repulsion** lived up to its title, a clear-eyed study of a girl (Catherine Deneuve) slipping into insanity, solitary in a large house in West London.

Three almost wholly British films were successes throughout the world. Sidney J. Furie directed **The Ipcress File** from Len Deighton's novel, making a star out of Michael Caine, playing yet another spy, one with glasses and a Sarf London accent. Like Furie, Richard Lester hails from the other side of the Atlantic, but he has made his career in Britain. His current feature was **The Knack**, a running and jumping film about love and young Londoners which has dated badly – something that might more readily be expected of **Darling**, set as it is in the world of fashion and centring on a model without much up there. But because of Julie Christie's performance in that role, and intelligent writing and direction, by Frederic Raphael and John Schlesinger respectively, it holds up pretty well.

From India came a film unlike any other, **Shakespeare Wallah**, an elegiac, melancholy look at a theatrical troupe touring in the post-Raj era. Produced by an Indian, Ismael Merchant, and directed by an American, James Ivory, it was not without an element of autobiography, since the Kendall family, playing the leads, had

themselves been taking Shakespeare to the odd school and concert hall.

All cinema in 1965, however, was overshadowed by two masterpieces from Japan: Kurosawa's **Red Beard** and Ichikawa's **Tokyo Olympiad**. Toshiro Mifune played the title role for Kurosawa, a doctor of the feudal era (the nineteenth century) who wielded a mean blade; but the film is more a panoramic study of a time and mankind's place in it. 'The Olympics are a symbol of human aspiration,' says a title in Ichikawa's account of the Games in Tokyo in 1964, but it is a statement which clearly amuses him. He is interested, instead, in the matter of nations gathering in peace, and thus has made one of the greatest of humanist films. The Olympic committee which had commissioned the film disapproved and prevented the original from being shown except in those countries which had already contracted to show it.

Left: Madhur Jaffrey and (behind her) Shashi Kapoor in **Shakespeare Wallah**, watching the Kendall family act. As in the film, the youngest daughter, Felicity, went to England; her sister, Jennifer, married Kapoor and sadly died not long after appearing in Aparna Sen's pleasing **36, Chowringhee Lane** (1981). Above: Bette Davis as **The Nanny**, directed by Seth Holt, and one of the better films turned out by Hammer, which specialized in horror. Opposite above: Anna Karina in Godard's science fiction tale, **Alphaville**, subtitled 'Une Etrange Aventure de Lemmy Caution'. Eddie Constantine played Lemmy. Opposite below: Catherine Deneuve (left) and Yvonne Furneaux in **Repulsion**, Roman Polanski's most brilliant film. With a couple of exceptions, his movies are violently uneven – either superb or unwatchable.

T he Motion Picture Association of America (MPAA, formerly the Breen Office) bowed to the inevitable. So many people had seen and admired **Who's Afraid of Virginia Woolf?** on the stage and so many had read and admired **The Group** that there was no point in doing a wholesale job of bowdlerization. The first was Edward Albee's play about

1966

an academic and his wife who fight and shout obscenities at each other through one very long night, watched by an apalled younger couple. The second was Mary McCarthy's novel which followed a group of Vassar graduates for twenty years from 1933, during which time many of them had marital problems, some of them caused by not using condoms. The films were respectively directed by Mike Nichols (fresh from Broadway), from a screenplay by Ernest Lehman (fresh from **The Sound of Music**), and Sidney Lumet, from a screenplay by Sidney Buchman. Richard Burton, Elizabeth Taylor, Sandy Dennis and George Segal comprised the cast of the first; several new actresses comprised the group, none of them to gain lasting fame, except Candice Bergen as the Sapphic member. Neither film stands up too well, especially the first, which is atrociously acted.

There is no blacker, funnier comedy in American cinema between Keaton's most pessimistic shorts and

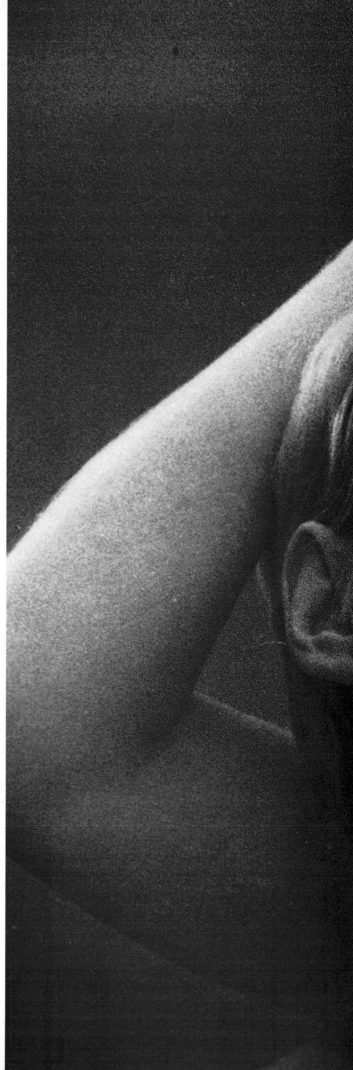

Above: Anouk Aimee and Jean-Louis Trintignant in Claude Lelouch's simple and romantic **Un Homme et une Femme**. Opposite: Bibi Andersson and Liv Ullman in Ingmar Bergman's **Persona**. Ullman plays an actress who has a nervous breakdown after offering one illusion too many; Andersson is her nurse, coming to the same conclusions – that illusions and mental breakdowns are preferable to human realities.

Billy Wilder's **The Fortune Cookie**. Wilder and I. A. L. Diamond had been working towards this since their collaboration began, and this would be the last wholly satisfying film they made. But it's more than that: its cynicism is awe-inspiring as a shyster lawyer, Walter Matthau, overrules his injured brother-in-law, Jack Lemmon, and decides to go for a million in damages.

In Britain too, it was a popular play which extended what was permissible on screen. Bill Naughton's **Alfie**, directed by Lewis Gilbert, has Michael Caine having it away with half the women in the cast list, including an over-age Shelley Winters and Millicent Martin. **Georgy Girl** didn't hurt the cause either, as Charlotte Rampling fucks with Alan Bates while her best friend, Lynn Redgrave (in the title role), looks after her bastard baby. James Mason played Daddy Long Legs to Lynn, and this amiable comedy was directed by Silvio Narizzano, from the novel by Margaret Forster, who wrote the screenplay with Peter Nichols. These were movies with which the British were discovering themselves as individuals. Another was **Morgan: A Suitable Case for Treatment**, written by David Mercer from his TV play and directed by Karel Reisz. Morgan, played by David Warner, was certifiable, but his wife, Vanessa Redgrave, still found him attractive enough to forget the man who had succeeded him in her life, Robert Stephens. The situations are treated with irreverence but no humour, which is why the piece has dated.

One historical film stood above several others: Fred Zinnemann's **A Man For All Seasons**, with Paul Scofield repeating his stage role as Sir Thomas More. Robert Shaw is too young as Henry VIII, but it is otherwise flawless since Robert Bolt reworked his play for the screen and omitted the awkward device of the 'common man'. Orson Welles is Cardinal Wolsey and Susannah York, Meg Roper.

Welles directed his best film since **Ambersons**, **Chimes at Midnight**, in which he was Falstaff, for this was his reworking of Shakespeare's two Henry IV plays. John Gielgud is the king and Keith Baxter is Hal. From the USSR came another superb literary adaptation, Josif Heifits' **In the Town of S**, from Chekhov's story, *Ionych*, about the provincial doctor who cannot quite bring himself to propose to the daughter of the local salon hostess. In Germany, Volker Schlöndorff wrote and directed his first feature, **Der Junge Törless**, from Robert Musil's autobiographical novel of life in a boarding school in a remote part of the Austro-Hungarian Empire. Since that was published in 1906, a last-minute analogy with the Nazis seemed rather odd. We were reminded of them in Erwin Leiser's companion piece to **Mein Kampf**, **Deutschland Erwache!**, a collection of sequences to show how

Left: Steve McQueen in Robert Wise's **The Sand Pebbles**, which attempted to find parallels with the current conflict in Vietnam as it detailed the adventures of a Yankee gunboat patrolling the Yangtse river in 1926. Above: Marlon Brando as the sheriff of a small Southern town in Arthur Penn's **The Chase**, a tale of tensions, some of them racial, from a novel and a play by Horton Foote. Opposite: Fred Zinnemann's **A Man For All Seasons**, with screenplay by Robert Bolt from his play about Sir Thomas More, which won great acclaim for Paul Scofield in New York and London.

they had actually distorted history.

In Japan Naruse made his penultimate film, a thriller described by the title, **Hit and Run**, and Imamura made **The Pornographer**, which is also self-explanatory, but also blacker than the title suggests. In Hungary, István Szabó directed **Father**, as seen by his son from the end of the war. The only Italian film of note was Gillo Pontecorvo's **La Battaglia di Algeri** or **The Battle of Algiers**, a stunning semi-documentary about the revolution on the streets which led to the expulsion of the French. That was one of the most popular foreign-language films of 1966, along with Czechoslovakia's

Closely Observed Trains, directed by Jiří Menzel. This concerned the problems of a young man working at a remote station – the problems concerned seduction by the station master's wife and premature ejaculation.

One film, however, was more popular, and the world over it was the biggest French success for as long as anyone could remember, helped by Francis Lai's theme tune. **Un Homme et une Femme** is the story of Jean-Louis Trintignant and Anouk Aimée, both widowed, he a professional racing driver and she a movie script girl. Claude Lelouch produced and directed, finding time for cars driving through rain.

1967

It was a year of many pleasures. There were many things Hollywood did well, and they were doing them even better this year. Jane Fonda and Robert Redford went **Barefoot in the Park** while honeymooning at the Plaza. There were some good one-liners by Neil Simon from his Broadway play, and even more in **The Graduate**, directed by Mike Nichols from a novel by Charles Webb. 'I find you the most attractive of all my parents' friends,' says Dustin Hoffman to Mrs Robinson (Anne Bancroft), aware that she wants to tear off all his clothes. And she does, too, to an endearing, folksy soundtrack of songs composed and sung by Simon and Garfunkel. The film declines as the young student returns to pursuing Mrs Robinson's daughter, but the public didn't care; it loved it.

More dubiously it adored **Guess Who's Coming to Dinner?** The man who was about to come was Sidney Poitier, who had this thing about the daughter of Spencer Tracy (in his last film) and Katharine Hepburn, both of whom had to be persuaded that he would be a worthy comer, in marriage as much as to dinner. William Rose, credited with the screenplay, later expressed his regret that he had pulled it from an old drawer when Stanley Kramer wanted something simple for Tracy, who was no

longer insurable. Kramer had no such regret: its platitudes were his own. He and Otto Preminger, his rival in fake social consciousness, were pitchforked into oblivion when their chief supporter, Bosley Crowther of *The New York Times*, was retired.

Crowther particularly loathed an artless but cunning movie about bank robbing and killing, **Bonnie and Clyde**, yet it took its two subjects and turned them into myths. Director Arthur Penn, writers David Newman and Robert Benton and stars Warren Beatty and Faye Dunaway made important contributions to the myth-making, as did Burnett Guffey, who photographed the dead middle of 1930s America so evocatively. The most highly acclaimed and popular thriller was Norman Jewison's **In the Heat of the Night**, with Rod Steiger as a prejudiced Mississippi police chief and Sidney Poitier as the Northern cop seconded to help him. Tense, and impeccable on race relations. John Huston directed the first film from a novel by Carson McCullers, **Reflections in a Golden Eye**. A glimpse into army life: Marlon Brando as an officer who, lusting after an enlisted man who rides naked in the woods, is afraid of his first

Left: A lady bent on seduction, Mrs Robinson, which was what the guy was calling her as she tumbled him into bed – after all, she was his parents' friend: Anne Bancroft in **The Graduate**. Above: David Hemmings in **Blow-Up**. Look at his eyes. Below the surface, Antonioni's picture was a dissection of a hollow man. Opposite: Faye Dunaway and Warren Beatty in **Bonnie and Clyde**, i.e. Bonnie Parker and Clyde Barrow, who 'robbed banks', as they proudly put it, in the 1930s. To the newspapers of the time, they were gangsters, if petty ones, but this was like no other gangster picture yet made.

homosexual encounter but unable to back away; Elizabeth Taylor as his wife, flaunting her affair with a colleague, Brian Keith; and Julie Harris as his wife, lost in a play-world with the Filipino houseboy. It should have been risible, but Huston had an unerring control and just enough humour to make it work.

Out of control in Britain was Charlie Chaplin, whose **A Countess from Hong Kong** made patsies out of Brando and Sophia Loren, diplomat and whore respectively, on an ocean liner. Chaplin's reported view of the reviews was that critics were idiots. Disaster struck several more times, but be content with only two: Desmond Davis's broad, vulgar picture of swinging London, **Smashing Time**, which reunited Rita Tushingham and Lynn Redgrave; and **Casino Royale**, a James Bond movie made not by the usual Bond team, but by a clutch of directors, including Huston (but no one ever owned up as to who did what), and with an all-star cast including William Holden, Deborah Kerr, Jean-Paul Belmondo, Orson Welles, Peter O'Toole, Peter Sellers, David Niven and Woody Allen, some of whom were 007 or pretended to be. The reason for this mishmash is that the producing company feared comparisons with Sean Connery, who had now grown beautifully into the role and whose fifth outing, **You Only Live Twice**, was the most lavish yet, the most exciting and the best received,

The reason for mentioning Davis's wretched little movie is because 'swinging London' was largely an invention of journalists and moviemakers, and no movie was more responsible for that image than **Blow-Up**, Antonioni's portrait of a photographer (David Hemmings) who swung with the best of them, coupling with a couple of naked ladies at the same time, and Vanessa Redgrave. She may be witness to a murder which he may have photographed: that is a problem left unsolved but in the event unimportant, since the film – like most of Antonioni's others – is a dissection of a hollow man and how, in the course of the action, he comes to realize this.

In France, Buñuel was telling quite a different story. In **Belle de Jour**, Catherine Deneuve is a respectable housewife who goes to work in a brothel simply for fun.

Among pretty movies, Sweden's **Elvira Madigan** holds a high place. Bo Widerberg directed this film, based on a true case about an army officer (Thommy Berggren) who deserts for love of a circus high-wire act (Pia Degermark). Since the ending is clearly signalled, the prettiness seems misjudged, but the film put its theme,

Left: Sean Connery in **You Only Live Twice**, the most expensive and the best of the Bonds – as he was, too: the best of the Bonds. He would play the part only once more for the producers that had set the whole bonanza rolling. Above: Rod Steiger and Sidney Poitier in **In the Heat of the Night**, an absorbing thriller about race relations – and ultimately a moving one, as Steiger admits how wrong his prejudices had been.

from Mozart's Piano Concerto No. 21, into the charts. If this was the most popular foreign language movie, Russia's **War and Peace** was the biggest. The King Vidor version had been so popular in the Soviet Union that the state-owned film industry was granted something like $100 million to film it, in an original version lasting 507 minutes. Sergei Bondarchuk, who directed, plays Pierre. The reception overseas was spotty, depending on how its buyer decided to promote it and on the attitude of the press. Some people found it *troppo*; others found it put the vastness of Tolstoy's novels on the screen. One thing is sure: one Napoleonic battle scene is very like another.

Japan's great age of cinema was coming to an end. Kobayashi's **Rebellion** is one of its last masterpieces (he and Kurosawa would be responsible for the few in the future). A lord's only son dies and he demands the return of an illegitimate one born to a lady who has married a samurai (Toshiro Mifune). When he is refused the lord commands an old friend (Tatsuya Nakadai) of the samurai to bring the boy back by force. This dark, brooding piece moves inexorably to their duel, one of the most exciting ever put on film.

1968

This was the year that boredom on the part of the public permitted one of the most minimal films ever made, **Flesh**, which, in turn, changed American cinema. It was 'signed' by the pop painter Andy Warhol and thus booked by respectable cinemas; but it was impossible to say what it was about, except a male hustler and his lovers of both sexes. Lots of nudity and sex. Anything was now permissible. When no moves were made to prevent it being seen, soft-porn turned to hard. When nothing was done to prevent this, legitimate film-makers wanted their share of the action. The reason for this permissiveness was again television. With films swarming the network schedules the public were inclined to want to remain at home. If nudity and sex would bring audiences into cinemas, then Hollywood would match the purveyors of porn. The industry's watch-dogs could no nothing. The MPAA Code was abandoned, and with it one of the movies' most sacred rules, that crime must not pay. Even murderers escaped punishment in the last reel.

It would be a while before movies would become explicit, and Hollywood made its way forward with sex enjoyed without the benefit of blessing by the clergy. Some steps on the way, most of which were popular but all of which were minor in terms of artistry: Norman Jewison's **The Thomas Crown Affair**, a thriller about a tycoon (Steve McQueen) who plans a heist and the insurance investigator (Faye Dunaway) who interviews him; **The Secret Life of an American Wife**, an intermittently brilliant comedy written by George Axelrod about a

Connecticut housewife (Anne Jackson) who decides to fulfil her fantasies by seducing her favourite movie star (Walter Matthau); a thriller about a gay murderer being hunted down by **The Detective** (Frank Sinatra), who has a nymphomaniac ex-wife (Lee Remick). **The Sergeant**, Rod Steiger, was another army man (like Marlon Brando last year) who sadly realized that he wanted to get into the pants of one of the men under his command; John Flynn directed, from a story and screenplay written by Dennis Murphy.

Funny Girl was brought to the screen with direction by William Wyler, with Barbra Streisand, its Broadway and London star, still singing the songs by Jules Styne (music) and Bob Merrill (lyrics) and still playing the Jewish comedienne Fanny Brice. Streisand, for all her verve, seemed a doubtful screen acquisition, though she could do the deprecatory humour. She had a draggy leading man, Omar Sharif, as the bad lot she married – and in that respect **Star!** did little better, since it was hard to care much about Michael Craig or Richard Crenna, the two husbands of the star in question, Gertrude Lawrence. Robert Wise directed and never understood why the film failed to draw a public: it wasn't the fault of Julie Andrews as Gertie, as enchanting a screen presence as Streisand was not. Blame the miserable screenplay.

Fox's failure with this was somewhat compensated for by the returns from the portentous **Planet of the Apes**, directed by Franklin J. Schaffner, with Charlton

Left: Unlike the 1938 version, **The Charge of the Light Brigade** could lay claim to historical accuracy, with one of the best portraits of Victorian life ever offered by films. David Hemmings was among the cast. Above: Katherine Hepburn as Eleanor of Aquitaine in **The Lion in Winter**, directed by Anthony Harvey from the play by James Goldman. Opposite: A street fight in Verona from Zeffirelli's version of **Romeo and Juliet**, which joined Olivier's three Shakespeare films and Mankiewicz's **Julius Caesar** to prove that the Bard could be successfully filmed. Commercially, it was even more popular than they had been.

Heston as an astronaut who lands in just such a place. There were more returns – sequels, that is. Heston had a better movie in Tom Gries's elegiac movie about an ageing cowboy, **Will Penny**.

Clint Eastwood made an excellent showing in **Coogan's Bluff** as a laconic Arizona sheriff out to get his man in the Big Apple. Don Siegel directed, and this veteran showed he might now be a master of this form, for **Madigan** was also very nearly top notch. Richard Widmark was Madigan, Harry Guardino his assistant and Henry Fonda the commissioner. Like Eastwood, they were up to their necks in police work. So was Steve McQueen in **Bullitt**, Peter Yates's superior thriller, with lots of car chases up and down the hills of San Francisco.

In Britain, permissive cinema was given its biggest lift with **The Strange Affair**, which may have been strange but was not very good. Still, it has Jeremy Kemp as a cop with a bad case of the psychotics and Michael York as a college-educated cop who bends easily after a

sexy young hippy (Susan George) throws herself at him. York was Tybalt in a sensuous, exciting **Romeo and Juliet**, eclipsing the lovers (Olivia Hussey, Leonard Whiting) in what was a triumph for Franco Zeffirelli, who had changed ideas about the staging of Shakespeare when he had originally directed this at the Old Vic. The most exciting, complex and satisfying history lesson from a British studio in many a year was **The Charge of the Light Brigade**, which examined not only that matter but a large section of the Victorian upper class. Tony Richardson directed from a script by Charles Wood; with Vanessa Redgrave, and Trevor Howard and John Gielgud as the two military twits whose conflict led to the blunder.

Encouraged by the spaghetti Westerns, Britain sent Edward Dmytryk to Spain to make **Shalako**, with a cast oddly joining up Sean Connery, Brigitte Bardot, Jack Hawkins, Woody Strode and Stephen Boyd. Among Anglo-American cooperations there was one triumph: Kubrick's **2001: A Space Odyssey**, which stretches its action over four million years – towards the end of which, inspiration unsurprisingly failed (as those who made the film recognized). But there are some marvellous images, such as the swirling spaceships and the psychedelic trip. If you haven't seen it, wait till they revive Cinerama.

In Sweden, Bergman was telling of **The Shame**, about a married couple and the nightmare that is civil war. This is a film of immense stature, perhaps Bergman's greatest to this date. Liv Ullmann and Max von Sydow play the couple.

Opposite: Liv Ullman in Bergman's **Shame**, set on a remote island. Somewhere a war is raging, and as it comes closer a film that is already powerful becomes overwhelming. Above: Mia Farrow in Roman Polanski's **Rosemary's Baby**, from Ira Levin's novel. The film provided plenty of shocks as it told of witchcraft in modern New York. Right: **Coogan's Bluff** was a superior thriller which gave new impetus to the careers of both director and star: Don Siegel, who had been directing with only occasional success since 1945, and Clint Eastwood (right), best known for television's **Rawhide** and spaghetti Westerns.

Larry Peerce's **Goodbye, Columbus** was based on Philip Roth's novel about the pursuit of a poor Jewish boy (here, Richard Benjamin) by a rich Jewish girl (Ali McGraw). She refuses him sex until she wants it, and when he wants it she says, 'Start without me.' 'Growing a penis' is how she spent the summer, she says. Neither line would have been allowed

1969

before. It's the first film to show a jock-strap, even if McGraw's brother is washing it, not wearing it. This film is honest about life in 1969, as is John Schlesinger's **Midnight Cowboy**, from the novel by James Leo Herlihy, with John Voight as a Southern boy expecting to make a fortune as a stud in New York. He goes to a few wild parties and does get to sleep with a lady or so; but in the end he's servicing men in cinema balconies. In Peter Yates's **John and Mary**, Dustin Hoffman and Mia Farrow meet in a singles bar and go to bed together. Sex was smart. In Paul Mazursky's **Bob and Carol and Ted and Alice** one suburban couple (Natalie Wood, Robert Culp) decides to swap partners with another; in the end they don't, but sing 'All the World Needs Now is Love, Love, Love'. The public lapped up all four films, despite the quality of the last; and they adored Dennis Hopper's **Easy Rider**, in which he and Peter Fonda jump on motorbikes to go off and discover America. They meet other hippies, do drugs and meet up with a drunken, courteous young lawyer, Jack Nicholson, who thinks their values are smashing. There had been

many hippy movies because there had been many hippies since American involvement in Vietnam had increased dramatically; the movement was also a protest against their parents, the television generation.

Ménages à trois turned up in two of the year's most successful pictures: George Roy Hill's **Butch Cassidy and the Sundance Kid**, with Paul Newman, Katharine Ross, Robert Redford; and Joshua Logan's **Paint Your Wagon**, with Lee Marvin, Jean Seberg and Clint Eastwood. Both were Westerns, the latter a singing one, from Lerner and Loewe's 1951 show. Let's come back to **Butch** and first despatch two other musicals, again from Broadway: Bob Fosse's **Sweet Charity**, based on **Le Notte di Cabiria**, with Shirley MacLaine as a hooker and John McMartin as the nice guy who makes off with her dough; and Gene Kelly's **Hello Dolly!**, in which Barbra Streisand played Dolly as a grotesque imitation of Mae West as she pursued Walter Matthau. Both were dangerously expensive, endangering the species.

Fox would have been in serious trouble with **Dolly** if it hadn't been for **Butch**. Neither he nor the Kid were remotely like the originals, who were dangerous. Audiences liked the jokey town and the Mexican settings, which were to be found again in Peckinpah's ultra-violent **The Wild Bunch**, who included William Holden, Ernest Borgnine and Edmond O'Brien, with Robert Ryan as their pursuer.

In Britain, **The Best House in London** is a Victorian brothel. It isn't very good and nor is Ken Russell's **Women in Love**, but these are the local film industry's

Left: Dennis Hopper and Peter Fonda in the immensely successful **Easy Rider**, directed by Hopper, produced by Fonda, and written and conceived by both with Terry Southern. Above: In **Goodbye Mr Chips**, Peter O'Toole and Petula Clark meet at Pompeii and then visit Paestum together. This film, from Terence Rattigan's screenplay, was better than the 1939 version. Opposite: Of the year's Westerns, **True Grit**, had the best material: John Wayne as a one-eyed gunfighter employed by a pert young girl, Kim Darby, and accompanied by a cocky Texas Ranger to avenge her dad's murder. Henry Hathaway directed.

chief contributions to the advance of sex in the movies, the latter for a nude wrestling scene with Oliver Reed and Alan Bates. Whether this is in the book – D. H. Lawrence's – is as immaterial as it is to the movie's actual plot, which is about the emancipation of two sisters, Glenda Jackson and Jennie Linden.

World War II and **The Battle of Britain** was relived by a star cast including Olivier, Richardson, Redgrave, Trevor Howard, Kenneth More and Susannah York, all of whom had been re-living World War I earlier in the year, albeit as a show on Brighton pier. This one had songs of the period, as it had had in Joan Littlewood's original stage production, **Oh! What A Lovely War**; but Richard Attenborough, in his first film as director, didn't get anywhere near the bitterness of that, despite Maggie Smith, two other theatrical knights (Gielgud, John Clements) and two more Redgraves (Corin, Vanessa).

George Lazenby played James Bond (Sean had gone)

On Her Majesty's Secret Service. Richard Burton was Henry VIII, marrying his **Anne of the Thousand Days**, Geneviève Bujold. Vanessa Redgrave was **Isadora** Duncan, a rather tiresome lady in this arid version, directed by Karel Reisz. Redgrave thus ceded her stage role of the strong-minded Edinburgh teacher of the 1930s in the dramatization of Muriel Spark's **The Prime of Miss Jean Brodie** to Maggie Smith, who played her, quite rightly, with no sense of the ridiculous. But equally rightly, Ronald Neame's film had some sly fun at her expense.

A boys' public school was the setting for **Goodbye Mr Chips**, with Peter O'Toole and Petula Clark singing away some fairly forgettable songs. Despite those, these performers, often resistible, were charming on this occasion, which was directed by Herbert Ross, who had been staging numbers in such films as **Funny Girl**. It was liked by the press neither as musical nor remake, but was superior to many for one reason: Terence Rattigan had

done a damned good job on the screenplay. The importance of this was re-emphasized by John Hopkins's script for **The Virgin Soldiers**, which was far better than the book on which it was based. It was directed by novice John Dexter (though he had many distinguished stage credits), and between him and Mr Hopkins it provided an authentic view of one army camp on Singapore during the Emergency. There is no better film on National Servicemen and their sniggering obsession with sex. Hywel Bennett was the chief culprit, with Nigel Patrick as his RSM.

With **Z** around, nothing else looked up to much. And **Z** was everywhere, except in Greece. It was the story of a political assassination (in an unnamed North African country) of a left-wing deputy (Yves Montand) who comes to speak in a provincial town. He was based on Grigoris Lambrakis, who had been murdered in 1963 in Greece with, it was thought, the connivance of the army and the police, an unholy alliance which eventually brought the colonels to power. The film was directed by a Greek, Costa-Gavras, and written by him with Jorge Semprun. Costa-Gavras did a number of revolutionary things, such as putting together an all-star cast and a documentary style, with shots that often arrived on screen like machine-gun bullets. The end titles, documenting the fate of the characters, would become standard practice in films about actual events.

It is not pleasant to turn from a film as bare and urgent to the excesses of Italy: **Fellini-Satyricon**, Sergio Leone's **Once Upon a Time in the West** and Visconti's **The Damned**, with Helmut Berger in a garter-belt to imitate Marlene Dietrich in **The Blue Angel**. Berger also

Opposite above: Paul Newman, Katharine Ross and Robert Redford in **Butch Cassidy and the Sundance Kid**. They look pretty respectable here, but they're on the run from the law. Above: Al Lewis and Gig Young in **They Shoot Horses, Don't They?**, directed by Sydney Pollack from the novel by Horace McCoy, set wholly during a dance marathon in the darkest days of the Depression. Right: Jon Voight (left) in **Midnight Cowboy**, as a Southern innocent who arrives in New York looking for ladies who will pay for his sexual prowess; but the only lasting relationship is with a dying down-and-out, played by Dustin Hoffman.

rapes a child and his own mother (Ingrid Thulin), while Dirk Bogarde shuffles around as her lover. The film's family, armaments manufacturers in Germany, is based on the Krupps and, given the material there, Visconti should have come up with something more than a catalogue of perversions. Ermanno Olmi proved there was still integrity in Italy with a beautiful film, **Un Certo Giorno**, about a middle-aged executive in advertising and how an automobile accident affects his perceptions about his life.

From India, **Bhuvan Shome** was a Godardian jingle about a railway official on a hunting trip. The director was Mrinal Sen, whom Ray despised; but then, it was around this time that Ray and Buñuel allowed a conversation of theirs to be quoted, to the effect that Godard would soon be forgotten. In time, Sen's work would lean much further toward that of Ray, who in 1969 came up with one of his most contemplative films, **Days and Nights in the Forest**, which are spent by four playboys from Calcutta, on vacation.

Analogies can be dangerous, but Bergman's **A Passion** (US **The Passion of Anna**) is one of his finest films, and it also takes its characters to an examination of their lives. Ray's film is tranquil but disturbing; Bergman's is violent – the island on which the characters live is stalked by a maniac who strikes at night – and equally disturbing. With Max van Sydow, Liv Ullman, Erland Josephson and Bibi Andersson, it featured his usual actors and his usual preoccupations, but never expressed so eloquently and fiercely.

Hollywood breathed a sigh of relief. The end of censorship had freed it not only of sexual inhibition, but also of reverence and respect. Audiences were getting younger and they didn't want what the French called the *cinéma du papa*. The industry, however, was sometimes uncertain of what the public did want.

1970

There was much blood in Robert Altman's **M*A*S*H**, set in a field hospital in Vietnam, with Elliott Gould, Donald Sutherland and no regard for anything or anybody. It was a huge success, leaving audiences little appetite for Mike Nichols' **Catch-22**, from Joseph Heller's satirical anti-army novel, with a large cast headed by Alan Arkin and including Martin Balsam, the first American actor to be seen sitting on a toilet. The military took another bashing in **Patton**, directed by Franklin J. Schaffner with George C. Scott in the title role, seen warts and all. Beyond that, the film was clear sighted on the general's battle strategy.

In this climate it was possible to make a movie favourable to **The Revolutionary**, even if he lived in an unnamed European democracy. Jon Voight played him, Robert Duvall was his mentor and Paul Williams was the director. Perhaps the film was too left-wing, though, since it was a box-office failure. The student hero, Gould, of **Getting Straight**, was a radical who slept around. Sutherland, in **Alex in Wonderland**, asks his wife after sex, 'When was the last time you made it twice?', and he

goes around asking his married male pals whether they masturbated (the answer was yes). Paul Mazursky directed and co-wrote this self-indulgent movie about a moviemaker (Alex).

It was otherwise an above-average year for comedy, and much of it was post-coital in Frank Perry's **Diary of a Mad Housewife**, who was Carrie Snodgress, having an affair with Frank Langella because she is tired of her pompous husband, Richard Benjamin. New York was beautifully used in Hal Ashby's **The Landlord**, with Beau Bridges as a dilettante who buys a house in a black ghetto in order to conform to his liberal convictions; in Herbert Ross's **The Owl and the Pussycat**, with Barbra Streisand as a Jewish hooker (at one point a client is waiting for her in his shorts – it had taken this long for Hollywood to admit that people took their clothes off to make love) squabbling with neighbour George Segal; in Carl Reiner's **Where's Poppa?**, with Segal as a mother (Ruth Gordon) dominated Jewish boy; and in Irving Kershner's **Loving**, with Segal as a commercial artist trying to pluck up courage to leave his wife, Eva Marie Saint. There was a lot of loving around, including **Lovers and Other Strangers**, about various comic antics of the guests at a wedding; and Arthur Hiller's **Love Story**, about the

Left: Martin Balsam, Art Garfunkel, Orson Welles and Martin Sheen in **Catch-22**. The acclaim for Joseph Heller's novel was one factor in **M*A*S*H** being made in the first place, but by the time it was filmed there had been too many military madmen on the screen. Above: Ryan O'Neal and Ali McGraw in **Love Story**. The press didn't like the book or the film, but this was one of those occasions when the public paid not the slightest attention. Opposite: George C. Scott, expressing some sort of military vainglory, in **Patton: A Salute to a Rebel**. It was retitled **Patton: Lust For Glory** for most overseas audiences.

lugubrious meeting, mating and parting (she dies) of two students (Ali McGraw, Ryan O'Neal), from a bestseller.

Dying in this maudlin way was something Hollywood could cope with. **I Never Sang for my Father** dealt with a family facing old age and mother dying. Melvyn Douglas was her husband, with equally sensitive performances by Gene Hackman and Estelle Parsons as the siblings. Gilbert Cates directed from Robert Anderson's screenplay, from his play. Another play filmed was Mart Crowley's **The Boys in the Band**, with bitchy New York gay humour because all but one of the guests at this birthday party are gentlemen who prefer gentlemen. Very nice performance by Laurence Luckinbill, who left his wife for another man but can't, dammit, be faithful to him. Directed stagily by William Friedkin.

Then there was heterosexual sex from Fox, whose shareholders complained. Needing a sequel to a popular movie, they called in Russ Meyer, known as the maker of some semi-porn boob movies. With a script by Roger Ebert, he came up with **Beyond the Valley of the Dolls** which looks at a pop group into drugs and every form of sex. It does liven up in the second half, which is more than can be said for **Myra Breckinridge**, based on Gore Vidal's novel about a movie critic who has a sex change. It has a scene where Myra rapes a jock with a dildo. The bad news continues with Rex Reed and Raquel Welch sharing the title role; it gets worse with the grotesque return to the screen of Mae West; and even worse with direction by a British pop singer, Mike Sarne. Fox realized both films were a mistake, and the new permissiveness was never abused quite so blatantly again.

Bob Rafelson's **Five Easy Pieces**, written by Carol Eastman, was recognized as a fine and serious film, even if there are some close-ups of Jack Nicholson's head while he's fucking. The film catches 1970 America truly, and so do two others which were disregarded at the time. James Bridges wrote and directed **The Baby Maker**, about one of those couples who have everything they want except a baby. The girl (Barbara Hershey) they employ is deeply into drink and drugs and so is her husband (Scott Glenn). Soon the nice square husband has fallen crazily in love with her. John G. Avildsen directed **Joe** from a screenplay by Norman Wexler. A well-off girl (Susan Sarandon) takes to drugs and disappears. Her father kills her lover/pusher in a fit of anger and confesses after some drinks to a hard-hat (Peter Boyle), who shares his views. They decide, as they search the underworld bars, that any further killing may not be accidental. These three films are about class and about changing America. More importantly, they told us that the America that Hollywood had been selling from the start had been a false bill of goods.

The real Britain had been seen on the screen from time to time, and Ken Loach put it there again in **Kes**, the story of a small boy living in a mining town who knows only too well what he'll do when he grows up. Meanwhile, childhood is enlivened by a pet kestrel. It was the only good British film of the year.

In France, Chabrol made his best film, **Le Boucher**. With life in a quiet provincial town overshadowed by a murder hunt, the local teacher (Stéphane Audran) begins a friendship with the butcher (Jean Yanne). We all know who did it. Much more complicated and hardly less watchable is **La Rupture**. In a boarding house, a lawyer (Jean-Pierre Cassel) is spying on the wife (Mlle Audran) of

Left: Elliott Gould, Donald Sutherland (both at left) and Tom Skerrit (in hat) in Robert Altman's **M*A*S*H**, which stood for Mobile Army Surgical Hospital. Above: **Ryan's Daughter** was a grandiose tribute by Robert Bolt to his wife, Sarah Miles, playing a colleen who commits adultery with a soldier during World War I. Even Robert Mitchum (pictured with her) and Trevor Howard couldn't save it. Opposite: Jack Nicholson (right) with Karen Black and Billy 'Green' Bush in **Five Easy Pieces**, an excellent free-wheeling picture which turned out to be a discussion of class distinctions – one of the very few American films on this subject.

a bourgeois thug (Jean-Claude Druout) because his father (Michael Bouquet) is paying him to do so. Will she find out? Costa-Gavras directed another powerful political thriller, **L'Aveu**, examining the Czech show trials of the 1950s, when a large number of people were accused of subverting the state. Prominent among them is Yves Montand, with Simon Signoret as his wife and Gabriele Ferzetti as his confused interrogator.

In Italy, Francesco Rosi continued his cause for committed cinema with **Uomini Contro**, set on the battlefields of World War I, but it wasn't exported. Nor was the best Italian film of the year, Bolognini's **Metello**,

which concentrates on the activities of a dedicated anarchist in turn-of-the-century Florence.

In Spain – the new Spain, that is, of tourists and prosperity – Berlanga made **Vívan los Nóvios!**, about an ill-matched couple preparing for marriage. The couple in Buñuel's **Tristana** were even more unsuited: the guardian (Fernando Rey) and the orphan (Catherine Deneuve). With lust and then disorder when she falls in love with an artist (Franco Nero), this was the master's last, dark masterpiece. In Poland, another great director was at work. **Landscape After Battle** was Wajda's study of the mental turmoil of the victims of the concentration camps.

1971

The industry's renewed confidence hardly outlasted 1970. It filmed Neil Simon (**Plaza Suite**, directed by Arthur Hiller, with Matthau) and Euripides (**The Trojan Women**, directed by Cacoyannis, with Katharine Hepburn, Vanessa Redgrave), both of which flopped. Deservedly. The new schizophrenia was exemplified by Hal Ashby's **Harold and Maude**, in which a seventy-nine-year-old woman (Ruth Gordon) and a student (Bud Cort) fall in love. The critics weren't shocked by this, only dismissive, but it became a cult item. Only a handful of movies with a high sex quotient found moviegoers equally eager to watch: Pakula's **Klute**, a murder mystery with Donald Sutherland as a cop and Jane Fonda as a hooker ('Wow, sounds like fun,' she assures a client); Mike Nichols' **Carnal Knowledge**, written by Jules Feiffer, which examined the sex lives over some years of college graduates Jack Nicholson and Art Garfunkel, one of whom can only – eventually – get it up with a blow-job (another movie first); Robert Mulligan's **Summer of '42**, with frustrated (her husband is in the army) Jennifer O'Neill seducing teenager Gary Grimes, who dutifully takes himself to the drugstore to buy condoms (another first); and Bogdanovich's **The Last Picture Show**, in which the smart set of a small Texas town like getting it off with each other or maybe one of the other's mothers. This was the last American picture in monochrome, though there would be others for special occasions. It's conten-

tious to say exactly when monochrome fell into disfavour, since the British had continued using it – if only a couple of times a year – for movies not intended for the American market. But now that televiewers were exchanging their black-and-white sets for colour at a zillion knots a second, the networks made it clear that they were only prepared to buy movies with the full prism.

To get back to sex, which was what the characters in these movies clearly needed to do, we alight on **Taking Off**, directed by Milos Forman, hot from Czechoslovakia, with a screenplay by Buck Henry, considered to be, along with Feiffer, the satirist of his age. The film proposed an exciting theory: that parents could be rejuvenated if they emulated their kids by taking off their clothes at parties and smoked pot. The kids in the plot didn't want to know, and neither did audiences.

Audiences wanted Clint, who represented a more assured America, even if it was touch and go for a while. In **Play Misty for Me** he was a disc jockey who sleeps with a fan who becomes homicidal when he finishes the affair. In **Dirty Harry** he was a San Francisco cop, a bruised martyr, out to get a petty but vicious crook who, at the end, hijacks a school bus for ransom. He himself directed the first of these two films, Don Siegel did the other. One other thriller rivalled **Dirty Harry** as box-office bait: William Friedkin's **The French Connection**, with Gene Hackman as an over-the-hill New York cop persevering in his pursuit of some drug smugglers. In the old days this would have been a superior B-movie: in 1972 it took Oscars for Film, Direction, Actor (Hackman's was deserved).

It was a cheerless year in Britain, but the following

Left: Peter Finch (left) and Glenda Jackson in John Schlesinger's **Sunday, Bloody Sunday** in which, in just over a week, Murray Head hops into bed with one or other of them. Mr Head seemed an unlikely object of sexual desire. Above: Donald Sutherland as **Klute**, a cop, and Jane Fonda, a hooker, who admits that she never comes at the same time as her clients. Thus the cinema came of age. Opposite: Julia Christie wasn't so much a whore in **McCabe and Mrs Miller** as the madam of the brothel where most of the action took place. Warren Beatty was her lover and Robert Altman directed.

were seen and talked about: Kubrick's **A Clockwork Orange**, a bleak portrait of a future Britain ruled by zombie-like thugs; John Schlesinger's dishonest **Sunday, Bloody Sunday**, with Glenda Jackson and Peter Finch (as a doctor) vying for the affections of the same young man; and Ken Russell's **The Devils**, with Miss Redgrave and Oliver Reed, which redefined vulgarity as it poked around at witchcraft in seventeenth-century France. Producer Sam Spiegel and director Franklin J. Schaffner took on the last of the Czars with **Nicholas and Alexandra**, with Michael Jayston and Janet Suzman in those roles. The complexities of Robert K. Massie's massive bestselling biography were up there on the screen, with players of the calibre of Olivier, Irene Worth, Ian Holm, Michael Bryant as Lenin and Brian Cox as Trotsky, but the public was hardly interested. **And Now For Something Completely Different**: well, that was it, wasn't it? Nor did the public care for this first movie outing for the Monty Python team which had changed television comedy. The best British film was about Barry Newman getting from A

to B, from Denver to Colorado, with some mild adventures and hallucinating scenery en route: **Vanishing Point**, directed by Richard Sarafian.

In France, Chabrol's masterly **Juste Avant la Nuit** has Michel Bouquet as a man who murders his mistress and confesses to his best friend (François Périer), her husband, and his own wife (Stéphane Audran), none of whom react very positively. France's most successful film abroad was Louis Malle's autobiographical **Le Souffle au Cœur**, about a youngster with a heart condition hospita-

lized in the 1950s. His mother, visiting him, decides that it is time he learnt about sex the practical way, but then when your mother looks like Lea Massari few are likely to be offended.

In Italy, Visconti did an elegant literary adaptation, **Death in Venice**, from Thomas Mann, with Dirk Bogarde as the composer who lingers on on the Lido despite an outbreak of cholera because he is obsessed with a handsome youth. Mahler swelling up on the soundtrack as the steamer crosses the Lagoon can make the situation

plausible. But Olmi made two films which dwarf even Visconti: **I Recuperanti** and **Durante l'Estate**. The first, echoing the theme of his first movie, is about the relationship of an old man and a young one as they scavenge for scrap metal – from the shells of World War I – in the Dolomites; the second is about another aged fellow who lives in a world of fantasy which makes him happier than an old friend who lives in a world of luxury, in Milan.

In India, Satyajit Ray made two movies with related themes, inasmuch as both concern urban life and the necessity of earning a living. Both, Ray conceded, were brought about because his critics had accused him of not being sufficiently political. He didn't want to be, as these films show: **The Adversary** is about a young man who needs to get a job but, like Olmi's 'professor', would rather dream; **Company Limited** is about a successful young executive. Political, no, but taken together they suggest that life can never be perfect.

Left: The situation of an older woman seducing a schoolboy first appeared in films in **Le Blé en Herbe**. The first American film to deal with this subject was **The Graduate**, and then **Summer of '42**, with Jennifer O'Neill and Gary Grimes. Above: Gene Hackman in **The French Connection**, the first film to spawn a sequel with a single digit, **The French Connection II** (1975). It wasn't a very imaginative solution.

1972

There's James Coco standing there in just a T-shirt, shorts, socks and garters. There's Dyan Cannon kneeling down and suddenly there's cum all over her face. Otto Preminger, no less, offered this glorious moment in cinema in **Such Good Friends**, written by Elaine May, understandably under a pseudonym. It has one good idea: as a man (Laurence Luckinbill) is dying, his wife (Cannon) discovers that he had been flagrantly unfaithful so she decides to make it with as many men as she can before he kicks the bucket. There are seven bad ideas in **Everything You Always Wanted to Know About Sex But Were Afraid to Ask**: seven episodes. Come back, Myra Breckinridge, all is forgiven. Writer-director-actor Woody Allen perpetrated this wet dream.

Two musicals benefited from the movies' new freedom: Sidney J. Furie's **Lady Sings the Blues**, a life of Billie Holiday, who was played by the plastic Diana Ross; and Bob Fosse's **Cabaret**, from the Kander and Ebb Broadway musical, which had Liza Minnelli having a good time in Berlin in the 1920s. The adaptation lost some of the original's bite, but Herr Issyvoo (Michael York) was now bisexual, which he wasn't before.

Of the year's better movies, there was John Boorman's **Deliverance**, in which four urban guys go canoeing in the Appalachians and one of them (Ned Beatty) is raped by some backswoodsmen, after which the others (Jon Voight, Burt Reynolds, Ronny Cox) find that escaping through the hostile terrain is increasingly desperate; Michael Ritchie's **The Candidate**, with Robert Redford discovering that he is only the patsy after being selected to represent California for the Democrats; and Martin Ritt's sympathetic **Sounder**, centring on a small black boy in Louisiana during the Depression who realizes that education is his only means of escape.

The year's biggest box-office success, critically admired and an Oscar winner, was Francis Coppola's **The Godfather**, with Marlon Brando in the title role, a Mafia chief whose family and counsellors include James Caan, Al Pacino, Robert Duvall. It is an excessively violent film, if apparently as objective as the films of Costa-Gavras. He, though, is not objective at all, but he understands the matters whereof he speaks; Coppola merely shows them.

In Britain, Roman Polanski filmed **Macbeth**, deliberately choosing young Macbeths, Jon Finch and Francesa Annis. It was a mistake. Finch was also in Hitchcock's **Frenzy**, as a suspected sex murderer (there hadn't been many of those in films in the past, but there would be a helluva lot in the future). We all knew that Barry Foster was guilty, which didn't help an occasion as tired and show-offy as this director's other recent efforts. Britain's best film, **A Day in the Death of Joe Egg**, went almost

Below: Burt Reynolds became a national figure when he posed discreetly nude for *Cosmopolitan*, the first 'name' to do so. He knew he could get away with it as he had just made a very good film, **Deliverance**. Opposite: The Western was in decline, except for those starring Clint Eastwood. Here he is as **Joe Kidd**, a mercenary embroiled in a struggle for land between a landowner and the Mexicans, led by John Saxon.

unnoticed, despite the fact that Peter Nichols' play had been successful both in London and New York. He wrote the screenplay, about a couple (Alan Bates, Janet Suzman) who try to confront the tragedy of their spastic child with laughter; Peter Medak directed.

In France, **L'Attentat** was a smashing political thriller in the manner of **Z**, by the same writer, Jorge Semprun, but directed in this case by Yves Boisset. Its starting point was the unsolved kidnapping of the exiled Moroccan leader, Mehdi Ben Barka, on the streets of Paris in 1967. Among those trapped in the spider's web plot are Gian Maria Volonté, Jean-Louis Trintignant and Jean Seberg; among those wanting them killed while they're there are Philippe Noiret, Michel Piccoli and Michel Bouquet, as nasty a group of right-wingers as you'd find anywhere.

Preoccupied with sex were Marlon Brando and Maria Schneider, but grimly, graphically and much concerned with butter up bums. With Brando's name attached, United Artists had invested, worried at first as scenes were improvised and then, in the current climate, convinced that they had a bigger moneyspinner than **The Sound of Music**. They reckoned without Bernardo Bertolucci, who spectacularly proved that his two admired films of 1970 were flashes in pans. A drearier film than **Last Tango in**

Paris could not be imagined, and audiences melted away. UA revised its estimates. Buñuel had fun with **Le Charme Discret de la Bourgeoisie**, an ironic title since the bourgeoisie on display were lethal and anything but charming. That was always his way and these were his usual targets. Like **Last Tango**, it was much discussed as an assault on the natural order of things. What it was was an assault on those who had disregarded most of his superior earlier films. Like his fellow-countryman, Picasso, he showed his contempt by offering something no longer challenging either to themselves or audiences.

In Ceylon, Lester James Peries made his two finest films. He had been much influenced by Ray since he began making films in 1956. In 1972 he approached Ray's level with **The Eyes** and **The Treasure**. In the first, the butt of the village jokes unselfishly weds a blind girl and at his mother's insistence takes her to a holy man for a cure, only to find that the latter's lust for her only complicates matters. The second is also about a marriage: a penniless landowner marries a virgin because of a local belief that if a virgin is sacrificed at a particular spot, a fortune can be found there; but he hadn't reckoned on falling in love with her.

This luminous, moving film would be the year's best were it not for one not remotely like it. Francesco Rosi's **Il Caso Mattei** or **The Mattei Affair** is the cinema of polemic and very angry. Enrico Mattei, played by Gian Maria Volonté, organized Italy's oil supplies, turning AGIP into a multimillion state-owned company: yet, when he mysteriously died in a plane crash, no one in government or elsewhere seemed curious to know why.

Opposite: Janet Suzman and Alan Bates as the worried parents in the moving film of Peter Nichols' comedy of hurt, **A Day in the Life of Joe Egg**. Nichols called it 'a very arty horror film that just isn't funny', but even so it proves that he is among the best of contemporary British writers specializing in theatre and television. Above: Liza Minnelli as Sally Bowles in **Cabaret**, originally one of Christopher Isherwood's *Goodbye to Berlin* stories, and then a play and film, **I am a Camera** (1955). Right: Marlon Brando as the Mafia chieftain in **The Godfather**, with Robert Duvall as the clan's lawyer.

Hollywood continues to grow up. In **The Exorcist**, directed by William Friedkin, with a screenplay from his novel by William Peter Blatty, a Catholic teenager (Linda Blair) gets possessed by the devil, gets blood all over herself masturbating with a crucifix, vomits, has her head in a whirl and is responsible for several deaths. Pretentious, moronic, much seen and, more sensibly, much-banned.

1973

The year's two most under-rated films both had the word 'blue' in the title. James William Guercio's haunting **Electra Glide in Blue** is a riposte to **Easy Rider** – hippies as seen by authority, in the person of a diminutive cop, Robert Blake, who swaggers around Monument Valley feeling very proud of himself. James Frawley's **Kid Blue** is a comic Western, with Dennis Hopper as the stranger who rides into town prepared to do anything rather than go back to being a bank robber. 'Anything' is what he does do, amidst the 'actress' (Janice Rule), who services the town's leading citizens; a bourgeois couple (Warren Oates, Lee Purcell), both of whom make a pass at him; 'Mean John' (Ben Johnson), the sheriff; and 'Preacher' (Peter Boyle), who has just invented the aeroplane.

There were two fine Westerns, both showing a dirtier, rougher West than in the past: Peckinpah's **Pat**

Above: Jack Nicholson as a petty officer in **The Last Detail**, the best film yet about service life – a claim made earlier in these pages, but this time they were allowed to leave in the four letter words. Opposite: Ryan O'Neal and Tatum, his daughter (though not in the film), in **Paper Moon**, a very funny comedy and the best film of its variable director, Peter Bogdanovich.

298

Garrett and Billy the Kid, with James Coburn and Kris Kristofferson in those roles; **High Plains Drifter**, directed by and starring Clint Eastwood, another stranger in town. Eastwood played Dirty Harry for the second time in **Magnum Force**, under the direction of Ted Post; 'Make my day,' he says to a punk pointing a gun at him. It was a year of good thrillers, including Sidney Lumet's **Serpico**, with Al Pacino as an unconventional member of New York's finest, the only one not on the take.

Hollywood remained determined not to face the modern world and Jack Lemmon only managed to get **Save the Tiger** made by taking no salary but a deferment. He played a man who looked around him and didn't like what he saw – porno cinemas, hippies and the ethics of his partner in the L.A. garment business. John G. Avildsen directed from a screenplay by Steve Shagan. James Bridges' **The Paper Chase** was about the perils of law school, with John Houseman as a supercilious professor and Timothy Bottoms as chief swot. Hal Ashby's excellent **The Last Detail** chronicled the adventures of three men in the peacetime navy, an old hand (Jack Nicholson) and a black (Otis Young), who are escorting a youngster (Randy Quaid) to the brig. Robert Towne scripted from a novel by Darryl Ponicsan.

Hollywood preferred to look at the past. George Lucas's **American Graffiti** was set in 1962 and concerned the antics, chiefly amorous, of some teenagers after graduation. These included Harrison Ford, Richard Dreyfuss, Ronny Howard, Bo Hopkins and Paul Le Mat. Terrence Malick's script for **Badlands**, which he directed himself, was based on a case in Nevada in the 1950s: when father (Warren Oates) tells Holly (Sissy Spacek) that she can't see Kit (Martin Sheen), she shoots him dead and the

two of them go on a joyride of killings. Peter Bogdanovich's delightful **Paper Moon** is set firmly during the Depression (hence like **The Last Picture Show**, he made it in black and white), when a conman (Ryan O'Neal) has to take a newly orphaned child (Tatum O'Neal) to Missouri, and *en route* discovers that she is brighter than he. 1973 was, **The Exorcist** apart, a good year for the American cinema.

This could not be said for Britain. **The National Health**, or **Nurse Norton's Affair**, was directed by Jack Gold from the screenplay by Peter Nichols based on his play, which contrasted life in a real hospital to life in hospital soaps. Very amusing were Jim Dale and Lynn Redgrave as members of the staff, and Bob Hoskins and Clive Swift as patients. Zinnemann's **The Day of the Jackal** concerns a plot to assassinate de Gaulle, as taken from Frederick Forsyth's thriller. Edward Fox was the would-be killer, among a large cast scattered all over Europe. This was hardly a British film, but Britain did have two dolls' houses. Claire Bloom had played Nora in London, just as Jane Fonda decided that the role was central to the Women's Liberation movement. The rush was on, and Miss Bloom was the clear winner: **A Doll's House** was directed by Patrick Garland, with Anthony Hopkins. Miss Fonda's version was directed by Joseph Losey.

In France, Costa-Gavras made another powerful

Left: Sissy Spacek in **Badlands**, one of the two beautiful, cruel evocations of life in the Mid-West and directed by Terrence Malick. The other is **Days of Heaven** (1978), after which he went to live in Paris – refusing all further offers till the present. Above: Cyril Cusack (left) as a gunsmith and Edward Fox as a would-be assassin in Fred Zinnemann's complex but riveting thriller, **The Day of the Jackal**. Opposite: Helmut Berger in the title role of Visconti's lavish, elaborate biography of the king **Ludwig**, dilettante, homosexual, castle-builder and patron of Wagner – for all of which reasons he died in mysterious circumstances.

protest, this time against American infiltration into the affairs of other countries. Again, the film was based on fact and again it took the form of a thriller: **Etat de Siège** or **State of Siege**, with Montand as an attaché at the American embassy who is kidnapped and murdered by terrorists. The film, like **The Mattei Affair**, takes the form of an enquiry, and although it never names the country, it is clearly Uruguay.

Visconti cast Helmut Berger as the king **Ludwig** of Bavaria, filming in many of his ornate castles, with Trevor Howard as Wagner and Romy Schneider as the empress Elisabeth, his cousin. It was laughed off foreign screens when MGM released it, but re-assembled (it was never clear whether or not Visconti had intended the plot to be told in chronological order) it improved considerably, which could never be said of Zeffirelli's film about St Francis, **Brother Sun, Sister Moon**. Marco Bellochio's **In the Name of the Father** looks at daily life in a

Catholic seminary, ensuring that no one who saw it would ever want to enter one. De Sica made one last bid to restore his reputation, with the help of Zavattini, **Una Breva Vacanza**, but it was too late. There were few foreign bookings. Yet this is a fresh, affecting movie, concerned as it is with a Milan factory worker (Florinda Bolkan) finding kindnesses in an Alpine clinic which she had never received from her husband (Renato Salvatori).

From India came Satyajit Ray's **Distant Thunder**, which examines famine in a remote Indian village in 1943, when over five million died because cargo ships could not get through. Soumitra Chatterjee is the village schoolmaster. In Germany, Fassbinder made **Fear Eats the Soul**, which charts the romance between a young Arab immigrant worker and a dumpy, middle-aged woman, Brigitte Mira. It was Fassbinder's eighteenth film and gave him an international reputation, for it is not only his best, but by far his best.

H ollywood was again glowing with confidence. So many new talents were touted, if soon to crash. Cash registers in box offices were ringing ... for films which wouldn't find a place today in the post-midnight television schedules. Some personal choices, more or less in preferential order, which brings us first to the thrillers, are: Alan J. Pakula's

1974

The Parallax View, a tense political one with a subtext on the mysterious disappearance of the many who knew too much about the assassination of Kennedy, with Warren Beatty on the spot because he's a journalist investigating a similar event in Seattle; Joseph Sargent's adroit **The Taking of Pelham One Two Three**, with Walter Matthau as an investigator for the New York subway system and a lot of scared passengers in the hijacked train; Gordon Parks' **The Super Cops**, the nth ultra-convincing movie about corruption in the New York police, with David Selby and Ron Leibman as the only two who aren't. Peter Hyams' **Busting** found the same situation in Los Angeles, with Elliott Gould and Robert Blake as the buddy-buddy partners who weren't; and according to Richard Rush's **Freebie and the Bean**, the San Francisco police were squeaky-clean. James Caan and Alan Arkin were the partners. It looked as though all

Above: **Chinatown** used a number of old movie situations and characters – the private eye, Jack Nicholson, and the Mr Big (played by John Huston) who is behind all the rackets. Right: Mia Farrow and Robert Redford in **The Great Gatsby**. F. Scott Fitzgerald's novel was admired by millions of readers; Paramount's budget and publicity reflected this, but the result was much less successful than their 1949 version.

of these had joined together for Steven Spielberg's **The Sugarland Express**, since you had never seen so many police cars in your life, chasing Goldie Hawn and William Atherton, the husband she had helped spring from jail. Polanski's **Chinatown** had Jack Nicholson as a 1930s private-eye sniffing out civic corruption. And Sidney Poitier's **Uptown Saturday Night**, the best of the proliferating all-black features, saw Poitier and Bill Cosby as a couple of nice guys who get caught up with rival gang leaders Harry Belafonte and Calvin Lockhart.

Martin Ritt's **Conrack**, from Pat Conroy's novel, had Jon Voight in beautiful form as a teacher whose individual way of handling his black pupils brings the wrath of inspector Hume Cronyn. Martin Scorsese's **Alice Doesn't Live Here Anymore** had Ellen Burstyn as a young mother who uses her new widowhood to go travelling in the hope that she can make it as a singer. Instead, it looks as though she'll settle down with a gentle bearded giant, Kris Kristofferson. Peckinpah's **Bring Me the Head of Alfredo Garcia** starred Warren Oates in a beautifully judged performance as a saloon pianist who agrees to do just that (for the father whose daughter Alfredo seduced); but when the film moves from reflection to bloody bodies, it goes downhill. Still, no other director could have made it, which can't be said of **The Towering Inferno**. This is not to discredit John Guillermin, since it's the perfect studio product. In fact, it was the product of two studios, the first time this had ever happened, but it was necessitated by the fact that Warner Bros and Fox owned similar properties, about burning skyscrapers. Paul Newman was the architect who designed this one, Steve McQueen the fire chief; and among the

many in peril are William Holden, Jennifer Jones and Fred Astaire who, as it happens, appears in the year's most enjoyable film, **That's Entertainment**, a collection of numbers from the great days of the MGM musical, with Garland and Kelly.

Other 1974 movies included Jack Clayton's over-produced **The Great Gatsby**, with Robert Redford and Mia Farrow; Coppola's **The Conversation**, a hollow Antonioni-esque enigma about bugging, with Gene Hackman; and **The Godfather II**. Billy Wilder's **The Front Page**, with Jack Lemmon, Walter Matthau and Carol Burnett, was broad and vulgar, but a miracle of taste beside Mel Brooks's Western spoof, **Blazing Saddles**, which had only two jokes, cowboys breaking wind after eating beans and kicking each other in the balls. Brooks obviously thought the latter funnier, because it was repeated every few minutes. The film was enormously popular, but each of Brooks's successive films showed a decline in interest, till those of the late 1980s raked in almost no audience at all.

In France, two film-makers were looking at the fate of the Jews during the War. Michel Mitrani's **Les Guichets du Louvre** is a simple study of that day in July in 1942 when the police cooperated with the Gestapo; Louis Malle's **Lacôme Lucien** was about a not-so-bright boy who is a collaborator and the Jewish family who suffer thereby.

In India, Satyajit Ray did a glorious boys' adventure yarn, set chiefly inside **The Golden Fortress**. For quality, this film-maker had been joined by Shayam Benegal, whose **Ankur The Seedling** deals with feudal-

Left: Ellen Burstyn with Diane Ladd in **Alice Doesn't Live Here Anymore**. The film is set in 1943, when Alice wants to be a singer like her idol, Alice Faye; but on her way to Hollywood she stops off in Tucson and gets some temporary work in a diner. Above: Warren Beatty in **The Parallax View**, which cleverly revamped one of the oldest ideas of movie thrillers – that of the journalist on a dangerous undercover assignment. Opposite: Paul Newman and Faye Dunaway in **The Towering Inferno**, which managed to be exciting for 165 minutes with only one situation: a skyscraper is on fire.

ism lingering in provincial villages and how it threatens to destroy the rather foolish young man sent to manage one of his father's estates. 1974 witnessed several new film-makers emerge, many of them from countries which had seldom before exported a film. They included Senegal, with Ousmane Sembene's **Xala**, about an executive whose go-get-'emism lands him in trouble; and Iran, with Dariush Mehrjui's low-key **The Cycle**, about a country boy learning the ropes on the streets of Teheran.

Above all, however, came movies from Australia.

The new Labour prime minister, Gough Whitlam, convinced his countrymen that it was time they stopped looking to Europe and America for their culture – a bold incentive for many young men who had learnt their trade in television. The first two fruits of his prompting were both very enjoyable. Ken Hannam's **Sunday Too Far Away**, about the sheep-shearer's strike of 1955, with Jack Thompson; and Peter Weir's **The Cars That Ate Paris**, a fantasy about a young man becoming a 'veggie' in a remote town being overwhelmed with car wrecks.

The French Connection **II**. Note the **II**. Hollywood had gotten away with it with its sequel to **The Godfather** which, though comparatively few people had turned up to see it, had won an Oscar. Hollywood movies began to be as reproductive as rabbits, and with each sequel the cinema died a little. At least **Jaws** had a few laughs. Steven Spielberg directed, from Peter Benchley's bestseller, with Richard Dreyfuss, Robert Shaw and Roy Scheider trying to trap the bloody thing as it threatened to savage unwary vacationers on Long Island Sound. High class thrills and box-office to match. More of the former in Lumet's **Dog Day Afternoon**, a companion piece to **Serpico**, also based on fact – an incident in 1972 when two gunmen held up a Brooklyn bank in order to get money for one of them (Al Pacino), in order to pay for a sex-change operation for his lover, who wasn't sure he wanted it in the first place.

1975

For originality, Robert Altman's **Nashville** would take some beating: a group portrait of visitors to the home of Grand Old Opry which managed by turns to be invigorating, bizarre, funny and melodramatic as its characters seek fame or just the perfect lay. Most of them are mediocre – as you realize when the film goes on too long. Also striking at the smug and small-minded heart of Middle America was Michael Ritchie's **Smile**, about a beauty competition; but it also manages to be witty and affectionate at the same time. The year's most popular comedy was Hal Ashby's **Shampoo**, with Warren Beatty

as a Beverly Hills hairdresser who uses his reputation as a gay to seduce all the ladies in sight. Beatty and Robert Towne wrote the script, which successfully attacks the myths surrounding American society – especially at an election night party (1968) when Julie Christie is under the table with her mouth at Beatty's fly as he listens to Nixon spouting clichés on television. 'Is this what it's all about?' Jack Warden asks, watching him. 'To make this country a better place to live in?' The question is central to most American movies of the 1970s, post-Watergate, and the answer would seem to be: Fuck some, drink some. It was certainly Jack Nicholson's attitude in **One Flew Over the Cuckoo's Nest**, in which he was a mental patient tormenting the acidulous, severe and petty Nurse Ratched. Much more than **Shampoo**, and with more depth, the film is a comic assault on the sort of people set in authority over us. Milos Forman directed nimbly, from Ken Kesey's novel, and the film was the first to win all four leading Oscars since **It Happened One Night** forty-two years earlier.

A notable expensive disaster occurred in Britain, and from a literary source. Thackeray's **Barry Lyndon** may no longer be much read, but those who do so will find a cunning satire on the bombastics of the eighteenth century. Stanley Kubrick alone knows what he was doing in turning it into this grandiose and pompous costume picture, with Ryan O'Neal simply overparted as Barry, the Irish mercenary. **The Rocky Horror Picture Show**, from a stage musical, took the oldest plot of porno movies, in which a stranded couple stumble into an old dark house and get variously seduced. In this one they're

Left: Jack Nicholson and Maria Schneider in Antonioni's haunting **The Passenger/Professione: Reporter** – which is what Nicholson is, and the film takes him from the North African desert to London, Munich and, finally, Spain. Above: An American couple (Barry Bostwick and Susan Sarandon) stumble into a Transylvanian castle and meet Dr Frank N. Furter (Tim Curry): **The Rocky Horror Picture Show**. The film immediately became a cult item on both sides of the Atlantic. Opposite: Roy Scheider and Robert Shaw in **Jaws**, which was so popular that there were three sequels, not one as hair-raising as the original.

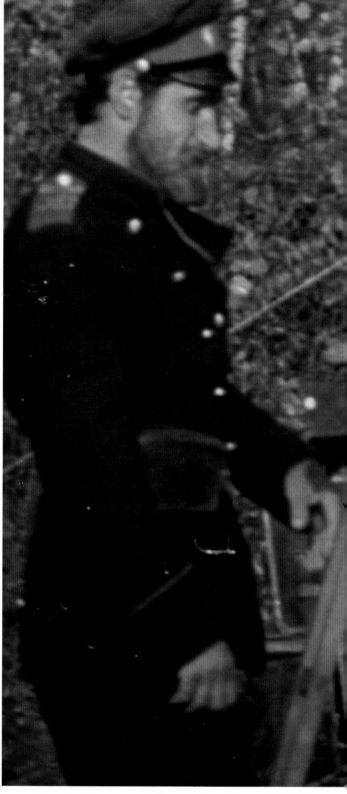

honeymooners, it's a Transylvanian castle and they're not so much seduced as beguiled – by motorcyclists and men in garter-belts, fishnet stockings and high heels. Junky, but the film has been a regular staple since of midnight matinées.

In West Germany, more persuasive perversions were paraded by Fassbinder in **Fox and His Friends**, in which he cast himself as a Joan Crawford-like homosexual involved with a bit of rough trade. Ironically, while foreign critics discussed the New German Cinema, it was ignored at home. The year's biggest success there was a sympathetic study of old age, Bernhard Sinkel's **Lina Braake**, about life in an old people's home. Also much better than anything being done by Fassbinder was **The Lost Honour of Katharina Blum**, written and directed by the husband-and-wife team of Volker Schlöndorff and Margarethe von Trotta from the novel by Heinrich Böll. It was an attack on the gutter press, who turn inside out the life of a nice young woman after linking her name with an anarchist; and **In Der Fremde**, directed by Sohrab Shahid Saless, a simple tale of a Turkish waiter in Berlin.

From India came three very fine films: Ray's **The Middleman**, about the dilemma of a university graduate who, unable to get a job, starts to think that the corruption around him is not so unappealing; Benegal's **Night's End**, based on an actual incident in 1945 when the wealthiest family in the village kidnapped the schoolmaster's wife for sexual purposes; and M. S. Sathyu's **Hot Winds**, which follows the fortunes of a Muslim family in Calcutta after Partition.

Spain sent out its best film yet: José Luis Borau's **Poachers**, a wry, ironic look at some provincials, from governor to poacher, caught up in a web of lust, treachery

and greed. Australia had its biggest success so far with Peter Weir's **Picnic at Hanging Rock**, about the disappearance in 1900 of three schoolgirls at that scenic spot. Another disappearance was the starting point of Antonioni's **The Passenger**, giving reporter Jack Nicholson the chance to assume the personality of another. It isn't easy, as enigmas mount up – in Morocco, London, Munich and Spain. This is perhaps Antonioni's most haunting film. In **Section Speciale** Costa-Gavras examined that French committee of 1941 appointed by the government, to find six citizens for trial to appease the Germans after one of their officers had been shot.

Opposite above: Jack Nicholson as a mental patient in **One Flew Over the Cuckoo's Nest**. A spirit of rebellion is in the air, and Nicholson has appointed himself the ringleader. Above: At the heart of Kurosawa's beautiful **Dersu Uzula** is a study of an unlikely friendship between a Russian officer (Yurl Solomin) and his guide (Maksim Munsuk).

A great director made a great film. Kurosawa's **Dersu Uzula** is about a Russian officer who, in 1902, was seconded to make a geographical survey close to the Pacific coast of Russia. He was given a native guide, and the film is an exhilarating and ultimately moving account of their growing friendship. It is also perhaps the best ever made about terrain – forest, field, snow, loneliness and darkness.

1976

The year was dominated by **All the President's Men**, one of the few movies about something important: the abuse of power (by President Nixon). It is also an extremely exciting detective story (of the Watergate burglary in 1972) by two journalists on *The Washington Post*, Bob Woodward and Carl Bernstein. Their book became William Goldman's screenplay, which Alan J. Pakula directed, and they were played by Robert Redford and Dustin Hoffman. Watergate had outraged the nation as nothing since the assassination of Kennedy. It had taken much longer for another misuse of power to reach the screen, even though it had affected Hollywood's own: the McCarthy witch-hunts of the late 1940s and early 1950s. Walter Bernstein saw the period from the point of view of the writer, and the end credits of **The Front** explained how so many people associated with the film, including Bernstein himself, had been treated. Zero Mostel, who also suffered then, played a comic driven to suicide. Woody Allen was the night cashier who becomes a front for one writer, and the left-wing Martin Ritt directed. It is often an amusing film, and never more so than when a government information agent is explaining Americanism. **Network** was the third film about corruption and the abuse of power, this time in television, as the title implies; but Paddy Chayefsky's script is too hysterical to have many laughs. Faye Dunaway was the ambitious dame on her way to the top; Peter Finch and William Holden were two of the losers.

There weren't many laughs around. The humour of Bob Rafelson's **Stay Hungry** was quite individual, with Jeff Bridges as an idealistic young millionaire living in Birmingham, Alabama. Like **Five Easy Pieces**, this is about a search for identity in a changing world, and Bridges finds his in a gym where he meets Arnold Schwarzenegger and falls in love with the receptionist.

In Hal Ashby's **Bound For Glory**, Woody Guthrie (Keith Carradine) leaves his wife during the Depression because a man's gotta do what a man's gotta do; he rides the freights and became famous as a folk singer. An excellent picture on a difficult subject. The song in **Ode to Billy Joe** is Bobby Gentry's, about the McAllister (Robby Benson) who threw himself off Tallahatchie Bridge – because of a gay experience. That was what Mississippi was like in the 1950s. The film, however, is mainly about Bobbie Lee (Glynis O'Connor) who aims to be a local legend like him.

There were good reasons why America wished to look back at the pre-Watergate years, and the Philadelphia of John G. Avildsen's **Rocky** looked as it might have done at any point since the War; so did the clothes. It was, said one of its producers, in the tradition of Capra, but

Below: Sylvester Stallone in **Rocky**, which he wrote for himself to direct – but he wasn't allowed to. He did, however, write, direct and star in the four sequels. Opposite: Robert Redford and Dustin Hoffman in **All the President's Men** as the two *Washington Post* reporters, Bob Woodward and Carl Bernstein, who uncovered the Watergate conspiracy. As filmed, it made a superb detective story.

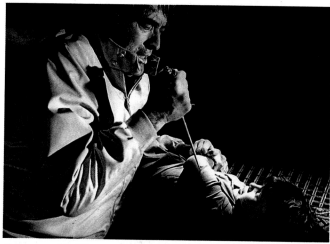

Sylvester Stallone, who wrote it and starred, wasn't much like a Capra hero. He played a punk who boxed part-time and won the big fight at the end. The film was a big success and had several sequels, but that was partly because the public showed no interest in Stallone unless he was in these or the **Rambo** films (first one: **First Blood**, 1982).

Taxi Driver contributed little to the gaiety of the nations. This gem was directed by Martin Scorsese from a screenplay by Paul Schrader and it starred Robert de Niro on brilliant form as a psychotic cabbie who eventually finds himself in a room looking like the cellar in Ekaterinburg. That dear little shower room in the Bates motel seems more than a generation away. Plus Jodie Foster as a thirteen-year-old hooker.

One unexpected success was John Guillerman's **King Kong**. It doesn't have the odd, haunting quality of its predecessor, but it is 'big' and often very amusing, due to the dialogue and the performances of Jeff Bridges, Jessica Lange and Charles Grodin.

The year also saw Brando bid farewell to his talent in Arthur Penn's Western, **The Missouri Breaks**, and the dreadful Russo-American co-production, **The Blue Bird**, directed by Cukor. It was the year, too, of **Gable and Lombard**, **W. C. Fields and Me**, **The Duchess and the Dirtwater Fox** and **Robin and Marian**, ageing Hoods played by Sean Connery and Audrey Hepburn, directed by Richard Lester.

Lester made the only British film of quality, and it was set in America – in a bath house and a gay one at that. A few of the characters hiding in **The Ritz** are gay, because that's what they're doing there – hiding. They include Treat Williams as an Alan Ladd lookalike

detective and Rita Moreno as an untalented chantoosie.

From India, two rural tales: Mrinal Sen's **The Royal Hunt**, about the headman's son and his friendship, in the 1920s, with the British district officer; and Shayam Benegal's touching, witty **The Churning**, in which a bewildered city official is trying to persuade some backward villagers to adopt a dairy collective. In Australia, **Don's Party** gets predictably out of control, directed by Bruce Beresford from David Williamson's play; and Henri Safran's **Storm Boy** lives by the sea and has friends in a pelican and an Aborigine, in that order.

In Italy, Francesco Rosi's dazzling **Cadaveri Eccellenti (Illustrious Corpses)** was a thriller which surpassed even **The Mattei Affair**. At first it does not appear to be political, even though the murders being investigated by Lino Ventura are of prominent citizens; but slowly he begins to realize that the victims are the responsibility of an unholy alliance of Church and Communists, who would rather unite, and kill, than lose an iota of power. A fine cast included Max von Sydow, Charles Vanel and Fernando Rey.

Wajda made **Man of Marble**, a film of the same quality, and one which also criticized the abuse of power – specifically Communist power. It took the form of an enquiry by a student (Krystyna Janda) into the disappearance of a folk hero of the 1950s, a bricklayer. As she gets closer to the reason for his disappearance she finds her own life threatened, since it is evident that the government was ruthless in its bid to cling to power. The government did not care for this film, but it was admired within the industry and Wajda as a world figure was unpunishable. The government prevented the film from being widely shown in Poland, and then let it out to prove to the rest of the world how democratic it was.

Opposite: Robert de Niro in **Taxi Driver** – enough to make anyone give up both taxis and cinemagoing. Above: Gregory Peck as the American Ambassador to Britain in Richard Donner's **The Omen**; he's being drastic because he has discovered that his son is the anti-Christ. There were sequels in 1978 and 1981. Right: Peter Finch (left) and William Holden in **Network**, Paddy Chayefsky's bitter study of the power games played in television. Sidney Lumet, directing, had known Chayefsky when they had both worked in that medium and could therefore vouch for his accuracy.

ollywood was in heaven. It could embrace mediocrity, which it had always understood better than anything, but had been prevented by doing so by the likes of Von Stroheim, Borzage, Capra, Wilder, Minnelli, a couple of Sturges, Kazan, Mankiewicz and Zinnemann. They had gone, except the last (see below), to be replaced by a generation

1977

reared on comic strips and B-movies. How else do you explain this lot? – George Lucas's **Star Wars**, a fairy tale set in Outer Space (which would have two sequels; originally eight more were promised); Steven Spielberg's **Close Encounters of the Third Kind**, in which UFOs appear over Wyoming and a space ship lands in Indiana; Woody Allen's **Annie Hall**, with him in his usual role, a Jewish jerk in love with a WASP girl, Diane Keaton, whose dialogue consists chiefly of 'Wow'; John Badham's **Saturday Night Fever**, with John Travolta as a Brooklyn store clerk who lives for evenings on the dance floor; and Hal Needham's **Smokey and the Bandit**, another road movie, with Burt Reynolds being pursued from Texas to Georgia by a vicious sheriff, Jackie Gleason. All were enormously popular, thus helping to kill literate cinema. The only one of much merit is the last, partly because it has Sally Field, who does have some good dialogue. It is also the only one without pretension. Of course there is room for all sorts of movies, but Hollywood narrowed its sights and lowered its standards; and while everyone was relieved that movies could be as frank as it liked, there was something unnecessarily gratuitous about Travolta asking his girlfriend for a blow job because he

didn't have a rubber.

George Roy Hill's **Slap Shot** certainly had its raunchier moments, being about an ice hockey team who call each other 'cock-sucker' all the time; one of the team also strips to his jock on ice when the band strikes up 'The Stripper'. Paul Newman was the easy-going coach and Molly Down wrote it.

There were some other pleasures in 1977: Joseph Sargent's under-rated General **MacArthur**, with Gregory Peck at his megalomaniac best, is quite the equal of **Patton**; and Jonathan Demme's **Citizens Band** is a random look at some users, out there in Middle America.

Zinnemann's film was **Julia**, who was Vanessa Redgrave, a left-wing activist who disappeared in Hitler's Germany. Zinnemann adopted a complex structure for what was basically a simple theme, her friendship with Lillian Hellman. In fact, Hellman never knew Julia, but they were both clients of the same lawyer, who told Hellman about her. Jane Fonda played Hellman, with Jason Robards as Dashiell Hammett. Friendship was also at the heart of Herbert Ross's **The Turning Point**, as it existed between prima ballerina Anne Bancroft and Shirley MacLaine, who had given up dancing years ago for domesticity – just as her husband, Tom Skerritt, had given up homosexuality for her. The world of ballet, however, was as nothing to the one created by Diane Keaton for herself after **Looking for Mr Goodbar** in singles bars. Among the weirdos and hopheads she beds – and not always one at a time – are William Atherton, Richard Gere and Tom Berenger. Richard Brooks wrote and directed, from Judith Rossner's bestseller.

Much was made of these three films after years in

Left: **Close Encounters of the Third Kind**, written and directed by Steven Spielberg, who re-edited it in 1980 and reissued it with **The Special Edition** added to the title. Above: Harrison Ford in **Star Wars**, directed by Spielberg's friend and colleague George Lucas, his last film in that capacity. But as producer he has collaborated on some of the films – including the three adventures of Indiana Jones – which have enabled Spielberg to dominate the American film industry ever since. Neither has done much more than **Star Wars** artistically. Opposite: John Travolta in **Saturday Night Fever**, another of the year's very popular films.

which almost every one was for, by and about men. It is easy to say that Neil Simon wrote **The Goodbye Girl** for Marsha Mason, as he was married to her at the time. Having just lost her man, she sublets a room in her flat to an eccentric off-Broadway actor, Richard Dreyfuss. Ross directed what was, overall, an old-fashioned occasion: it took them five reels to realize they're in love and a little longer to get to bed. Hip Hollywood gave Oscars – Best Picture, Screenplay, Direction – to **Annie Hall**; audiences preferred **The Goodbye Girl**, which was the most enjoyable American film of 1977.

Britain didn't have one. Something went wrong with Richard Attenborough's film about the battle of Arnhem, **A Bridge Too Far**: it sank under the weight of star names such as Sean Connery, Robert Redford, Ryan O'Neal, Gene Hackman, Laurence Olivier and Michael Caine, fine as some of them were. It was an excellent year for French cinema, with four feminist tracts, three of them by women: Paula Delsol's **Ben et Benédict**, on the perils of marrying the wrong man; Agnes Varda's **Une Chante, L'Autre Pas**, which chronicles the friendship of a minor pop singer and a girl who starts a birth control clinic; Diane Kurys' autobiographical **Diabolo Menthe**, a study of Jewish adolescence; and Claude Goretta's **La Dentellière/The Lacemaker**, from Pascal Laine's best-selling novel about supposing that a holiday affair can last for ever, with Isabelle Huppert in the title role. Cabourg

in the rain is not much like the Côte d'Azur in the sun, so Claude Berri's **Un Moment d'Egarement** is not like the film of the other Claude: Victor Lanoux and Jean-Pierre Marielle are on vacation together when Marielle begins an affair with the daughter of Lanoux, who desperately wants to know whom she is secretly seeing. This is 1977's funniest French film, along with de Broca's **Tendre Poulet**, with Philippe Noiret as an unworldly professor and Annie Girardot as a leading detective. They had been friends when young and look like becoming lovers as he reluctantly helps her in a murder hunt.

M. Lanoux and Andrea Ferreol had been lovers, and when she inherits a château he moves back in and treats her as before, loftily. Her response is to buy him a valet's jacket. The games start then, and Bruno Gantillon's **Servante et Maîtresse** is quite the most chilling and appealing of the game-playing and role-reversal films.

It was a memorable year for movies elsewhere, and Canada, usually noted for its duds, sent out good ones, including Zale Dalen's **Skip Tracer**, about the adventures of a debt collector in Vancouver, a city for which the director seems to have ambivalent feelings; and Richard Benner's **Outrageous**, from Margaret Gibson's book about her relationship with a drag artist, Craig Russell, who plays himself, moving from Toronto to New York.

In India, Mrinal Sen made **The Outsiders**, about an unruly old man and his son who prefer to live in poverty on their own terms than under those imposed by the villagers, who are equally poor. And Benegal pertinently examined the life of a movie star, her ups and downs, her

Left: Diane Keaton was **Looking for Mr Goodbar**, and she found it with the then-unknown Richard Gere. Richard Brooks wrote and directed, from Judith Rossner's bestseller – both somewhat awed by their revelation that women liked sex. Above: Marsha Mason and Richard Dreyfuss getting it together in **The Goodbye Girl**, one of Neil Simon's handful of original film scripts. In 1993 it became an unsuccessful Broadway musical. Opposite: Jacqueline Bisset and Nick Nolte in Peter Yates's **The Deep**. They played lovers in Bermuda, involved with drug-runners and hunters of buried treasure, most of them very nasty.

smiles and frowns, in **The Role**. The downs mostly concerned her domineering, small-minded husband.

From Tunisia came Ridha Behi's affecting **Hyena's Sun**, a film much concerned about a fishing village targeted as a holiday resort with high-rises. And in Finland Risto Jarva made **The Year of the Hare**, a beguiling portrait of a man who finds contentment in a forest with a hare after walking away from Helsinki, a rotten marriage and a world contemplating nuclear warfare. In Poland, Feliks Falk made **Top Dog**, a satire on the small-minded bureaucracy controlling show business in a provincial town and on the young man ambitious enough to use western culture to subvert it. It was a brave film, as was Krzysztof Zanussi's **Camouflage**, in which a lecturer is forced to take on the commissars by his students, who are indignant that the university prize is going to an idiot who toes the party line instead of the guy who really deserves it.

The times they were a-changing, and only with the passing of Franco (in 1975) could Spain produce a film as virulent about the Right as these Polish films were about the Left. The people who made them knew what the Soviets and Nazis had realized: cinema could provide heady propaganda. The idea had remained dormant until the attacks on totalitarian regimes by Costa-Gavras and Francesco Rosi spurred on others. The thing about extremists of any kind is that they believe themselves to be on the side of the angels; so in **Camada Negra** or **Black Brood** Mañuel Gutierrez Aragon made his fascists choirboys who believed in their divine right to smash up Madrid's new left-wing bookstore. The film's under-age protagonist is too young to join them and uncertain whether he wants to wank, rape or just beat up his girlfriend.

In Italy, specifically Sardinia, **Padre Padrone** focused on another young man unsure of himself, in this case a shepherd's son who wants an education but dare not ask it of his stern father till conscription on the mainland gives him the courage. This is the best of the films written and directed by the Taviani brothers, Paolo and Vittorio. In Ettore Scola's **Una Giornata Particolare** the day referred to is that when Hitler came to Rome. Everyone has left to see the historic meeting with Mussolini except Sophia Loren and Marcello Mastroianni. She's unhappy because she's overworked, he because he has been fired because he is homosexual. She decides to seduce him.

In West Germany, Wolfgang Petersen's **Die Konsequenz** follows much the same idea. A young convict (Jurgen Prochnow) learns that one of the guard's sons is gay. He has a handy bottle of schnapps and they're happy – for a while. The sexual tides which had overwhelmed Hollywood had had little effect on other movie industries, untroubled by a prurient, puritan past; they now knew they could be franker without losing the chance of American distribution, and this particular film does have a strong sequence in which the boys of the reformatory school gang-rape the local whore.

The sexual mores of Berlin in the 1920s were examined in detail in **The Serpent's Egg**, directed by Ingmar Berman, who had quarrelled with the Swedish tax authorities and exiled himself till he received an apology. This film is also homage to many German Silent films of his youth, a murder mystery and an attempt to find the roots of Nazism. The stars are David Carradine, as a Jewish-American trapeze artist and, as his brother's widow, Liv Ullmann. The evils of Nazism are addressed as few films have dared to do by Theodor Kotulla in **Aus Einem Deutschen Leben**, or **Death is My Trade**, from the novel by Robert Merle, based in turn on the notes left by the first commandant of Auschwitz, Rudolf Hoss. Here is his life, from the end of the First World War to that of the Second, when history delivered its verdict. He pretends not to know what is going on in the gas chambers, and this film is an indictment not only of him but of the nation, with its concern for conformity and order. Without these, there would not have been the Holocaust. Not only is it the most important film of 1977, because it tried to explain how the incredible could happen, it is the most important film of the decade.

1978

The American cinema took several turns for the worst, and here are three of them. John Landis' **National Lampoon's Animal House** was a campus comedy using only crude stereotypes, having divided pupils and staff into squares or slobs. The latter smoked pot, conversed in four-letter words and showed a taste for physical humour which Mack Sennett would have rejected. Randal Kleiser's **Grease** was based on a long-running but otherwise un-noticed Broadway musical about school in the 1950s. The pupils are better behaved than those above, but hardly more literate or intelligent. One of them is John Travolta, and since he was floating on **Saturday Night Fever**, the film owed its popularity to him. Both he and co-star Olivia Newton-John were soon to have quick flops. If the critics had had their way, the public wouldn't have gone to either of these. **The Deer Hunter** was more serious. It had a fine actor, Robert de Niro, and an important subject: the experience of the Vietnam War, which it managed to trivialize and make portentous at the same time. It was also an ego trip for director Michael Cimino, who won golden opinions and awards – but not

from people who had been in Vietnam.

Hal Ashby's **Coming Home** was a much better film on the same subject, even if it presented it as a simple triangle drama: a Marine captain (Bruce Dern) is sent to Vietnam and his wife (Jane Fonda) does voluntary work in a veterans' hospital, where she falls in love with a paraplegic (Jon Voight). The film was explicit on their sexual relations. Sex was being seen to be enjoyed in Louis Malle's **Pretty Baby**, since the action takes place in a Storyville cathouse, in 1917. The story, such as it was, told of the relationship between a photographer (Keith Carradine) and a twelve year-old (Brooke Shields) imminently set to follow the example of her mother (Susan Sarandon). Schrader's **Blue Collar** was more satisfying, as it looked at the lives of three factory workers (Richard Pryor, Yaphet Kotto, Harvey Keitel), their night-time pleasures of whoring and smoking pot, and of their troubles with the taxman and the union.

There were laughs to be had from **Foul Play**, a murder mystery written and directed by Colin Higgins, with Chevy Chase as a San Francisco cop setting up

Below: Jon Voight and Jane Fonda in **Coming Home**, probably the best film about Vietnam veterans re-adjusting. Opposite: Christopher Reeve in **Superman**, the first of the spate of movies derived from comic strips in recent years. Made in discord – between the producers on one hand and cast and crew on the other – it still managed to be genuinely lighthearted.

Goldie Hawn, the possible next victim, to help him; Stanley Donen's **Movie Movie**, with George Scott in two spoofs of films of the 1930s, a musical and a boxing story, neither of which should work as well as they do; and Robert Altman's **A Wedding**, a look at the guests.

Two British films deserve a place. Alan Parker's **Midnight Express** observes the brutal life inside a Turkish jail, seen through the eyes of Billy Hayes (Brad Davis), who was interned in one for drug-running. His autobiographical account of such matters was somewhat less than honest. Not, obviously, a lovable film, but the adjective can be applied, after a pretentious opening, to **Superman**, as directed by Richard Donner. The case for filming comic strips had not been made since the serials and B-Movies of the 1940s (apart from the 1966 **Batman**, brought about by a TV series), and it is not a strong one, even with audiences getting ever younger. Justification can be strong, however, if the film doesn't take itself seriously and if it has the special effects which must be the *raison d'être*. This one soars when Superman flies. He is Christopher Reeve, wide-eyed as the flying guy's *alter ego*, accident-prone journalist Clark Kent; even in his blue leotard he is not invincible.

From Italy, Ermanno Olmi's **L'Albero Degli Zoccoli**, better known as **The Tree of Wooden Clogs**, was his biggest success since **Il Posto**. It is simply an account of peasant life in Lombardy towards the end of the nineteenth century and, at over three hours, an extremely detailed one. It was the only foreign-language film to create much stir, except for Ingmar Bergman's **Autumn Sonata**, with his namesake, Ingrid (in her last film),

playing a concert pianist on a visit to her daughter, Liv Ullmann, and trying to assuage her guilt because she has considered her career more important. Given the bitterness of their arguments, she can hardly have been a welcome guest.

France seemed obsessed by crime. Chabrol's **Violette Nozière** was based on a true case of 1933, with Isabelle Huppert doing a Lizzie Borden job on her parents, Stéphane Audran and Jean Carmet; Christian de Challonge's **L'Argent des Autres** was a reflection of the large number of high-level financial scandals of this decade, with Jean-Louis Trintignant as scapegoat for the respectable but irresponsible bank for which he works; and Michel Deville's frightening view of the new world of computer technology, **Le Dossier 51**, showed a man's soul and sexuality being laid bare as the software accumulates on details of both. Um, it turns out he's gay ... if not so defiantly as the middle-aged couple of **La Cage aux Folles**, one (Ugo Tognazzi) owning a night club in St Tropez, the other (Michel Serrault) being its drag queen star. And the latter has to get into drag in real life to meet the prospective in-laws of his lover's son. As a play, this ran for years in Paris; the film, though clumsy, was France's most successful export since **Un Homme et une Femme**; and it became a Broadway musical.

The US, in particular, took to another unexpected ménage, from Brazil: Bruno Barreto's **Doña Flor and Her Two Husbands**, in which the first comes back from the dead to excite her sexually as she tires of the second.

Left: Brooke Shields and Susan Sarandon in Louis Malle's **Pretty Baby**, which gave Paramount some headaches, since it was chiefly set in a brothel. It had only been greenlighted because of Malle's reputation – it turned out to be a quite respectable affair. Above: John Travolta and Olivia Newton-John in **Grease**. Opposite: Brad Davis, handcuffed, in **Midnight Express**, based on the experiences of a young American who had done time in a Turkish jail.

Shayam Benegal's **The Boon** completes his remarkable quartet of studies of life in rural India, and it has whimsy, which the others do not. The title refers to a root with magical qualities, as a result of which the villagers regard its otherwise useless protagonist, who owns it, as a god. The film also contains Benegal's usual bemused attitude towards indolence, superstition and the corrupt powers of the *zamindars*.

Turkey joins the movie exporting countries because of one man, Yilmaz Güney, a former movie matinée idol who, like De Sica, had turned to making films about the dispossessed, most of them from jail (the authorities considered him subversive, communist, anarchist, or all three), and in the case of **The Herd** and **Enemy**, 'signed' by Zeki Ökten, who followed his detailed instructions. The first is a study of the feudal rivalry between two nomadic Kurdish tribes, and of the corruption one herdsman finds in Ankara when he escapes there with his wife, born to the other side. It is a powerfully persuasive movie, but **Enemy** is astonishing. On the surface it is concerned with a man whose education has left him without a capacity to work, though he would do any menial task. His wife had been a prostitute and becomes one again; but as they move from apathy to hopelessness, Güney regards them with hope and affection. The title is finally revealed as having three meanings: Greece, Turkey's traditional enemy; the country itself, always boxing itself into a corner; and Güney's protagonist, too supine, despite his intelligence, to react positively to his situation. Some sources state that both films were made in 1979, but it is impossible to check. Güney died in 1984 (in Paris, aged forty-seven), and the government suppressed all documentation about him. It banned these films at home, but allowed them out, as in the case of Wadja in Poland, to refute allegations that it was not a democracy.

Wadja himself made **Without Anesthesia** aka **Rough Treatment**, which is the way a man may feel when his wife suddenly ups and leaves him for another. He is a journalist who begins an affair with a student admirer (Krystyna Janda), only too anxious that his tirades against the political regime should lead to its downfall.

From Australia, two sinister weekends. In Colin Eggleston's **Long Weekend**, a disgruntled married couple (Bryony Behets, John Hargreaves) knock down a kangaroo and find that natures strikes back; in Tom Jeffrey's **Weekend of Shadows** a farmer's wife has been murdered and the chief suspect, a Polish labourer, has vanished. From New Zealand, two tales of frustration. Geoff Steven's **Skin Deep**, about the perils arising when the Chamber of Commerce resolves to install an experienced masseuse in the town gym and sauna. It decided she was 'havable', but she knew how to take care of herself. A very funny comedy about hypocrisy. Tony Williams' **Solo** may be a masterpiece. Certainly there is no other film like it. A feckless girl (Lisa Peers) starts a forest fire, and thus starts a relationship with a pilot (Vincent Gil) in charge of fire-fighting, and his adolescent son (Perry Armstrong). The film moves from an investigation into parts of their lives into why they've met and why they are living in the first place.

The new generation of Hollywood film-makers were now being called 'the movie brats', both because they were young and because they were obsessed by movies. They were also not perhaps as gifted as some of their admirers claimed. Evidence: two lumbering war films: Francis Coppola's **Apocalypse Now** and Steven Spielberg's **1941**. The first is loosely based on Conrad's *The Heart of Darkness*, and has Martin Sheen journeying through the jungles of Vietnam, till he can seek the truth from a sage, Marlon Brando, who gives a performance as inept as the whole sequence. The second is a comedy portraying Los Angeles in a panic because a Japanese submarine has been spotted offshore. Both films were ridiculously expensive, but only Coppola's film looks as if it was, and at least the box-office returns justified the cost. Spielberg's film, which drowned the many names in its cast, was avoided by the public. Both films were visually spectacular, but it helped if you left your intellect behind. 1979 was also depressing because of a film called **"10"**, which was how Dudley Moore rated his women. Bo Derek, a nine days' wonder, was the glamorous creature he foolishly preferred to his steady girl, Julie Andrews, whose husband, Blake Edwards, wrote and directed, with vulgarity and no wit in either function. The public rolled up, but the public isn't stupid; with one exception it refused to turn up to see poor Moore in anything else.

Having got those three out of the way – you could add, if you like, Woody Allen's pretentious **Manhattan** –

1979

you'll find that 1979 was an excellent year for the American cinema: responsible, no Westerns, only one real musical, a handful of thrillers. And nothing was more responsible or more thrilling than James Bridges' **The China Syndrome**, which imagined an accident at a nuclear power station. Jane Fonda and Michael Douglas were the new team attempting to penetrate the cover-up, and Jack Lemmon was the employee they're hoping will talk. Just below this came Jerry Schatzberg's **The Seduction of Joe Tynan**, with Alan Alda, who also wrote it, as a senator who discovers that idealism can be contentedly replaced by corruption; Harold Becker's **The Onion Field**, a disconcertingly concerned thriller by Joseph Wamburgh, based on an actual case in 1963 when two petty crooks killed one LA cop (Ted Danson), leaving his partner (John Savage) to years of recriminations of cowardice and court battles; **Hardcore**, written and directed by Paul Schrader, concerned an adolescent girl who disappears into the porno parlours of Los Angeles, where her father (George C. Scott) goes miserably to search for her; and Hal Ashby's **Being There**, with Peter Sellers as a dim recluse who comes to be regarded as the equal of Kissinger.

There was more than a fair share of films about the relationship between the sexes, the best of which was Robert Benton's **Kramer Versus Kramer**, with Mr Hoffman as a one-parent father determined to fight when his wife, on whim, demands custody of the boy. The worst was Zeffirelli's **The Champ**, with exactly the same plot. A remake of the 1931 movie, it did, however, contain a remarkable performance by Jon Voight as a broken-down boxer. The others, most of which invited rueful laughter, included Alan J. Pakula's **Starting Over**, with Burt Reynolds settling down with Jill Clayburgh, till Candice

Left: Australian cinema continued to blossom, notably with Gillian Armstrong's **My Brilliant Career**, with Judy Davis as the strong-willed heroine offered an escape from poverty when landowner Sam Neill proposes. Above: Diane Keaton and Woody Allen in Allen's **Manhattan** – filmed in monochrome. Opposite: Richard Gere in **Yanks**, about the Americans stationed in Britain during the War.

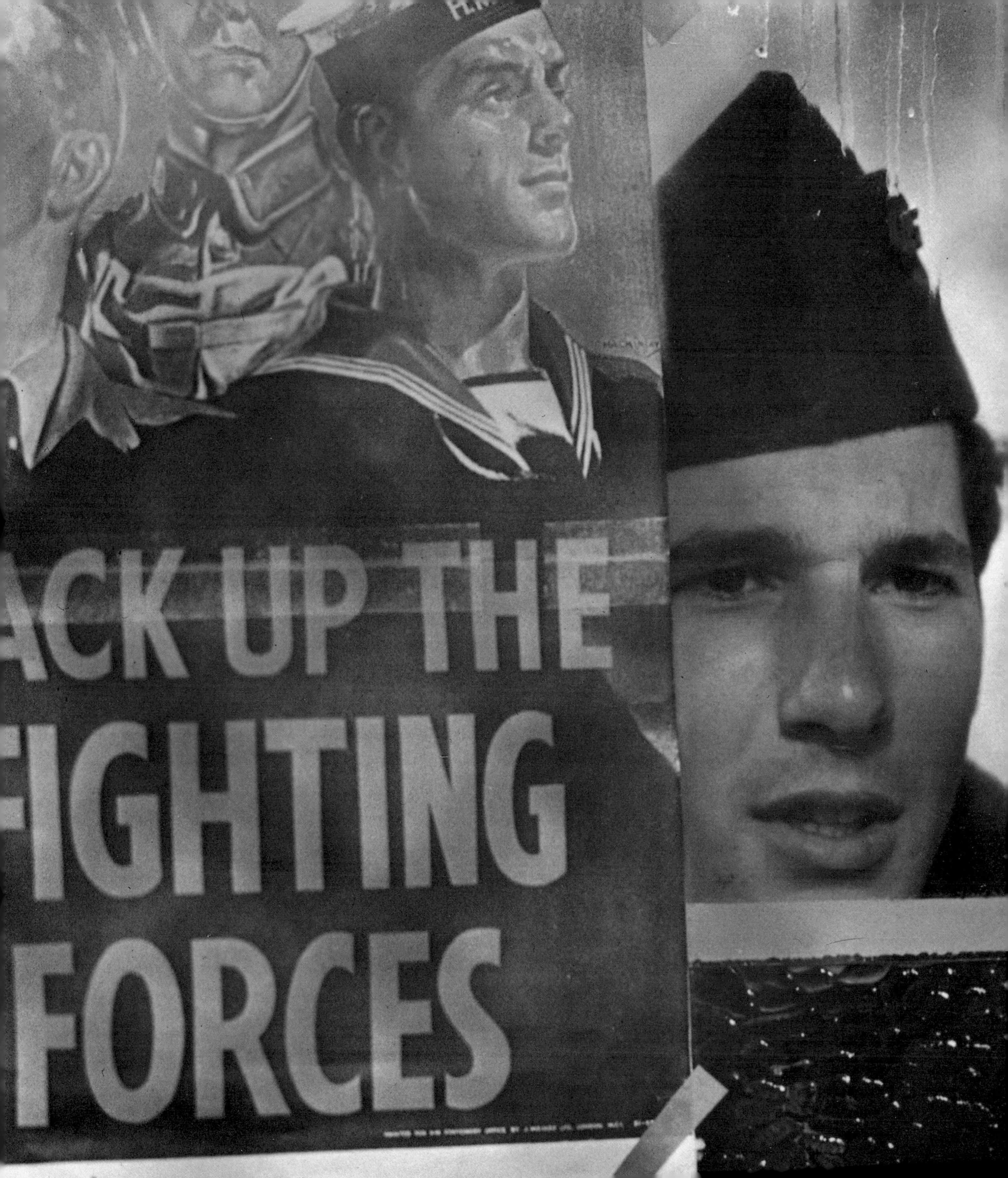
ACK UP THE
IGHTING
FORCES

Bergen decides that their marriage isn't over, after all; and Robert Moore's **Chapter Two**, from Neil Simon's funny autobiographical screenplay, with James Caan as him (more or less) and Marsha Mason as herself.

Steve Martin arrived on the big screen as **The Jerk**, emulating Mel Brooks by kicking most of the male characters in the balls. He would learn to do better. The best thick-ear melodrama was Jonathan Demme's **Last Embrace**, with Roy Scheider as a man marked for murder, which has twist after twist and its tongue in its cheek. And then there was Ridley Scott's **Alien**, which has lodged itself inside a spaceship and tends to destroy the crew when it decides to make its presence felt.

Another autobiographical piece, even more taking than Simon's, was **Breaking Away**, directed by Peter Yates from Steve Tesich's script. Memories of schooldays in a town in Indiana in the 1960s centre on four boys, the girls they chase, and the annual cycle race. Audiences love it. More autobiography, which was not likeable at all but more riveting, was Bob Fosse's **All That Jazz**, with Roy Scheider as a Broadway director/choreographer with a giant ego. The only true musical was **Hair**, based on that marvel of the 1960s which has always resisted revival — because it was rotten in the first place. Recognizing this, Milos Forman kept it in period and ensured a satiric plot line, about an Oklahoma cowboy (John Savage) on his way to Vietnam who is befriended by some Central Park hippies who soon have him smoking pot. It was too late: audiences stayed away in droves. But they flocked to Carroll Ballard's **The Black Stallion**, based on Walter Farley's 1941 novel about a boy shipwrecked with a fierce Arab horse on a desert island. They become friends, and back home the boy is coached to ride him. The trainer is Mickey Rooney; the boy, Kelly Reno, is one of the most

fetching ever to appear in an American movie; and the first hour is sheer magic, a quality unexpected in 1970s cinema.

Britain cold-shouldered **The Riddle of the Sands**, not a good augury for Rank, as it was by far the best of the films with which this company had returned to production after a decade concentrating on exhibition and distribution. Furthermore, Erskine Childers' novel had never been out of print since it was published in 1903. Michael York and Simon MacCorkindale were perfect as the secret servicemen poking about in the Baltic to see whether the Germans were preparing war, and it was all well-managed by Tony Maylam. The same could not be said of the Merchant-Ivory team, starting their generally dismal attacks on the classics of modern literature with **The Europeans**, from Henry James, with Lee Remick. Other Americans round and about included: Otto Preminger for **The Human Factor**, his best film in years (and his last), from Graham Greene's novel about spies and cock-ups in the Foreign Office, with Richard Attenborough, John Gielgud, Nicol Williamson and Robert Morley; and James Frawley for **The Muppet Movie**, which enervatingly brought Kermit the Frog and Miss Piggy to the big screen.

Television was the source of **Monty Python's Life of Brian**, which was a life of Christ in comic terms. There were cries of blasphemy from all over; but the objections

Left: Dustin Hoffman with Justin Henry in **Kramer Versus Kramer**, written and directed by Robert Benton from Avery Corman's novel about the consequences of divorce. Above: Martin Ritt's excellent **Norma Rae**, with Sally Field as a Southern mill worker persuaded into action by a New York Jewish intellectual activist, sent by Textile Workers Union to investigate conditions. Opposite: Dennis Christopher, Jackie Earle Haley, Daniel Stern and Dennis Quaid in **Breaking Away**, directed by Peter Yates from Steve Tesich's autobiographical script: schooldays in a town in Iowa in the '60s . . . the girls chased, the annual bicycle race.

should have been about the childishness of the finished product, for it was a good idea.

The big British film of 1979 was about **Yanks**, GIs in Britain during the Second World War. Vanessa Redgrave pairs with William Devane; Lisa Eichhorn with Richard Gere. John Schlesinger directed from a screenplay by Colin Welland and Walter Bernstein, which trades on nostalgia but has no bite. Two small films by new directors delighted their patrons by putting working-class teenagers on the screen without patronage: Bill Forsyth's **That Sinking Feeling**, about a Glaswegian on the dole who persuades his chums in joining him to steal ninety-three steel sinks; and Franc Roddam's **Quadrophenia**, about a Londoner who hangs around the pubs and clubs and gets involved in Mods and Rockers fights in Brighton.

In France, intertwined male nude bodies interested Philippe Vallois. In the summer of 1942 one of them is a German soldier, in **Nous étions un Seul Homme**. In the summer of 1939 **L'Adolescente** goes to stay in the country with her grandmother (Simone Signoret) and she has her first crush, on a young Jewish doctor (Francis Huster). Jeanne Moreau directed.

There was murder in Japan: Imamura's **Vengeance is Mine** is no thriller, but a dark and graphic study of a man compelled to murder, as examined by the police after his capture, anxious to understand his motives. And in India, in Mrinal Sen's most compassionate film to date, **And Quiet Rolls the Dawn**, about an impoverished Calcutta family, anguished when the daughter, the only breadwinner, fails to return from work.

In the USSR, a **Declaration of Love**, by Ilya Averbakh, is about an aged couple reminiscing. As poet, crime reporter and inspector of collective farms, they have been kept apart despite their love for each other, by her family circumstances and his need to earn a living. Wadja in Poland takes a more romantic view of the same subject, as Daniel Olbrychski deliberately revisits **The Young Ladies of Wilko** fifteen years on, to find that they have different perceptions of the past than he. Wajda's **The Conductor** (John Gielgud) also revisits his past – Poland – which he hasn't seen for years. His presence in a small town almost destroys the marriage of a local musician and his wife, but this is an allegory on the state of the country. The Polish hierarchy was something Krzysztof Kieślowski handled head on in **Camera Buff** – a man who becomes a movie-maker for his factory, which brings him into confrontation with the authorities.

Films about Germany's recent past were tumbling out of the studios from a generation too young to remember the Nazis. Most of them were indignant. The two most significant were chronicles: Schlöndorff's **The Tin Drum**, from Günter Grass's novel, which had (often sexual) adventures in Danzig, as seen by a boy who couldn't grow, set against the period from the rise of Nazism to the end of the War; and Fassbinder's **The Marriage of Maria Braun**, with more adventures, for Hanna Schygulla, from the end of the War through the economic miracle.

From Australia came Donald Crombie's **Cathy's Child**, based on the Cathy Baikas affair of 1974, when Cathy's Greek, separated husband abducted their child and took it to Athens, a matter the Australian government didn't want to know about. Tom Jeffrey's **The Odd Angry Shot**, by far the best film yet on the war in Vietnam, had Bryan Brown and John Hargreaves among the guys who are stalking the jungle, terrified, or larking around or, most of the time, bored. Fred Schepisi's **The Chant of Jimmie Blacksmith**, from Thomas Keneally's novel, was based on the true story of a half-caste aborigine in a whites' world who revolts against one injustice too many and takes an axe to it. Peter Weir wrote and directed a clever, keep-em-guessing horror about a suburban housewife (Judy Morris) increasingly certain that **The Plumber** is not only a psychopath, but a dangerous one; and she's not quite sure what to do about it.

None of these was a load of laughs, which came instead from the other antipodean country, with **Middle Age Spread**, directed by John Reid from Roger Hall's play about a dinner party for six. The hostess is a snob who regards her husband (Grant Tilly) not with malice but as one might a backward child. The two male guests are smoothies who put him in the shade. During the course of the evening, flashbacks alert us to the fact that the activities of two colleagues have caused him to cut loose without his wife knowing. We're glad for him.

It was the year that **Heaven's Gate** changed the American cinema, but before that there were other, more interesting films. Jonathan Demme's **Melvin and Howard** (Hughes) stars Jason Robards Jr, who is given a lift by a milkman Paul LeMat, who subsequently believes that Hughes has left him his fortune; so he marries again the wife, Mary Steenburgen, who had called him a loser but who believes that the money can help her achieve her dream of becoming a movie star. Sharp script by Bo Goldman. Michael Apted's **Coal Miner's Daughter** is about Loretta Lynn, who came from a Kentucky shack to become a big star of Country and Western. Sissy Spacek plays her and Tommy Lee Jones is her husband; and the film is essentially about the effects of fame on a couple only just qualified to handle it. **Hide in Plain Sight** was directed by James Caan, who plays a Buffalo factory worker in search of his children, spirited away by the new man in his wife's life because he needs to hide out after spilling the beans on his Mafia pals.

Richard Gere was winning as an **American Gigolo**, and he had to be because he was paid to be. This was another of Paul Schrader's warning on the perils of modern life. You get unjustly accused of murder, but you get an Armani wardrobe and redemption at the end in the form of Lauren Hutton. He bows to the inevitable when his pimp orders him to service a gay, and the inevitable was what happened between Michael Ontkean and Ray Sharkey in Paul Mazursky's **Willie and Phil** – but only briefly, since they're both in love with Margot Kidder in this homage to **Jules et Jim**. Something more prolonged

was going on between **Nijinsky** and Diaghilev, George de la Pena and Alan Bates, in Herbert Ross's biopic of the dancer. More attention was paid to re-creating the famous decor than the dance or the exact nature of that relationship. William Friedkin's **Cruising** was more explicit: Al Pacino was a cop who dons a leather jacket to search for a murderer in New York's gay bars. This was the first movie to feature a black cop who hangs around the precinct wearing nothing but a Stetson and a jock strap. Pacino didn't seem surprised. Audiences didn't come to any of these four films, which isn't surprising either since Hollywood's ability to shock was no longer a novelty. They are by no means bad, that is boring. Nor is another reject, **Can't Stop the Music**, produced by Allan Carr, hoping for a follow-up to **Grease**, and the only film directed by the comedienne Nancy Walker. It takes as its premise the wish of such as Valerie Perrine and Steve Guttenberg to make stars of the Village People, a handful of gay stereotypes – they sing, lustfully, of the joys awaiting them at the Y.M.C.A. – then enjoying their brief brush with fame.

The most popular comedy was Colin Higgins' **Nine to Five**, with Dabney Coleman as a male chauvinist pig who is kidnapped by three of his staff (Jane Fonda, Lily Tomlin, Dolly Parton) and put into a dog collar. This was supposed to be funny, and was, intermittently, but 1980 wasn't a great time to be alive: witness the **Ordinary People**, Momma (Mary Tyler Moore), who has it all and wants even more, and her son (Timothy Hutton), whom she has turned into a psychiatric mess. There has to be room in movies for the ordinary, but not in this spurious way. Robert Redford directed, to be rewarded by an

Left: Tatsuya Nakadai in **Kagemusha**, which marked Kurosawa's return to movies after an absence of five years. Above: Richard Gere, with Lauren Hutton, in **American Gigolo**. Paul Schrader chose his title carefully, knowing that a few years ago it would have been considered a contradiction in terms. In fact, a few years ago such a film could never even have been made. Gere suffers and suffers throughout, not for selling his body but by being suspected of murder. Opposite: William Friedkin's **Cruising** took an extensive tour of New York's leather bars as a detective, Al Pacino, is sent undercover to hunt for a serial killer.

Academy award for Best Picture. Incredible.

Jake LaMotta didn't have it so good, either, even if he had the good fortune to be reincarnated by Robert de Niro. **Raging Bull** is not the worst picture about prizefighting – though it's a near thing – but is the most humourless and the most superficial. A decade or so later, American critics voted it the best film of the 1980s. Even more incredible.

Heaven's Gate. At last, and last is right. It had its admirers, and the Old West never looked so splendiferous ... or less convincing. It was before its time, said its perpetrator, Michael Cimino, faced with the fact that the most costly American film till now couldn't draw flies. United Artists went under, and no wonder.

Britain had its own **Heaven's Gate**, inasmuch as both films opened big but by the end of the second week you couldn't give them away. Both, too, are careful about hiding any merits they have; and they're flashy. **The Shining** had Jack Nicholson as a caretaker of an empty Colorado hotel in winter, swinging an axe around wife (Shelley Duvall) and child after seeing a few ghosts. Stanley Kubrick co-wrote and directed.

Apart from **Superman II** (directed by Richard Lester and even better than the first one), a moribund industry had a few more moments. Tony Garnett's **Prostitute** takes a clinical look at a lady who serviced in Birmingham and a social worker who would like the profession legalized. A co-production with Pakistan wasn't much seen, certainly not there, for it was about the misuse of power, and General Zia was not about to have anyone reminded that that was what he was doing. Jamil Dehlavi wrote and directed **The Blood of Hussain**, with

Salmann Peer in the dual role of brothers, both wealthy, one countrified and the other a government adviser. Dehlavi is mostly concerned with their love affairs, but he is also questioning Pakistani mentality, with symbolism, mystery and much visual beauty. It was seen at several festivals and won the Grand Prix at Taormina, without making any subsequent impact on the international repertoire.

West Germany sent Wolf Gremm's **Fabian** to Cork, but Cannes turned it down. United Artists bought it for the US but didn't open it. A great film which, for all its magic, **The Blood of Hussain** isn't, lies in limbo. Its source is the novel by Erick Kastner and its subject the rise of Nazism, so it too is concerned with a national mentality and the abuse of power. Fabian (Hans Peter Hallwach) is a copywriter, drifting from brothel to nightclub, aware but indifferent to what is happening. Nevertheless, he is shocked at the end to find that his childhood chum has joined 'the steel helmets'; and then he drowns. In West Germany Bergman made **From the Life of the Marionettes** and announced that he would only make one more. It was tempting to say that it was just as well if they were all as grim as this. It is masterly, peeling off layers like an onion skin as Bergman again confronts the conflict between appearance and reality; but in the end, after examining the mentality of a man who has murdered a whore, he decides that that was because he

Left: Kris Kristofferson in **Heaven's Gate**, a failure of such proportions that it brought the virtual demise of United Artists and damaged Kristofferson's career – unfairly, since he was one of its few virtues. Above: Robert de Niro in **Raging Bull**, directed by Martin Scorsese with his usual feeling for the vernacular and lack of humour. Its subject was Jake LaMotta, middleweight champion of the '40s. Opposite: Bruce Beresford's **'Breaker' Morant** was based on fact – an incident in the Boer War when an officer was court-martialled for killing some prisoners. Edward Woodward (centre) played him; behind him is Bryan Brown.

would rather have been homosexual and that the cause lies in childhood, which echoes two lesser film-makers, Bertolucci (**Il Conformista**) and Welles (**Citizen Kane**).

Canada had **Atlantic City** with a French director, Louis Malle, and an American writer, John Guare. On the surface a thriller about a hidden stash of drugs, it was more a look at some of the quirky individuals of the New Jersey resort, including an old man (Burt Lancaster) who claims he knew Bugsy Seigel and a waitress (Susan Sarandon) who aspires to becoming a croupier. It was, along with **Mon Oncle d'Amerique**, one of 1980's more satisfying films. Malle's contemporary, Resnais, made the latter in France, also content to do little more than regard characters' lives changing over the years, as Nicole Garcia, Roger Pierre and Gérard Depardieu become successful in their careers.

Kurosawa returned with American money in **Kagemusha**, a lavish tale of feudal life centring on a powerful warrior who employs a double (Tatsuya Nakadai) to fool his enemies; the man concerned is then tempted to seize the power conferred on him.

In Poland, Krzysztof Zanussi made a notable duo:

The Contract, a group portrait of some guests at a wedding; and **The Constant Factor**, a close-up of a young man who has integrity while all those about him are losing theirs. He frequently travels abroad and can see how much better democracies work. Encouraged by the Polish film industry's continuous cries of rage against the regime, the other Soviet bloc industries were opening up. For over thirty years they had been churning out dutifully dull films, but in 1980 this stopped. In Yugoslavia, Goran Paskaljević made **Special Treatment**, in which a home for alcoholics is a metaphor for the country. From Hungary came Janos Zsombolyai's **Duty Free Marriage**, which is chiefly in English, because that is the common language of the Budapest heroine and the Finn she marries. In the Soviet Union itself, Vladimir Menshov's **Moscow Does Not Believe in Tears** focuses on a woman who has a brush with a handsome man from television, who then seduces her. She also sees many changes in her life, from 1958 to the present, eventually becoming director of a factory. This was as enjoyable as it was enlightening, and it had the warmest welcome in the US of any Russian film in over two decades.

1981

The bravest film of the year, as well as one of the longest and most expensive, was **Reds**, with which Warren Beatty directed himself as John Reed, who admiringly witnessed the Russian Revolution and wrote a book about it, *Ten Days that Shook the World*. In the end, Beatty and his writer, Trevor Griffith, can't quite decide whether the changes it wrought were a Good Thing, but they offer many matters once unthinkable in an American film, such as the defence of agnosticism – by Reed's lover, Louis Bryant (a miscast Diane Keaton).

Alan J. Pakula and Sidney Lumet also examined some important issues, albeit in thriller form, respectively **Rollover** and **Prince of the City**. The former entangled Jane Fonda and Kris Kristofferson in a web of intrigue involving high finance, and the latter caught Treat Williams in a net of police corruption. The best of some other superior suspense tales was **Body Heat**, with which writer Lawrence Kasdan made a stunning directorial debut. As William Hurt and Kathleen Turner plotted to kill her elderly husband there were echoes of **Double Indemnity**, but it proved yet again that only the best talents can steal profitably from the very best. Sydney Pollack's **Absence of Malice** found menace in Miami, as journalist Sally Field suspects Paul Newman of having Mafia connections. Ulu Grossbard's **True Confessions** was true enough, since the starting point of the screenplay by John Gregory Dunne and Joan Didion (from Dunne's novel) was a Los Angeles murder case of the 1940s. In the film, the murder is of special significance to a monsignor (Robert de Niro) and his brother, a cop (Robert Duvall), and since the Church figures so largely in the action it was interesting to find it attacked, having been one of Hollywood's sacred cows for so long. Ivan Passar's **Cutter's Way** and Michael Mann's **Thief** were highly individual thrillers, which may be why both died at the box-office.

A literary adaptation, Milos Forman's version of E. L. Doctorow's **Ragtime**, had too many events and characters to cover, so was forced to take the panoramic approach, so that too little came into focus for long. Similarly, Arthur Penn tried to pack too much of '60s angst into **Four Friends**. **All the Marbles** looked rewardingly at the underbelly of American life, with Robert Aldrich more in command of his material than usual in what turned out to be his last film.

Among the year's deserved box-office disasters were Peter Bogdanovich's mirthless **They All Laughed** and Herbert Ross's **Pennies from Heaven**. Faye Dunaway played Joan Crawford in **Mommie Dearest**, proving that Crawford was better off dead, and Julie Andrews played a movie queen who bears her breasts to the camera in Blake Edwards' semi-autobiographical **S.O.B.** It was a comedy which flailed in all directions, as did **The Cannonball Run** and **Arthur**, but they, on the other hand, were very popular.

The year's biggest success by far was an expensive comic strip, **Raiders of the Lost Ark**, directed to the hilt by Steven Spielberg but with no regard for simple logic. Harrison Ford was the intrepid hero. Also highly popular was Mark Rydell's **On Golden Pond** which, like last year's **Ordinary People**, thought it was telling life as it is

Left: The disaster that we known as **Gallipoli** has haunted Britain, Australia and New Zealand since it happened in 1916. It was recreated, badly, in **Tell England** (1931) and movingly in this film, conceived by Peter Weir when he visited the beach in 1976. With Mel Gibson. Above: Ian Charleson and (far right) Ben Cross, who were the dual protagonists of **Chariots of Fire**; based on fact, it won awards and admirers the world over. Opposite: William Hurt and Kathleen Turner as the clandestine lovers in Lawrence Kasdan's **Body Heat**.

without having the least idea how to do so. It was also highly sentimental and may have owed its appeal to the teaming of Henry Fonda, in his last film, with both his daughter Jane and Katharine Hepburn.

Britain's film industry was boosted by the worldwide success of **Chariots of Fire**, directed by Hugh Hudson, which blended the stories of a Cambridge-educated Jew (Ben Cross) and a Scot (Ian Charleson) of missionary stock. Both ran in the 1924 Paris Olympics, to give the film its climax. Peter Hyams' **Outland** was a revamping of **High Noon**, with Sean Connery at his best as the marshal isolated on the space station. He also put in a guest appearance in Terry Gilliam's **Time Bandits**, which moved a small boy about in time – an over-crude film, but with some terrific ideas. It was disliked by critics, but was a success with the American public. **Clash of the Titans** contained some of Ray Harryhausen's most accomplished special effects, and with its unstuffy respect for the Greek myths it became one of the best films with which he was associated. James Ivory made one of his better pictures, **Quartet** – based on one of Jean Rhys's novels – about her affair in Paris with Ford Madox Ford, but John Fowles's fetching pastiche on Victoriana, **The French Lieutenant's Woman**, fell to the leaden talents of director Karel Reisz, screenwriter Harold Pinter and star Meryl Streep.

From Australia, Peter Weir's story of World War I, **Gallipoli**, starred Mel Gibson. From New Zealand, Mike Newell's grim **Bad Blood**, based on a true murder of 1941, and Geoff Murphy's cheerful 'road' movie, **Goodbye Pork Pie**.

Opposite: Hollywood had flirted for years with the story of John Read, the American journalist who witnessed the Russian Revolution. The facts were dramatic enough, but in all the years of red scares could only come to the screen garbled. Warren Beatty, here with Diane Keaton, took the plunge, as star, producer-director and co-writer of **Reds**. Above: Philippe Noiret and Stephane Audran in **Coup de Torchon**, one of the films of Bertrand Tavernier which evoked the great days of French cinema. Right: Treat Williams in **Prince of the City**, which completed Sidney Lumet's unofficial trilogy about the New York police force.

Perhaps the most successful foreign language film was Hector Babenco's study of a streetwise boy criminal, **Pixote**, but it was rivalled by István Szabó's **Mephisto**, the story of an ambitious actor but a shallow man, who stayed on in Nazi Germany though he had a chance to leave. In the title role Klaus-Maria Brandauer became a world-class actor.

West Germany had two of its biggest successes in a long time, **The Boat**, Wolfgang Petersen's Second World War movie, and Frank Ripploh's semiprofessional, semi-autobiographical **Taxi zum Klo**, with its graphic portrait of homosexual life in Berlin.

One great director was on towering form, Andrzej Wajda, with **Man of Iron**, his sequel to **Man of Marble**, while another, Italy's Francesco Rosi, was in reflective mood in a tale of a family reunion, **Three Brothers**.

From France, Bertrand Tavernier sent one of his best films, **Coup de Torchon**, an atmospheric tale of murder set in West Africa in 1938, with Philippe Noiret as the town's police chief. The only other French film widely seen was a devilishly clever thriller, **Diva**, with which director Jean-Jacques Beineix made his début. Because it was made in English, in Scotland, Tavernier's **Death Watch** received some overseas bookings; but these were denied to the umpteenth and most intelligent version of **La Dame aux Camélias**, with Isabelle Huppert and Gian-Maria Volonté (as her father), perhaps because Mauro Bolognini's handling was found to be too square. The same fate awaited Claude Lelouch's **Les Uns et les Autres**, despite the presence in the cast of James Caan. Deprivation was a mixed blessing, for its excesses and banalities were epoch-making.

1982

One American film overshadowed all the others. **Missing**, directed by Costa-Gavras, caused the State Department to issue a formal rebuttal. The missing man (John Shea) is an American in Chile in 1973, in the coup which ousted the socialist government. His wife (Sissy Spacek) and his right-wing father (Jack Lemmon), in uneasy alliance, discover that their embassy is not as dis-interested as it pretends, since it has conspired with the right-wing victors.

Another foreign direc-tor, Australian, made a considerable contribution to American cinema in 1982. Fred Schepisi's **Barbarosa** was a deliciously fresh comic Western, with Gary Busey as a Texan farmboy who becomes an outlaw and teams up with Willie Nelson, reputed to be a ruthless killer.

Lumet's **The Verdict** had a sharp screenplay by David Mamet, and Paul Newman at his best as an unsuccessful, alcoholic lawyer who jumps at what might be his last chance, prosecuting a Catholic Hospital for malpractice. Its portrait of Boston was splendid and if outmatched by Baltimore in Barry Levinson's **Diner** that was because Levinson's express design had been to re-create the city of his youth (in the late 50s), with the teenage kids talking about sex, indulging in it or getting married so that it was legal. Among these were Steve Guttenberg, Kevin Bacon, Mickey Rourke and Ellen Barkin.

1982 was a promising year for screen comedy, if only because it marked the maturing of Steve Martin in one of

his own screenplays, directed by Carl Reiner. **Dead Men Don't Wear Plaid** was a spoof of the crime films of the 1940s which managed to have such as Bogart, Davis, Bergman, Ladd and Stanwyck appearing with him. There were several laughs in George Roy Hill's **The World According to Garp**, with John Irving's novel much restrained and tamed in Steve Tesich's screenplay. It's well acted by Robin Williams, who has a strange upbring-ing and an adulterous marriage, and by Glenn Close as his unmarried mother, who writes a feminist bestseller. There is also John Lithgow as a transvestite ball-player, a situation reworked in Sydney Pollack's **Tootsie** so that Dustin Hoffman can become a star of soaps; till then he'd been an unimportant actor. Teri Garr is super as his girlfriend, as is Jessica Lange as the girl he falls for after donning dresses. Making passes at him in drag are Lange's father, Charles Durning, and an actor, George Gaynes. Much of the film was very funny.

1982 also had a locker room scene which raised eyebrows, but it's the best thing in the film as the jocks sing lustily preparing for their evening at **The Best Little Whorehouse in Texas**. When they're there the girls' frocks fall off while they're dancing. Colin Higgins directed from a Broadway show with C & W songs. Dolly Parton is the madam, Burt Reynolds her boyfriend, the sheriff, and there's a plot about someone trying to close the place down. Another long-running show was filmed, based on the 1930s comic strip, Little Orphan **Annie**, nominally directed by John Huston. Mr Finney was the millionaire who adopts the child, with Carol Burnett, Tim Curry and Bernadette Peters all O.T.T. as the villains. Both films were expensive and popular; but the second, in

Left: A year of outstanding films included Yilmaz Guney's **Yol/The Way**, which in any other would have towered over the competition. The leading role was played by Tarik Akan, seen here with Serif Sezer. Above: Peter Weir's **The Year of Living Dangerously** – which was 1965, when the communists attempted a coup in Manila. Mel Gibson played a dedicated reporter, and Sigourney Weaver the British girl with whom he falls in love. Opposite: Greta Scacchi in **Heat and Dust**, a Merchant-Ivory production written by Ruth Prawer Jhabvala, usually the kiss of death – at least artistically – for this team. This was an exception.

particular, did nothing for the cause of screen musicals. Even less was done by Coppola's **One From the Heart**, a film so misconceived that no survey of the cinema's first hundred years can afford to ignore it. Difficult to know which was worst: the stylized Las Vegas sets, the songs or the quartet of quarrelling lovers, who would doubtless prefer to be unnamed.

Spielberg's **E.T.: The Extra-Terrestial**, an odd creature who come to earth and is befriended by a child. It took, in comparative terms, more money than any other movie yet made. Ridley Scott's **Blade Runner** was, on the other hand, scifi for adults, a haunting view of a dystopic Los Angeles, with robots arriving in human shape and able to self-destruct after their killing games. Rutger Hauer and Sean Young were two of them, doubtless prevailing had Harrison Ford not happened along to help the world.

In Britain there was another musical and more transvestites. Blake Edwards' **Victor/Victoria** was a remake of the old German movie, with Robert Preston as a drag artist who persuades Julie Andrews that she can become a star. She does, and acquires a gangster admirer in James Garner, who gets a bit worried because he also feels the same about Victor. Henry Mancini wrote the excellent songs (lyrics, Leslie Bricusse), which get the treatment they deserve from Andrews and Preston. Most of the cast of **Privates on Parade** want to get into drag, but then they belong to a concert party in Singapore in 1948. They're headed by Denis Quilley as a screaming queen, repeating his outrageous performance in the Royal Shakespeare Company's production of Peter Nichols' very funny play. Michael Blakemore directed; John

Cleese did a neat turn; and it would all have been much better if they hadn't had to perform in an English football field with some palm trees stuck in it.

Merchant-Ivory made their best film in a long while, **Heat and Dust**, lovingly re-creating the India of the 1920s, with Greta Scacchi and Christopher Cazenove as a couple enjoying the formal life and the friendship of a local nawab, Shashi Kapoor. Julie Christie, a researcher curious about the letters Scacchi wrote to her grand-mother, comes to India in the present day, and the contrasts are splendidly evoked. **Gandhi**, too, is set in this land of heat and dust, though it begins in South Africa. John Briley wrote the screenplay of Richard Attenborough's film, which errs only in stressing its anti-Imperialism. It manages important matters (Home Rule, the conflict between Hindus and Muslims) with skill and without oversimplifying, and has an eloquent Mahatma in Ben Kingsley. A large-name cast subdued itself to the task, clearly loving it as much as Sir Dicky.

Bill Forsyth's sweet-minded **Gregory's Girl** sees a fifteen-year-old Glaswegian footballer (Gordon John Sinclair) discover sex in the person of his replacement on the team – a *girl* (Dee Hepburn). **The Long Good Friday** is a tale of East End gang wars. This was more like it. It had a new director, John MacKenzie; a new star, Bob Hoskins; and, as in the good old days, a box-office success that owed nothing to transatlantic cousins.

Eire had a brilliant new writer-director in Neil Jordan, whose **Angel** is a complex tale of terrorism in South Armagh, with Stephen Rea as a saxophonist unwillingly caught up in it.

Australia sent out several films of quality: Paul Cox's

Left: Walter Hill's **48 HRS** was a conventional but exciting thriller with Nick Nolte as a San Francisco cop who springs Eddie Murphy from the pen to help him catch some punks. Above: Harrison Ford, a Bogart for the future, in Ridley Scott's stunning **Blade Runner**. It has come to be regarded as one of the key films of the Eighties. Opposite: Graeme Clifford's **Frances** Farmer was a grim biography of the 1930s star – an outstanding Jessica Lange – whose left-wing views and drinking took her from the studios into a series of mental homes. It is a harrowing story.

Lonely Hearts, about the romance between two people who never expected one, a thirty-five-year-old bank teller (Wendy Hughes) and a piano tuner (Norman Kaye); Peter Weir's **The Year of Living Dangerously**, with Mel Gibson as a reporter and Sigourney Weaver as the girl with whom he falls in love; John Duigan's **Far East**, which may also be set in Manila, with Helen Morse walking into the bar of an old flame, Bryan Brown (and you know where they got that from); David Stevens' very funny **The Clinic**, about a cross-section of people with V.D. and those who nonchalantly offer cures; Michael Robinson's **The Best of Friends**, about a childhood friendship between Angela Punch McGregor and Graeme Blundell, which flounders when now grown up, they introduce sex; and Carl Schultz's **Goodbye Paradise**, one of the few successful parodies of Chandler, with Ray Barrett as a Queensland ex-cop discovering corruption in high places.

In Italy, Antonioni returns to filming with **Identification of a Woman**, with Thomas Milian as a director undecided whether or which of his two lovers is the ideal woman for his next film. Zeffirelli does an over-stuffed **La Traviata**, the first really successful filmed opera . . . and it does have Teresa Stratas and Placido Domingo as the leads.

In France, Daniel Vigne's **Le Retour de Martin Guerre** was based on the bizarre case of 1542 (much discussed in 1982, since there was a book on the same subject) when Martin was welcomed back by his wife, Nathalie Baye, when he probably wasn't Martin at all. Gérard Depardieu played him; he was also Wajda's **Danton** in his coruscating review of the immense, exhilarating and bloody events of 1792–4. It was the first film Wajda had made since his imprisonment at the time of the suppression of Lech Walesa's Solidarity movement. Although Wajda denied it, the analogies resound, for this, too, questioned the wisdom of a government prepared to ride roughshod over the will of the people.

When the state refused funding for Ryszard Bugajski for **Interrogation**, Wajda's company supplied it. The woman (Krystyna Janda) being interrogated – tortured and raped (willingly, perhaps, to relieve the boredom of prison) – is an actress, and the authorities want to know whether she knew that the army officer with whom she had a one-night stand was a spy. That is what they say they want to know; she cannot, as they put it, 'stop the march of history'. In effect, they are subjugating her to prove that People's Power can make no mistakes. By setting the film back in 1951, Bugajski suggested that such matters were ancient history. He finishes with the death of Stalin and the inference is that there is no longer any need for communism. In the Soviet Union, the veteran director Yuli Raizman made **Private Life**, about a

middle-aged executive who loses his job and is especially at a loss because his wife is successful at hers. In Hungary, Karoly Makk made **Another Way**, which is what a married woman finds she likes after kissing another lady. Unlike **Interrogation**, these films were not banned because they were more subtle in predicting that the communist way of life was a rotten one.

In India, Benegal made **Ascending Scale**, whose starting point is the 1967 government declaration that three out of five land shares must be ceded to the people. One man (Om Puri) cannot claim because of a loan secured from a landowner. He spends ten years in fruitless court battles because it is clear that no one in authority is really keen to have the peasantry own the land. A masterpiece. As is **Yol/The Way**, directed by Şerif Gören in Turkey. It is, in fact, a Yilmaz Güney film and the one that would make his worldwide reputation – a telling picture of a country under martial law and of five prisoners who are temporarily released. Their fortunes are various – rebellion, romance, marital anguish – but the film ultimately concentrates on one man's struggle across the mountains to recover his wife, who has become a prostitute.

Finally, **Fanny and Alexander**, who are two children. But the subject of Bergman's last film is Sweden itself, represented by two contrasting families. A widow from one (Ewa Froeling) – spirited, affectionate, outgoing – marries into the other – small-minded, sanctimonious, hypocritical. The first is of the theatre, the second of the church; and connected to both is a foreigner, a Jewish man (Erland Josephson) who can make magic happen. Bergman's last film, as he intended, is his greatest.

1983

Hits and misses. It was ever thus. Some films are critic-proof and others aren't. Two things are certain: the age of the super-cinema is over and the age of video has arrived. Only large cities can support large movie houses; others are closing everywhere, to be replaced by complexes, usually in suburban shopping malls. Video rental shops are proliferating; the price of video cassettes is coming down; and we're coming to the point where every home has to have a player/recorder. The time between cinema showings and release on video is shrinking. Parents remain at home with a choice of movies on network, cable or rental; but children love video cassettes. And the increasingly young audiences are going again and again to see films they like. This year they overwhelmingly liked **Return of the Jedi**, which became the third-biggest money maker of all time. **Star Wars** was second; and the second of the series. **The Empire Strikes Back** (1980), was fourth, reflecting the fact that it was the least well received of the three.

Among the failures were two with Burt Reynolds: **The Man Who Loved Women** and **Stoker Ace**; two by Coppola, **The Outsiders** and **Rumblefish**; Scorsese's **The King of Comedy**; the remakes of **Scarface** and **To Be or Not to Be**; **The Sting II** and **Cannonball Run II** (which makes a third for Reynolds); **Brainstorm** and **Deal of the Century**.

Also failing to attract audiences were the year's two best films. **Daniel** was directed by Sidney Lumet from

E. L. Doctorow's screenplay (from his book) about the execution of the Rosenbergs (Mandy Patinkin, Lindsay Crouse) for treason in 1953. The film was much criticized for not tackling the question of their guilt, but the title tells you that growing up left-wing and Jewish is not exactly an advantage. Timothy Hutton plays Daniel, with Amanda Plummer his sister. The voice of Paul Robeson on the soundtrack is exactly right. The songs in **Tender Mercies** were sung by Robert Duvall as a C & W star who gives up drink and minds the petrol pumps for their owner, Tess Harper. He proposes and the film has no other plot than whether he'll take up booze again and ruin the marriage.

Three good films were popular. Lawrence Kasdan's **The Big Chill** gathered together some friends one weekend at the home of two of them, Kevin Kline, Glenn Close. They've made it as they all hoped when they were together at the University of Michigan, but none of them is quite sure if they're happy and they're concerned about the suicide of a friend, which has brought them all here in the first place. The others include Jeff Goldblum, William Hurt. Those who had **The Right Stuff** – the first men to go to the moon – were being chosen and trained: Ed Harris (as John Glenn), Scott Glenn, Fred Ward and Dennis Quaid with Sam Shepard as their trainer. Philip Kaufman's film concentrates on only four of the seven, and he has carved a winning film out of Tom Wolfe's long book, managing to be romantic and yet funny, with occasional satirical digs at the military or the enterprise itself. In 1974 Karen **Silkwood** was found dead, and Mike Nichols' film asks, absorbingly and terrifyingly, why? She was the apparent victim of a car crash but, as a union

Left: **Tender Mercies** has the slimmest of plots, but it works because of Robert Duvall's performance and the response of Bruce Beresford (in his first American film) to the vastness of Texas. Above: Kevin Kline and Glenn Close in **The Big Chill**, host and hostess for a weekend reunion of their college friends. Opposite: **The Right Stuff** with Philip Kaufman had carved a winning film out of Tom Wolfe's book about the military and the first American astronauts. Down to earth and a hero's welcome: Ed Harris as John Glenn, with uncredited players as President Lyndon Johnson and his wife.

activist at the Kerr-McGee plutonium plant in Oklahoma, had been given information on what she considered to be poor safety standards. In the title role Meryl Streep gives her only acceptable screen performance. Kurt Russell is her live-in lover and Cher a lesbian chum.

John Sayles's **Lianna** was the most perceptive yet on this subject. Lianna (Linda Griffiths) has two children and a husband (Jon DeVries) who teaches cinema and literature. He says it's just 'playing around' when caught having sex at a party. A few days later her psychology teacher, Ruth (Jane Hallaran), asks her about crushes; when Ruth touches her, she takes a moment to respond, then falls in love. Her husband is contemptuous when she tells him during a quarrel. The film's true subject then emerges, which is not whether Ruth wants her (she doesn't), but whether she can come out and keep the respect of her friends.

Two comedies were highly popular. John Landis's **Trading Places** found two millionaire brothers (Don Ameche, Ralph Bellamy) playing a joke on their protégé (Dan Aykroyd) by refusing to recognise him and then replacing him with a penniless black (Eddie Murphy).

James L. Brooks's **Terms of Endearment** found a middle-aged love affair between an ageing astronaut (Jack Nicholson) and his neighbour (Shirley MacLaine). Also liked was Michael Ritchie's **The Survivors**, with Robin Williams and Walter Matthau, executive and gas station attendant respectively, linking up on the dole and going to a gun school after being robbed in a restaurant; Stan Dragotti's **Mr Mom**, a glorified sitcom, with Tom Hanks and Teri Garr changing places; Paul Brickman's **Risky Business**, with Tom Cruise left alone in a Chicago mansion and asking the girls in, one of whom, a whore (Rebecca de Mornay), decides to stay; and there are laughs in **Staying Alive**, the sequel to **Saturday Night Fever**, with John Travolta now a Broadway dancer.

There were two clever comedies by men who wrote their own material. One of them directed as well: Woody Allen, in a documentary about **Zelig**, one of the forgotten men of history, via newsreels and those who knew him. The piece is a cod, but a masterpiece of technical skill. Carl Reiner directed **The Man with two Brains**, which takes Steve Martin all the way to Vienna to see his idol, Dr David Warner. Martin's new wife, Kathleen Turner, is with him, apparently keen to consummate the marriage with anyone but him.

Sean Connery returned to playing James Bond, under his own management, in **Never Say Never Again**. Roger Moore was playing him for the old management and when **Octopussy** came along simultaneously there was much discussion. They still looked like the same film. **Yentl** didn't look like a British film since it was set in old Russia, with Barbra Streisand donning knickerbockers in

Left: Dan Aykroyd and Eddie Murphy – who were **Trading Places** in a snowy Boston for a comedy that wanted to be cruel, but couldn't quite manage it. Above: Jack Nicholson offering **Terms of Endearment** to Shirley Maclaine – a film that managed to be funny about the monstrous pretensions of this opinionated woman. It was much less successful when turning sad because her daughter (Debra Winger) is dying. Opposite: Carl Reiner's **The Man With Two Brains**, which took Steve Martin all the way to Vienna to see his idol, a professor who has designs on his body – strictly in the cause of medical science.

order to study the Talmud. She also sang and directed, co-wrote and co-produced. It was not as embarrassing as expected, though that was not a view shared by Isaac Bashevis Singer, the author of the original story.

In France, Güney directed his final film, **Le Mur**, a study of the men, women and children herded together in a Turkish prison. He views them compassionately, but for the warders he has only scorn and contempt. Costa-Gavras makes **Hanna K**, set in Israel with Jill Clayburgh as an American-Jewish lawyer who is defending a terrorist and falling in love with Gabriel Byrne, who is defending him. A little glib, but it makes a strong statement for the Palestinian cause. **J'ai Epousé un Ombre** is **No Man of Her Own** (1949) remade, by Robin Davis, with Nathalie Baye in the Stanwyck role. Guy Trejean plays the father-in-law and Francis Huster the brother. These films were little seen abroad. These were: Pialat's **À Nos Amours**, proof that family life is not for him, since he himself plays a man who is a failure as both husband and father; and Euzhan Palcy's **Rue Case Negres**, proof that growing up poor and black in 1930s Martinique was no joke. This last is nevertheless a charming film, adapted by Palcy herself from an autobiographical novel by Joseph Zobel.

In Australia Carl Schultz filmed **Careful He Might Hear You**, based on another autobiographical novel, Sumner Locke Elliott's 1963 bestseller. Nicholas Gledhill is unforgettable as the child deserted by his father (John Hargreaves) and fought over by several of his dead mother's sisters, including the one who has taken her place and the wealthy one (Wendy Hughes) who believes it her right to look after him.

In India, Mrinal Sen made a movie about the death of a boy from asphyxiation while working for a bourgeois family. As the police investigate, this becomes an excellent thriller, and an indignant one, as you can tell from the title Sen chose: **The Case is Closed**. And Benegal's attitude towards his subject can be discerned by his title, **Market Place**, life in a brothel studied in over two and a half hours which gives time for much detail and humour since it and its inhabitants have seen better days.

In Japan, two veteran directors look back to the War and its aftermath: Kobayashi's **The Tokyo Trial** consists only of documentary footage of those prosecuted for war crimes and it lasts 265 minutes, all of them riveting; and Kinoshita's **The Children of Nagasaki** recreates, rather clumsily, that night when the city was destroyed by an atomic bomb.

Some diverse European films would make you feel only marginally better about the human race. In Hungary, **Daniel Takes a Train** at the time of the unsuccessful 1956 uprising, with Pal Sandor earning admiration for acknowledging that it had ever happened in the first place.

In the Netherlands, **The Fourth Man** is loose, though it is unclear who he is. Paul Verhoeven's edgy, excessive thriller concerns try-anything writer Jeroen Krabbe, who moves in with Renee Soutendijk because he has the hots for her boyfriend. He also thinks the young man may be Christ and, seeing him on on the crucifix, pulls off his swimming briefs. Like Bergman, Verhoeven believes that our enslavement to religion and sexuality are two of God's blunders, but he is more lighthearted about them, which may be why he is now working in Hollywood.

Alain Tanner was in Portugal, **In the White City** (Lisbon), where a sailor (Bruno Ganz) drinks, becomes disorientated, has an affair with a maid and writes letters to his wife. The dialogue is in German, French, Portuguese and English. Another hybrid, and a magnificent one, was **The Mission**, with West German nationality, shot in New York and directed by Parciz Sayyad (producer of **In der Fremde** and **The Cycle**), who also plays a colonel who had been in the Shah's secret police. The title refers to the assassin sent to kill him. It is a film of great tension, only apparently unwilling to say whether it is for the Shah or the Ayatollah.

A s the cinema approaches its centenary, there will be few people around who saw it start. There are very many around responsible for the successes and failures of these last years – many of them, in both cases, inexplicable. The videocassette had dramatically increased movie culture, and movies were more frequently discussed than ever. Everyone read the critics, but they could no longer call the shots (as they had since the 1950s). It might be most revealing for these last years to look at the significant American films roughly in order of popularity – as it is measured in box-office terms.

1984

Ivan Reitman's **Ghostbusters** becomes the sixth most popular film ever made, a broad comedy with special effects, with Dan Aykroyd, Bill Murray and Harold Ramis in the title roles, plus Sigourney Weaver and Rick Moranis as welcome company in the building in which they're working. Joe Dante's **Gremlins**, produced by Spielberg's outfit, had more special effects as bugs eat up a small town till they're vanquished as miraculously as they came. Michael Brest's **Beverly Hills Cop** was released in November, but by the time it had finished its run in the spring of 1985 it had surpassed **Gremlins** at the box office. The reason was Eddie Murphy, coming into his own as a Detroit cop who takes himself off to LA to

Above: Sexual tensions abounded in **The Bounty**, the best movie reincarnation of its mutiny. Not only was Captain Bligh obsessed with Fletcher Christian, but Christian hoped to use that banked-up emotion to spend more time with his native princess: Mel Gibson and Tevaite Vernette. Right: Sam Waterston and Haing S. Ngor, American journalist and his Vietnamese minder, in Roland Joffe's noble, moving film **The Killing Fields.**

investigate the death of a pal. There, and this is the best of it, he comes up against some phonies, some dangerous villains and a local police force which doesn't like him. John G. Avildsen's **The Karate Kid** was pleasing stuff about a despised boy (Ralph Macchio) who gets the condo's handyman (Noriyuki 'Pat' Morita) to show him how to give his enemies the chop. In Hugh Wilson's **Police Academy**, more goons get laughs; George Gaynes tries to make a speech to VIPs while being blown under the table – the high spot.

Ron Howard's **Splash** was Disney's first smash in years, about a mermaid (Darryl Hannah) in New York and a vegetable wholesaler (Tom Hanks). It had all the expected jokes, but was none the worse for that. Hugh Hudson's **Greystoke: The Legend of Tarzan, Lord of the Apes** had magical views of Africa and something similar blown into the old tale. Christopher Lambert took the title role.

2010 was the sequel to **2001**, this time directed by Peter Hyams, and very much more tense and original than we had a right to expect, but while David Lynch's **Dune** looked marvellous it was actually hard to tell what was going on. Carl Reiner's **All of Me** had Steve Martin both writing and starring, as a lawyer who finds nasty, dead Lily Tomlin inside him. Mr Martin was getting funnier all the time. Taylor Hackford's **Against All Odds** was a remake of **Out of the Past** (1947), with Jeff Bridges hired by James Woods to look for a girl. What Bridges finds is danger and massive civic corruption. This was Bridges' year: in **Starman**, another excellent movie and his best work to date, he was an android looking so much like a human that the scientists want to lock him up.

Robert Benton's **Places in the Heart**, which he also wrote, saw Sally Fields as a widow in Waxahachie, Texas in 1935, coping, helped by John Malkovich (a little: he's blind, and this is the movies' most convincing portrayal of that condition) and by a black (Danny Glover) who is glad to get work because of the Depression. Coppola's **The Cotton Club** was supposedly a synthesis with black musicians, gangsters, Richard Gere and Gregory Hines as its joint heroes. Norman Jewison's **A Soldier's Story** concerned a murder in a Louisiana army camp in 1944. The victim was black and so is the investigating officer (Howard E. Rollings), which sets off some rumbling among the whites. Since the black GIs are pleased to see him, it's a movie with more than its share of tension.

Anyone wanting comedy couldn't have done better than Charles Shyers' **Irreconcilable Differences**, written by him and Nancy Myers, with Shelley Long and Ryan O'Neal looking back on their marriage, with some keen satire at the expense of Hollywood, since he's in films; Garry Marshall's **The Flamingo Kid**, written by him and

Neal Marshall, with Matt Dillon as a Brooklyn boy who makes the acquaintance of a showy millionaire (Richard Crenna) and begins to emulate him; and Woody Allen's **Broadway Danny Rose**. Allen's films have always had spotty box-office success, but this is by far his funniest – and most endearing – film. He plays the least talented talent-agent in New York, only too happy to oblige his only (half)-famous client by escorting his girl (Mia Farrow, surprisingly accurate as a harpy) to hear him sing; he's much less happy to learn that she had been married to a member of the Mafia which, thinking her his, decides to rub him out.

Murder is very much at the centre of **Blood Simple**, after a bartender (John Getz) sleeps with the wife (Frances McDormand) of the owner (Dan Hedaya). When said owner employs a private eye (M. Emmet Walsh) to keep an eye on them, it's a sure thing that someone will wind up dead. This was a stunning début for Joel Coen, who wrote the screenplay with his brother Ethan, who also produced. For his second film (the first was a spaghetti Western) the British-born Alex Cox, writing and directing, came up with something equally fine, **Repo Man**, who is Emilio Estevez, repossessing autos in a seedy LA, with Harry Dean Stanton on particularly fine form as his partner. Not as bloody as the Coens' film, but, despite a touch of whimsy, equally black.

Since no one involved in those two films was well known, it's not surprising that they did little business; but the failure of the next two is more problematic. It could be that audiences didn't want to see a picture about an English drunk or a subject whose earlier movie manifestations had been on television too often. John Huston tamed Malcolm Lowry's novel about a consul drinking himself to death **Under the Volcano**, in Mexico. It contained Albert Finney's best screen work in years, with strong support by Jacqueline Bisset as his ex-wife and Anthony Andrews as his brother. Robert Bolt's screenplay made much sense of that naval incident that we know as the mutiny on **The Bounty**. Roger Donaldson's direction took care of both the sweep of the tale and Bolt's contention that the dissension arose because Captain Bligh (Anthony Hopkins) was in thrall to Mr Christian (Mel Gibson), who wanted to use that to his own ends. Both were major movie achievements when there were no longer many around.

David Lean had worked for years on **The Bounty** before the producers decided that his version would be too expensive. He turned his attention to **A Passage to India**, which looks beautiful but does not show much understanding either of the country or E. M. Forster's novel, which he scripted himself. Victor Bannerjee was Dr Aziz, responsible for what may or may not have happened in the darkened cave, and Judy Davis was the girl to whom it may have happened; Peggy Ashcroft was perfect as the mother of her intended fiancé, Nigel Havers. He and James Fox, as a teacher, were hardly less so. The Brits were also in the East for a very different matter, **The Killing Fields**, directed by Roland Joffe from Bruce Robinson's screenplay, based in turn on reporting by Sydney H. Schanberg on the inhuman conflict in Cambodia. Sam Waterston was Schanberg, determined to find Dith Pran (Haing S. Ngor), friend, guide, translator, and travelling into dangerous Khmer Rouge territory to do so. The result wouldn't be dwarfed if programmed with the other great movies on the terrible foolishness of war.

The British looked to the past, to **Another Country**, as L. P. Hartley called it, which was the title Julian Mitchell used for his play on the morals and mores of a public school in the 1930s. There were no morals; the mores were those governing religion, the equally sacred game of cricket, and military life. Rupert Everett played a character based on the spy Guy Burgess, a dedicated homosexual at the start of the film and a committed Communist at the end of it. Mitchell wrote the script, which was directed by Marek Kanievska.

Elsewhere others also looked back. Argentina in 1847: Maria Luisa Bemberg's backdrop for the moving **Camila**, the true tale of a girl who loves a priest, who loves her back, knowing that they can only self-destruct. India *circa* 1907: Ray's setting for **The Home and the World**, from a Tagore story about a kindly man (Victor Bannerjee) who wants his wife to share his westernized culture, so he encourages the visit of an old friend (Soumitra Chatterjee) who is both a philanderer and a dangerous political activist. China in 1939: Chen Kaige's studied **Yellow Earth** tells of a soldier preaching Communism in a remote province and of the girl whom he thinks he can save from an unwanted marriage by getting her permission to join the Red Army. Germany in 1941: Wajda's magnificent **Eine Liebe in Deutschland** has Hanna Schygulla courting disaster by falling madly for the Polish POW doing odd jobs about the house; with Marie-Christine Barrault, Daniel Olbrychski and Armin Mueller-Stahl as the SS officer who would like to get the lovers off the hook.

There were two wry comedies of today. From Australia, Bruce Best's **Warming Up** takes the mickey out of the macho image by having a football team start to win again after being taught ballet. From Spain, in Manuel Gutiérrez Aragón's **La Noche Mas Hermosa**, the woman for whom a TV producer wants to leave his wife (Victoria Abril) is a transvestite actor, Bibi Andersen.

In **Paris, Texas**, in English (dialogue by Sam Shepard, directed by Wim Wenders), Harry Dean Stanton collects the child he deserted years ago and they go off in search of his wife (Nastassja Kinski), whom he's delighted to find has become a whore. **Les Ripoux** or **Le Cop** is a lovely thing about the most cynical, most corrupt cop on the beat and his permanently astounded partner, with Philippe Noiret and Thierry Lhermite both splendid in those roles. It was written and directed by Claude Zidi, whose films hitherto had been loathed by the critics and adored by the public. This time they agreed. Agreement, too, that Francesco Rosi's **Carmen** was the best filmed opera yet, imaginatively shot in Andalusia in an adaptation beautifully aware of the demands of cinema, story and music. It starred Julia Migenes-Johnson, Placido Domingo (Don José) and Ruggero Raimondi (Escamillo).

Opposite above: Michael Douglas and Kathleen Turner, both having high jinks in the Brazilian jungle in **Romancing the Stone**. Douglas produced and Robert Zemeckis directed. Right: Milos Forman's **Amadeus**, from Peter Shaffer's play, studied the supposed rivalry between the young, foul-mouthed Mozart (Tom Hulce) and the older, jealous Salieri, played by F. Murray Abraham. It was sumptuous to ear and eye.

Back to the Future is the year's most popular movie. It's the year's most entertaining movie, inventive, genial and perfectly judged by Robert Zemeckis, director, and Bob Gale, producer, who wrote it together. Michael J. Fox is a teenager and Christopher Lloyd the mad inventor responsible for sending him back to 1955. He's astonished to

1985

find what his home town was like then and appalled to find that he won't be born unless he persuades his mother to go after his father instead of himself. This is the best film yet from the Spielberg factory and Richard Donner's **The Goonies** may well be the worst, a loud and aimless thing about children looking for buried treasure. Ron Howard's **Cocoon** is more scifi fun: some androids (including Brian Dennehy) land near a Florida geriatric home and store their pods in its pool. After swimming, three old boys (Don Ameche, Wilford Brimley, Hume Cronyn) get hard-ons and their wives (Gwen Verdon, Maureen Stapleton, Jessica Tandy) are delighted. Sydney Pollack's **Out of Africa** has Meryl Streep as the Danish baroness Karen Blixen on a farm, married to the interesting Klaus Maria Brandauer and carrying on after his death with the bland Robert Redford.

Among the thrillers is Michael Ritchie's **Fletch**, which is Chevy Chase's break-through movie, playing one

Above: The Western shuddered to its close in the '70s, killed by excessive violence, too-real realism and, on the other hand, too much facetiousness. Clint Eastwood revived the form in **Pale Rider**, helping Carrie Snodgress, deserted by her husband when her life is threatened by a greedy landowner. Right: Mel Gibson in **Mad Max Beyond Thunderdome**, the third, last and most popular of the thrillers set in a dystopian Australia.

of those foolishly bold reporters likely to be shot at any moment. The laughs come from his impersonations. **Mad Max Beyond Thunderdome** has biker violence in a future Australia, with Mel Gibson pitted against corrupt Tina Turner. There are better ways of spending your time. George Miller directed the three movies in this series, of which this was the last. The first (1979) attracted little attention, but when **Mad Max 2** did well, Warner poured big bucks into this one.

Lawrence Kasdan's approach to the Western is the reverse of Eastwood's, realistic instead of epic, and **Silverado** may be the first to have its hero show fear. He's Kevin Kline; Scott Glenn and Kevin Costner are his friends, and they have other chums like Danny Glover, Jeff Goldblum, Rosanna Arquette and Linda Hunt, with a plot that involves stolen bullion. But John Cleese's unfeeling sheriff and Brian Dennehy's corrupt town boss aren't formidable opponents. Taylor Hackford's **White Nights** has some individual moments and a confused plot about defectors – Russian dancer Mikhail Baryshnikov, and American Gregory Hines. When the dancer's plane crash-lands in Siberia, a KGB officer (Jerzy Skolimowski) has him lodge with Hines.

The youth film in full cry, both set firmly in 1984 and for what it's worth both containing Emilio Estevez, Judd Nelson and Ally Sheedy: **The Breakfast Club**, written and directed by John Hughes, responsible for many more in the future, few as pleasing as this; and Joel Schumaker's **St Elmo's Fire**, which is rather better. There is a reason for this: the first is set almost wholly in the school library where some pupils in detention (others: Molly Ringwald, Anthony Michael Hall) discuss sex, parents, etc. The seven subjects (others: Rob Lowe, Demi

Moore) of the second are older, graduates, and life has already fucked them up.

Susan Seidelman's **Desperately Seeking Susan** looked freshly at New York and has a plot to match. Miss Arquette, a fed-up housewife, is mistaken for the tacky Madonna and thus finds herself in a life she'd never dreamed of, of mayhem and romance with Aiden Quinn, who is the reverse of her jerk of a husband.

There were two responsible movies by British directors: John Boorman's **The Emerald Forest** and John Schlesinger's **The Falcon and the Snowman**. Boorman thinks the Amazon worth saving and sends Powers Boothe up its accompanying river to search for his son, who after being lost for ten years has gone native. Schlesinger has a tall but true story of two guys, Timothy Hutton and Sean Penn, so incensed at learning of CIA involvement around the world that they are going to sell what they know to the Russian embassy in Mexico City. Among the things they know: that the CIA destabilized the Whitlam government in Australia. They probably shouldn't have given **A Chorus Line**, Broadway's longest-running musical, to Richard Attenborough. The critics didn't like it; the public didn't come, but the show was there all right. Perhaps Sir Dicky should have been tougher in his approach.

The Trip to Bountiful, directed by Peter Masterson from Horton Foote's play, follows Geraldine Page as she journeys to her home town and finds kindnesses *en route* to make up for the hurts inflicted by her daughter-in-law. Sissy Spacek is **Marie**, an abused wife who goes into Nashville politics to find herself being used. Roger Donaldson directed from a true report, originally by Peter Maas.

An essential pairing: Martin Scorsese's **After**

Left: Jonathan Pryce and Kim Greist in Terry Gilliam's **Brazil**, a scifi story by turns tired and inspired, comic, thrilling and tedious – but always ambitious. Above: Peter Weir's **Witness** to a murder is a small boy; detective Harrison Ford hides with him and his Amish mother, Kelly McGillis, after realizing two of his superiors are implicated. Weir made refreshing use of old tricks, like the getaway car that won't start.

Hours, his best movie in years, with Griffin Dunne, and John Landis's **Into the Night**, with Jeff Goldblum. Both protagonists unexpectedly find themselves in mysteries. So do we: why more people didn't come. They would have found style, menace, surprise in two entertainments which don't take themselves seriously. And in the second, dangerous Michele Pfeiffer and several well-known actors and directors in walk-ons. **Lost in America**, these people, and that was the title of Albert Brooks' comedy (director, co-writer, star) about a couple who go in search of it – as we're forcibly reminded when a cop stops the pair for speeding and Brooks mentions **Easy Rider**. The cop's eyes fill with tears. That movie was long in the past, but these three are virtually the first since then to say that nothing was comfortable, understandable anymore.

A non-essential pairing, except that nobody came and that wasn't a mystery: Karel Reisz's life of Patsy Cline (Jessica Lange), **Sweet Dreams**, and Bruce Beresford's life of **King David** (Richard Gere). The last was an honourable and long-gestating attempt to revive the Hollywood Biblical after the success of Zeffirelli's television **Jesus of Nazareth** in 1977. It was too late. Much, much too late.

The British cinema was said to be in a state of revival. The evidence was provided by two larky, fairytale efforts; Chris Bernard's **Letter to Brezhnev** and Stephen Frears' **My Beautiful Laundrette**. For Bernard, two Liverpool factory workers (Margi Clarke, Alexandra Pigg), one of them unemployed, spent a night on the town with two Russian sailors (Alfred Molina, Peter Firth), while for Frears a miscegenetic gay couple (Daniel Day Lewis, Gordon Warnecke) had each other while casually minding that laundrette – it was better than being out of work – which wasn't beautiful at all, but seedy and Pakistani-owned. Britain had not come to terms with the consequences of the immigration of millions of colonial coloureds since the 1950s, reflected in this movie for the first time. Thatcher had been in power six years, during which time race riots had reduced inner city areas to boarded-up ghettos.

Thatcher's Britain was superbly expressed in **Defence of the Realm**, Martin Stellman's script directed by David Drury, who said that it was better to show these matters in compromised or melodramatic form than not show them at all. 'These matters' are a cover-up by the Establishment of a nuclear explosion on an American air base; Gabriel Byrne was the investigative reporter discovering a vast conspiracy amongst mundane high-ups prepared to kill rather than have the facts revealed. The view conveyed was little different from that in Terry Gilliam's **Brazil**, imagining a future, department-store world of bureaucrats who killed at will. Jonathan Pryce was on the staff, dreaming of bucking the system; Robert de Niro was a renegade spirit encouraging him for a while.

In Argentina, Luis Puenzo's **The Official Story** was a powerful polemic on the country under the colonels, with hundreds of people 'disappearing'. The plot itself was somewhat simplistic, since it was hard to believe that the intelligent heroine – she's a professor – could not have realized that her husband was among those responsible.

In Japan, Kobayashi confronted contemporary problems in **The Empty Table**, in which a liberal-minded electronics engineer, Tatsuya Nakadai, has to come to terms with the knowledge that his son has become a terrorist. Kurosawa turned his back on the present and went to Shakespeare for **Ran**. The title means chaos, but this is *King Lear* transferred to feudal Japan, heavily adapted (this lord has sons, not daughters), visually breathtaking, and strikingly acted by Nakadai as the deceived father. This was probably the most discussed foreign-language film of the year, rivalled only by Sweden's **My Life as a Dog**, about a boy of twelve discovering the delights of sex, whether it's being paid to poke his dong in a Coca-Cola bottle, or with a girl of his own age, or by watching a couple through a roof-top window, through which he falls. Lasse Hollstrom directed. It's strange: this became a popular favourite despite press indifference, whereas Czechoslovakia's **My Sweet Little Village**, however, simply did not live up to the enthusiasm of the foreign distributors and those who saw it in preview. According to *Variety*, Jiří Menzel's film 'elicited a rarely heard ovation' at the Cannes Festival. It is very funny as it compares the lives of two contrasting truck drivers, a gormless youth and his knowing partner. The Hungarian film of the year was István Szabó's **Colonel Redl**, a follow-up to **Mephisto** and again based on fact, with Klaus-Maria Brandauer as the Jewish man of humble origins who, against the odds, became head of Imperial intelligence and sold what he knew to the Russians because they threatened to disclose his homosexuality.

From France, enigmas in Luc Besson's **Subway**, a clever, flashy rejig of **A Bout de Souffle**, set in the Métro, with Christopher Lambert and Isabelle Adjani. Pialat had his greatest success (on his home ground) with **Police**, a study of one of them, played by Dépardieu, who is exceptionally brutal and unethical but all mushy at heart. He's also sex-obsessed, as is everyone in Edouard Molinaro's **L'Amour en Douce**. Daniel Auteuil's wife throws him out after finding him with one woman too many; she moves in Jean-Pierre Marielle and Auteuil has to make do with his boss's girl, Emmanuelle Beart, who is also a prostitute. He falls in love with her. Before **Pretty Woman** (see 1990) and funnier.

1986

om Cruise in Tony Scott's **Top Gun**, taking part in high jinks in amongst the military airborne set; Eddie Murphy in Michael Ritchie's **The Golden Child**, as a detective looking for an Oriental princeling; Rodney Dangerfield, a pompous, self-made millionaire going **Back to School** in Alan Metter's comedy; Matthew Broderick in John Hughes's **Ferris Bueller's Day Off**, joy-riding around Chicago in his dad's borrowed Ferrari – these were all harmless entertainments but were nothing memorable. Among the 1986 movies the public liked best, **The Karate Kid Part II** was second, if taking almost $30 million less than **Top Gun**'s $82 million. The picture in the third position was Australian (see below). It's not till you get down to **Ruthless People**, directed by Jim Abrahams, David Zucker and Jerry Zucker, that you find much merit, with Bette Midler being kidnapped and husband Danny DeVito happily refusing to pay ransom. (The idea came from a British film of 1959, **Too Many Crooks**.) Another Disney comedy, Paul Mazursky's **Down and Out in Beverly Hills**, was an acknowledged remake of **Boudu Sauvé des Eaux**, and it had more stuffing, with nice performances by the leads: Nick Nolte as the bum given shelter by a bourgeois couple, Richard Dreyfuss and Miss Midler.

Ivan Reitman's **Legal Eagles**, a thriller with Robert Redford and Debra Winger falling in love while fighting in court, flew on star power. So did **The Color of Money**, Martin Scorsese directing Paul Newman and Tom Cruise in a sequel, all these years on, to **The Hustler**. No one

could pretend it had the same guts. **Three Amigos!** had its moments, notably when a bush sings one of Randy Newman's cod songs. Others are sung by Steve Martin, Chevy Chase and Martin Short as Western movie heroes of the Silent days, taken for the real thing down Mexico way. David Cronenberg's **The Fly** was Jeff Goldblum, an expensive remake of the 1958 movie, with Geena Davis. Molly Ringwald was **Pretty in Pink** for director Howard Deutch and writer John Hughes, remembering all those movies of the 1920s when a poor girl was courted by a rich boy, Andrew McCarthy. **Hannah and her Sisters**, about adultery in the family, was Woody Allen's most successful film in years (those who had missed the others didn't know they were getting the same jokes). Coppola's **Peggy Sue Got Married** sent middle-aged Kathleen Turner back to the future, to her college days, to see whether she'd make the same mistake twice. She does; she marries Nicolas Cage.

'About Last Night' didn't have the nerve of David Mamet's play *Sex and Perversity in Chicago*, on which it was based but, directed by Edward Zwick, it had some funny and touching moments for Rob Lowe and Demi Moore, meeting in a singles bar and shacking up, but unsure how far they wish to commit themselves. Mike Nichols' **Heartburn** looked instead to the end of a

Left: Daniel Auteuil and Yves Montand in Claude Berri's **Jean de Florette**, the sequel to **Manon des Sources**. Above: **Salvador**, with James Woods as a reporter, was the first of the two 1986 films with which Oliver Stone signalled his concern with big issues – an indictment of the atrocities being committed by right-wing factions in South America. Opposite: Tom Cruise (right) with Val Kilmer and (behind) Anthony Edwards in **Top Gun**, the year's most popular film. No one was quite sure whether that was because it was a return to the hawkish values being preached in the White House or because of Cruise's appeal.

relationship, and seriously, as taken from Nora Ephron's autobiographical novel. Jack Nicholson was the adulterous husband and Meryl Streep was the Wronged One. Randa Haines's **Children of a Lesser God** saw William Hurt, a teacher of deaf-mutes, concerned that one of them is a cleaner and not in his class. Marlee Matlin, who is deaf-mute, played her, and they fall in love but do not live happily ever after. In Michael Mann's **Manhunter**, from a novel by Thomas Harris, an ex-cop (William Petersen) is asked back in order to track down a serial killer. To do so, he consults another, now in jail, Dr Hannibal Lektor (Brian Cox).

Sweet Liberty was Alan Alda's second picture as director and his third as writer, a gentle satire, in which he himself is a professor advising on the American Revolution as his novel on the period is being filmed. Splendid performances, too, from Michael Caine as a look-at-me movie star; Michelle Pfeiffer as his yielding leading lady, but hard-as-nails underneath; and Bob Hoskins as a terminally sycophantic screenwriter. And a cameo from a lady who had been around almost from the beginning of cinema's first hundred years, Lillian Gish, in her penultimate film.

Peter Weir's **The Mosquito Coast** is taken from a novel by Paul Theroux, with a screenplay by Paul Schrader. Harrison Ford is the Massachusetts man who opts out and takes his wife (Helen Mirren) and two kids to a jungle village. Nothing, however, could persuade anyone that this is a bright idea – see the title – so the film did little business. There were only small audiences for Bill Sherwood's **Parting Glances**, a study, made independently, of a group of gay friends, some of whom die of AIDS. This was the first important film on the subject.

The year's two best American films were both directed by Oliver Stone. **Salvador** was co-written by the journalist Richard Boyle – played by James Woods – in Salvador with James Belushi and appalled at the poverty, the open atrocities of the right-wing régime and the refusal of the American embassy to admit that anything is wrong. The film is jagged, often an action adventure. Coming to American involvement in another country, Vietnam, Stone is serious, partly because the film is autobiographical, with Charlie Sheen as the man who volunteered for patriotic reasons. A graphic account of what it was like there, the actual plot concerns a **Platoon**, whose leader (Tom Berenger) has been savaging and killing the villagers till another sergeant (Willem Dafoe) arrives. He is determined to report this and the men split into pro and con factions.

The New York critics thought the Best Picture was British, **A Room with a View**, showing that, like Merchant-Ivory, they hadn't read E. M. Forster's novel. For his reasons for writing it had been carefully excised, i.e. that Lucy, born in the Old Queen's reign, was looking for a meaning in the new century and was drawn for the suffragette movement. In that role Helena Bonham Carter is a disaster; some usually excellent players – Judi Dench, Maggie Smith – give stock performances, leaving Daniel Day Lewis to save the day, as Lucy's stuffy fiancé.

The Australian film the world went mad about was **'Crocodile' Dundee**, with Paul Hogan in that role, a guy from the Outback who goes to New York and puts the phonies in their place. It was the year's feel-good movie, but the 1988 sequel was anything but – to the extent that Hogan's next movie (1990), made in Hollywood, disap-

Left: Steve Martin was a Silent cowboy star in John Landis's **Three Amigos!**, used to faking it on the set – but he doesn't have that option when he strays South of the Border. Above: **'Crocodile' Dundee** was a vehicle fashioned by Paul Hogan and his friends to make him a movie star – and it did so, surprisingly, the world over. Opposite above: Oliver Stone's second important film of 1986 was **Platoon**, dealing with the American intervention in Vietnam of which it firmly disapproved. Charlie Sheen played Stone's own version of his younger self. The film won Oscars for Best Picture and Best Director.

peared within days. Oz had a quieter triumph with **Travelling North**, directed by Carl Schultz from a play by David Williamson. Leo McKern is the traveller, moving from Melbourne to the Queensland coast on retirement, discovering middle-aged love and experiencing heart spasms. As always, Williamson illuminates humanity, Australian-style.

In Canada, the variable Denys Arcand got his act marvellously together for **The Decline of the American Empire**, which is none the worse for being all talk – by some academics as they prepare a meal, and by their wives as they work out at a health club. In India, Benegal is on form with **The Essence**, a study of a cooperative of handloom weavers where corruption reigns – this director's usual preoccupation, though this time he blames nobody.

In West Germany, Margaretha von Trotta had bigger things on her mind: the troubled life and times of **Rosa Luxemburg** (Barbara Sukowa), who questioned the values of old Europe and believed that if the workers of the world united they would not be marched off to be cannon fodder. The film may be cavalier with the truth (it ignores both her Jewishness and her husband), but it is beautifully crafted and absolutely persuasive.

Two mischievous talents asked some awkward questions about sex. Yes, again. In Mexico, Jaime Humberto Hermosillas researched the motives of **Doña Herlinda y su Hijo**. The doña is a lady quite happy to see her son married, but who would be happier still with a *menage à quatre* if the presence of his (male) lover will keep him closer to her. This is uncomplicated stuff beside – from Spain – Pedro Almodovar's **Matador**, an unholy *mélange* of murder, masturbation and a Maria who plans to push a needle into her lover's neck after experiencing the greatest orgasm ever. And she does, too.

In France Lelouch had little success with a sequel, **Un Homme et une Femme: Vingt Ans Déjà** with Trintignant and Aimee, and it was a pity, since he sent himself up unmercifully – as if to atone for the many pretentious epics he had made in those twenty years.

Claude Berri saluted Pagnol with **Jean de Florette** and **Manon des Sources**, Provençal stories set some years ago. In the first, Depardieu is a city lad who inherits a patch of land without water; and he dies in his attempt to make it work. Responsible are a cunning peasant, Yves Montand, and his devious but stupid nephew, Daniel Auteuil. In the sequel, Depardieu's daughter, Emmanuelle Beart, plots her revenge. In Pagnol's own **Manon des Sources** (1952) the entire **Jean de Florette** is an anecdote told in the village square, and his Manon not a goatherd but a chic, abrasive Parisian. Never mind. Berri's two films were absorbing, beautiful and marvellously acted. The world over, they were the most admired and loved French movies in a generation.

O f the 'top' movies for this year, there were only two of any account: **Beverly Hills Cop II**, a grim rehash of the original; and Adrian Lyne's nightmarish **Fatal Attraction** in which a married lawyer (Michael Douglas) has a weekend fling with a publisher (Glenn Close), whose efforts to hang on to him turn from desperate to dangerous. The rest included Leonard Nimoy's unsubtle, unfunny **Three Men and a Baby**, with Tom Selleck, Ted Danson and Steve Guttenberg as bachelors; Brian De Palma's exciting **The**

1987

Untouchables, re-creating Chicago in the 1920s with Robert de Niro as Al Capone, Kevin Costner as Eliot Ness, the Treasury man determined to get him, and Sean Connery as the seasoned Irish cop who helps him; John McTiernan's violent, nonsensical **Predator**, with Arnold Schwarzenegger as a mercenary destroying jungle villages at whim; Tom Mankiewicz's loutish **Dragnet**, based on the old TV cop series, with Dan Aykroyd and Tom Hanks; Herbert Ross's **The Secret of My Success**, with Michael J. Fox making it; and Richard Donner's **Lethal Weapon**, with Mel Gibson and Danny Glover. Just another cop movie.

Let's make it four among the top movies, since two December releases would eventually end up there. Barry Levinson's **Good Morning, Vietnam** was the break-through movie for Robin Williams, playing an Army disc-jockey in Saigon in 1965. The piece had comments to make on the War and the military mentality, but it owed its success to Williams' often-improvized monologues. It eventually took more money than **Three Men and a Baby**

while Norman Jewison's **Moonstruck** would take in more than many another. It deserved to, with its funny and original sceenplay by John Patrick Shanley, centring on a New York Italian family and the divorced daughter, Cher, who is engaged to boring Danny Aiello but falls headlong for his wild brother, Nicolas Cage.

Steve Martin was in two comedies: John Hughes's **Planes, Trains and Automobiles**, a rather strained effort in which he's landed with a slob of a fellow passenger, John Candy; and Fred Schepisi's **Roxanne**, in which he's a modern Cyrano, fire chief in a small town, wooing Darryl Hannah on behalf of Rick Rossovich. Both films took approximately the same amount at the box office, which is surprising – Hughes's film is by no means his worst, but **Roxanne** is special. Martin wrote it.

Roger Donaldson's **No Way Out** was a tense and imaginative remake of **The Big Clock** (1948), transferred to the Pentagon. Sean Young is mistress to Gene Hackman; she is also having an affair with one of his underlings, Kevin Costner, who finds himself instructed to find the murderer when she is discovered dead. Oliver Stone's **Wall Street** was a dark comedy about wheelers and dealers, with Michael Douglas as the chief shark, Gordon Gekko, and Charlie Sheen as the young guy studying his methods. Bob Rafelson had a clever thriller, **Black Widow**, who was Theresa Russell, leaving behind her a trail of husbands; Debra Winger was the cop detailed to nail her, and when the two become friends, it's a question of who will learn the truth first.

Barry Levinson's **Tin Men** are Richard Dreyfuss and Danny DeVito, rival salesmen in Baltimore in 1963.

Left: The streets of Chicago in the 1920s, with (from left to right) Andy Garcia, Sean Connery, Kevin Costner and Charles Martin Smith. They were **The Untouchables** – four fighters against the evil of mobster Al Capone. Above: Michael Douglas, wheeler-dealing in **Wall Street** and power-hungry – braces were back in fashion. Opposite: Denzel Washington as the murdered black rights leader, Steve Biko, in **Cry Freedom**. The South African government allowed only token showings of the film, but world-wide it created more discussions on Apartheid than anything else – and that led to the end of Nelson Mandela's long imprisonment.

Mainly a comedy, this has some melancholy notes as Dreyfuss makes for the other's wife, Barbara Hershey. James L. Brooks wrote and directed **Broadcast News**, a satire on television and the various ambitions therein, the biggest of which is Holly Hunter's, who is loved by both William Hurt and Albert Brooks. Jack Nicholson did an unbilled walk-on as a vastly self-satisfied anchorman. With **Roxanne**, it rates as the year's funniest comedy.

Alan Parker's **Angel Heart** was set in 1955, with Mickey Rourke as a private-eye and Robert de Niro as the devil. Some of it was set in New Orleans, as was **The Big Easy**, which used the city better. Jim McBride directed Dennis Quaid and Ellen Barkin, police rivals and lovers hoping to get to the bottom of some gangland killings. Both did only fair business, which was a disaster in the case of Parker's film, given its budget. But there are a handful of thrillers at the bottom of the list even better than **The Big Easy**. In Ridley Scott's **Someone To Watch Over Me** Mimi Rogers is the murder witness and Tom Berenger the cop detailed to guard her. She's rich; he's an ordinary, married guy from Queens, and when they get a sex thing going, he's in as much danger as she. Arthur Penn's **Dead of Winter** has Mary Steenburgen as an actress hired to replace another whom she resembles; but when she arrives on location there is no film equipment in the house, and she's soon pretty sure the girl is dead. Kim Basinger is **Nadine**, who has left some 'art studies' with a photographer, now murdered. Asking her estranged husband, Jeff Bridges, to help her retrieve them, they take some civic plans by mistake and are thus a threat to Rip Torn, who keeps rattle-snakes in his office.

Two trips to the Orient were a waste of time. Steven Spielberg directed **Empire of the Sun**, from J. G.

Ballard's novel about an English boy separated from his parents through the Second World War. Bernardo Bertolucci followed **The Last Emperor** from boy to manhood to Communist prisoner, reducing a fascinating subject to zilch, though the scenes inside the Forbidden City are spectacular. These films were not, of course, failures, though Spielberg's did much less than was expected of it; the other did slowly till it picked up its nine Oscar nominations. It won all of them, including Best Picture and Best Direction. You never saw a worse directed film in your life.

In Britain, a small boy's experience of the Second World War was the subject of John Boorman's **Hope and Glory**, but it wasn't very convincing. David Leland wrote and directed **Wish You Were Here**, about a teenager (Emily Lloyd) discovering sex in 1951, which wasn't too hot on period detail. It was taken from an autobiographical book by Cynthia Payne, whose suburban bordel was the subject of **Personal Services**, written by Leland, directed by Terry Jones, with Julie Walters in the role of the Madame. There was more interesting autobiography in Harry Hook's **The Kitchen Toto**, memories of Kenya in 1960 set round the home of the police commissioner (Bob Peck), living with the terrorism of the Kikuyu. The film opened at the same time as another, more ambitious, African biography, **Cry Freedom!**, directed by Richard

Left: Patrick Swayze and Jennifer Grey in Emilio Ardolino's unpretentious, invigorating **Dirty Dancing**, about two youngsters finding romance in a Catskill resort in the 1960s. Above: James Wilby (at the piano) as **Maurice**, with Hugh Grant and (at left) Mark Tandy in a Cambridge study. Opposite: A dumpy lady, Marianne Sagebrecht, is deserted in the Arizona desert by her husband and puts up at **Bagdad Café**'s dilapidated motel run by bad-tempered Brenda, C. C. H. Pounder. She dislikes it as much as we dislike her, but all will change: a local artist (Jack Palance) is as much in love with her at the end as we are.

Attenborough from Donald Woods's reminiscences of the murdered activist, Steve Biko, roles played respectively by Kevin Kline and Denzel Washington. The film is awkwardly shaped, because it can only flashback to Biko as it follows Woods from the time he championed him till his escape from house arrest and flight from the country. But the shape doesn't matter because the film is not really about the two men, but about Apartheid, shown here in all its grisly injustice. It towers over every other British and American film made in years.

Two veterans of the First World War spend **A Month in the Country**, directed by Pat O'Connor from the novel by J. L. Carr. Colin Firth is there to uncover a wall-painting and Kenneth Branagh to search for a family grave. Their friendship is tenuous because Firth is troubled by memories of the conflict and Branagh is homosexual. This was a subject tackled in superior films adapted from very different books by homosexual writers. **Maurice** was Merchant-Ivory going at Forster again. Blessed for once with a sensitive screenwriter, Kit Hesketh-Harvey, it manages an even portrait of the time and of its hero, James Wilby, rejecting the advances of a fellow undergraduate and panting at the end after the gamekeeper, Rupert Graves. **Prick Up Your Ears** was a favourite phrase of Joe Orton (here, Gary Oldman), who was murdered at the height of his fame by his jealous lover (Alfred Molina). Alan Bennett wrote the mordantly funny script; Stephen Frears directed. Writer-director Bruce Robinson only goes back to 1969 for **Withnail and I**, Richard E. Grant and Paul McGann are two perky out-of-work actors spending a month in a sodden cottage in the Lake District. They're not gay, but Uncle (Richard Griffiths) is. Grant makes trouble and McGann has to sit barricaded in his room all night.

In New Zealand, there was a **Starlight Hotel**, never reached by two itinerants, Greer Robson and Peter Phelps, who have thrown in their lots together in 1932 and try to pretend they're not falling in love. Sam Pillsbury directed from Grant Hinden Miller's screenplay and there's magic here, as there is in the **Bagdad Café**, a West German production directed in English by Percy Adlon.

In Italy, Guiliano Montaldi's **The Gold-Rimmed Spectacles**, from Giorgio Bassani's novel, is set in a small town near Ferrara in 1938. A bachelor doctor (Philippe Noiret) becomes friendly with a rich set of youths and their girls; one of the boys begins to accept the doctor's presents and then goes on vacation with him. This is a movie about the loneliness deriving from the fear of ostracism should the relationship become public.

In Denmark, Bille August made **Pelle The Conqueror**, from the first volume of Martin Anderson Nexo's four-novel autobiographical cycle, 1906–10. Everything is seen through the eyes of a Swedish child, the eponymous Pelle, including his weak, widowed father (Max von Sydow) and other people's sex lives. Here we go again, you may say, but you'd be wrong. August had decided that if this wasn't better than all the other rural dramas it wasn't worth doing. And then there was **Babette's Feast**, based on a novel by Isak Dinesen (the Karen Blixen of **Out of Africa**). She set **Babette's Feast** in a pretty Norwegian fjord town and writer-director Gabriel Axel transposed it to a bleak part of the Danish coast, but if he got that wrong, he has everything else marvellously right. Two old spinsters dispense food and spiritual comfort to their father's parishioners, when there arrives in their midst Stéphane Audran, a Communard fleeing Paris with a letter. She requires no salary to prepare the daily fare of dried fish and bread-and-ale stew, but the sisters fear she will leave when she wins a 10,000 franc lottery. She cooks a meal of such splendour as no one had ever dreamed of, and no one comments. She is content: 'I am a great artist.' The money has gone. Movies are almost a hundred years old and there had never been one remotely like this.

Nor had there been anything quite like **Pathfinder**, from Norway; the closest you'd get might be **Seven Samurai** or Sjöström's epics. It was based on a Lapp legend and set among primitive peoples living near the Arctic Circle, some of them barbarian, killing on sight. Our hero sees his family slaughtered and has to stand alone when his tribe flees to the coast. He can only escape annihilation if he can stop the bloody horde. The director, Nils Gaup, had worked only in children's television, but his grasp is complete: of narrative, tension, mysticism and Dolby stereo, which had never trapped the sound of wind whipping through snow to more enthralling effect.

1988

The year's most popular film was a calculated, expensive job about a seedy LA private-eye, Bob Hoskins, enlisted to discover **Who Framed Roger Rabbit** by Roger himself, as wacky a bunny as ever got animated. Snow White and the seven dwarfs had walk-ons, as did Mickey, Donald and a few animals from the cartoon menageries (and Betty Boop) of other studios. Impossible not to like the result, as animated by Richard Williams, the British animator called in to prevent the film from an attack of the cutes, and the architect of the duel-to-the-death climax. Impossible to love it either, since it was a slam-bang noisome thing with little sense of the 1940s thrillers it attempted to parody. Robert Zemneckis directed for a co-production between Disney and Spielberg. Even noisier was **Coming to America**. Eddie Murphy came, as an African prince happy to clean up in a hamburger joint; directed by John Landis. Much, much better was a breakthrough for Tom Hanks in Penny Marshall's **Big**, even if the success was due to a clever, funny script about a boy who gets his wish to become a man and is then only employable as an expert with a toy factory.

Stars were very much back in favour after years when the scripts went to the same half-dozen people. Barry Levinson's **Rain Man** had high-living Tom Cruise getting to know his brother, Dustin Hoffman, who has long been in a home. Hoffman is selectively bright and Cruise begins to enjoy being with him as they travel across the country. Another couple were doing that: Robert de Niro and Charles Grodin in Martin Brest's **Midnight Run**, the

former a bail bond man required to bring the latter safely to LA before the Mafia goons get him. One of the joys of George Gallo's brilliantly original script is that Grodin is never the sort of man to take on the Mob (he embezzled $15 million). Stephen Frears' **Dangerous Liaisons**, from a dramatized version of that novel, had John Malkovich and Glenn Close as the eighteenth-century French aristocratic schemers and Michelle Pfeiffer as their victim.

Frank Oz's **Dirty Rotten Scoundrels** saw Steve Martin and Michael Caine as conmen struggling for supremacy on the Riviera. Martin was never funnier, even when simulating physical disability and idiocy, which Brando did not manage in **Bedtime Story** (1964), on which this is a vast improvement. Michael Apted's **Gorillas in the Mist** was based partly on the memoir by Dian Fossey, played here by Sigourney Weaver, the American anthropologist whose mission was to preserve the species in central Africa and who was murdered because of it. This actress had a smallish role in Mike Nichols' **Working Girl**, being both stylish and loathsome at the same time. It was the clever interpretation needed, as Melanie Griffith – from a different strata of society – steps into her job while she's away and into bed with her man, Harrison Ford.

Costa-Gavras's **Betrayed** had many important points to make but didn't quite work. A murder is committed in Chicago and an undercover cop (Debra Winger) is sleeping with the redneck (Tom Berenger) whom she thinks is responsible; she also accompanies him to midnight fascist meetings. **Punchline**, written and directed by David Seltzer, takes an affectionate look at a housewife who wants – *needs* – to be a stand-up comic:

Left: Alan Parker's passionate, moving **Mississippi Burning** had Gene Hackman and Willem Dafoe as two FBI agents in danger in 1964 as they investigate the murder of three Civil Rights workers. Above: Philippe Noiret and Salvatore Cascio in Giuseppe Tornatore's **Cinema Paradiso**. One of the film's incidental virtues was the picture of Sicily gradually dragging itself into the twentieth century. Opposite: Melanie Griffith in **Working Girl**, a cunning reworking of **All About Eve** (1950), set amongst New York's stockbrokers.

lovely work by Sally Field, by John Goodman as her bemused but compliant husband, and Tom Hanks as the man she chooses to train her.

Keep from any list of good movies **The Unbearable Lightness of Being** which must, however, have a place here because it was directed by Philip Kaufman and co-written by him with Jean-Claude Carrière, who used to write for Buñuel, and produced by Saul Zaentz (whose record includes **One Flew Over the Cuckoo's Nest**, **Amadeus** and **The Mosquito Coast**). The film is a lot of old cobblers, with Juliette Binoche as a country waitress who arrives in Budapest and, without any experience, becomes a magazine photographer overnight. There are scenes of kinky sex, and what makes the matter worse is that much of it takes place against the Czechoslovakian invasion of 1968. Daniel Day Lewis had the lead.

It did not do well, nor did the film of another modern European novel, but in this case a lot of people made sure that it didn't – Kazantzakis's **The Last Temptation of Christ**, very well brought to the screen by Paul Schrader and Martin Scorsese. It was a perfectly valid revisionist account of some famous matters. Paul (Harry Dean Stanton) is a poseur and Jesus (Willem Dafoe) an exhibitionist. So what?

A few other films which did poorly deserve a mention: Clint Eastwood's **Bird**, a life of Charlie Parker (Forest Whitaker); Pat O'Connor's **Stars and Bars**, from William Boyd's novel, with Day Lewis as an art dealer up to this neck in Li'l Abner types when he goes to buy a Renoir in Georgia; Errol Morris made an extraordinary documentary on the Adams case in Dallas in 1976, when a man was convicted for murder on the evidence of the actual killer: **The Thin Blue Line**. Paul Bogart's **Torch**

Song Trilogy was a romantic comedy about a drag queen, played by Harvey Fierstein, who also wrote it, and who had acted in the original in both New York and London. Anne Bancroft was his mother; among his lovers are Matthew Broderick, who is killed, and Brian Kerwin, a laid-back bisexual in search of gratification. Fierstein deliberately made no mention of AIDS.

Britain had its biggest success for years in the US with **A Fish Called Wanda**, starring and written by John Cleese, who chose Charles Crichton to direct in the mistaken belief that he had written an Ealing-style comedy. It's a story of cross and double-cross, prevented from failure only by the verve with which Kevin Kline imbues his performance; Jamie Lee Curtis has little to do; and Cleese plays his trade-marked pompous twit. Mike Figgis's **Stormy Monday** is much more fun, if not a comedy – a crime movie set in Newcastle, where Tommy Lee Jones controls the rackets: among those to whom he may be dangerous are Melanie Griffith, Sting and Sean Bean; plus Alison Steadman as the mayoress in cahoots with Jones.

Real crime was on screen in David Green's **Buster** Edwards, one of the Great Train Robbers, at its best after he and wife (Phil Collins, Julie Walters) are in South American exile, homesick. The government, represented by Anthony Quayle, wants long sentences to smooth over public feeling after the Profumo **Scandal**, inadequately raked over in Michael Caton-Jones's film, with Ian McKellen in that role, John Hurt as Ward, Joanne Whalley-Kilmer as Christine Keeler and Bridget Fonda as Mandy Rice-Davies.

James Dearden, who wrote **Fatal Attraction**, made

Left: Jodie Foster in **The Accused** – who are the men who raped her in reel one; but the film's true subject is one desolate woman finding pride in herself. Above: Tom Hanks (right) and his boss, Robert Loggia, dancing 'Chopsticks' on a giant keyboard in Penny Marshall's engaging **Big**. Opposite: After two movie flops, Bruce Willis had a success in John McTiernan's **Die Hard**, though it really owed its popularity to its high-tech action in a skyscraper: a battle to the kill between a lone, dogged Willis and a gang – superb villains in Alan Rickman and Alexander Godunov – bent on a multi-million dollar robbery.

his directing début with **Pascali's Island**, the first-ever English-language movie about an island in the Aegean in 1908 under Turkish rule. Charles Dance was a mysterious archaeologist, Helen Mirren a widow who keeps the wolf from the door with her paintbox, and Ben Kingsley someone fishy from the Levant. Martin Donovan, an Argentinian, set **Apartment Zero** in his native country and put Colin Firth in it as a movie nut lonely after his mother is hospitalized. He advertises for someone to share and gets Hart Bochner, the antithesis of his fussy self. Matters become murderous. The cinematographer Chris Menges turned to directing with **A World Apart**, written by Shawn Slovo from her childhood experiences in Johannesburg, where her parents (Barbara Hershey, Jeroen Krabbe) opposed Apartheid, foolhardy, brave and dedicated in the face of a thug-like police force.

In South Africa itself the German-born Oliver Schmitz managed to make a movie on the same subject because ostensibly **Mapantsula** is about the life of a petty black thief, played by Thomas Mogotlane, his co-writer; but later they cut into their material some harrowing sequences of prison life. Mira Nair, married to an American, returned to India to make **Salaam Bombay!**, a sympathetic and telling tale of a country boy who grows up quickly among the whores and drug addicts of the city.

The Dutch director George Sluizer was in France for **The Vanishing** of a Dutch girl, at a gas station, while travelling with her boyfriend: a real jigsaw this, nail-biting, and remade by Sluizer in Hollywood in 1993. The French director Jean-Jacques Annaud was in British Columbia for **The Bear**, a motherless cub befriended by a grizzly and hunted by nasty white men: much fakery, but essential viewing for the kiddywinkies. Wajda was in Poland making a sweeping film of Dostoevsky's **The Possessed** in French, with Isabelle Huppert, Lambert Wilson and Omar Sharif among a huge cast. Lelouch came up with one of his bizarre ones, **Itineraire d'un Enfant Gaté**, but it also has wit and tension as it examines why a self-made millionaire should have disappeared. Like it or not, Lelouch remains a master of cinema language. Belmondo played the man, returning to world screens after years of non-exportable action films and acting on the stage. He left us a young man; he returned looking like Michel Simon.

In Spain, Pedro Almodóvar was doing the same as Lelouch, making somewhat unlikeable but high-spirited, inventive films which are subject to his god-like whim. **The Law of Desire** and **Women on the Verge of a Nervous Breakdown** were two of the most cunning he had done. The first concerns a movie director, Antonio Banderas, who seduces an admirer who protests all the while that he isn't gay; but Antonio becomes obsessed and, after the boy has disappeared, accidentally kills the guy who has succeeded him. The second has Banderas as a thoughtful, bespectacled youth caught in the coils of Carmen Maura, who dubs movies for a living and has an exceptionally turbulent private life, which includes a friendship with a Shi'ite terrorist.

It was all very different in old Denmark. **Katinka** is happily married to the town stationmaster, somewhat older than she, but when the new foreman on the farm flashes his handsome fish-eyes and moustache at her, she's ready for a rendezvous in the summer-house. Pelle-territory, but whereas that film looked keenly at village life this one is lyrical: but the two films have in common an ability to re-invent familiar material, to do it better than before; the luminous photography is by Bergman's Sven Nykvist and the direction by Bergman's von Sydow.

In Italy, or rather, Sicily, there was a **Cinema Paradiso**. Philippe Noiret was the cinema's projectionist and Salvatore Cascio the small boy who helps him. The films change too, and the self-satisfied censorship by the local priest has to surrender to the audience's wish to see sex on the screen. The film was Italy's biggest international success since – at least – **The Tree of Wooden Clogs**. Olmi, who directed that, made a movie which gave new meaning to the word 'hybrid'. **The Legend of the Holy Drinker** was filmed in Paris in English with a Dutch actor in the lead, Rutger Hauer; and its source was a German story by Arthur Roth. Hauer played a down-and-out drunk who is suddenly given a large amount of money by a stranger, Anthony Quayle: that sets him looking at life, Paris, religion and sex – he seeks out an old girlfriend, goes to bed with a casual pick-up – before he dies. A magical film.

1989

There were rumblings from the Soviet bloc throughout the Autumn. Although Poland had been fitfully moving towards democracy after it became clear that the public would have Lech Walesa for president and no other, the tradition of Communism was strong – and the Soviet Union's presence too near. But the rumblings suddenly became a roar. Growing complaints of cruelty and corruption against the President of East Germany, Honecker, resulted in riots. The Soviet President, Mikhail Gorbachev, had been making gestures of friendship to the West for some time – admittedly because he could see no way of solving the country's overwhelming economic difficulties without help – and he took this opportunity to announce that the Soviet Union would not, as in the past, send in tanks to restore the regime. Honecker resigned in October and, as the Berlin Wall began to come down in November, Gorbachev announced that the Soviet Union was renouncing Communism. The other countries fell like dominoes, culminating in revolution in Romania and the summary trial and killing of its brutal president, Ceauşescu, on Christmas Day.

The year's most successful film was **Batman**, snakes alive. You weren't supposed to take it seriously, but the people who put it together had been only too serious: they were making Big Popular Art. Clearly they succeeded. Tim Burton directed; Michael Keaton was effective in or out of the bat-cloak and Jack Nicholson had a great time as the villain, the Joker. Since he had a percentage of the gross and the merchandise, he made over $50 million,

probably the highest sum earnt by one individual for any movie. The film's closest competitor for big earnings was **Indiana Jones and the Last Crusade**, the third of Indy's adentures and they – Spielberg directed – got it right at last: no cheating to get the thrills, which were genuine, much spoofing, and a lovely double-act for Harrison Ford and Sean Connery, who played his father. **Lethal Weapon 2**, **Back to the Future Part II**, **Ghostbusters II**: you couldn't blame the studios for turning out formula stuff if audiences turned up in these numbers. In there somewhere are **Honey, I Shrunk the Kids** – Rick Moranis did, for Disney, with Joe Johnston directing. A one-joke comedy. Amy Heckerling's **Look Who's Talking**. Another one-joke comedy. Ron Howard's **Parenthood**, with Steve Martin, had a bit more substance, but not much. Heckerling's film had a baby with Bruce Willis's voice, but its popularity was almost certainly due to good, old-fashioned sentiment: Kirstie Alley's married lover, George Segal reneges on his promise to marry her, so she becomes an unmarried mother looking for a husband without realizing that there's one right under her nose – attentive cabbie John Travolta. **Parenthood** has some satire at the expense of several members of a large family, including (again) Moranis, very funny as a father trying to bring up his tot as a genius. Martin is wasted in a role anyone could have played. **When Harry Met Sally** was written by Nora Ephron from an autobiographical idea by its director, Rob Reiner. They (Billy Crystal, Meg Ryan) dislike each other intensely, till a third meeting has them becoming 'best friends'. Sex would only spoil things, they agree, so this become a movie only about fucking, for they and we have nothing else on our minds, waiting for

Left: Tom Cruise in Oliver Stone's **Born on the Fourth of July**, as Ben Kovic, on whose autobiographical book it was based. He joined up to serve in Vietnam from the highest patriotic motives, to emerge maimed for life, disillusioned and then bitter, having been flung on the scrapheap. Above: Andie McDowell and James Spader in **Sex, Lies and Videotape**, a seriocomic sex story which foolishly ends like the old Hollywood, where perverts must reform and adulterers be punished. Opposite: Morgan Freeman and Jessica Tandy in **Driving Miss Daisy**, both giving exemplary performances.

the actual moment. These comedies are amiable, sharing a tendency to search far for a joke, no matter how unlikely or unfunny in the event.

Hollywood, however, did present two civilized pleasures to which posterity may look kindly. Peter Weir's **Dead Poets Society** has Robin Williams as a teacher at a posh, traditional boys' school whose unorthodox methods delight his pupils but also lead them into troubles which will overwhelm them. This is one of the best school movies ever made; an original screenplay by Howard Schulman. **Field of Dreams**, written and directed by Phil Alden Robinson, has Kevin Costner as an Iowa farmer hearing a disembodied voice instructing him to tear down several acres of corn to make a baseball field: and after spectral players of the past appear he sets out to seek happiness in the manner of Maeterlinck's 'The Blue Bird'; with Amy Madigan as his wife and James Earl Jones as a reclusive novelist.

Driving Miss Daisy came from a stage play about the relationship between a Southern Jewish widow (Jessica Tandy) and her black chauffeur (Morgan Freeman) over a twenty-year period from the first stirrings of the civil rights movement. It sounds yukky, but Alfred Uhry's screenplay reworks his original, with Bruce Beresford pulling back all the while till it's a piece about two people showing common sense, with some statements on racial prejudice always worth restating. Unsettling: Harold Becker's **Sea of Love**, as several naked men are shot at the point of orgasm. They had all advertised for 'company', so Al Pacino does the same, quickly infatuated by Ellen Barkin, who would seem to be the chief suspect; nice performance by John Goodman as his oppo.

A great anti-war movie was **Born on the Fourth of July**, directed by Oliver Stone from a screenplay by him and Ron Kovic, who went to Vietnam with gung-ho motives and returned permanently crippled. Tom Cruise plays him in this film about the darkening of the American dream; he does not become a pacifist from idealism but from bitterness at being flung on the scrapheap.

The Dream Team are four oddballs (Michael Keaton, Christopher Lloyd, Peter Boyle, Stephen Furst) from a mental home inadvertently let loose in New York; but what seems like being a rehash of **One Flew Over the Cuckoo's Nest** becomes something more, due to director Howard Zieff's sense of humanity and of New York (though some of it was shot in Toronto). **Sex, Lies and Videotape** is a chamber piece for four players. Three of them are Peter Gallagher, married to Andie McDowell, whose frigidity has sent him into the bed of Laura San Giacomo. The women become trapped by James Spader, an old chum of Gallagher's who wants them to act out their sex fantasies for his video camera – which they can safely do because he's impotent. The movie was not a satire on voyeurism, but a thriller which is itself voyeuristic – and foolishly like the old Hollywood, where perverts must reform and adulterers be punished: but it was an ingenious debut for writer-director Steven Soderbergh. As was **The Fabulous Baker Boys** for Steve Kloves, with only one screenplay to his credit. The boys were Jeff and Beau Bridges, not fabulous at all but with a piano act so lousy they hire a blonde to help them get work, Michelle Pfeiffer. She makes waves – especially

Left: Kevin Costner (right) with James Earl Jones, the reclusive novelist whom he seeks out to help him solve the secret of the **Field of Dreams**. Above: Daniel Day Lewis as Christy Brown in **My Left Foot**, with Ruth McCabe as the nurse who marries him. It was curious that 1989 should see two films about young men in wheelchairs, with Day Lewis pitted against Cruise in the Oscar Derby. Day Lewis, in particular, gave a performance of immense compassion and power. Opposite: Robin Williams in **Dead Poets Society** which, aided by Howard Schuman's screenplay, is one of the most perceptive movies on school life.

towards bachelor Jeff. The piece is funny on the lower rungs of show business, tentative when it tries for old-style romance and awkward as it tries for a 'modern' ending.

Casualties of War has four men on patrol under the command of corporal Sean Penn, who takes prisoner a local girl to 'service' them, claiming she is a whore. Only Michael J. Fox resists, to be predictably called 'a faggot'; back at base his life is in danger and officers won't listen as he tries to bring charges. A Vietnam veteran, David Rabe, wrote the screenplay, which was directed by Brian De Palma, usually responsible for showy, derivative thrillers. This film was expected to do great business, but O. Stone's two movies had used up audiences for the Vietnam War; the true subject of this one is the dehumanisation of young men induced by war.

Woody Allen's **Crimes and Misdemeanors** had schizophrenia, on one hand the usual rondelay of adulterers, but on the other, as much fun as he's ever offered. He plays his usual nerd, terminally jealous of his brother-in-law, Alan Alda, a lecherous, self-opinionated TV producer who, if he notices Allen at all, is patronizing. He gives him a chance to make a documentary about him, and Allen uses it to get even for all the slights over the years. The last laugh, however, goes to Costa-Gavras's **Music Box**, another movie which should have done better. A Hungarian immigrant (Armin Mueller-Stahl) is wanted in Europe for war crimes and his daughter (Jessica Lange), a lawyer, assuming a mix-up, decides to fight his case; Joe Eszterhas's script takes her into detective work, but the courtroom scenes say as much as can be said in a work of fiction. But perhaps **A Dry White Season** didn't deserve to do better, and perhaps the blame is due to director Euzhan Palcy, who reworked Colin Welland's script from Andre Brink's important novel on Apartheid. This is a subject which doesn't interest schoolteacher Donald Sutherland till his black gardener's son is tortured and killed. He employs an activist lawyer, Marlon Brando, and his family ups and leaves him.

My Left Foot is about a Dublin Catholic boy born with cerebral palsy and condemned to life as a vegetable. His father (Ray McAnally) is confused, angry; his mother (Brenda Fricker) understands him; his siblings help. He escapes from his handicap by learning to paint with his foot, but nothing in 1980s cinema is so moving as the moment when a professional therapist is called in. Jim Sheridan directed, from a screenplay by himself and Shane Connaughton from Christy Brown's autobiography. Hugh O'Conor plays Christy as a boy and justly should have shared the prizes so richly deserved by Daniel Day Lewis, the adult Christy.

Fellow Traveller examines the McCarthy blacklistings as they affected one screenwriter (Ron Silver) who managed to get a job scripting a TV 'Robin Hood', recreated in all its ghastliness. The piece shuttles between a Britain recovering from austerity and an earlier Hollywood, when left-wing fund raising was in fashion; at its heart is a psychiatrist (Daniel J. Travanti; based on fact) who shopped left-wingers to the FBI after claiming to share their views and who turns up in GB later claiming to be a liberal. Philip Saville directed from a screenplay by Michael Eaton. It was made for the BBC, but shown in cinemas first, as was Kenneth Branagh's **Henry V**, reclaiming the play 'from jingoism and its World War II associations'. There were thirty-six other plays to choose from. Olivier's cast had been imbued with a sense of occasion, while this one seems merely tired. Chief exceptions were Paul Scofield (the King of France) and Ian Holm (Fluellen). Branagh's Henry is a head prefect, which may suit this particular play, but he emerges as vacuous.

In adapting Ibsen's **An Enemy of the People** and transferring the action to India, Ray was recognizing that pollution was still a serious problem in the country; Soumitra Chatterjee was the doctor who faced contumely by trying to expose it. The only other foreign film of note was Tavernier's **La Vie et Rien d'Autre/Life, and Nothing But**, choosing to bring it out as the French were celebrating the bicentennial of the Revolution. He takes a time when *la gloire* had gone stale, after the First World War, when everyone pretended it hadn't by erecting war memorials. One tired but dedicated officer (Philippe Noiret) is trying to put names to the corpses still littering the battlefields.

1990

Home Alone: Macaulay Culkin was, and why millions wanted to share their time with the least talented child since Shirley Temple has to be the greatest mystery of the cinema's first hundred years. The premise was idiotic (his parents mislay him on a trip to Paris) and he is even more so (he goes to the supermarket not to buy candy but detergents, which he is never seen using). Of course it wasn't meant to be taken seriously, you mutter to yourself as he takes a blow-torch to the incompetent crooks (Joe Pesci, Daniel Stern) trying to get in. No fun, no fantasy, no nothing. Directed by Chris Columbus from a screenplay by John Hughes, who also produced. Patrick Swayze, killed, was a **Ghost** trying to get unghosted to warn his wife, Demi Moore, that she's in for the same fate. This is better already. Whoopi Goldberg was a hopeful medium; Jerry Zucker directed. Julia Roberts was a radiant thing called the **Pretty Woman**. She's a hooker given a week in a penthouse by corporate raider Richard Gere although, as he says, he doesn't have 'to buy sex'. Hardly Bogart and Bergman, but Garry Marshall's film works because Gere's a Pygmalion teaching her the ways of his world and she's the eternal whore redeemed by true love. Anyway, who wouldn't want to pay for her?

The year's movie of real quality, though it made

Above: Patrick Swayze and Demi Moore in **Ghost**, with which Jerry Zucker ingratiatingly blended fantasy and thrills. This was the most spectacular sleeper of recent years, mildly commended by the press and building to giant box-office sales by dint of word of mouth. Right: Kevin Costner as the Civil War soldier who finds a new meaning in the wastes of the unexplored West in **Dances With Wolves**, which he also directed.

most of its money in 1991 after getting twelve Oscar nominations and winning seven, was **Dances With Wolves**. It is a great film, with glimmerings of W. S. Hart, Sjöström, **Pathfinder** and the best Japanese samurai movies, since Kevin Costner confronts a universe which is at the same time empty, mysterious and menacing; and he, like Mifune so often, has to obey some primeval directive from his subconscious. He is a nineteenth-century man, a soldier fulfilling a wish to explore the Frontier. His gradual adoption by the Sioux and absorption of their culture is of different calibre, but still superbly entertaining and magnificently done, with a sweep seemingly missing from movies for decades. Not since Olivier with **Henry V** had a debuting director attacked so large a canvas with such confidence, also when playing the lead.

Somewhere around here on the list there's a replica of a '40s B movie in undeniably pretty colours, based on a comic strip, **Dick Tracy**, also directed by its lead actor, Warren Beatty. It also has a B movie vamp, Madonna, and many more talented people hidden under make-up. Equally horrible experiences are to be had with two incoherent and violent thrillers: Coppola's **The Godfather, Part III** with Al Pacino, and Scorsese's **Goodfellas**, which would be 45 minutes shorter if they cut the shots of bloody bodies and the word 'fuck'. It is the more pernicious of the two, since Ray Liotta shops Robert de Niro to save his skin, facing a dull, anonymous future in hiding. Hadn't he told us that 'Being a gangster was all that I wanted to be. Being a gangster was better than being President of the United States'? And hadn't his wife (Lorraine Bracco) said 'after a while, it didn't seem like crime, more like Henry was enterprising', as if he was

shoplifting from Woolworth?

At least an intelligent thriller was more popular than all but the first of that trio: Alan J. Pakula's **Presumed Innocent**, written by him and Frank Pierson from Scott Turow's novel. Harrison Ford was the police officer suspected of killing a colleague (Greta Scacchi in flashbacks) and thereby finding his career and marriage in jeopardy. There was further good news (or not, if you consider the ending) in **Awakenings**, directed by Penny Marshall from Dr Malcom Sayer's account of his attempts – using drugs – to bring his brain-dead patients back to life. How he succeeded and how they regressed again is charted in brilliant performances from Robin Williams as the doc, Julie Kavner as his stoic assistant, Robert de Niro as the chief of his patients and Ruth Nelson as de Niro's mother. More mothers appeared in **Postcards from the Edge**, which also came along at just the right time to prove that literate, intelligent movies were still being made. Mike Nichols directed from Carrie Fisher's autobiography about growing up fucked-up in Hollywood. Meryl Streep is a blank in this role, but Shirley MacLaine is funny in a role based on Debbie Reynolds, and there are terrific bits by Simon Callow as a pretentious British director and Rob Reiner as an unctuous producer. What gives the film itself an edge is that there is barely a character in it with any sense of reality.

Mike Figgis's **Internal Affairs** is about a cop so corrupt that he uses not only blackmail but murder to amass a fortune in real estate; he also likes sodomizing women and either boasting of this to their husbands or making them watch. What is it with these people? Still it's an exciting picture. This cannot be said of Barbet Schroeder's **Reversal of Fortune**, which has magnificent material in the Claus von Bulow affair – in 1980, his wife

Left: Gérard Depardieu and Anne Brochet in Jean–Paul Rappeneau's version of **Cyrano de Bergerac**, lovingly and absorbingly recreated for a new generation. Above: Richard Gere and Julia Roberts in **Pretty Woman**, which had some new – well, fairly new – comments to make about the world's oldest profession. Opposite: Ray Liotta and Robert de Niro in Martin Scorsese's **Goodfellas**.

Sonny (Glenn Close) went into a coma and two years later he (Jeremy Irons) was sentenced to thirty years for administering drugs. She was beautiful, rich, a drinker and a drug addict; he was always unfaithful and stood to gain from the will; and he had the good sense to get a Harvard law professor who worked for the underprivileged to fight his case (played in the film by Ron Silver and on whose book Nicholas Kazan's screenplay was based). The piece fascinates for a while because the material is so riveting.

Bob Rafelson's **Mountains of the Moon** is a companion picture to Costner's triumph: again nineteenth-century man exploring uncharted territory, in this case Sir Richard Burton (Patrick Bergin) and Speke (Iain Glen) searching for the source of the Nile. But it had a success the reverse of that film after being savaged by inaccuracy. Whether the men had been lovers is unclear but that could be the reason for the famous quarrel; both were homosexual and far from never being seen publicly without his wife (as the film claims) Burton spent most of his life trying to get away from her. But as a romance – of the feeling the men had for Africa – it is the equal of **Dances With Wolves**.

Britain's only two notable films are non-fiction, more or less. Less in the case of Peter Medak's **The Krays**, about the East End bully boys (Gary and Martin Kemp) who went too far and finally murdered for fun. Grittier than **Buster** and better on period detail. Also less in the case of **Memphis Belle**, directed by Michael Caton-Jones for David Puttnam, whose only real successes had been Anglo movies for American audiences. He had returned from a difficult spell as a Hollywood bigwig more determined about this than ever, so here's an American crew going from Britain on their last raid on Bremen (Reading stood in). The historical detail is rotten, but towards the end we may come to admire the young men who risked their lives for freedom in the horribly cramped conditions of a Flying Fortress – a feeling kicked back at us when an end-title informs us that the film is dedicated to all airmen of any nation who fought in the War. Can't have empty cinemas in Japan or Germany, can we?

Not that two better movies about the War found audiences. Wajda, who had returned to Poland to become a senator, made **Korczak**, who was the Jewish doctor (Wojciech Pszoniak) who accompanied the children of his orphanage to a concentration camp – though ultimately this is a film about choice, since the doctor's distinction was such that he was clandestinely offered passports to enable him to leave the country. Jiri Weiss, returning to Czechoslovakia after years of exile, had the temerity to make a second 1990 film on the same subject, **Marthe und Ich**, a memory piece about a boy farmed out to an uncle

(Michel Piccoli) – also a doctor – who, after a messy marriage, weds his housekeeper (Marianne Sagebracht); she is also a gentile, standing by him after he has been herded into the ghetto in Vienna and committing suicide after he has been deported. An ingratiating movie.

Francesco Rosi's exciting **To Forget Palermo** concerns Mafia control of the drug trade in New York. James Belushi runs for mayor on a ticket including the legalization of drugs so that the murder-rate is curtailed. He is accordingly a marked man when he takes Mimi Rogers on honeymoon to Palermo. That doesn't suggest that he was wise enough for the job, but an exciting film, Italian, in English. No audience. Sicily features again in Gianni Amelio's **Porte Aperto**, based on a 1937 case when a clerk walked in the judicial building and plunged a knife into a lawyer before raping and killing his wife. Turns out that she and the lawyer had been having trysts. Gian Maria Volonté is the judge who wants him to be psychologically examined in order to avoid the death penalty.

In India, Ray made his penultimate film, **Branches of the Trees**, in which a dying man gathers his family around him, only to find that the only son with any values is the Beethoven-loving Soumitra Chatterjee, a dummy. Among the backers is Gérard Depardieu, who became **Cyrano de Bergerac** for Jean-Paul Rappeneau. They went all out for this: huge budget kept lower by filming in Hungary. They went for perfection and got it. Depardieu, a huge, clumsy man, is delicate as the man with the nose. Why be surprised at its total success, the world over, with critics and audiences alike? The French gave us **La Kermesse Heroïque** and **Les Enfants du Paradis**, but the precedents are Olivier's three Shakespeare films, with their subtle blend of action, romanticism and humour.

With the appalling, exciting pictures of the Gulf War being pumped into every home, who needs to go out to see the movies faking it? Obviously, many. **Terminator 2** is what the 'many' most wanted to see: Schwarzenegger, dazzling special effects and no indication that those who assembled this thing had any advice than that beamed to

1991

them from the screen of a backward computer. Ditto **Robin Hood: Prince of Thieves**, or Kevin Costner *v*. Errol Flynn. Poor Kev hasn't a chance. Nor has Peter Pan, but if he's going to grow up it must be nice to be Robin Williams; Dustin Hoffman was Captain **Hook**, Julia Roberts was Tinkerbell and Steven Spielberg directed this vulgar, misconceived movie. They were all on a percentage, so work it out: No. 3 at the box office, it took around $65 million but cost about $10 million more than that. But there's even worse to follow. **The Silence of the Lambs**, a squalid rehash of **Manhunter**, with Jodie Foster as the rookie cop who consults a jailed psychotic, Anthony Hopkins, in order to find a serial killer. Both are from novels by the same writer; Jonathan Demme, like Michael Mann, is a talented director, but nothing on screen shows any desire but to be as lacking in taste, humour and believability as seems humanly possible. The film's popularity and its several Oscars rebounded when it came to be regarded as the nadir of Hollywood's obsession with violence (Hopkins himself spoke out against it).

Above: Ron Underwood's **City Slickers** was a comedy about three middle-aged men who elect to take their annual holiday following the cattle drive from New Mexico to Colorado. Chief of them is Billy Crystal, seen here with Jack Palance, the old cowpoke they meet on the trail. Right: Geena Davis and Susan Sarandon in Ridley Scott's liberating **Thelma and Louise**. With one bound, Scott had become a major director.

Matters improve considerably with a thriller that does have those qualities, Joseph Ruben's **Sleeping With the Enemy**. Julia Roberts so loathes husband Patrick Bergin, with good reason, that she fakes her own death off Cape Cod and moves to Iowa, where she seems like finding true love with Kevin Anderson – till Bergin finds her, as we knew he would: unlike Demme's film, this is logically worked out.

Bad news: **Beauty and the Beast**, which was popular, the first Disney cartoon Oscar-nominated for Best Picture. Beauty is cute, the Beast isn't scary and there are talking teapots and such.

Something wonderful: **JFK**. Whether or not there was a plot to kill Kennedy, this film will make you believe there was, as seen through the eyes of Jim Garrison, the New Orleans DA. Mr Costner plays him, with Sissy Spacek as the wife who wants him to give up. Why Oliver Stone allowed this ancient device in an otherwise mature film is unclear: it's far-reaching and absorbing for every minute of its 189.

Thelma and Louise: not since **Bonnie and Clyde** has there been a movie like it. Susan Sarandon and Geena Davis are the girls on the run, after Susan shot a man who tried to rape Geena. Now the plot may be full of holes and Callie Khouri's script naught but a feminist tract, but the piece is rousing, funny and beautifully made – by Ridley Scott – piling up telling detail. As the cop in charge of finding the girls, Harvey Keitel manages to be even better than he usually is.

Two bright comedies. Michael Hoffman's **Soapdish**, written by Robert Harling and Andrew Bergman, much fun at the expense of people who star in and perpetuate soaps, including Sally Field, Kevin Kline, Robert

Downey Jr and Whoopi Goldberg. Mick Jackson's **L.A. Story** was written by Steve Martin, who knew his Rostand in **Roxanne** and who here proves that he knows his Woody Allen. He's as sharp on LA as Allen is on NY, and his British wife, Victoria Tennant, plays a British Annie Hall, a reporter whom Martin, a TV weatherman, grows to prefer to Marilu Henner, who can't stop chasing the latest fads.

In Britain, **Meeting Venus**, produced by David Puttnam, was an autobiographical piece by István Szabó, who once directed *Tannhauser* in Paris, about coping with a multilingual company and any number of union restrictions. A Hungarian movie director becomes a Hungarian conductor, and Niels Arestup plays him. Glenn Close is the Swedish soprano (Dame Kiri te Kanawa dubbed her) with whom he fights before tumbling into bed with her.

In Spain, bed supplies the problems in Vicente Aranda's **Amantes/Lovers**, based on an actual case of 1955: Trini won't sleep with Paco before marriage, but a *very* experienced widow (Victoria Abril) is only too ready to teach him all she knows; by the time Trini decides to fight back in kind her fate has been sealed.

Left: Kevin Costner (centre) in Oliver Stone's persuasive **JFK**, a detailed examination of the most famous assassination of the century. Many considered it biased and untrue, but it caused such a furore that Congress ordered the FBI and CIA files on the case – sealed until 2029 – be opened at once. Above: Kevin Costner as **Robin Hood: Prince of Thieves**, directed without much subtlety by Kevin Reynolds. Opposite: Arnold Schwarzenegger in James Cameron's **Terminator 2: Judgment Day**, about which there were two opinions – either it was a miracle of modern technology or a showcase for new brutal ways of killing.

s the year ended, the top ten American box-office films were 1) **Home Alone 2**: **Lost in New York** 2) **Batman Returns** 3) **Lethal Weapon 3** 4) **Sister Act**, which has Whoopi Goldberg as a murder witness hiding out in a convent, dressed as a nun 5) Disney's animated **Aladdin** 6) **Wayne's World**, a 'wacky' teen comedy for teens and about teens 7) **A League of Their Own**, with Madonna and Tom Hanks in a story about a female baseball team 8) Paul Verhoeven's **Basic Instinct**, in which a mentally unstable detective, Michael Douglas, becomes involved with Sharon Stone, a bisexual psychopath, as are all the female characters 9) Mick Jackson's **The Bodyguard**, who was Kevin Costner, falling in love with his client, Whitney Houston, and 10) **A Few Good Men**, to which we'll return.

1992

These were followed by Coppola's **Bram Stoker's Dracula**, an unnecessary and silly remake, taking the latest special effects into the nineteenth century; **The Hand that Rocks the Cradle**, in which Rebecca De Mornay has deadly designs on the family whose child she is 'nursing'; and Philip Noyce's **Patriot Games**, in which Harrison Ford is an ex-CIA agent trying to prevent a VIP from being assassinated by the IRA. With the Cold War over, Hollywood had to look for new villains. Most of these films were excessively violent, as was Michael Mann's **The Last of the Mohicans**, despite the fact that the basis of the screenplay was that of the 1936 version. The film was visually striking, but it needed every one of Daniel Day Lewis's acting muscles to hold it together.

Two experts in the business of churning out massive mass entertainments, Spielberg and Disney, combined to make **Noises Off**, based on Michael Frayn's farce about the backstage antics of a third-rate company touring a fourth-rate farce. Despite a cast of delightful people, including Michael Caine, Carol Burnett, John Ritter and Christopher Reeve, they couldn't give it away – and that was all the more ironic since the director, Peter Bogdanovich, had only once before made a comedy as witty and disciplined; and he had many which were the reverse.

Among the year's other civilized pleasures was **Bob Roberts**, a pop singer turned politician whose knowledge of Dirty Tricks would leave even Nixon's ruffians gasping. Contributing hugely were Bob's rival for office, Gore Vidal, and Bob's campaign manager, Alan Rickman, supposedly a CIA man at the time of the Iran-contra hearings; Bob himself was played by Tim Robbins, who also wrote and directed. Robbins was equally devious in **The Player**, as a Hollywood executive who will stop at nothing to prevent his being accused of a murder he has committed. Decorating this beautifully crafted film were more than two-score Hollywood players, as Themselves and others; and it was another return to form for Robert Altman, directing from Michael Tolkin's screenplay. The whole was a throwback to the days when Hollywood flattered its audience instead of indulging it. As much might be said of **Lorenzo's Oil**, except that back then a movie like this couldn't have been made, for its subject is a boy with a rare form of muscular sclerosis and his parents' quest – against professional advice – to find anything to prevent it worsening. They were played by Susan Sarandon, in the year's best female performance,

Left: Forest Whitaker and Stephen Rea in Neil Jordan's **The Crying Game**, which dazzles because virtually nothing in the film turns out as expected. Jordan had planned it years before, taking each of Antonioni's themes and twisting inwards. Above: Emma Thompson and Anthony Hopkins in **Howards End**, bringing to life E. M. Forster's Margaret Schlegel and Henry Wilcox, whose second wife she becomes. Opposite: Sharon Stone and Michael Douglas in **Basic Instinct**, directed by Paul Verhoeven from a screenplay by Joe Eszterhaz – which was little more than **Jagged Edge** with voyeurism and a sex change.

and Nick Nolte; and it was directed by a former doctor, George Miller. It was based on fact, as was – obviously – Spike Lee's ambitious biography of **Malcolm X**, taking the Black Rights leader from his days as a petty hood to murder and martyrdom. Aided by a magnificent interpretation by Denzel Washington, the year's best male performance, Lee pulled it off with flair, acumen, daring and skill. Both artistically and commercially it towered over its rival screen biographies, Danny DeVito's **Hoffa**, a study of the Teamster leader, played by Jack Nicholson and written by David Mamet, and Attenborough's **Chaplin**, a hagiographical slog through Charlie's life, played by Robert Downey Jr and written by some people who should be ashamed of themselves. So should Sir Dicky, who explained his motives in making his film: 'It wasn't as if he was *merely* [author's italics] Buster Keaton or Harold Lloyd.' Where has he been for the last forty years?

Earlier in the year, two biopics celebrated a certain quincentenary: **Christopher Columbus: The Discovery**, directed by John Glen, with George Corraface as Chris, and Tom Selleck and Rachel Ward as Ferdinand and Isabella; and **1492: The Conquest of Paradise**, directed by Ridley Scott, with Gérard Depardieu as Columbus and Sigourney Weaver as the Queen. Serious thought and care had gone into the second, not to mention a lot of money; and its credits suggested that if you could only see one of the two, it would be this one. As it turned out, the public wanted to see neither.

A Few Good Men was one of the five candidates for the Oscar for Best Picture, a tolerable piece about a miscarriage of justice among soldiers – but how it gleamed

with self-importance. Tom Cruise again, the lawyer righting wrongs, and Demi Moore as his superior and accomplice, not to mention an eye-swivelling turn from Jack Nicholson as the CO, the villain of the piece. Rob Reiner directed. Martin Brest directed another of the nominees, with a screenplay by Bo Goldman, **Scent of a Woman**, which took its title and its leading character from a 1974 movie with Vittorio Gassmann. Gassmann played a blind ex-army officer who is accompanied to Naples by an adolescent. In this revamp, Chris O'Donnell is a schoolboy 'minding' Al Pacino when he decides upon one last fling in New York. The film, equally compounded of perception and idiocy, is watchable as long as the boy is on screen; Pacino gives a performance more misconceived and mannered, more showy and yet more shallow, than any other in the cinema's first hundred years. Why was he talking like W. C. Fields?

And why did he win an Oscar? – over Clint? Eastwood was up there for Best Director and Best Picture with **Unforgiven**, a self-conscious (and violent) revenge Western, which nevertheless shows his mastery in this field. The film beat the two entries from Britain, **Howards End** and **The Crying Game**. Given the sheer amount of blood, violence, gore or simple inanity of most of 1992's output, the first of these seemed better than it was. Another of Merchant-Ivory's linen-suit literary adaptations, it was taken from E. M. Forster's novel, again by Ruth Prawer Jhabvala. As with **A Room With a View** she has removed the common assumption about culture, class and politics which drew the characters together in the first place, but her otherwise omit-nothing approach to the stronger material of this novel means that it suffers

Left: Tim Robbins as a top Hollywood executive caught up in a murder in Robert Altman's **The Player**. Like **The Crying Game**, it celebrated movies as the supreme purveyor of illusion and mystery. Above: **Malcolm X** is a long and exhaustive study of the Black Muslim leader, taking in, as here, his days as a petty crook before prison and conversation. Denzel Washington was Malcolm X and his youthful companion was played by Spike Lee, who also directed. Opposite: Daniel Day Lewis as Hawkeye in Michael Mann's **The Last of the Mohicans**, which had some spectacular scenery but was somewhat confusing.

less; and the performances of Anthony Hopkins, Prunella Scales and Samuel West, at least, come close to Forster's intention.

The Crying Game is, on the surface, an ingenious tale concerning the thugs and misfits of the IRA; but the true subject of Neil Jordan, who wrote and directed, is identity. Jordan's first film, **Angel**, contains a homage to Antonioni, and **The Crying Game** is the best film Antonioni never made. It may not be a great film, but it is brilliant, daring and exciting.

So the cinema's first hundred years finishes on a film worthy to stand alongside the best efforts of those who have toiled and created for it: Bergman, Antonioni, Ray, Buñuel, De Sica, Zavattini; the great Japanese directors; Renoir, Clair, Lamprecht; Carné, Prévert, Davivier; Bauer, Eisenstein, Pudovkin, Sjöström, Kazan, Keaton, Capra, Mankiewicz, Wilder, Preston Sturges, Zinnemann.

Those among them still alive are no longer working, so we may suppose the cinema's greatest days are over.

Yet, in the last ten years it has produced more works of quality – which entertain, illuminate and/or project an individual intellect – than any of the other arts put together. Maybe the worthwhile movies of the 1980s and 1990s are fewer than in any one year of the 1930s or 1940s (and maybe we should set against them the extraordinary number of violent, infantile comic strips that the industry persists in perpetrating). What is cheering is that so many of them are factually-based – and not on some distant historic event. The cinema came along just as modern society needed a record of the sweeping changes being made. It provided a more vivid, cogent account than the press – ironically, since for so long its coinage was a combination of dreams, fantasies and romance. Since the horrendous events of the century, from the Boer War to the civil war in Bosnia, have increased our demand for reality, the cinema's role was inevitably superseded by television. Admittedly, the two mediums function differently, but television cannot capture the imagination in quite the same way.

1993

Eastwood had brought the Western back, and there were two more: **Geronimo: An American Legend**, Walter Hill's best movie in a while, notable for old hands Gene Hackman and Robert Duvall, and **Tombstone**, the best film yet made by George P. Cosmatos, another look at the oft-told tale of Wyatt Earp (Kurt Russell) and Doc Holliday (Val Kilmer). Other factual dramas included three studies of marriages, in ascending order of merit: **Tom and Viv**, directed by Brian Gilbert, about the unhappy match between Anglicized-American poet T.S. Eliot (Willem Dafoe) and his first wife (Miranda Richardson); Richard Attenborough's tender **Shadowlands**, which concerns the writer and don C.S. Lewis (Anthony Hopkins) who weds an American fan (Debra Winger); and **What's Love Got To Do With It**, Brian Gibson's searing account of the relationship between pop ikon Tina Turner (Angela Bassett) and husband Ike (Laurence Fishburn). Jim Sheridan's **In the Name of the Father** looked at corruption in the British police, as it affected one Irishman (Daniel Day Lewis) unjustly jailed for an IRA bomb.

The ultimate feel-good movie was Phoebe Ephron's disarming **Sleepless in Seattle**, in which Tom Hanks and Meg Ryan don't meet till the last reel. Comedy offered Harold Ramis's **Groundhog Day**, in which TV commentator Bill Murray finds himself living the same day over again, and Chris Columbus's **Mrs Doubtfire**, really an excuse for Robin Williams to show off *and* don drag so that he can be nanny to his children. Woody Allen's spoof of old movies, **Manhattan Murder Mystery**, was his best film in an age while, in contrast, **The Age of Innocence** was the best thing Martin Scorsese had done, with another flawless performance by Day Lewis. Edith Wharton struck it lucky twice, for John Madden did an equally beautiful job on **Ethan Frome**, who was Liam Neeson.

Tom Hanks was also on fine form in Jonathan Demme's **Philadelphia**, as an AIDS victim unjustly sacked, with Denzel Washington equalling him as his lawyer. For thrills, there was: Andrew Davis's **The Fugitive**, with Harrison Ford eluding cop Tommy Lee Jones; Wolgang Petersen's **In the Line of Fire**, with Clint Eastwood eluding would-be assassin John Malkovich; and John Dahl's twisty film noir, **Red Rock West**. There was tension, too, in Steven Spielberg's dinosaur-infested **Jurassic Park**, the year's most popular film. But this director also made the humbling tale of the concentration camps, **Schindler's List**, not only his best film but one that overshadows every other one in Hollywood's history.

1994

Forrest Gump, directed by Robert Zemeckis with Tom Hanks as a mentally retarded Southerner reliving recent US history was '94's second most popular film – though why must be a mystery, even if it lacked the terminal pretension of some recent items: last year's **The Piano** and **House of the Spirits**; this year's idiotic **Interview with a Vampire**, unaccountably directed by Neil Jordan; and Edward Zwick's **Legends of the Fall**, which attempted to do for Montana and Brad Pitt what **Giant** had done for James Dean and Texas. **That's Entertainment III**, came eighteen years after the last, and proved that the first had been a celebration, the second a rip-off and this a requiem. If they no longer make musicals, the Western was still with us, with Richard Donner's **Maverick**, in which Mel Gibson, Jodie Foster and James Garner reminded us that Westerns can be fun. Lawrence Kasdan's **Wyatt Earp**, with Kevin Costner, mostly reminded us that they can be too long. As comparisons go, John Dahl's **The Last Seduction** was even more satisfying than **Red Rock West**, because it wasn't trying so hard to pack ten surprises into every reel.

Four Weddings and a Funeral was also quite relaxed, in this case in getting its laughs, even if it was only an extended sitcom as directed by Mike Newell. Commercially, it was the most successful film ever made in Britain, which also sent out a fine historical in **The Madness of King George**, written by Alan Bennett and directed by Nicholas Hytner, with Nigel Hawthorne tremendous as the King. Australia offered **The Adventures of Priscilla, Queen of the Desert**, three drag queens in the Outback, and strangely sweet as directed by Stephan Elliott.

Ed Wood also liked to drag up, though in this case he was hetero – and the maker of some of the cruddiest movies ever. With Johnny Depp as Wood and Martin Landau as Bela Lugosi, it was a fond tribute from the quirky mind of Tim Burton, who last year gave Disney the brilliant, animated **The Nightmare Before Christmas**. Disney's trailer for that suggested that the highlights of its history were **Snow White**, **101 Dalmations**, **Aladdin** and **The Lion King**, but where **Aladdin** dazzled, the last seems pompous and sentimental; the animation, however, is extraordinary and it was the year's most popular film. From Disney came two other outstanding movies: Quentin Tarantino's parody of **Pulp Fiction**, which was called just that; and Robert Redford's **Quiz Show**, an examination of the way they were rigged by TV in the 1950s. It was the year's best film.

Index of film titles

Page numbers in italic refer to illustrations.

Sources

Sources include *Variety, The Motion Picture Almanac, The Film Daily Yearbook, The New York Times, The Monthly Film Bulletin, Le Cinématographie Français, Deutsche Spielfilmalmanac 1929–50* and *Deutsche Stummfilme.*

Acknowledgements

The publishers would like to thank the following for supplying the pictures used in this book:

Hulton Deutsch Collection: pp. 3, 8 (above and below), 10, 12 (above), 15, 17, 34, 38–39 (below), 49, 77, 79, 82, 85, 86 (above and below), 96 (above), 97, 99, 100, 102 (above), 107, 118 (above), 126 (below), 132 (above), 143, 145, 146, 150 (above), 158 (below), 159, 166, 168, 182 (below), 185 (below), 189, 190 (below), 191, 192, 196, 197, 198 (below), 200 (above and below), 202, 205, 206, 208 (above), 211, 212.

Photofest, New York: pp. 9, 11, 13 (below), 16 (below), 21, 24, 29 (below), 31, 37, 39 (above), 52, 53, 55, 56, 57, 58, 59, 60 (above), 62, 63, 64, 65 (below), 69, 72, 74, 78, 80, 81, 83, 84 (above), 87, 89 (below), 90, 91, 93, 98, 101, 103, 104 (above and below), 105, 106, 108, 109 (above and below), 110, 111, 112 (below), 113, 114 (below), 115, 116, 117 (above and below), 118 (below), 119, 120 (below), 121, 122 (above and below), 123, 124 (above and below), 125, 128 (above and below), 129, 130 (above and below), 131, 132 (below), 133, 134, 135, 136 (above and below), 137, 138 (below), 140 (above and below), 141, 142 (above and below), 144 (below), 147 (above), 148, 149, 150 (below), 151, 152 (above and below), 154 (above and below), 155, 156, 157 (above and below), 160, 161 (below), 162, 163 (above and below), 164 (above), 165, 167, 169 (above and below), 170 (above and below), 172, 173, 174 (above and below), 175, 176, 177 (above and below), 178, 179 (above and below), 180 (above and below), 182 (above), 183, 184, 185 (above), 186 (above and below), 187 (above and below), 188 (above and below), 190 (above), 193, 194, 195 (above and below), 198 (above), 199, 203 (above and below), 204 (below), 208 (below), 210 (above and below), 219, 220, 221, 222, 223, 225, 226, 228 (above and below), 229, 230 (above and below), 231, 232, 233 (above), 235, 236 (below), 237, 239 (above), 240 (above and below), 241, 242 (above and below), 243, 244 (above and below), 245, 246 (above and below), 248 (above), 249, 250, 251 (above and below), 252, 254 (below), 255, 256, 257, 258, 259, 260 (above and below), 261, 262, 263, 264 (above and below), 265, 266, 267, 268 (above and below), 269 (above and below), 270, 271, 272 (above), 273, 276, 277, 278 (above and below), 280, 282 (above), 283, 286 (below), 288 (above and below), 289, 292, 293, 295, 298, 300 (above and below), 301, 303, 304 (above and below), 306 (above and below), 309, 310, 311, 312, 313 (below), 314, 315, 316 (above), 317, 318, 320 (above and below), 321, 322 (above), 324 (above and below), 326 (above), 327, 328 (above), 330 (below), 331, 332, 333 (above), 334 (above and below), 335, 336 (above and below), 338 (above and below), 339, 340 (above and below), 341, 342, 343, 344, 345, 346, 347, 348 (above and below), 350 (above and below), 351, 352 (above and below), 353, 354 (above and below), 355, 356 (above and below), 357, 358 (above and below), 359, 360 (above and below), 361, 362 (above and below), 363, 364 (above and below), 365, 366, 367, 368 (above and below), 369, 370, 371, 372 (above and below), 373, 374 (above and below), 375, 376 (above and below), 378.

Syndication International: p. 5.

Grateful thanks also to the British Film Institute, Kenneth Carroll, Tom Graves and the author.

Finally, the publishers are indebted to the following production companies for the use of their stills: Alcina; Archers Film Productions; Argyle British; Artcraft Pictures Corporation; Associated British Pathé; Associated R and R Films; Avco Embassy; Avenue; Biograph Company; Breathless Associates; British International Pictures; British Lion Films Ltd; Cineguild; Cino Del Duca; Columbia Pictures Corporation; Comicque Film Company; Cristaldi; Crown Film Unit; Daiei Motion Picture Company; Walt Disney Productions; EMI; Ealing; Enigma; Film Polski; Films 59; Films De La Tour; Films du Carrosse; Films Victoria; Filmsonor; First Studio Goskino; Foreign Film Productions; 40 Acres and a Mule Filmworks; Fox Film Co; Franco London Film; Gainsborough; Gaumont-British Picture Corporation; Goldcrest; Samuel Goldwyn; Governor Films; Granada; Greenberg Brothers; Hemdale Holdings; Holiday; Images; Inspiration Pictures; Buster Keaton Productions; Jesse L Lasky Feature Player Company; Lenfilm; London Films; Lorimar; Lumière; M.A.I.C.; Majestic; Mega; Merchant Ivory; Metro; Metro-Goldwyn-Meyer; Mezhrabpom-Russ; Miko Prod.; Kennedy Miller Entertainment; Minerva; Mutual; NSW Film Corporation; Nero Film; Orion Pictures; Outlaw; Pabst; Palace Productions; Palomar Pictures International; Panthéon; Paramount Pictures Corporation; Pathé Consortium; Pathé Entertainment; Pelemele; RKO; Rank; Carol Reed Productions; Reliance Majestic; Remus; Ren Productions; Republic Pictures Corporation; Riama; Rimfire; Rizzoli; Romulus; Selznick International Pictures; Sheffield Photo Company; South Australian Film Corporation; Speva Films; Svensk Filmindustri; Theatrecraft; Tobis; Toho; Touchstone Pictures; TriStar; Twentieth Century-Fox Film Corporation; UFA; UNINCI; United Artists; Universal; Vestron; Vitagraph; Walter Wanger Productions; Warner Bros; Warner-Pathé; Woodfall Film Productions; Saul Zaentz Production Company.

First published in 1993 by
George Weidenfeld & Nicolson Ltd

This paperback edition first published in 1998 by
Phoenix Illustrated,
Orion Publishing Group, Orion House
5, Upper St. Martin's Lane, London WC2H 9EA

British Library Cataloguing-in-Publication Data
A catalogue record for this book is available from
the British Library

ISBN 0-75380-130-2

Designed by Carrol Associates
House Editor: Coralie Hepburn

Phototypeset by Keyspools Ltd, Golbourne, Lancs
Printed and bound in Italy

Prelim illustrations
Frontispiece Clark Gable
Title Page Margaret Lockwood in *Bank Holiday*, 1938
Page 4 The cast of *Behind Two Guns*, 1924
Page 5 Marilyn Monroe in *How to Marry a Millionaire*, 1953
Page 7 Bette Davis